Introducing
Urban Design:

Interventions and
Responses

This boo

P
3

5

Series: Exploring Town Planning

Series editor: Clara Greed

Introducing Urban Design:

Interventions and Responses

EDITED BY CLARA GREED &
MARION ROBERTS

With contributions by Hugh Barton,
Matthew Carmona, Sue Cavanagh, Robert Cowan,
Richard Guise, Tony Lloyd-Jones, Sandra Manley,
Henry Shaftoe and Ian Thompson

 LONGMAN

Addison Wesley Longman Limited
Edinburgh Gate, Harlow
Essex CM20 2JE, England
and Associated Companies throughout the world

© Addison Wesley Longman Limited 1998

The right of Clara Greed, Marion Roberts, Hugh
Barton, Matthew Carmona, Sue Cavanagh, Robert
Cowan, Richard Guise, Tony Lloyd-Jones, Sandra
Manley, Henry Shaftoe and Ian Thompson to be
identified as authors of this work has been asserted by
them in accordance with the Copyright, Designs and
Patents Act 1988

First published 1998

British Library Cataloguing in Publication Data
A catalogue entry for this title is available from the
British Library

ISBN 0-582-28534-8

Produced by Longman Singapore Publishers (Pte) Ltd
Printed in Singapore

Contents

A key feature which differentiates this book from other collections on urban design is its emphasis on user responses to urban environments. The editors make no apologies for this shift: too many accounts of design initiatives and schemes stop with the triumphant photographs of openings and do not consider how well such schemes have fared in the long run. This book seeks to make a small step in redressing the balance of academic discussion away from the first part of the design process to an examination of the whole, which includes design in use. As a consequence it inevitably integrates social issues within the design agenda.

Clara Greed
Bristol, 1996

List of contributors

Hugh Barton Dip TP, MPhil, MRTPI is a senior lecturer in environmental sustainability studies in the School of Planning, and course leader of the MA/post graduate diploma course in town and country planning, within the Faculty of the Built Environment, University of the West of England. He has a long-standing interest in environmental and energy issues, founding the Urban Centre for Appropriate Technology and Bristol Energy Centre in the 1980s. His recent research and consultancy projects have included *The Good Practice Guide on the Environmental Appraisal of Development Plans* for the Department of the Environment, and contributing to the EC-funded Bristol Energy and Environment Plan. Current projects are a book on local environmental auditing for Earthscan, and a design guide for sustainable development for the Local Government Management Board.

Matthew Carmona is an architect/planner and lecturer in planning (urban design) at the University of Nottingham's Department of Urban Planning. After spells in both public and private architectural practice, Matthew worked from 1993 to 1995 as research officer on the DoE-sponsored research project 'Best Practice for Local Plan Policies on Design' and on a follow-up ESRC-sponsored project at Reading and latterly Strathclyde University. The results of this work have been published widely and are to be found in a book (co-authored by Professor John Punter) – *The Design Dimension of Planning: Theory, Content and Best Practice for Design Policies* (E & FN Spon., 1997). Since taking up a lectureship at Nottingham in 1995 Matthew has maintained an active research presence in this area. Since 1992 he has also been undertaking a University of Nottingham-sponsored research study entitled 'Controlling the Design of Private Sector Residential Development'.

Sue Cavanagh originally undertook a career in art and design and trained at Camberwell School of Art. She subsequently gained teaching qualifications and a BA Degree from the Open University, and lectured in ceramics and three-dimensional design. In her mid-thirties she enrolled in the 'Women's Access Course into Architecture and Building' and went on to take a part-time degree in architecture. In 1986 she became an architectural researcher for Women's Design Service. Publications have included, *Thinking of Small Children: Access, Provision and Play; Shoppers' Crèches: Guidelines for Childcare Facilities in Public Places,* and *At Women's Convenience: A Handbook on the Design of Women's Public Toilets,* and *Designing Housing for Older Women.* She is also convener of the 'London Women and Planning Forum', which meets regularly to discuss the impact of planning issues and policies on women's lives. In 1994 she joined the Medical Architecture Research Unit at the University of North London as a PhD student and is currently researching the planning and design of primary health care buildings. She has two children.

Robert Cowan is a writer and consultant on urban affairs, Senior Research Fellow in the Department of Architecture at De Montfort University, and a trustee (and former chairman) of Vision for London. He was joint leader of the team at Urban Initiatives writing the manual *Good Practice Guidance on Design in the Planning System* for the Department of the Environment. He is a former editor of *Town and Country Planning* and Shelter's housing magazine *Roof*, and a former deputy editor of the *Architects' Journal*. His publications include the manifesto *The Cities Design Forgot*.

The series editor, **Clara Greed** BSc (Hons), MRTPI, FASI, FRGS, PhD, is a senior lecturer in town planning in the Faculty of the Built Environment, University of the West of England, previously working in the Department of Surveying, and in local government. She is the author of the first volume in this series, *Introducing Town Planning*, editor of Volume II, *Implementing Town Planning* and *Investigating Town Planning* Volume III, and has published widely on built environment matters, including *Women and Planning* (Routledge, 1994) and *Surveying Sisters* (Routledge, 1991) on women chartered surveyors. She is a chartered town planner, Fellow of the Architects and Surveyors Institute, and a member of several committees dealing with education and practice issues in the built environment professions. She is a member of the CISC (Construction Industry Standing Conference) Planning and Strategy Group which produced Part A (Planning) of the CISC map. She is interested in all aspects of equal opportunities issues, and is chair of the Faculty Access Initiative. She has always been interested in art and design and studied three-dimensional design at Bath Academy of Art before embarking upon a town planning degree at the University of Wales, Cardiff.

Richard Guise is an architect and planner, and currently award leader of the MA urban design course at the University of the West of England in Bristol. He has substantial experience of urban conservation practice, both within Somerset County Council, and as a consultant. He is involved with the English Historic Towns Forum and has given papers and run workshops for regional seminars of the Association of Conservation Officers. He is a co-author of *Sustainable Settlements*, a design guide for sustainable development, published by the Local Government Management Board in 1995. Currently he is undertaking research and auditing of traditional paving design and its contribution to the street scale of historic areas. He has published articles and presented conference papers on this topic as well as organising short courses on the practical aspects of paving design and laying. With his colleague Sandra Manley he has conducted numerous short courses and in-house courses for local authority planners on character appraisal and design policy in conservation areas.

Tony Lloyd-Jones is an architect with extensive international experience. He originally studied architecture at the University of Bath, and currently combines professional practice with lecturing in urban design at the University of Westminster in London. He has worked on a range of residential and community schemes involving both new-build and conversion schemes within various London boroughs. As an architect in private practice he has worked on schemes as diverse as solar housing in Greece, town planning in Nigeria and student housing and sports and recreational buildings in Finland. He has been successful in several international architectural competitions, producing prize-winning schemes for the Ecole Jean Jaures, Chatenay Malbry; Centre Socio-culturel, La Chartre; the Rectorate of the University of Amiens in France, and, with Sir Percy Thomas, Bristol, for an International Organisation Headquarters and Conference Centre in Vienna, Austria.

Sandra Manley is a chartered town planner and currently a senior lecturer in the school of town and country planning in the Faculty of the Built Environment, at the University of the West of England, Bristol, and course leader for the undergraduate town planning degree. She has extensive experience of local government town planning departments. Her particular interests are development control, local plans, urban design, and planning for disabled groups. With her colleague Richard Guise she has conducted numerous short courses and in-house courses for local authority planners. She has developed various audit exercises in relation to disability access to specific sites and buildings. Along with Richard Guise Sandra Manley has been responsible for the development of the new RIBA-approved, combined architecture and town planning degree at UWE, bringing 'architecture' back to Bristol, after a twenty-year gap which followed the much-regretted closure of the Bristol University School of Architecture. She has also played a key role in the development of her urban conservation group in Bristol, within the Kingsdown area of the city.

Marion Roberts BSc(Hons), Dip Arch, Reg Arch, PhD, is an architect who studied at the Bartlett School, University College London and the Welsh School of Architecture. She has had a range of professional experience, specialising in the field of community architecture and housing. Her research interests and funded projects have moved from gender issues and housing design to public art and cultural regeneration. These have resulted in publications which include *Living in a Man-Made World: Gender Assumptions in Modern Housing Design* (Routledge, 1991), *Public Art in Private Places: Commercial Benefits and Public Policy* (University of Westminster Press, 1993) and articles in learned journals and the professional press. Her educational activities include membership of the editorial boards of *Urban Design Quarterly* and *Journal of Urban Design* and course leadership of the BA(Hons) Urban Design at the University of Westminster.

Henry Shaftoe's educational background incorporates degrees and other qualifications in social work, social planning, community development, and architecture and design. He has worked as a freelance architectural designer, undertaking a wide range of projects and research activities. While undertaking local authority work he has specialised in neighbourhood-based approaches to crime and design issues. He has undertaken neighbourhood research in Edinburgh, Middlesbrough, Leeds, Bristol and Notting Hill, London. He is co-ordinator of NACRO's Inner Cities Community Safety Unit. He has specialised in running training courses and seminars for local authorities, police authorities and a range of universities. He was a contributor to the Home Office Standing Conference on Crime Prevention Working Group on *Fear of Crime*. He has developed a series of training packs and videos. Publications include *Crime Prevention through Housing Design* (Spon, 1991) and *Creating Safer Neighbourhoods in Wales* (Welsh Office, 1994), and *High Expectations:*

A Guide to the Development of Concierge Schemes and Controlled Access to High Rise Social Housing (Department of the Environment, 1994). Currently he is involved in developing courses in Community Safety and Crime Prevention at the University of the West of England.

Ian Thompson is a landscape architect and town planner, who currently lectures in landscape architecture in the Department of Town and Country Planning, University of Newcastle upon Tyne. Before taking up his academic post in 1992, he spent much of his working life on windswept sites in Glasgow and on Tyneside, clutching soggy plans and looking at wet holes in the ground. He is now working on a PhD thesis which explores the aesthetic, ecological and socio-political value systems held by landscape practitioners. He has written numerous articles about landscape architecture for academic and professional journals.

Acknowledgments

The contributors and publishers are grateful for permission to reproduce material from the following sources:

Figure 2.2: *Cornell Journal of Architecture* (1982); Figure 2.4: Foundation Le Corbusier and Nation Fender Architects; Figure 2.5: Tschumi (1994) *Event Cities*, MIT Pres; Figure 2.7: Burrell Foley Architects; Figure 2.8: Max Lock Archive, Auckett Associates; Figure 2.9: Tibbalds Munro Ltd; Figure 2.10: MacCormac, Jamieson and Prichard; Figure 2.11: Calthorpe (1993) *The Next American Metropolis*, Princeton University Press; Figure 3.1: Cartoon by Louis Hellman first published in *Building Design*, 16 June 1995; Figure 3.2: Glasgow Development Agency; Figure 4.9: Map reproduced from the Ordnance Survey (Bridgwater conservation area) mapping with the permission of The Controller of Her Majesty's Stationery Office © Crown copyright (399582); Figure 5.2: Barcelona Holding OLímpico, S.A; Figure 5.4: Euralille; Figure 5.6: CZWG Architects. Figure 5.7: Birmingham City Council; Figure 5.8: Group 91 Architects and Temple Bar Properties Ltd; Figure 5.9: Presse- und Informationsamt des Landes Berlin; Figure 5.10: Bill Erickson; Figure 6.1: Bill Erickson; Figure 7.1: Lisa Harty, Artangel; Figure 7.3: *The Economist*; Figure 7.8 and 7.9: Artangel; Figure 7.10: Wolfgang Neeb, Esther and Jochen Gerz; Figure 8.4: Map reproduced from the Ordnance Survey (Bradley Stoke) mapping with the permission of the Controller of Her Majesty's Stationery Office © Crown copyright (399582); Figures 8.6 – 8.10: Barton et al. (1995) *Sustainable Settlements: a Guide for Planners, Designers and Developers,* UWE/Local Government Management Board; Figure 9.1: Cartoon by Louis Hellman first published in *Access by Design*; Figure 10.2: The London Transport Unit for Disabled Passengers; Figure 11.2: City of Portsmouth; Figure 12.2: Neighbourhood Initiatives Foundation and the Joseph Rowntree Trust.

We have acknowledged the source for each illustration in its caption and in doing so we have tried to contact all the known copyright holders. If there are any whom we have missed, we would be eager to acknowledge them in any future editions of this book.

Thanks are also given to Peter Monk, access officer for Thamesdown Borough Council, Swindon, for information on the role of the Building Regulations in the enabling or preventing of access. The contribution of other access officers is also gratefully acknowledged.

Finally, the editors would like to thank James Newall of Addison Wesley Longman for his patience and unfailing courtesy.

I SETTING THE SCENE

1 Definitions and perceptions of urban design

Clara Greed

Expectations

How to take the book

The purpose of this book, as its title suggests, is not to provide a prescriptive design guide, but to introduce key aspects of the urban design agenda, from among an ever-expanding range of other equally eligible topics. A further volume on urban design is under preparation which will be more prescriptive, relatively speaking, and will constitute more of a primer on urban design. But one cannot provide detailed standards, codes and guidelines until one has discussed and established the criteria, policy considerations, objectives and 'visions' upon which these factors should be based. That is the function of this present volume. The intention is to present a selective range of contributions, comprising discussions, accounts and some case studies, which are indicative of the current agenda. Although urban design as a subject has experienced a renaissance in recent years, in terms of college courses, and in numbers of practitioners undertaking urban design work within both public and private sector contexts, it is still an evolving area which is difficult to define and delimit. Many people equate urban design variously (and inaccurately) with townscape, urban conservation, architecture, town planning, and, inevitably, Prince Charles! As will be explained, however, there is a great deal more to urban design than these popular impressions and associations might imply.

In this book, one will not generally find dedicated chapters on topics or types of development such as retail, commercial, leisure and recreation, and residential development, although one will find information on these aspects – particularly the latter which, after all, represents 70 per cent of all development (Greed, 1996a, Chapter 1) – within the various chapters. The book will first identify current issues in the development of the professional urban design agenda, and then look at user demands and response within the community to this evolving agenda. The aim is to take a more holistic approach, based on understanding urban design as a philosophy and way of seeing entire cities, and thus as a basis for developing policies concerned with the design, management and planning of urban form and space.

Because of the evolving nature of the field and the debates which rage around the question of 'What exactly is urban design?' and 'Who are the urban designers?' the first half of this chapter is devoted to discussing what urban design is and what it is not. Definitions are provided to give the reader a clearer idea of how to approach the subject and what to expect from it. This introduction will also provide an opportunity to provoke some discussion as to the relative contribution of the 'designer' (the professional, the providers) as against the 'designed' (the community, the users) in the design process. Trends towards participatory, bottom-up, as against top-down, approaches to decision-making are often assumed to be 'better' than more traditional approaches, but, taken to their logical conclusion, may make the role of the professional urban designer redundant. These debates need airing in Part I to provide context to the two main sections of the book, Part II which is written, relatively speaking from the 'top-down', provider perspective, as against Part III which incorporates 'bottom-up' user perspectives.

Conceptualising urban design

This book investigates urban design as the fourth volume in the series, *Exploring Town Planning*, which with each volume seeks to move to a new, and relatively more advanced, level of understanding of current conceptual and policy issues. This begs the question of whether urban design is, in fact, part of town planning. As will be seen from subsequent chapters, there are several different viewpoints as to what urban design actually is, particularly among the built environment professions. For example, town planners may imagine that urban design is a component, or function, of modern town planning. Architects may believe it is simply 'architecture writ large' across the whole urban fabric. But some urban designers may believe that urban design is not necessarily about architecture (the internal and external design of individual buildings) but about strategic, city-wide urban policy issues. Many would argue that urban design exists as a subject and profession in its own right, which is located somewhere between planning, architecture, landscape architecture, and transport planning. Linked to this, environmental 'green' issues, especially in relation to 'sustainable cities' have, nowadays, become part of the agenda of urban design and landscape architecture and this will be reflected in various chapters.

On the other hand, if urban design is more than 'big architecture' is it also bound to be something less than full-blown town planning? Interestingly, some urban designers may see town planning as a mere subset of urban design, and a fairly recent twentieth-century development at that. Although the agenda of urban design may appear new and different relative to other more established aspects of late-twentieth-century town planning, in fact, urban design is an ancient profession which has shaped towns and cities over the centuries in many different cultures and continents. Arguably, in the past urban design was the chief form of town planning, in which architectural and aesthetic issues predominated. Of course, a range of wider, practical issues were taken into account, as defined by the needs of the affluent classes who effectively commissioned town planning, but many of the design principles utilised are timeless in relevance. Curiously, this heritage appears to be unknown among some planning graduates, so to them ancient principles of urban design may appear as modern revelations. As will be seen from the various approaches of the contributors, urban design can be as broad or narrow, as traditional or modern in its ambit as the designer wants it to be.

Equally, there is much confusion about how urban design relates to the overarching areas of 'Art and Design', three-dimensional design, and, more broadly, urban culture itself. Likewise, there are links to be explored between landscape architecture and urban design. The latter has been traditionally concerned with the physical form of cities, buildings *and the space between them*, whereas the former concerns itself both with the 'soft' landscape, that is greenery, vegetation and water and also with the 'hard', that is the design and treatment of open spaces using hard surfaces such as granite setts, paving and elements such as street furniture. The history of landscape architecture is a rich one and there has been much interchange with the structure of urban form, and thus with urban design, and these relationships will be explored within the book.

Urban designers clearly do not exist in a vacuum, but are players in the decision-making processes which shape the built environment, they are also interacting with those concerned with property development, investment finance, town centre management, community politics, environmental sustainability and urban governance. All of these other groups bring with them a diversity of other agendas, representing a range of professional bodies, community groups and political interests involved in the development process, some of whom, at worst, may never have heard of urban design, or, at best, may hold overoptimistic or muddled views as what urban design is for and what urban designers can do.

It is important, therefore, at the start of the book to give a definition of what urban design is, and to alert readers to the fact that urban designers, architects and town planners may not entirely agree as to what should be included in, or excluded from, its scope. The following introductory section discusses both what urban design is and does and considers who the urban designers are, and what issues are of concern to them. This introductory section grew from a dialogue between the two editors Marion Roberts (urban designer and architect) and Clara Greed (town planner), as to definitions of urban design, and also reflects the diversity found among the contributors. The introduction concludes with an explanation of the purpose, scope and content of the book with reference to a summary of each chapter.

Definitions and perceptions of urban design

What is urban design?

Controversy exists over definitions of urban design. To characterise the most extreme positions, some urban designers think that planners imagine urban design consists of prettifying the detailed aspects of planning – pedestrianisation, bollards, townscape schemes, or that planners have a remote and rather vague idea that any matter concerned with aesthetics and architecture is somehow 'urban design'. Conversely, architects may see urban design as a larger extension of architecture; rather as they might argue that an architect should be able to design everything from the door knobs upwards, designing a city is rather like designing a door knob, only a bit larger – 'Big Architecture'. Traffic engineers have a very precise view of urban design – to them it is traffic calming. Landscape architects, on the other hand, are convinced that landscape architecture is urban design – landscape in the city. To non-professionals it is baffling, but the 'urban' is explicable, even if design is not.

Each of these views contains a grain of truth. The definition of urban design used by the Urban Design Unit at the University of Westminster in the context of 'teaching' urban design is as follows:

> Urban design is concerned with the physical form of cities, buildings and the space between them. The study of urban design deals with the relationships between the physical form of the city and the social forces which produce it. It focuses, in particular, on the physical character of the public realm but is also concerned with the interaction between public and private development and the resulting impact on urban form. (Source: Current University of Westminster MA Urban Design Course Documentation)

As can be seen, this definition does incorporate city design, pedestrianisation and traffic schemes, hard landscaping and a mysterious process called 'design'. It also implies the concepts of management and stewardship and calls for an understanding of the processes of land assembly and building procurement. The problem with the definition of urban design is that it lies both outside and inside conventionally-defined professional boundaries. Thus, it cannot be tidily defined as the 'left over' parts of these professions, although it might indeed deal with some of the problems that are thrown up by the 'gaps' between professional spheres of interest – such as the spatial problems produced by building an urban motorway.

Rob Cowan, who has written a chapter later in this volume about the process of urban design, has previously defined urban design as: 'everything to do with planning that is not covered by the Town and Country Planning Acts.' Whilst this definition is useful for those who are familiar with the Acts, it is still rather baffling to those who are not. But reading between the lines, this statement appears to allude to the fact that town planning has become so obsessed with narrow, physical, land use control, that there is need for another, freer perspective, to be furnished by the urban design movement, that allows for a more holistic, integrated approach to the understanding and planning of urban form. Another way to express the idea might be to say that each planning decision has a design implication and it is in this implication that the urban designer's sphere of influence lies.

To give an example to illustrate the role of the urban designer: the siting of any major new development is of great importance to town planners, transport planners and urban designers. The town planner might be concerned about the environmental and economic impacts – will the activities on the site affect residents? How many jobs will it provide? Will it destroy natural countryside and agricultural land? What services can it provide? How will it blight or regenerate a region? The transport planner will consider the development's relationship to surrounding large developments and existing highway provision, as to the traffic congestion it might cause, and the impact of increased volume on existing road capacity. The urban designer would be thinking about the design of the scheme itself, its layout, the relationships between buildings and space within the scheme and related access and circulation patterns, how it 'works' as a scheme, and the design implication of its potential for growth and its future impact on the structure and layout of neighbouring areas – as well as its visual appearance – which, incidentally, is often erroneously typified as the only thing that interests urban designers.

To give another example at a different scale: the layout of a smaller regeneration area, perhaps an inner-city site, would also be of interest to planners and urban designers. Whereas a planner would consider questions of land-use, job creation and equity in a two-dimensional sense, the urban designer would also be thinking about how to make the area work as a place which is memorable and pleasant in a three-dimensional sense. An urban design brief would not only consider the uses which are appropriate to a site, but would prescribe how they should be arranged, the overall massing or building envelope, the fronts and backs of buildings, the arrangement and positioning of routes and linkages, landmarks and open spaces. In this example, far from urban design being seen as a subset of planning, planning might be viewed as subordinate to urban design. However, some town planners might argue that the above has described what they were doing already, or what used to be thought of as 'good town planning' in years gone by, and that urban designers are really only reclaiming a currently undervalued dimension of 'real town planning' ...

This exploration of definition is beginning to suggest that there may be a clash between professions over their 'ownership' of problems and solutions. This is a sub-current which underlies much urban design thought. Two examples bring out these areas of conflict: mixed development and design guides. Mixed development has had a distinguished history in the urban design thinking of the last three decades. Its most famous advocate was Jane Jacobs (1961), whose *Death and Life of the Great American Cities* should be on every urban design student's reading list; more recently it was promoted by Alcock et al. (1985) in their influential primer *Responsive Environments* and Peter Calthorpe (1993) has been raising the torch in the US with his concept of transport-oriented development in *The Next American Metropolis*. The mainstream of town planning has made only rather tentative steps towards accommodating mixed use however and the General Development Orders classification of uses remains an essential part of the town planners' battery of controls.

From the point of view of architecture, the adoption of design briefs remains a thorny topic. As will be discussed by Matthew Carmona (in Chapter 3) there is often a professional clash of wills accompanying efforts to control architectural design. Many architects are very unhappy with any attempt to regulate their individuality and, with architectural education moving more in the direction of individual subjectivity, such clashes seem likely to be more frequent than ever. Indeed, if some urban designers argue that they are concerned with more than just townscape, visual issues, and 'architecture writ large' some town planners would ask why this clash has arisen. Why don't they trust the planners? Clearly, urban design is a fraught field, where boundaries and definitions are still evolving.

It is significant that in recent years the Department of the Environment has responded to the growth of interest in urban design and has instigated an Urban Design Campaign, producing reports such as Department of the Environment *Quality in Town and Country, a Discussion Document* (DoE, 1994a) and *Quality in Town and Country, Urban Design Campaign* (DoE, 1995a). Significantly, the 1995 revised draft of PPG1 (Planning Policy Guidance) *General Policies and Principles* includes a section on the importance of urban design for the first time, giving a definition in para.12 (set out below) and further guidance in Annex A 'Design' of the PPG. (See Appendix II for List of current PPGs.)

> For the purposes of this Guidance, urban design should be taken to mean the relationship between different buildings; the relationship between buildings and the streets, squares, parks and other spaces which make up the public domain; the nature and quality of the public domain itself; the relationship of one part of a village, town, or city with other parts; and the patterns of movement and activity which are thereby established: in short, the complex relationships between all the elements of the built and unbuilt space. As the appearance and treatment of the spaces between and around buildings is often of comparable importance to the design of the buildings themselves, landscape design, whether hard or soft, should be considered as an integral part of urban design. (para 12, draft PPG1, 1996)

In conclusion to this introductory section it must be admitted the problem of definition has not been solved, but the alternatives provided above may prove helpful whilst reading the book.

Who are the real urban designers?

Professionals?   The field of urban design is a contested area in terms of its scope, its intentions and its processes. The question of who is, or who should be allowed to call him/herself, an urban designer, and on the basis of what qualifications, is even more controversial. In a sense, everyone has the potential to 'do' urban design either individually or in collaboration. For example, partnerships may be developed within the course of the design process between big business and local authorities, between voluntary groups and local authorities and between communities and professionals, as will be illustrated by various contributors. As urban design is concerned about the interaction between people and urban space, it seems clear that one strand of urban design thought will be focused on extending the participation of non-professionals in urban design.

The most powerful exponent of this view, in terms of wealth, land ownership and influence, is of course the Prince of Wales. His support of the Urban Villages Forum and the support which his own School of Architecture, the Prince of Wales Institute, gives to a number of 'planning for real projects' suggest the keenness of his interest, albeit without formal qualification. However, it is worth while to remember that a number of other, less famous, 'folk-heroes' of architecture were practising community design decades before His Royal Highness got in on the act and there are many other unsung heroines and heroes battling on to this day in unfashionable areas which do not receive media attention.

At the moment there is no professional grouping which controls urban design in the way in which the RTPI controls entrance to the town planning profession and the Architects Registration Act (1931) controls the title of 'architect'. There is no official urban design 'profession' as such with its own chartered body. British society is still obsessed with the importance of professional status, and no more so than within the built environment sector, where to belong to a chartered/royal professional body is a prerequisite of being seen to 'exist' (as discussed in Greed, 1994).

The Urban Design Group is a voluntary association with (approximately) one thousand members. Professionals and non-professionals are encouraged to join. At the moment the Group acts as a cross between a learned society and a pressure group, organising talks, events and conferences, publishing a journal, *Urban Design Quarterly*, organising community participation schemes and lobbying Government to take on the ideas offered in its *Manifesto*.

Much debate has taken place within the Urban Design Group about its role and purpose. A strong current within the membership would like to see it incorporated formally as a professional association, with accreditation of courses. At the point of going to press these ideas have not been accepted as policy within the group. Controversy exists over the extent to which professionals from a background which has not contained a substantial design content, such as the majority of planners, can ever become fully fledged designers. There is also a view that it is necessary to educate not only designers, but also potential 'clients' or patrons, such as surveyors and investors, about the context of urban design proposals and how to evaluate them.

The voluntary nature of the Urban Design Group suggests the looseness which accompanies the stylisation 'urban designer'. In the past the Group has published a source book in which it invites members to publicise their services. Of the 54 practices listed in the 1994 edition, all offered a range of multidisciplinary services. Practices included the lone practitioner and the large multidisciplinary company. Whilst some practices were better known for their work in transport, others included high-profile architects. Services offered were mainly in the fields of masterplanning and site planning, urban regeneration and development frameworks, but a varied menu of specialisms were also available, ranging from horticultural services, through community participation, public inquiries, conservation, energy implications, environmental design, landscaping, cultural regeneration and user studies.

Many local authorities nowadays have departments, officers or activities which they entitle 'urban design', but whether all these are actually doing real urban design is open to investigation. Much of the impetus for this development has come as a result of a widely developed, prior interest in urban conservation within historical areas, and associated legislative controls on development in such areas. In turn, concern has spread to a greater consideration of new development too, especially when there is a need for integration with historical environments. The various Single Regeneration Budget initiatives, many of which contain funding for urban renewal within inner-city, and thus architecturally sensitive areas, have given further government support, and generated a measure of private property investment (Greed, 1996b).

Community groups? There has been considerable interest from community groups, minorities, and residents' groups in urban design issues, because they affect the quality and 'feel' of the areas in which people live. This has resulted in an amateur, but often well-informed, activist strata of ersatz urban designers. Within certain sections of the community, there is a greater expectation that in the urban design process more emphasis will be placed upon their demand and upon the needs of particular so-called 'minorities' within society. For example, the 'women and planning' movement has laid great stress upon urban design which provides good access, especially for carers accompanied by small children and babies. Likewise, ethnic minority groups have challenged urban conservation policies in which there is no 'visual space' for Islamic architectural requirements, and different cultural needs.

Whilst many people welcome these developments, others question the value of such 'bottom-up' involvement within urban decision-making processes. Indeed, whilst many non-professionals do urgently want to have their say over the shape and form of the built environment, others have neither the time nor, often, are they in a position to be consulted. For example, in the Maritime Quarter in Swansea, where the old docks were regenerated, it was not possible to consult local residents about proposals because the old residents had long gone and the new had not even been defined. Likewise, in the past, in the postwar reconstruction

THE URBAN DESIGN GROUP

The forum for debate, ideas and action for civilised places

1. OBJECTIVES OF THE URBAN DESIGN GROUP

The Urban Design Group (UDG) promotes the creation of high quality urban environments. Seeing beyond the narrow perspectives of individual disciplines, agencies, ideologies or styles, it demonstrates practical alternatives to the type of design that pays no regard to context, and decision making which is driven by bureaucracy. The objectives of the UDG are:

- To promote the understanding and appreciation of cities and towns and how they work (urbanism).
- To promote and engage in research, debate and collaboration between citizens, professions and institutions.
- To influence and guide decision-makers at all levels, and to educate both practitioners and the public.
- To encourage best practice in urban design.

2. GUIDING PRINCIPLES FOR URBAN DESIGN

The UDG promotes principles of:

EMPOWERMENT: building the sense of identity of the people who live and work in a place, and their involvement in caring for or changing its fabric or character.

DIVERSITY: encouraging the variety that enlarges the interest or choices a place can offer.

EQUITY: making places (and their facilities and amenities) accessible to people beyond the owner and immediate users.

STEWARDSHIP: taking a broad and long term view of the costs and benefits of any change.

CONTEXT: building on the best of what already exists.

3. APPROACHES TO URBAN DESIGN

The UDG believes that successful urban design depends on:

IDENTIFYING COMMON INTERESTS: taking account of the interests of the city as a whole, not just a development's immediate client or users.

COLLABORATION: bringing together a wide range of disciplines, expertise and experience throughout the design and development process.

CREATIVE THINKING: drawing on the creativity and imagination of professional and citizen alike.

SHARING VISIONS: using graphic, written and spoken media as well as three dimensional design to communicate and share ideas.

LEARNING: making the shaping of the environment a learning process for everyone, from school children to communities and decision-makers.

5. PROCESSES OF URBAN DESIGN

The processes of successful urban design include:

ANALYSIS: understanding and defining the character of a place, its history and development, its physical and social structure, its routes and landmarks. its strengths and weaknesses.

VISION: setting goals for a place that relates to its three dimensional form and planning objectives.

STRATEGIES: developing urban design strategies for cities or areas, establishing principles on which local design decisions can be taken in the wider context of issues such as transport, the public realm, building heights and the location of landmarks.

GUIDELINES: drawing up urban design guidelines to show how local action can support strategic policies. The guidelines will cover issues such as building heights, principles of frontage design, access points, open space, tree planting, street design, floorscape, safety and security.

BRIEFS: drawing up more detailed urban design briefs for particular sites.

period of new town building, most of the residents did not live near or in the new town until they moved into their new house, and then it was virtually too late to comment upon the design of the neighbourhood. The extent to which urban design, in particular, has been concerned with user needs is a sensitive point for discussion. Urban designers contributing to this book have argued that urban designers have always really been concerned with the needs of users, and it is a false distinction to suggest that, in the 'bad old days', 'the great designer' was more concerned with creating his own visually stunning ego-trip, than with the specific needs of the residents and users.

The user-orientated approach is exemplified within the wider realms of town planning itself, in a more sensitive approach to public participation activities based on 'Planning for Real' principles (as expressed in the work of Tony Gibson and Mike Parkes and innumerable 'women and planning', community, and ethnic minority initiatives (cf. Parkes, 1996; Askew, 1996; Nisancioglu and Greed, 1996 and see Chapter 11), and in concepts such as 'citizens' juries which 'judge' planning decisions for their area (*IPPR*, 1996). But the big question, which has also been the subject of much discussion in the process of producing this book, is whether in fact urban design is bound to be better, and more 'human' because of such participatory approaches, or whether in fact they reduce the process to single-issue campaigns, slow it down, and narrow the agenda. Conversely, particularly if one looks at historical examples of famous urban designs (Bath, for example) relative lack of public participation did not appear to make the design worse – indeed it gave the designer the freedom to get on with the job. After all, the urban designer, especially the architect/urban designer, is expected to have had around seven years of professional education, and practical experience, before he/she is in a position to make urban design decisions. All this must be worth something in terms of being able 'to see the whole picture', possessing 'know-how', and making balanced and informed professional judgments, when developing urban policy for a particular area.

Indeed, 'design' is definitely a skill, quite possibly an art, and also has its scientific, technical aspects. The process of imagining something which does not exist has its difficulties as well as its highlights. To learn how to design is as much an opportunity to practise, to reflect and to criticise, then to practise some more, than learning in a more formal sense. Design involves synthesising ideas and transforming that synthesis into three-dimensional form. Even if the local people in an area know more about their area than the urban designer,

that does not, therefore, necessarily make them better able to design their area. Community participation cannot, then, replace the role of the designer: rather, as Tom Woolley argues, it acts as an education for the non-professional in the process of understanding how buildings and places get built (Markus, Teymur and Woolley, 1988 and Woolley, 1985). At its best, it can also act as a means for political empowerment, by creating opportunities for people to take key decisions out of the hands of politicians and officials (for example, how much office space? how many houses?) and to have a voice. But when some of the residents are also urban designers, planners or architects themselves, as is the case in some 'middle class' urban conservation areas, then the situation is different again.

In thinking around these issues and the validity of community and more participatory approaches to the urban design process, the reader should consider the following questions. Do too many (unqualified) cooks spoil the broth? Are community approaches always appropriate? Arguably, much depends upon the nature of the situation in question, the power relationships between the designers and designed, and related class, gender, wealth, and lifestyle differences. These relationships might be very different in a socially deprived area than in, say, a gentrified urban conservation area.

One cannot ignore the overall context of governmental and regulatory powers which overarch the planning, design and management of the built environment nowadays. Urban designers cannot necessarily depend upon fellow professionals and other regulators of the built environment to understand what they mean, nor can they assume they will be supportive of their views. Indeed, is the urban designer actually an inspired individual genius, or is he/she really a 'team', perhaps a bureaucratically restricted local authority department, or a private practice consultancy more worried about financial overheads and management deadlines than purely about design issues?

Another aspect of concern is that new forms of user-orientated and generated, problem-solving 'urban design' have emerged which may be seen as not complete or valid by urban designers themselves but which have, nevertheless, gained popularity among a wide range of other built environment professionals and with user groups, who may assume that what they are witnessing is representative of real urban design. In particular certain single-issue elements can become the subject of campaigning by residents, or for that matter by other governmental and official groups responsible for 'problem solving' in an area. For example, many are critical of 'quick-fix' solutions to crime and design which disregard other vital components of the urban design agenda.

Other Professionals?   Another issue which will come up in various chapters in relation to the definition of urban design and the appropriate role of urban designers is the extent to which the design and architecture of individual buildings is a proper concern for urban design. Or to turn it around, one must admit that a fair amount of what is effectively urban design is being done by default, and often in ignorance, by other built environment professionals.

A key aspect of this is the effects of 'planning for the motorcar', which still have such a major influence on the nature of city form as a whole and on the scale and design of individual areas. Yet, the culture and objectives of highways engineers and transportation planners are not necessarily compatible with those of urban designers, although, by default, they have had a such a major input into the nature of urban design by their actions and policies. For example, for many years road design was based upon the presumed need to make the traffic go faster, and thus wide roads, long visibility splays and pedestrian segregation were key components of layout standards, destroying the human scale of urban environments. Nowadays, traffic calming is the order of the day (Trench and Ball, 1995). But in seeking to make streets safer it has not followed that they have become either more usable for human beings, nor more aesthetically pleasing (see J Hanna 'Whose streets are they anyway?', *The Geographical Magazine*, June 1996, pp.18–20 with reference to the 1993 Traffic Calming Act, which made all this possible). Bumps and bends are being purposely put back into residential streets but the approach is not necessarily based on a comprehensive urban design strategy (cf. Hass-Klau et al., 1992). Unfortunately, the general public may be unaware of the power of the highways engineer and attribute blame to the town planners, and expect solutions from urban designers.

Another form of what many people see as an aspect of 'urban design by default' is the influence of building design and control. Urban designers themselves may argue that this whole issue of building regulation and control is not part of their pitch, as it relates to 'architecture' of individual buildings. However, they would point out that the gradation between public and private space is often subtle and that the insides of privately owned public buildings such as shopping malls, places of worship and office atria are of just as much interest to the urban designer as the conventional street or piazza. In addition, many 'ordinary people' – and some town planners – assume that urban design is not limited to the outsides of buildings and the wider built environment, but expect the principles and issues inevitably to affect the insides

of buildings as well. For example, this has been a major issue in respect of designing for disabled access, in which it has often been argued that a more holistic approach is needed to facilitate free flow between, through and within buildings. The argument that the role of the town planner stops at the entrance to a building and responsibility for the insides is taken over by the building regulation authorities has been much criticised. Likewise, many 'women and planning' issues relate not only to overall land use principles but to how individual buildings are used and designed, not least in respect of the provision of social facilities such as crèches, baby buggy access and storage, and general crime, surveillance and safety issues. Again, this is a matter for debate, for, as will be seen, some contributors are clearly of the view that the proper place of urban design is 'outside' whilst other contributors cannot prevent their chapters and proposals for change flowing 'inside', particularly in relation to disability, sustainability, childcare, and crime and design issues. Statutory town planning, as explained in earlier volumes, is, strictly speaking, concerned only with overall land uses and outsides, whilst the building regulations are meant to be responsible for the insides. Yet many town planners concerned with the social aspects of urban design (in the broadest sense of the term) have questioned and sought to challenge this dichotomy. The reader should therefore be aware of this controversy as another debate going on throughout the book. Whatever urban design is, it is certainly not a static field, but is still evolving, and it is for the readers to decide what they consider should be included in or excluded from its scope. The various contributors will cast further light on the points raised above in their respective chapters, giving their own perspectives and insights on the nature of the beast.

The place and contents of the book

The relationship with the series, *Exploring Town Planning*

Earlier volumes have put considerable emphasis upon, variously, the spatial, social, economic and political aspects of town planning. The visual and design aspects were featured in Volume I *Introducing Town Planning* (Greed, originally 1993, now 2nd edn., 1996c, Part III: The Visual and Design Aspects of Planning). This was intended to give an elementary, quick run through the centuries on the history of town planning and architecture. In particular, Table 8.1 (p. 147) in *Introducing Town Planning* provides a handy 'ready reckoner' on the chronological sequence of the development of architectural styles which may be of use when reading this book. *Introducing Town Planning* may also be of interest to those seeking basic background before tackling the more advanced text found in the present volume. For example, in discussing urban conservation the contributors emphasise urban design issues, not the technicalities of listing buildings or designating conservation areas. Background information on these topics may be found in *Introducing Town Planning* which also covers the wider development control system in Chapters 8 and 9. Alternatively, the reader might consult one of the many planning law textbooks which are available nowadays, for instance, Heap (1996), Telling and Duxbury (1991), Moore (1995), Morgan and Nott (1995) and Grant (1995), as given in the bibliography. Likewise, those who need more legislative background upon environmental planning, as context to the discussions on 'sustainability and urban design', are advised to consult Ball and Bell (1995) and Lane and Peto (1996).

It is one thing to have ideas about urban design, even solutions, it is quite another to put these into effect within the constraints of the British statutory planning system. Previous volumes in this series have majored upon the issue of implementation of policy, and have sought to show the linkages between theory and practice. The theme of implementation, as stated earlier, is continued, to some extent, within this present volume, where examples of what can be achieved are given throughout. But in view of the *avant-garde* nature of the subject, and of the fact that, arguably, the existing town planning system is not an adequate 'container' to encompass all aspects of the scope and nature of modern urban design, emphasis is put upon presenting new ideas, concepts, and possibilities. Those readers who are interested in implementation of policy should consult Volume II of this series *Implementing Town Planning*, where, for example, the chapter on York Gate by Robin Tetlow deals with an architecturally sensitive, historical area, containing residential, commercial and retail development.

Part I: Introduction

This section contains the present chapter, and Chapter 2 which gives an overview of the development of urban design, within the context of Part I which constitutes the introductory section to the whole book.

Chapter 2 The scope of urban design   In this chapter Tony Lloyd-Jones argues that urban design is not just 'big architecture' but that its subject matter is concerned with all aspects of the production and use of the three-dimensional built environment. He also refutes the misapprehension that urban design is only practised at the level of urban street and square, and instead argues that urban design principles and strategies may be applied to all levels of planning from a small urban space to an entire city. In the course of this chapter he provides a contextualising history of the development of modern urban design.

Part II: Urban design interventions

Part II comprises five chapters, which investigate different aspects of how 'planning' policy has been used to intervene in the design, and especially the visual quality, of the built environment. A uniting factor among the chapter topics chosen is that all of these aspects of urban design are officially accepted within the modern discourse of town planning (to a degree), as evidenced by the receipt of government funding and legislative powers, which have given urban designers unprecedented opportunities 'to make a difference'. Whether current policy initiatives are really what urban designers would want to be doing in an ideal world, or what the ordinary people want, are issues which will be discussed further in Part III. Whereas Part II looks at urban design 'top-down' from the planners' perspective, Part III will look at urban design in terms of 'bottom-up' user responses and demands from residents, community groups and interested parties among the public.

Chapter 3 Urban Design and Planning Practice Matthew Carmona considers the role of design guidance and aesthetic control in town planning practice in shaping British townscape, with particular reference to government guidance, illustrated by detailed tables and text boxes. Consideration is given to the way in which design guidance policy operates within the hierarchy of the governmental planning system. From the point of view of architecture, the adoption of design briefs remains a thorny question. Carmona describes the professional clash of wills which accompanies efforts to control architectural design. Many architects are very unhappy with any attempt to control their individuality. With architectural education moving more in the direction of individual subjectivity, such clashes are likely to be more frequent in the future. For example, the role of PPG's (Planning Policy Guidance notes), circulars, and other central government policy directives issued by the Department of the Environment is investigated and categorised through the presentation of a series of extremely informative diagrams and tables. The role of urban development plans, local plans, and local authority-level design guidance is also considered and illustrated by a detailed case study of initiatives in Glasgow. The place of design guidance within the planning system is elucidated and recommendations are made for future good practice. At the same time, awareness of the constraints and opportunities of the private commercial property market context (from which the initiative for most large-scale development derives nowadays) is acknowledged and integrated into the debate.

Chapter 4 Conservation in the built environment
Richard Guise and Sandra Manley draw on their extensive experience of urban conservation issues to discuss the relationship between conservation, urban design, and town planning. Conservation may be seen as one of the few effective mechanisms still available to the urban designer within the statutory planning system which may be used to implement his/her policy agenda, albeit 'only' with reference to worthy historic areas and buildings. This chapter is, relatively speaking, more prescriptive than other contributions to the book, as the many examples and illustrations provided are used to present and critically interrogate accepted wisdom, checklists and principles of good urban design.

Chapter 5 Urban design and regeneration   Marion Roberts investigates the opportunities which the current policy priority of 'urban renewal' has offered the urban designer. The last fifteen years have seen many examples of design-led regeneration taking place throughout Western Europe. This chapter considers the topic in relation to holistic urban design strategies as against the mere creation of architectural landmarks, and discusses the dangers of creating an 'architectural zoo', rather than urban places in which human beings might live, work and feel at home. It will be argued that although British practice may be rightly criticised for being too conservationist in outlook (compare the previous chapter), conservation-led renewal strategies are also valid if treated in a sufficiently robust fashion. Finally, the problems of creating renewal areas which are too homogeneous and similar in appearance are considered and it is argued that best practice creates new authentic regional style by using the existing heritage to create a new visual future. Examples are drawn from a variety of locations, ranging from the urban development programme associated with the hosting of the Olympics in Barcelona; the urban design opportunities afforded by the reunification of Berlin; Euralille; to Temple Bar in Dublin and other community-based urban renewal pro-

grammes in Britain, thus encompassing a wide span of scales, and levels of urban renewal.

Significantly, many of the examples used in this book are not British, because, as stated above, an urban design agenda has not yet been fully integrated within the British town planning system, though, perhaps this book will assist in this process. Examples are drawn particularly from other European countries, not because of a narrow Eurocentric perspective, but because of their potential applicability to the comparable British situations, in view of the similar cultural context and historical urban heritage. Nevertheless, as will be explained, many of the seminal ideas in the postwar period which shaped the discipline of urban design were derived from the North American situation, where, paradoxically, urban development is generally much more recent, and on a much larger scale (Lynch, 1960; Jacobs, 1961).

Chapter 6 Landscape and urban design   Urban design and landscape architecture converge in their focus upon the public realm. In this chapter Ian Thomson argues that good landscape design is essential in the creation of a high-quality urban environment. The benefits of parks, open spaces and vegetation in urban areas will be discussed. Landscape design has traditionally been concerned with issues of aesthetics and amenity, but a new set of values related to ecological sustainability has now been superimposed, which is already influencing the way places are designed and managed. This chapter therefore looks at past examples of landscaped space in the urban situation, such as Victorian parks, and at modern aspects and examples of landscape design.

Chapter 7 Art in the public realm   Nowadays, over 70 per cent of urban planning authorities in Britain have policies which encourage the provision of public art, thus the integration of art into the urban environment has become an important issue. In this chapter Marion Roberts draws on the author's recent research and consultancy experience and includes examples from Britain, North America and Europe. The discussion is set within the context of investigating the reasons for local authorities' recent interest in public art, and explains the motivation of both the public and private sector towards its provision. The chapter considers the components of good practice by means of a review of four key requirements: the site, the provider, the audience and the artist. The relationship of such policies to wider issues of the social, community and cultural role of town planning will be considered in the course of illustrating developments in public art. Significantly, issues such as public art often overlap with the interests of other 'minority' groups, such as 'women and planning' or ethnic minority community groups (see WDS, current publications, No.17). For public art to be 'real' and 'wanted', of course, there needs to be congruence between the intentions of providers and artists, and reception by the audience and community. This is not necessarily achieved through consultation, but sensitivity and awareness needs to be built into the whole process.

Part III: Urban design: current issues (user requirements and responses)

This section comprises six chapters which are characterised by a focus upon the demands and ways in which people use cities. This emphasis continues a theme which has been building up in earlier volumes in this series, namely the importance of looking at how people use land and the need to question the narrow preoccupation of traditional town planning upon land uses (see Part VI: *Alternative Perspectives* of *Implementing Town Planning* (Greed, ed. 1996b) for full discussion of this matter). It also strongly reflects the 'user' theme present within urban design as reflected in the definitions given in this book.

Chapter 8 Design for sustainable movement   In this chapter Hugh Barton develops further concepts first introduced in the previous volume *Investigating Town Planning*, now bringing them to bear specifically on urban design issues, with particular reference to transport, movement and sustainability. He shows that in order for detailed, local planning policies to be effective they must be tied into a higher-level city-wide strategy which relates to overall urban densities, location of amenities and facilities, and public transport policies. This chapter is concerned with far more than just transport, but with user-orientated concerns of movement, accessibility and therefore location and design of the components which comprise the whole city.

Chapter 9 Design for accessibility   Sandra Manley continues the theme of accessibility, relating it to the demands of campaigning groups of people with disabilities, who have become a major force in questioning and seeking to reshape so many assumptions basic to town planning and urban design. A central theme of this chapter is that the creation of a barrier-free public realm, which is accessible to those with disabilities and to those who have difficulties in personal mobility, would in fact benefit everyone in society. It is argued that accessibility should not be seen as purely a technical matter related to

the limited requirements of the Building Regulations, but there is a much wider agenda which affects all aspects of town planning and urban design, and challenges the very culture of the built environment professions. Accessibility is seen as a civil rights issue, essential to giving people a better quality of life, and therefore too important to be left to Building Control. After statistically defining the types of users in relation to disability groups, she draws on her research and training experience with local authorities. She discusses the gaps in existing policy and makes comparisons with the situation in the United States. She explains a notation system and checklist for use in analysing accessibility of the built environment. Again, like Chapter 4, this chapter is somewhat more prescriptive in nature and is based upon current examples with illustrations. Some additional background statutory material is provided in Appendix II at the end of the book.

Chapter 10 Women and the built environment   Despite the fact that women make up over half the population, they are poorly represented in the built environment professions. Even when urban design and town planning appear to be enlightened and concerned with users and people, it is likely that the models used of the average human being will be based on men, or if women's needs are taken into account, it is likely that outdated and stereotyped gender images will be used. Sue Cavanagh considers some recent initiatives which have attempted to redress the balance, with reference to key areas of women's use of the city, namely housing, shopping and town centres, safety and transport. Finally, prospects for future change are reviewed.

Chapter 11 Planning for crime prevention   Henry Shaftoe begins by discussing the way in which designed environments of the last forty years have encouraged crime, or not, in ways which were quite unforeseen. Current approaches to reduction of crime are critically reviewed. The key issues which planners need to bear in mind when they are addressing community safety are then discussed and examples are given of how good planning and informed urban design practice can contribute to safer environments. Finally, safety issues are reviewed in context, providing a more prescriptive conclusion to this chapter. Because of the topicality of 'crime and design', its extreme concern to citizens, high-profile media coverage, and the enduring popularity of the topic for student dissertations, a little more background is given here to clear the air about some of the criticisms. In seeking to assess the role of urban design in combatting crime one is inevitably drawn into historic debates about environmental determinism, that is, the extent to which the environment might influence people's behaviour, and this theme is returned to in the last section.

Chapter 12 The people and the process   Rob Cowan provides a bridge between the preceding chapters' emphasis upon user responses, and the next chapter which provides a case study of how people actually use what has been designed for them in relation to residential development. This is discussed with reference to UDAT, that is the activities of Urban Design Assistance Teams, in design in/with the community. Written by a well-known planning journalist who has been involved in many community initiatives himself, the chapter gives a wider perspective on what is going on in terms of varied manifestations of community involvement.

Chapter 13 Conclusion   In the concluding section, Clara Greed reviews the issues raised in Parts II and III, which could be characterised as the 'top-down' and 'bottom-up' approaches, respectively, to urban design. The chapters have revealed the scope of issues covered by urban design, and the range of scales and types of area, incorporating city-wide macro-level; meso-level district and neighbourhood planning; and micro-level housing estate and individual building design. The question of who the urban designers are, what they do, and what qualifies them to do it will be revisited. The relative importance of innate qualities as against educational training to make a good urban designer will be discussed, with reference to the underlying cultural concepts of the artist, inspired designer and genius. The impact of urban design on the people, that is 'the designed' will be re-evaluated in a discussion of environmental determinism in the light of the expectations as to the power and role of urban design expressed by the various contributors in their chapters.

Unresolved issues such as the appropriate levels and means of urban design intervention are reconsidered. Related to this is the question 'What do urban designers want [instead]?' This is a complex question; the answer depends upon one's perceptions of the problem, upon the priorities and values of the designer in question, the unique characteristics of the area under consideration, and the views of its community and users. The purpose of this book is not to give definitive or prescriptive solutions, but guidelines for the future are presented in relation to a discussion of the changing urban situation.

Checklist of dualisms

To conclude, here is a list of dualisms (or opposites) to bear in mind in reading the book, which may help the reader to reflect upon and organise his/her ideas as to what the scope, nature and purpose of urban design is:

town planner/urban designer
whole city/local area
insides/outsides
public/private
spatial/aspatial
social/visual
townscape/landscape
elite/popularist
urban/suburban
grands projets/ordinary areas
historical/modern
bottom-up/top-down
participatory/paternalistic
old/new
conservation/renewal
sustainability/decentralisation
genius/teamwork

2 The scope of urban design

Tony Lloyd-Jones

A new discipline in an era of professional change

This chapter looks at the historical, professional and policy context of urban design. This overview is intended to provide a framework for exploring the meaning and scope of urban design in contemporary planning and urban development. At the same time, it aims to provide the reader with a 'route map' to further reading about contemporary urban design ideas.

The central argument is that urban design is neither project-focused 'big architecture', nor limited to urban landscape issues. It does not operate solely at the interface between planning and architecture (that is, as 'small planning'), but is a problem-solving activity with applications to spatial decision-making at all scales of urban planning. Recent urban design practice, justifiably, has focused on the public realm and its three-dimensional quality. This has involved a timely reappraisal of the public face of urban architecture and a preoccupation with the aesthetic and perceptual character of the landscape of public spaces. There has been some neglect, however, of the role of design in the larger process of urban structuring of both public and private development.

Only fairly recently has urban design been identified as a specific discipline in the United Kingdom. It encompasses practices which have always had a central place in city planning and urban development, though with new techniques and different points of emphasis related to contemporary urban issues. The need for such a discipline has arisen as a result of the fundamental cultural, political, social and economic changes. These have focused attention on environmen-tal issues and the quality of life, on the nature of the city and on how urban form can best be adapted to our current and future needs.

During the 1960s and 1970s, town planning, transport planning and architecture were subject to considerable public criticism. During the 1980s and 1990s, they have been buffeted by the effects of economic change and government policy on the development industry as a whole, and on the public sector in particular. As with many other areas of professional practice, the boundaries of disciplines concerned with urban development, which had remained fairly constant for the best part of this century, have recently become more fluid. Architects have abandoned some of their traditional dominant roles (for example, in town planning) and had their dominance of others undermined by new disciplines such as project management. Town planning has been reduced to a largely regulatory, advisory or moderating role.

All professions have responded by developing new areas of specialism so that the traditional professional training commonly represents only the first step in developing a marketable skill. The pace of technological and organisational change has added to the confusion. It is unclear which of the new specialisms are transient and which may evolve to become an established part of a restructured system of professions, or whether, in fact, the whole concept of professionalism as we understand it may be under threat.

It is within this professional flux that the discipline of urban design has emerged. It overlaps a number of existing professions and incorporates elements of planning and architecture, landscape design, transportation and infrastructure planning. With such undefined boundaries and shifting points of focus, it has proved difficult to provide a simple, commonly accepted definition of the scope of urban design. At its broadest, urban design is about the form of cities. We may regard it as that element in the planning process that is concerned with finding an appropriate physical framework for human activities in cities. Such a definition is commonly qualified with the term 'three-dimensional'. In the larger sense in which we are using it in this chapter, however, urban form may be viewed in two or three dimensions, depending on the scale or level of resolution at which the design process is operating.

Origins of recent urban design theory in America and Europe

Contemporary British urban design practice can trace many of its influences to the United States, which was the crucible for new ideas in urban design in the postwar period. Many of the new theories, however, owed as much to European influences, including the long-established British tradition of physical planning and townscape design.

As American urban areas grew rapidly during the twentieth century it became increasingly difficult to distinguish the boundary between city and country. By the postwar period, the functional city of expanding metropolitan regions no longer coincided with an easily identified dense urban settlement. The term 'urban planning' was introduced to place a growing body of theory and practice in a suitably general geographical context (Branch, 1975). 'Urban' was a description of what had become a culture and lifestyle rather than a particular geographical territory. Urban planning could comfortably accommodate city, town and suburb, no matter how these were administratively defined or physically constituted.

It was within this larger framework of urban planning theory that ideas of a broad new approach to city design were evolving. The American Institute of Planners set up a committee to outline their policy towards urban design in the late1950s, with a growing debate about the topic in the planning journals (see, for example, Crane, 1960). Paul Sprieregaen's book, *Urban Design: the Architecture of Towns and Cities* was published in 1965, by which time the term had come into common usage in the United States. The conventions of urban planning at this time favoured rigidly-defined, functionally-zoned urban development. This was largely an inheritance of the International Modern Architecture Congress (CIAM), a forum for the development of modernist architecture and urbanism set up in the 1920s by the leading, mainly

European, architects of the time, including Le Corbusier, Walter Gropius and others. This paved the way for what came to be known as the 'International Style' in architecture. The CIAM came under the sway of Le Corbusier and his ideas of wholesale renewal of the contemporary city through zoned, single-use (mono-functionalist), high-rise developments. These were the ideas that were codified in the 1931 Athens Charter of CIAM, providing the basis of the new orthodoxy for city centre development. Simultaneously, an alternative, organic view of urban form, originating in the English Garden City movement, was being developed in the United States by Olmsted, Mumford, Perry and others (Lynch, 1987). This suggested a regional model of the city, decentralised, low-density and more suburban in character, hierarchically organised on the basis of semi-autonomous, community-based neighbourhood units or 'super-blocks'.

These very different concepts, it was suggested, had a similar effect in reinforcing the growing destruction of the traditional dense urban fabric of cities and were beginning to be widely challenged. In America in 1961, the economist Jane Jacobs published her powerful critique of both currents of modern town planning in *The Death and Life of Great American Cities*. This laid the ground for looking at the complexities of land use arrangements, and high-density living in traditional city blocks and the shared activities of the traditional city street in a new light. The first 'fully articulated women's view of the city' in the twentieth century (Berman 1984, p.322), Jacobs' book is a rich compendium of observations and analysis of the design, social use and economies of cities. Many current initiatives in urban regeneration and urban design take their inspiration from Jacobs' work. Most recently, her ideas about mixed development and density have seen a renaissance and an application in strategies for the revitalisation of city centres, the provision of natural surveillance ('eyes on the street') and compact, environmentally sustainable, urban form.

Within the CIAM itself, a group of younger European modernist architects which included Alison and Peter Smithson, Aldo Van Eyck, Giancarlo De Carlo and Ralph Erskine, alienated by the dominant high-rise, mono-functionalist concepts of the city, had formed Team X in 1953. They dedicated themselves to exploring new low- and medium-rise, high-density interwoven urban structures that would allow opportunities for social exchange and encounter that the International Style excluded (Zucchi, 1992). While, through the ideas and work of people like De Carlo, Erskine and Van Eyck, Team X had a humanising influence on modernist urban design, the interpretation of the Team X philosophy varied widely in practice. In Britain, the Smithsons called for a new way of structuring cities that fully expressed the motor vehicle as the generator of contemporary urban form (Smithson, 1968). This laid the theoretical basis for an approach to urban renewal which emphasised vehicular and pedestrian segregation and built upon Le Corbusier's idea of 'streets in the air'. Such ideas were realised in high-density public housing schemes including Park Hill in Sheffield, and in numerous other 'deck access' and 'megastructure' approaches to urban development. At a city scale, the Team X approach can best be seen in designs like that of Candilis and Woods for Toulouse-Le Mirail, an extension for the existing city of Toulouse, planned to accommodate 100,000 people (Kostof, 1991). The influence of such ideas spread well beyond those involved in the group, however, affecting the conceptual planning of a new generation of British new towns, such as Geoffrey Copcutt's 1961 design for Cumbernauld Town Centre and the 1970 proposals by Maitland, Gosling and Lowe for Irvine New Town central area (Gosling and Maitland, 1984, pp. 56–7). The acquiescence to the needs of the car evident in many of the schemes at this time led many architects and urban planners into yet another and, in many ways, more destructive cul-de-sac of modernist design theory.

Meanwhile, new ideas about urban design based on quite different sources were germinating within American universities. At the Massachusetts Institute of Technology during the 1950s, Kevin Lynch and Donald Appleyard began to devise new techniques for analysing and representing the perceptual structure of cities. Here again, the influence of European modernism was significant, in particular the tradition of abstract graphic symbolism developed at the famous Bauhaus design school in prewar Germany and represented at MIT by the émigré professor, Gyorgy Kepes (Gosling and Maitland, 1984, pp. 43–6; Appleyard, Lynch and Myer, 1964). Kevin Lynch's first, and most famous work, *The Image of the City*, dates from this period, providing an account of a research project, undertaken over a number of years and carried out in three American cities (Lynch, 1960, new edition 1988).

The project resulted in the evolution of the concept of legibility, based on five elements which, Lynch contended, people use unconsciously to organise their 'mental maps' of an urban area. The concepts of legibility have proved invaluable as an analytic and design tool. *The Image of the City* helped give rise to a new science of human perception and behaviour in the city (see Walmsley, 1988). For urban designers, however, it is Lynch's innovative use of graphic notation to link quite abstract ideas of urban structure with the

Figure 2.1 'Organic modernism' Team X-inspired megastructure in Irvine New Town, Scotland. Central area project by Barry Maitland, 1970, model. (Gosling and Maitland (1984) *Concepts of Urban Design*, Academy Editions)

human perceptual experience which has proved the strongest legacy of this work, liberating them from the previous straightjacket of the physical masterplan. David Crane, at the University of Pennsylvania, drew on the work of Lynch, Jacobs and others and brought these ideas together in his concept of the 'Capital Web', a physical and perceptual mechanism for structuring the city at a metropolitan scale, combining the main components of public space (the public realm) with the main elements of physical urban infrastructure (Crane, 1960; Buchanan, 1988; Caulton, 1995). A new generation of younger urban designers studied under Crane, together with social science theorists like Herbert Gans, Paul Davidoff and Britton Harris who were profoundly critical of the physical bias of CIAM-type urban planning. They included the South African architect, Denise Scott Brown, previously influenced by Team X ideas during her studies at the Architectural Association in London.

Scott Brown later joined Robert Venturi in a partnership that had a singular influence on popular concepts of architecture and urbanism (Scott Brown, 1990; pp. 9–20). Venturi's book, *Complexity and Contradiction in Architecture*, questioned the whole purist, minimalist and elitist dogma that, in his view, the International Style in architecture had become. It provided the philosophical basis for the catholic approach to the use of architectural styles and symbolism seen, for example, in his design for the National Gallery extension in London, an approach which later came to be known as post-modernism. Venturi, Scott Brown and Izenour (1996) also re-evaluated the popular urban architecture of commercial 'strip development', development that most typified the postwar American urban landscape and suggested, in *Learning from Las Vegas*, that urban designers should draw on the neon light symbolism of the Nevada desert city, as experienced in car journeys.

Ideas of a morphological approach to urban design, which related new urban development to the historical structure of the city and typologies of urban space, were explored in the work of students in the Graduate Urban Design Studio under Colin Rowe at Cornell University from 1963 onwards. In these studies the figure-ground drawing, as an urban design tool, was used to powerful effect (Middleton, 1982; Rowe and Koetter, 1984). This typological approach to the urban context was already being explored in parts of Europe in the ideas of the Italian Rationalist School (in particular, Aldo Rossi and Carlo Aymonino) and other theorists, such as Rob and Leon Krier from Luxembourg and the Austrian architect Ungers. The typological approach was

interpreted in Berlin, for example, as a new urban planning method called 'Critical Reconstruction', which became established during the International Building Exhibition in the 1980s (see Chapter 6 for a fuller discussion). The basic idea was to maintain and restore the traditional nineteenth-century street pattern and form of urban block, street and square, without constraining the contemporary architectural expression of new building additions.

Aldo Rossi's *The Architecture of the City* introduced the notion of the collective memory of the city, with urban form as a repository of culture from generations past and for generations to come (Rossi, 1989). Whilst attacking modernism, the book was not a plea for unthinking preservation or for regarding the city as a museum. Rather, Rossi aimed to explore the 'deep structure' inherent in building types and how built form accommodates changing, living uses over time. Rob Krier also adopted an anti-modernist stance in his book *Urban Space*, which sought, among other things, to catalogue all possible forms of urban space generated from the geometric fundamentals of circle, square and triangle (Krier, 1984). His brother, Leon, is known for his recent work in the United Kingdom and his influence in this country is discussed later in this chapter, but these type of rationalist ideas in general had a widespread influence throughout Europe (Economakis, 1992).

Contextualism and townscape in the United Kingdom

In Britain, a strong impetus to the contextualist type of approach to city design, relating new development to an analysis of existing urban structure, came from a rather different direction in the work of Gordon Cullen. Cullen's highly influential *Townscape* was first published in the early sixties (Cullen, 1961). This drew on the aesthetic of the Picturesque, with its emphasis on the three-dimensional compositional character of sequences of urban spaces and collections of buildings, found in traditional European towns. The influence on urban planning of the Picturesque approach to urban design was already evident in the ideas of Camillo Sitte at the end of the last century and subsequently developed through the work of Barry Parker and Raymond Unwin, Clough Williams-Ellis and others (Broadbent, 1990, pp. 270–5).

Unwin and Parker were largely responsible for giving tangible form to the Garden City idea in a series of masterplans that included Letchworth and

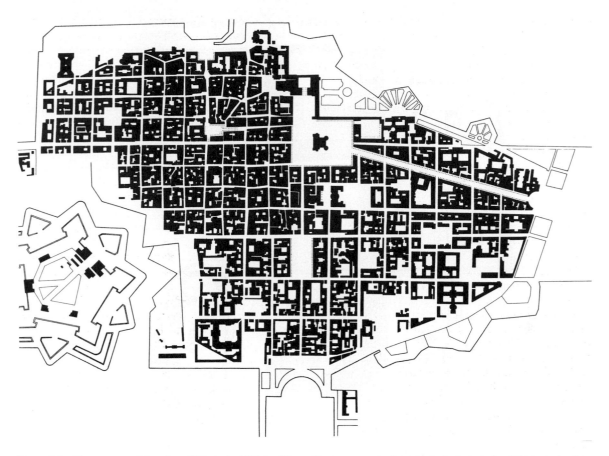

Figure 2.2   Figure-ground drawing of Turin in 1840 by Wayne Copper as part of a morphological study of historical urban form at the Cornell Urban Design Studio in 1967. (*Cornell Journal of Architecture*, 1982)

Hampstead Garden Suburb and which influenced town planning ideas in many countries across the world. Raymond Unwin, who transposed Sitte's ideas to the British context, combined formal and informal approaches to urban design, though he is best known as a proponent of the low-density garden suburb laid out according to Picturesque principles (Miller, 1992). Perhaps the single most influential figure in British twentieth-century urban design, Unwin had an acute grasp of the whole range of urban design and town planning issues. The ideas set out in his work, *Town Planning in Practice*, still find a resonance, for example, in the approach of the 'New Urbanists' in the United States outlined at the end of this chapter.

The term 'Townscape' was first used in the study of Oxford by Thomas Sharpe in 1948 and a number of writers have made significant contributions to contemporary townscape theory (see, for example, Gibberd,

1953; Worskett, 1969; Tugnutt and Robertson, 1987). It is Gordon Cullen, however, who dominates postwar British urban design thinking in this respect. Cullen's townscape ideas were developed in the period of the 1950s when, in the context of Ian Nairn's 'Outrage' column in the *Architectural Review*, Cullen's drawings highlighted the absence of urban design in and lost opportunities of much of the postwar reconstruction work that was going on at the time in many of Britain's cities. Out of this work arose perhaps the best known of Cullen's concepts, that of serial vision, which stresses the sequential and unfolding nature of the urban experience. In later studies in the 1960s for Alcan Industries, focused around the hypothetical town 'Alcan', Cullen developed his own method of recording townscape, the Notation, and a systematic framework for human and physical urban design criteria called the Scanner (Gosling, 1996).

CASEBOOK: SERIAL VISION

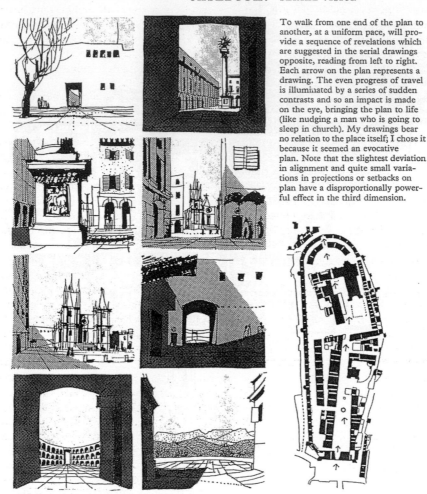

To walk from one end of the plan to another, at a uniform pace, will provide a sequence of revelations which are suggested in the serial drawings opposite, reading from left to right. Each arrow on the plan represents a drawing. The even progress of travel is illuminated by a series of sudden contrasts and so an impact is made on the eye, bringing the plan to life (like nudging a man who is going to sleep in church). My drawings bear no relation to the place itself; I chose it because it seemed an evocative plan. Note that the slightest deviation in alignment and quite small variations in projections or setbacks on plan have a disproportionally powerful effect in the third dimension.

Figure 2.3 Gordon Cullen's record of a walk through a hypothetical Mediterranean hill town is his first introduction to readers of *Townscape* of the concept of 'serial vision'. (Cullen (1971) *The Concise Townscape,* The Architectural Press)

Lacking the interdisciplinary framework which fuelled the early development of urban design teaching and theory in leading American universities, the first urban design courses in the United Kingdom did not get started until the early 1970s. Courses in five schools of architecture started as a result of an RIBA initiative. In 1976, the departments of architecture and planning at Oxford Polytechnic (later Oxford Brookes University) set up a Joint Centre for Urban Design which provided a curriculum that proved to be more resilient and successful than earlier initiatives. Other important academic developments in the early seven-

ties included the theoretical work on land use configurations and built form by March and Martin at the University of Cambridge School of Architecture. This lent support to the conviction that the medium-rise perimeter (courtyard) block could achieve the densities of high-rise pavilion-type blocks and slabs with a much greater effectiveness of the use of urban land (Martin and March, 1972).

By the end of the 1970s the team at Oxford Polytechnic were formulating a contextualist method of urban design which drew liberally on American sources (Lynch's theory of imageability, Jane Jacobs' ideas about permeability and small perimeter blocks, Rowe and Koetter's stress on public/private distinctions and Standford Anderson's (1978) notion of adaptability or 'robustness') as well as the British townscape tradition, with its emphasis of perceptual variety. This was later published as *Responsive Environments* (Alcock et al., 1985). A similar concern with making the public environment in towns and cities more 'user-friendly' using townscape ideas was behind Francis Tibbalds' *Making People-Friendly Towns* published in 1992.

The impact of the contextualist approach to urban design has varied with geographical location and cultural influence. In many parts of the world today, particularly in rapidly urbanising countries, the old International Style modernism, with its high-rise blocks, urban motorways and disregard for the traditional street form, still holds sway. In Europe and in many parts of the more industrialised world, however, a general change in the approach to urban form reflects a new view of how the car and pedestrians should be accommodated in cities. Despite the diversion into the pastiche historical styles of post-modernism, architects have, by and large, retained the architectural language of modernism. The mainstream of building design, however, has undoubtedly been strongly influenced by contextualism in terms of a new respect for the overall form of the traditional urban street and block and a concern for the public realm. This can be seen in some of the recent work of major mainstream modernist architects' practices like those of Richard Rogers and Norman Foster, both of which have carried out major studies of the public environment in Central London during the 1990s.

New modernist approaches to urbanism

Even in the areas where it has had most impact, however, it would be wrong to say that contextualism is universally accepted. A radical, neo-modernist approach to urbanism has persisted in the ideas of the architectural avant-garde since the mid-eighties. In this view, the city is primarily a canvas or 'text' for a formalistic, critical and artistic comment on the culture of modernism. This intellectual approach, however, is usually quite removed from any functional understanding of urban processes. The new modernism encompasses a wide range of approaches. It departs radically from International Style modernism in its emphasis on complex, ambiguous and often discordant and unstable architectural forms and on dynamic and anti-functionalist approaches to design, which contrast strongly with the rationalism and functional-

ism of conventional modernism. The impact of earlier epochs of avant-garde architecture, however, is important. The influence of the Russian Constructivism of the 1920s is evident, for example, in the work of the Iraqi-born architect Zaha Hadid, known for her competition-winning but unbuilt design for a new opera house for Cardiff.

A common theme in the work of some of the new modernists is the attempt to 'deconstruct' modernist architectural forms, making use of a series of unconventional formal techniques to create urban interventions that express the essential fragmentation or spatio-temporal complexity of our age. Thus the Swiss architect and urbanist, Bernard Tschumi, for example, interprets the contemporary city as patterns of events which occur within frames of reference or 'circuits' that have no intrinsic relationship to one another, and his designs exploit the random collisions that result from the layering of such frameworks (Tschumi, 1994). The American theorist, Peter Eisenman, also uses unusual formal techniques, but of a more mathematical and rational kind (Eisenman, 1993). Such approaches share a predominance of the formal over the functional and a rejection of any hint of historical contextualism.

Also strongly influenced by Constructivism, the Dutch architect and writer, Rem Koolhaas, makes free use of the typologies of modernism, recombining them in new and ironic ways (Koolhaas, 1990; Lucan, 1991). Moving from a position that shared much with the deconstructionist approach of Hadid and Bernard Tschumi, Koolhaas has propounded an influential view of the late-twentieth-century city as requiring a response that recognises both its dynamic and indeterminate character in the face of global market forces and the continuing need to impose a minimum ordering principle (Koolhaas and Mau,1995).

The recurrent themes of technology, flexibility and indeterminacy in the new modernism derive from the urban concepts of a previous generation of architectural visionaries. This includes groups like the Metabolists in Japan, Superstudio in Italy and Archigram in the United Kingdom who were active in the late sixties and early seventies. Both Hadid and Koolhaas studied at the Architectural Association at the time that the influence of Archigram was at its height. Archigram's future cities took the form of megastructures inspired by contemporary developments in technology (Banham, 1976). Since such ideas were unlikely ever to be realised in practice, the emphasis in most of this theoretical urbanism was on the quality of the graphics rather than the substance of the ideas.

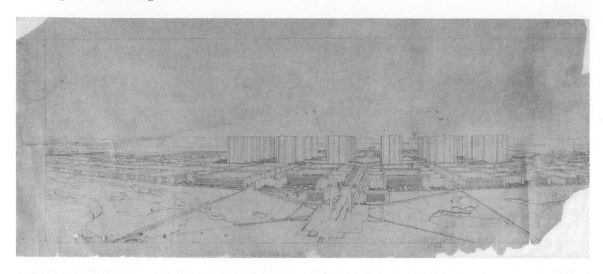

Figure 2.4   International Style modernism then and now: Le Corbusier's 1925 vision of the Contemporary City and Muang Thong Thani, a new city planned for one million people under construction near Bangkok by Australian architects Nation Fender. (Fondation Le Corbusier; Nation Fender Architects)

The new modernism has only a few manifestations in terms of built form and its theoretical influence has generally far outweighed its actual impact on the urban development process. One place where such concepts have been realised is in the masterplan for an international business centre – Euralille – in northern France (see Chapter 6). This reflects the interests of Rem Koolhaas, and his Office of Metropolitan Architecture, in encompassing a variety of urban functions within the envelope of large buildings. In its integrated approach to linking transport and other activities, the plan for Euralille adopts a more conventional attitude towards the practical requirements of the development.

The origins of modern city design lie in the attempts of planners and engineers, architects and social reformers to come to grips with the problems created by rapid industrialisation and urbanisation in the nineteenth century. Prior to the eighteenth century, cities were usually structured in a comprehensible and legible form, clearly reflecting the culture of the society that created them. The layout of cities was commonly based on cosmological symbols, ordered around ceremonial procession routes or focused on military, religious and civic landmarks. This enabled their inhabitants to adapt to the larger social, physical and spiritual order in which they lived. Communication was face-to-face and public life took place in public places. The web of public thoroughfares, of commercial avenues and market

places, of social promenades and meeting places, what we would now call the public realm, was placed within a broader structure of civic space expressing larger cultural dimensions and housing the grander public ceremonies. According to Kevin Lynch (1987, p. 13), in the historic city 'ritual and place fitted together.' Life in the cities, as centres of civilisation, was always dynamic and complex but held within this larger order. In addition, most people continued to live in small towns and villages where life changed little and people were bound to and secured by the established life of the local community.

The pattern of a city was frequently determined by the founders and the efficiency of the grid and other geometric layouts as urban structuring mechanisms was recognised in some of the earliest examples of urban civilisation (Lynch, 1987, pp. 81–7). However, most urban development did not follow a predetermined plan but rather responded to the configuration of land ownership and the evolution of the urban road and infrastructure system (see Kostof, 1991). The decision-making about this type of public structure can be described as a kind of 'unconscious urban design' in which most of the urban development consequences were not considered in any detail.

With the growth of capitalism and rapid urbanisation, the cities of Europe and America grew rapidly and this old order broke down. The main concerns of city development in the nineteenth century became how to obtain efficient access within cities, to provide modern

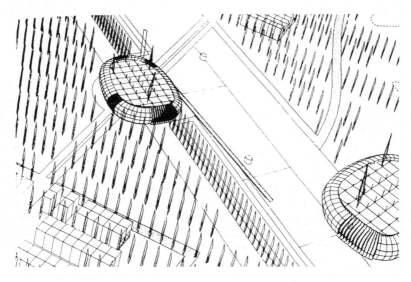

Figure 2.5 Bernard Tschumi: project for a business park extension to Lausanne, 1991. (Tschumi (1994) *Event-Cities,* MIT Press)

public services and to allow them to expand and function more effectively as engines of economic growth. The role of giving form to cities passed to engineers and reforming politicians like Baron Haussman who laid the system of boulevards that dissected the old medieval centre of Paris. This combined wide roads, promenades and a modern sewerage system with opportunities for property speculation on an immense scale and for reinforcing the public order (Vidler, 1978).

The demands for social reform, which gave rise to the town planning movement in the early part of this century, were largely based on a view of the burgeoning industrial cities as increasingly disordered and incomprehensible. The new planning profession saw its role primarily as regulating market forces which provided unequal access to the social benefits of the city and controlling its growth. Industrial growth and urbanisation in the nineteenth century had created huge areas of slum dwelling where people lived in insanitary and overcrowded conditions. The focus was thus primarily on public health and how to address the housing needs of the poor (Cherry, 1988).

The changing postwar perspective

The role of urban design within a broader planning framework needs to be set against the backdrop of the subsequent changing fortunes of the town planning profession in the twentieth century (Cherry, 1974; Hall, 1982). At the metropolitan scale, from an early stage, planners advocated policies that were directed at containing the growth of large cities and the loss of the countryside to new suburban development by the imposition of green belts, combined with a programme of new town development to relieve the overcrowded central areas of cities. The incorporation of these ideas in the town planning legislation of 1947 left its stamp on the larger form of British cities.

New town development also provided an immense stimulus for British planners and architects to explore new ideas of urban design on a large canvas. After the prewar experiments at Letchworth and Welwyn which were directly inspired by Ebenezer Howard's Garden City concept, 'second generation' new towns began to take shape in the 1950s. As noted in the previously mentioned Scottish examples of Cumbernauld and Irvine, these reflected the aspirations of a new generation of urban designers. They expressed a romantic fusion of machine-age modernism with the picturesque aesthetic of traditional, high-density, pre-industrial towns (Williamson, 1995, p.17). A

megastructure approach was not always evident but nearly all new towns conceived at this time were rationally planned around a sophisticated public transport system linking high-density centres, while providing good car access to lower-density residential settlements. Arthur Ling's plan for Runcorn in Cheshire, for example, with its figure eight busway is a model that has lessons for today's urban designers concerned with environmental sustainability and efficiency (ibid.).

This approach was still evident in the original 1970 masterplan by Llewelyn-Davies, Weeks, Forestier-Walker and Bor for Milton Keynes, the last and biggest of the postwar new towns, with its highly built-up city centre and strong emphasis on the public transport system. In the event, the development of Milton Keynes was driven by the logic of the city's 'super grid' road network. The team responsible for realising the plan, led by Fred Lloyd Roche and Derek Walker, were increasingly inspired by 'Autopia', the dispersed urban form found in the car-based, consumer metropolis of Los Angeles. According to Walter Bor, these were 'arrogant architects who had turned the Milton Keynes Master Plan inside out' (quoted in Williamson, 1995, p. 25).

At the local scale, attention was concentrated on city and town centre renewal, slum clearance and new housing. Much of the public housing that was constructed represented a marked improvement in living conditions. Much also was relatively successful in design terms and has provided a rich seam of urban design ideas through most of this century. However, the creation of ever larger housing estates reinforced segregation along social class lines. With the growing scale of such developments and the increasing demands of private car ownership in the postwar period, the physical and social problems inherent in this type of approach began to take on an acute form.

The architecture and urban design of sixties and seventies housing estates has probably been overemphasised as a factor in their failure. It has proved easier to blame designers and generic housing solutions like 'high rise' than to admit the true ongoing impact of inadequate management and maintenance. Nevertheless, problems undoubtedly did arise from the design philosophies adopted. Almost every estate that was built using the segregated pedestrian decks or 'pedways' principles that were popular during the 1970s, for example, subsequently needed major urban design surgery. The more physically cut off estates were from the general ebb and flow of city life, the worse the social problems that were likely to ensue. The impermeability of the housing estate and lack of spatial integration within it were almost uni-

Figure 2.6 Hook New Town proposals by London County Council Architects' Department, 1961-2. Early, unbuilt but influential examples of second-generation new town planning with concentrated commercial development on a raised pedestrian podium above segregated traffic circulation. (Banham (1976) *Megastructures: Urban Futures of the Recent Past*, Thames and Hudson)

versal features that derived from the underlying ideology of the town planning movement (Hillier and Hanson, 1984, p. 130).

Debate over growing crime and vandalism on council housing estates prompted a polarisation of argument over what urban design strategies should be used to address them. On the one hand was the view, put forward by Oscar Newman in the United States and Alice Coleman in Britain, that the solution lay in the transfer of communally-used space to private ownership ('defensible space' – see Newman, 1973 and Coleman, 1985). On the other side were solutions that favoured more intensive use of public areas, building on Jane Jacobs' concept of 'eyes on the street'. Spatial integration in housing estates and the relationships of pedestrian movement to patterns of built form was one of the areas explored by Bill Hillier and his colleagues at the Bartlett School of Architecture in the 1980s using a quantitative and graphical method known as 'space syntax' (Hillier and Hanson, 1984).

The growth and subsequent decline in the influence of town planning in the twentieth century has been linked to the fortunes of the welfare state, with which it shared the same interventionist ideology (Cherry, 1995). The framework of the modern welfare state and

the mixed economy were set in place during the Second World War and gave a powerful boost to town planning in the postwar period (Hall, 1995). The period of reconstruction and population growth, however, had came to an end by the 1970s. Large-scale public investment in housing and urban road improvements began to be cut back concurrently with a growing recognition of the social and physical problems associated with large-scale urban renewal and growing public reaction to these.

Around this time evidence of long-term structural economic change and decline became evident, with substantial increases in unemployment and a shift from manufacturing industry, particularly heavy engineering and basic industries, to services. Sociologists talked of the advent of the 'post-industrial' society, promising a vast increase in leisure time, but the main consequence for urban policy was the negative impact on those towns and cities and parts of cities that had been dependent on a manufacturing base. Planning, which had hitherto been driven by the perception that the growth of cities needed to be constrained and directed in an environment of expansion, faced an altogether different agenda. Cities increasingly found themselves being forced to compete on a global scale for limited

Figure 2.7   Angel Town Estate, Brixton, London: low-rise, medium-density deck-access housing with 'pedways', since demolished; Burrell Foleys' pilot scheme for transforming the estate. (Burrell Foley architects). Photo: Dennis Gilbert

capital investment and planners were forced into the unfamiliar role of managing decline and promoting growth. The tendency towards decentralisation with the exodus of people and jobs to the suburbs and beyond intensified the plight of the inner cities and helped set the conditions for the urban regeneration agenda which has dominated the 1980s and 1990s (see Chapter 6).

Peter Hall (1995) sees 1973 and 1974 as pivotal years because of the energy crisis which, though largely political in origin, focused attention on the energy-dependence of western economies and on the environmental agenda which had been set out dramatically a few years earlier in the Club of Rome's report, *Limits to Growth* (Meadows, 1968). This brought about a new emphasis on energy conservation and a debate on the car-based, high-consumption economy which gathered momentum in subsequent decades.

Political changes may have heralded the decline of town planning. Confidence was already being shaken, however, by a powerful shift in the cultural perspective throughout the sixties (the growth of the 'counter-culture', with its focus on local, community action and libertarian ideas). And, as has already been remarked, the ideas of planning commentators like Jane Jacobs were seriously questioning aspects of modernist town planning during the late fifties and early sixties.

With the growing reaction to the effects of large-scale interventions in the urban fabric in the sixties, these ideas helped focus attention on the failures of simplistic landuse planning methods, in particular masterplanning and the rigid zoning derived from the functionalist outlook of orthodox modernism. There was a radical shift in planning theory and practice which involved five related trends:

- The shift from design-based planning to social science-based planning
- The related move to a larger scale of problem conceptualisation
- The subsequent move towards a more participatory and partnership-based planning at the local scale
- A much stronger emphasis on the qualitative aspects of the urban environment
- The emergence of a preservationist mentality and new conservation-oriented planning mechanisms.

Planning as science, design as art?

Partly as a reaction, partly perhaps because of the decline of the proactive role of planning, with the loss of faith in physical planning social scientists began to

Figure 2.8a Modernist master planning of Brentford's riverfront in West London in 1965 by Max Lock and Partners (Max Lock Archive)

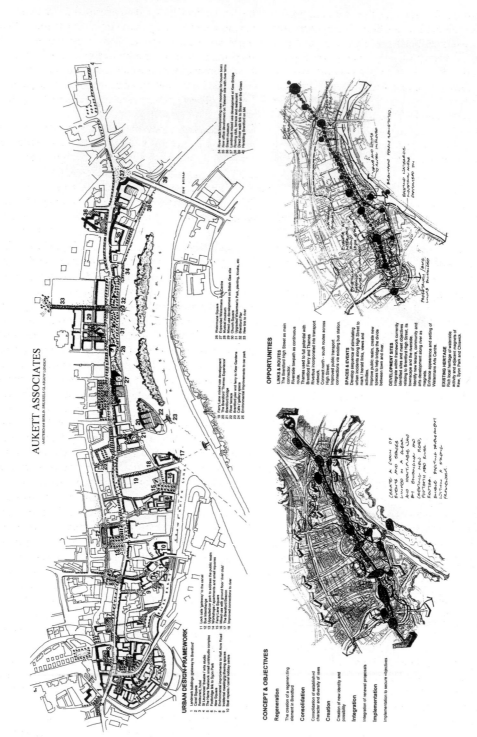

Figure 2.8b Contemporary urban design framework for the same area (as 2.8a) by Aukett Associates (Aukett Archive)

have an increasing influence over the planning profession, hitherto dominated by architects, engineers and surveyors. However, while social science appeared to offer powerful techniques for diagnosing urban problems, it offered no clear method for generating solutions. The great advantage of a design-based approach is its problem-centred focus and development of problem-solving skills (Businaro, 1994, pp. 5–6). The sidelining of urban design at this time was thus a factor in the subsequent loss of planning influence, a deterioration in planners' understanding of design issues and a growing alienation of the architectural and planning professions from one another.

In the UK and some other low-growth economies of the developed world, the emphasis in the late 1960s began to move away from traditional land use-based masterplans at the urban scale towards strategic planning at the regional scale. This was a recognition that masterplanning was insufficiently dynamic to deal with urban change but rested on a continuing belief that urban development, as a global system, could be understood and controlled. With structure plans, the aim was to avoid being geographically specific and rigid. Physical plans, where they existed, were diagrammatic and conceptual and the stress was on written policy.

The preparation of structure plans during the 1970s was often associated with the computer modelling of urban 'systems' (Devas and Rakodi, 1993, p. 85). This systems view of planning reflected the increasing influence of rational methods drawn from management science and cybernetics (see Chadwick, 1978). Such an approach offered social scientists techniques for making their statistics meaningful by looking at city systems in a structured way. At the same time, it seemed to offer an opportunity to spatial planners to model the impact of design options in an objective way and to overcome the subjective bias of the design disciplines. Rather than rely on highly prescriptive masterplans that were unworkable (except in a highly centralised, command economy), it was suggested that planners could, through an enhanced scientific knowledge of behaviour patterns in cities, influence their development through more strategic interventions. For a brief period, this approach drew together people from both a social science and design background with the lure of turning planning into a new urban science.

In practice, however, the promise was not realised and the retreat from the complex issues of the physical design of the city and the attempt to model spatial systems at ever larger levels paved the way for the virtual abandonment of spatial planning. Already, in the late 1950s, Jane Jacobs had foreseen that this approach, which promised a new future for town planning, was just as likely to hasten its demise. As she described it, 'there is a widespread belief among many city experts today that city problems already beyond the comprehension and control of planners and other administrators can be solved better if only the territories involved and problems entailed are made larger still and can therefore be attacked more broadly. This is escapism from intellectual helplessness.' (Jacobs, 1984, p. 422).

Political and economic change, more decentralisation, an emphasis on public participation and action-orientated planning and economic deregulation were all undermining the basis upon which planners could assume to control and regulate the development process. With the move from 'blueprint planning' to action or 'process-planning' the systems view of planning fell by the wayside (Devas and Rakodi, 1993, p. 87).

In the 1980s, the government adopted more laissez-faire approaches to counter the effects of industrial decline. The scientific approach rapidly gave way to market-led planning by appeal and 'leverage planning', where planning restrictions were largely abandoned in selected development areas and central government attempted to stimulate private development through strategic public investment (Brindley, Rydin and Stoker, 1989). This was aimed at triggering economic and physical regeneration of the inner cities through public–private partnerships but involved a continuous scaling down of public capital investment (Bailey, Barker and MacDonald, 1995). Along with the creation of relatively planning-free development zones, intervention at the local scale was increasingly limited and fragmented, relying on a market-based development site-led approach to regeneration.

There were a few notable exceptions to this site-based approach. Large provincial cities such as Glasgow and Birmingham adopted district-wide design-led or design-informed urban regeneration strategies with some success (see Chapter 6). More recently, Manchester has embarked on a major city centre renewal project following the devastation of the 1996 IRA bombing, through the medium of an urban design competition won by EDAW, an international planning and landscape grouping. Glasgow's development of an urban design strategy for the city centre came on the heels of a highly successful marketing campaign to change public perception of the city ('Glasgow's miles better'). The critical intervention, following a study by Gordon Cullen in 1983, was the upgrading of Buchanan Street as the city's 'hinge', the north–south axis linking together the existing east–west axis along the north bank of the river, and to the north of the city, along the route of Sauchiehall Street (Galloway and Evans, 1991).

Birmingham employed consultants Tibbalds, Colbourne, Karski and Williams who used Lynchian concepts to suggest ways in which the public realm of the city centre could be 're-imaged' and reinforced within a series of clearly-defined urban quarters. This proved to be the starting point of a highly successful transformation of a metropolitan centre that had suffered more than most from urban motorway schemes. This is still in progress with the recent mixed-use Brindley place development (see Coupland, 1996, pp. 247–8) and plans for transformation of the central Bull Ring site. For the most part such strategies were part of an image-building or 'civic boosterism', concentrating on marketing central business districts and therefore having little impact on more problematic run-down inner-city and suburban areas.

The project-focused policies of the 1980s were one of the factors leading to a revival of interest in urban design. This was very much driven, however, by a view of the city as a work of art and an approach which focused on the visual impact of the major individual architectural statement. In stark contrast to and perhaps partly in reaction to the scientific and rationalistic approaches of functionalism and the systems-based approaches, an inspirational view of design took hold.

The construction boom of the late eighties saw a huge wave of commercial development and redevelopment in the business centres of cities. In London, the most notable examples were the Broadgate development at Liverpool Street Station and the Canary Wharf development on the Isle of Dogs. This type of large-scale, primarily office development raised issues of impact on the public realm which were addressed to a degree by the designers of Broadgate, though hardly at all in Docklands (see Edwards, 1992), with private corporate image naturally playing the central role in determining their character.

What was most definitely not addressed in such developments were broader social and planning issues: how the adjacent communities could benefit, the problems of creating large areas largely devoted to office-based activities and related issues of sustainability and vitality. It was these type of issues that held back similarly scaled developments on the Spitalfields market site, adjacent to the Broadgate development and on the huge railway site north of Kings Cross Station.

At Spitalfields, in London, there was an attempt by architects MacCormac, Jamieson and Pritchard to knit together the interests of developer and community with an ingeniously configured mix of uses across

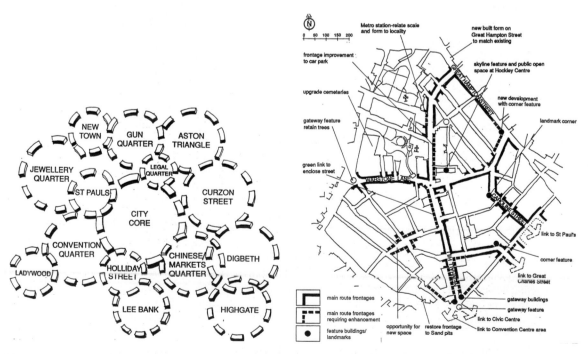

Figure 2.9 Townscape opportunities for Birmingham's Jewellery Quarter from the City Centre Design Strategy by Tibbalds/Colbourne/Karski/Williams, 1990. (Tibbalds Monro Ltd)

the site. A grandiose masterplan for the Kings Cross site by Sir Norman Foster and Partners incorporated a new public park and some low-cost housing but was too commercially orientated to satisfy the local authorities or communities living in the area. Both schemes were scuttled by a failure to resolve the conflicts of public and private interest before the boom turned to slump in the early nineties.

Shaping policy: urban design concepts in the 1990s

During the early 1990s, with the financial collapse of the Canary Wharf development and a growing recognition that a laissez-faire and market-led approach to the urban environment could not be sustained, there was some discernible shift in government attitudes towards urban planning issues. The new local plans and unitary development plans represented a strategic approach to spatial planning at the local scale, without the prescriptiveness and detail of the old zoning plans. Since they lacked any integral three-dimensional conceptualisation of the urban fabric, however, there was nothing to bridge the land-use 'blobs on the map' with the details of brickwork and fenestration at the development control level (Rowland, 1995, p. 23).

A new emphasis on a more coordinated, area-based approach, if one which increasingly rationed public investment to the lucky few winning bidders, was evident in the Conservative government's City Challenge initiative to promote inner-city regeneration. This paved the way for the Single Regeneration Budget schemes which enlarged the geographical and functional scope of the coordinated approach and which were linked to a more integrated and regional urban policy. These measures undoubtedly led to an increased demand for the integrated, team-based spatial approach of urban design. However, the increasing spatial focus of a diminishing pot of public investment implied that an ever larger section of the population was left out in the cold and did not benefit from resulting improvements.

Figure 2.10 Proposed redevelopment of Spitalfields Market, 1989 by MacCormac, Jamieson and Prichard. (MacCormac, Jamieson and Prichard)

In Britain during the 1980s, the crusade against architectural modernism had found its most prominent exponent in Prince Charles, who advocated a nostalgic view of urban design which drew strongly on the neo-rationalist ideas of Leon Krier. In Krier's opinion modern architecture has produced 'a cultural tragedy for which there is no precedent in history' (Economakis, 1992). The logical consequence of this position turned out to be a reversion to by-gone architectural styles such as classicism.

Of more significance, subsequently, for mainstream urban design, was the influence of Krier's concept of the mixed-use urban quarter as the basic unit of the city. Krier pictured the historic city as a federation of such quarters, which never exceed 33 hectares in extent and which provide for all the working, social and leisure needs of their inhabitants within an easy walking distance. This has been reinterpreted in the UK by the urban villages movement (Aldous, 1988) and in Krier's design for the new settlement of Poundbury extending the existing town of Dorchester, in Dorset.

The rather questionable thesis that large numbers of people can live in cities within walking distance of their place of work has meant that the urban village has been propounded as planning tool for sustainable urban development. More important, perhaps, has been the influence of the ideas of people like Krier and Jane Jacobs on government attitudes during the 1990s towards zoning and recognition of the need for a policy of promoting mixed uses to revitalise the centres of towns and cities threatened by out-of-town commercial development.

The adoption of the mainstream urban design agenda almost wholesale by the Department of the Environment under John Gummer's ministry came as a welcome surprise to many practitioners, although it was perhaps helped along by the fortuitous convergence of a number of strategic planning factors.

Following the UN Conference on the Environment in Rio de Janeiro in 1992, sustainable urban development became a central issue in British planning, seen increasingly in terms of curbing the growth of car movements on the urban periphery. This was compounded by the strengthening environmental policy in the European Union, with the 1990 European Commission Green Paper on the Urban Environment strongly advocating a 'compact city' approach to sustainable development. In addition to the environmental agenda and the problem of the threat to town centres from out-of-town developments have been the projections of an increase of more than four million in the number of households within twenty years. The natural constituency of the Conservative Party in and beyond the green belts of large cities was seen as under increasing threat from pressures for large-scale, 'greenfield' housing developments. Thus, the 'compact city' approach involving intensifying development within existing city areas, which was already implicit in Planning Policy Guidelines 6 and 13, was given added impetus.

The Department of the Environment's Quality in Town and Country Urban Design Campaign of the mid-1990s, together with the redrafted PPG1 on general policies and principles of planning policy guidance had an explicit urban design content, however. There has been a clear recognition of more general concerns with urban environmental quality and the role of good urban design in addressing it. It remains to be seen whether this will be extended to a recognition for spatial policies at the larger scale of urban structuring addressed by this chapter, though all the aforementioned strategic planning concerns point in this direction. Rather, the focus is on issues of local development and suggests a rather larger role in the future for local design control mechanisms. Here, the substantial research by John Punter (1995a) during the past decade, including more recent work with Matthew Carmona which is described in Chapter 3, is likely to have a major impact.

Bridging the interdisciplinary gap and professional divide?

Recent activity has tended to focus the concerns of contemporary urban design at the local level, the level of the site or the urban quarter. The necessity for a new design discipline operating at this scale was evident as early as the 1960s when Reyner Banham noted the need for an intermediate field of urban design to fill the interdisciplinary gap between architecture and planning concerned with 'urban situations about a half a mile square' (Gosling and Maitland, 1984, p. 7).

In urban design practice, this need has been expressed in the focus on the mechanism of the urban design brief, intended to be more prescriptive in spatial terms than the planning and development brief, and to resolve in advance any contradictions in written planning policy and standards (typically, as between townscape needs and density and parking requirements). The overlap between urban and architectural design occurs, then, at the level of the site planning which is required in compiling an urban design brief. This broadly corresponds to the early feasibility stage of building design. At the feasibility stage decisions need to be made as to the distribution (in three dimensions) of land uses across a site, and how these relate to the requirements of the site developer and the local community, the densities and broad patterns of circulation which determine the basic characteristics of the overall built form, and the intensity of activity on and around a site.

Where the urban design approach can vary from a purely architectural one is in its stress on the urban context. It differs from a purely planning approach, on the other hand, by visualising that context in integrated three-dimensional, spatial terms, rather than in terms of a set of separate, often unrelated general policy requirements for land use, density, transportation, etc. However, 'context' is something that has no clear or common spatial definition and reliance on the urban design brief for particular development sites is an inadequate substitute for a coordinated, area-based approach. In this respect, the idea of urban design guidelines or codes or, more strategically, of an urban design framework covering a given district or urban area has gained credence. This notion of urban design as a discipline sitting astride the boundaries of various existing professions brings into play issues of professional territory. Planners tend to regard broader questions of city form as their exclusive preserve. A typical planner's view is that urban designers should be engaged in turning the local and urban district plans into a three-dimensional reality.

The contrary view is of urban design as 'big architecture'. According to Peter Hall, there is a view that architects have moved into planning since the end of the 1980s building boom as a result of a lack of architectural commissions and an interest in 'flying a few planning kites' (Hall, 1995, p. 14). This reflects a shift in the view of the city as process to one of the city as product, more specifically as vision or image. In Hall's view, the most obvious explanation for this is 'the post-modern vision of the city as a place of images, images that are designed to protect the city in competition with other cities'. Certainly, the notion of vision is central to current urban design practice, although most urban designers would argue that finding an appropriate image can have a role beyond that of commercial promotion in giving authentic expression to a common meaning that a city has for its inhabitants. Nevertheless, the design competition has become enshrined as a method of dealing with large-scale urban problems. A leading exponent of 'planning as architecture', Richard Rogers, was able to supply a Thames-based vision of London which provided a focus of the Labour Party's 1992 environmental manifesto while winning the competition for revamping the South Bank cultural complex (Hall, 1995).

Many architects are typically arrogant in their attitude to planning issues and see urban design as architecture writ large. The excessively formalistic approach of most architectural schools in recent years has only intensified this problem. There is often a lack of recognition that urban design is a different discipline that requires additional skills and knowledge of the urban context, although an increasing number of architects are making use of the post-graduate urban design courses that have sprung up in universities around the country.

At the same time, it could be argued that urban design is filling a vacuum in the planning profession itself, created by a neglect of those very design skills which Hall sees as forming, in combination with a knowledge of social science, the hallmark of 'grown-up' town planning. One of the greatest potential values of urban design is as a means of overcoming the great professional divide. In so many instances, the interface of architecture and planning, which is most commonly found in the area of local authority development control, involves a vicious cycle of misinterpreted intentions.

Many planners have problems with the language of design and feel intimidated by architects. Planners who are not fully able to understand a design proposal adopt a defensive position, resorting to simple formulas, rigid interpretation of policies and overemphasis on copying the existing context. This is above all a problem of communication and one which the language of urban design should have a role in bridging. Urban design is defined pragmatically, according to the needs of the epoch, its tools and concepts used selectively by the established professional disciplines. The recent exclusive concern with the locality and professional exclusivity have implied a loss of understanding of the larger processes affecting urban form and of the possibility of making informed design decisions at urban scales and within environmental disciplines that are currently excluded and isolated from urban design.

The activities of traffic planners, for example, have a major impact on urban form. Streets structure the city and are usually its most enduring artifacts. The public realm has borne the brunt of the uncoordinated efforts of traffic engineers. Access and parking requirements have determined the form and density of new housing developments. Urban design, then, needs to link the perspectives of architecture, landscape design and planning with other disciplines such as surveying, property management and investment, transport planning, infrastructure planning and engineering. In the complex framework of contemporary urban development and management, traditional professional rivalries are increasingly irrelevant.

The current and future agenda in urban design

The relatively recent emergence of urban design as a distinct discipline can be seen as a response to planning issues which increasingly demand a spatially-based approach. A number of these issues are dealt with in this volume, from the immediate demands of meeting the skills needs of development and design control and conservation (see Chapters 2 and 3) to more general planning issues outlined in subsequent chapters. While the focus of this book is largely at the local scale, many of the current planning issues also require consideration in urban design terms at more regional levels. These include:

- Problems of transport pollution and congestion and the relationship of transport/land-use planning to environmental sustainability
- urban 'compaction' and intensification – increasing housing densities in existing urban areas
- The revitalisation of city centres (and, in many cities, designing to accommodate a successful renaissance of the centres)
- Issues of quality of life in cities and the need for competing cities to be marketed as leisure and business investment destinations
- The role of mixed-use development relating to security, vitality and sustainability in cities
- The redevelopment of large, redundant 'brownfield' industrial sites
- The regeneration of inner-city areas, including the renovation and revitalisation of run-down inner-city housing estates
- The pressures for new out-of-town housing developments and the increasing commercial development on the suburban periphery

All of these issues have brought urban design into the local planning arena but also have, to a greater or lesser extent, a strategic spatial component. The pressure to begin to address this strategic aspect in the UK is starting to be felt, particularly in response to new

transport developments (for example, new light rail systems in a number of cities and new road, tube and rail-based transport links and interchanges, particularly in relation to the Channel tunnel and the 'Thames Gateway' corridor) and in relation to the general demands on environmental sustainability.

Because of the restrictions on – and, in the case of the metropolitan counties, abolition of – institutional frameworks for considering such issues in strategic spatial terms, and diminished pressures in terms of urban growth and expansion, the notion of urban design at the metropolitan or even district scale has been noticeably absent from the planning perspective in the last twenty years. Milton Keynes represents the final chapter of the postwar new towns movement in the United Kingdom and the most recent attempt at urban spatial planning on a city-wide scale, one in which the civic design content of the original plan was dramatically diluted by the laissez-faire approach of its executors.

The 1980s saw the demise of the local authority house-building programme. It was replaced by a much enfeebled programme of new housing by housing associations held hostage to ever more stringent cost limitations and to a low-grade 'design and build' approach to housing design. This has cut off a potent source of urban design idea development, the public housing programme. Large-scale private housing developments have continued in synchronisation with economic cycles but with a pitiful lack of concern for the urban design character of housing form and layout on the part of the mass house-builders (see Biddulph, 1996 for one exception that proves the rule). The Essex *Design Guide,* published in 1973 and since updated, represents the last, much criticised but widely referred to attempt by a strategic authority to produce three-dimensional, urban design guidelines for influencing private housing development in a positive direction (Stones, 1992).

Both Glasgow and Birmingham used successful urban design-based regeneration strategies in the 1980s for revitalising their city centres but (unlike the notable example of Barcelona described in Chapter 6) no city-wide spatial strategies for wider-scale regeneration. If we look for ideas of urban design operating at a strategic, metropolitan or district scale in the 1990s we have few points of reference in the United Kingdom. The new agenda described above has generated a handful of projects which are as yet unrealised, such as the Kent Thameside development around the proposed Ebbsfleet International station in Kent by David Lock Associates (Thomas and Cousins, 1996).

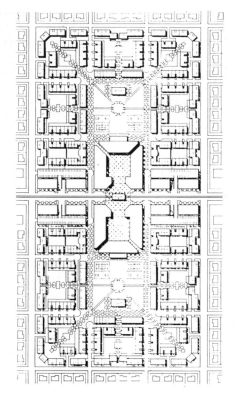

PEDESTRIAN POCKET

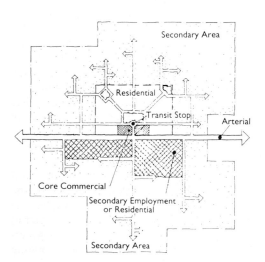

TRANSIT-ORIENTED DEVELOPMENT

Figure 2.11 Urban design for sustainable communities: integrated spatial planning of transport, land use and built form in Peter Calthorpe's model Pedestrian Pocket and TOD (transport-oriented development). (Calthorpe (1993) *The Next American Metropolis*, Princeton University Press)

In the main, however, we need to look outside the United Kingdom, to the recent urban design ideas being developed in Australia or the new planned communities in the United States. Here the 'New Urbanism' of Peter Calthorpe, Andres Duany, Elizabeth Plater-Zyberk, Peter Katz (1994) and others has been most significant (Kelbaugh, 1989; Katz, 1994). This small group has set up a Congress for New Urbanism with a charter that aims rather self-consciously to challenge the Athens Charter of the CIAM (Murrain, 1996). In this, the focus is on environmental sustainability and 'community building' at the macro level of the metropolitan region, the middle level of neighbourhood, district and corridor, and at the local level of block, street and building.

Duany and Plater-Zyberk are known for their application of rigid urban design codes in the planning of new communities of Seaside and Wellington in Florida. These are strongly influenced by the ideas of Leon Krier and somewhat exclusive and nostalgic in character. Nevertheless, they do incorporate a variety of dwelling types, including higher densities than are normal in contemporary American suburban developments. Peter Calthorpe's concept of the Transit-oriented Development (TOD) represents an adaptation of Garden City philosophy to suburban regional planning for more sustainable development in the American metropolis. It involves building a network of higher density, mixed-use, centres with a mix of housing types connected by a rapid transit system and feeder bus routes (Calthorpe, 1993).

We might look too, to the some of the so-called developing countries, where continuing rapid urban growth is promoting, alongside vast tracts of unplanned sprawl, new models of sustainable urban design, like the integrated transportation and land-use spatial planning approach of the Brazilian city of Curitiba (Lloyd-Jones, 1996; Rabinovitz and Leitman, 1996).

Environmental demands, dramatic shifts in the global economic structure and the impact of new developments in information and communications technology will have far-reaching impacts on the spatial form of our cities. This is likely to form the urban design agenda of the future, one which will necessarily demand an interdisciplinary, team-based approach, integrating the problem-solving skills of designers with the analytical skills of social scientists. Urban designers, of necessity, must operate at local and city-wide levels and in close liaison with the other disciplines within a relevant institutional, policy and participatory framework.

II URBAN DESIGN: CURRENT ISSUES

3 Urban design and planning practice

Matthew Carmona

Who shall decide on the nature of good design in the built environment? 'Me!' 'Me!' 'Me!', come the cries of response from Prince and planner, councillor and consultant, architect and accountant. It seems that each must believe in the virtue of their own opinion at the expense of others, must believe that there can be only one right answer. ... This intolerance does not apply in other arts.

(HBF & RIBA, 1990, p. 6)

Design and planning practice

The extent to which design is recognised as a legitimate interest of the planning system has been a matter of great controversy, dating back to the evolution of planning in Britain. In reality, the majority of decisions planning authorities make will be design-related in one form or other, from those dealing with settlement form and transportation, to those concerning land use mix, those aimed at defining an appropriate public realm and those on individual site layout and detailed design. To this extent planning is undoubtedly a design discipline.

If the cumulative result of such decisions is to preserve and enhance the environment which the planning profession seeks to protect, then a mastery of planning practice and its impact on urban design in terms of the planning system's operation, scope, mechanisms and procedures is absolutely essential. In particular, authorities should recognise how the powers granted to them can be used in a positive light, to encourage the best in design that respects its visual, social, functional, and environmental context, while intervening to improve the mediocre and actively discourage and effectively control the worst.

Fundamen-tal to achieving this aim is the need for authorities to recognise that it is through a concern for urban design that they can maximise their impact – albeit at very different scales of operation (strategic to site-specific) – while at the same time minimising unnecessary interprofessional conflict. The case is made that such a concern can most easily be addressed through the adoption of a wide-ranging conceptualisation of urban design, based on a thorough appraisal of locality, expressed through a full hierarchy of design policy and guidance, from design policy in development plans to supplementary design guidance and individual site briefs. Such a hierarchy requires consistent and robust backing from above in the form of comprehensive national and strategic advice.

Urban design as a developing control mechanism

At the heart of design control lies a concern for urban design, a discipline mentioned for the first time in an official Department of the Environment publication as late as 1994 (DoE, 1994a, p. 2) and in actual planning guidance only in 1995 (DoE, 1995b, and 1995c, para. 2.27). Historically, government guidance has tended to concentrate on encouraging control of basic environmental 'amenity', whilst discouraging the control of detailed design (still seen as design interference by central government – DoE 1997a, para.18. Within these limitations design control has evolved through a number of distinct stages and polar swings from pro- to anti-control since its evolution out of a concern for public health and amenity in the nineteenth and early twentieth centuries (see Table 3.1).

Table 3.1 The historical development of design control

Date	Publications	Impacts
Public health and amenity		
1909	Housing and Town Planning Act	Suburban 'amenity' and convenience
1925	Bath Corporation Act	Peer review (RIBA, RICS, JPs)
1930s	–	'Battle of the styles'
1932	Town and Country Planning Act	Non-static areas and areas of high amenity – design and external control
1933	Circular 1305/33	Only to prevent 'outrages'
Standards and Utopia		
1947	Town and Country Planning Act	Comprehensive planning introduced, key test – 'injurious to amenity'
1950s	–	'Prairie planning' and birth of the 'townscape' movement
1960	Homes for Today and Tomorrow	MHLG established minimum public sector residential standards
Conservation counter attack		
1961	Townscape (Gordon Cullen)	'Townscape' movement took hold
1967	Civic Amenities Act	Established conservation areas
1968	MHLG conservation studies	Conservation area appraisal (Bath, Chester, Chichester, York)
The design guides		
1970s	–	Spread of the design guides
1973	Essex Design Guide	Spawned a generation of residential design guidance, rejected standards approach for contextual approach
1977	Design Bulletin 32	Guidance on more innovative residential road layouts
Free-market backlash		
1977	House of Commons Expenditure Committee	Call for new advice on design control and for design freedom (from the RIBA and HBF)
1980s	–	Free-market approach to design control
1980	Circular 22/80	Reactionary – design is subjective; authorities should not impose their tastes
A New Deal		
1989	A Vision of Britain	The design debate rekindled by HRH the Prince of Wales
1990s	–	Consensus view on design control established
1990	Birmingham Urban Design Study	City-wide strategy, and hierarchy of guidance established
1990	Planning for Beauty (RFAC)	Advocates design guidelines and a positive approach to design control
1991	RIBA/RTPI Joint Statement	7-point agreement on design control
1991	Planning and Compensation Act	Section 54A gives development plan priority
1992	PPG1 Annex A: Design Considerations	Design – a material consideration, new implicit emphasis on urban design issues
A possible renaissance?		
1993	Suffolk Design Guide	Urban design prioritised over architecture
1993	Design Policies in Local Plans: A Research Report	Research on the writing of design policies in local plans commissioned (published 1996)
1993	PPG13: Transport	Sustainable agenda actively promoted through government guidance
1993	What Makes a Good Building	RFAC attempt to define 'good' architecture
1994	Quality in Town and Country	Emphasis on urban design rather than on suburban development, on 'quality pays' and on mixed use
1994	Vital and Viable Town Centres	The value of mixed use, of social vitality and of preserving the urban realm
1995	Sustainable Settlements (LGMB)	Explores the link between sustainability and design
1995	Quality in Town and Country: Urban Design Campaign	Urban design defined, development briefs used as means to strengthen emphasis on urban design
1996	Promised Good Practice Guide	Good practice guide on design in the planning system promised by DoE
1997	Draft (Revised) PPG1 issued	A new emphasis on urban design, mixed use and local distinctiveness

Figure 3.1 'The Architect's View of Planning'. (Louis Hellman, 1995)

In this regard the 1990s might be seen as heralding a new renaissance for design control – at least when compared to the retrenchment of the 1980s – with design control more widely understood to encompass a new and wider social, functional and environmental agenda. This move reflects the increasingly widespread acceptance by government (Gummer, 1995, p. 7), planners (Griffiths, 1995, p. 6), and the development professions alike (HBF & RIBA, 1990, pp. 10–12) that control of urban design – rather than architecture – represents the most appropriate and effective means through which local authorities can influence the quality of new development.

Any in-depth historical review of design control would reveal that the key actors in the process often display entrenched and contrasting positions. This is partly due to the fact that any changes to the built environment affect a wide range of interests, including the public (whether they like it or not), and consequently have the potential to stir up considerable passion. Secondly, the interests of and powers wielded by the different actors in the process are rarely equal. For example, architects and developers often have an interest in producing distinctive developments which stand out, while planners and amenity groups are more concerned to ensure that development blends into its surroundings (Hall, 1990, p. 6). Third parties such as

residents will frequently favour the status quo, but are often the least equipped to object to development, and run the unfair risk of being branded NIMBY (not in my back yard) when they do. For them design is the easiest target against which to vent their frustrations.

Against such a background a wide range of often inconsistent practice exists, as many authorities regard even detailed control as quite legitimate, whilst others practise little or no control over design. Furthermore, the system itself perpetuates such inconsistencies, as an essentially two-tier approach to design control guarantees maximum intervention in areas benefiting from a variety of conservation designations (conservation areas, national parks, the setting of listed buildings and the like) and frequently almost no intervention in other non-designated areas. Such a situation has been criticised as in essence undemocratic as higher-income households tend to live in conservation areas and therefore benefit from higher standards of control in what are already high-quality environments, while lower-income households suffer under an impoverished system of control in already relatively impoverished surroundings (Townshend, 1995a, p. 3).

Over the years the case against design control has frequently been made with great force, primarily by those in the architectural profession and development industry. After a truce in hostilities between the architectural and planning professions in the early 1990s, following the preparation of a joint statement on design control by the RIBA and RTPI – which largely formed the basis of PPG1 Annex A (DoE, 1992a) – hostilities have recently been rejoined. The cause on this occasion was a working party report from the RIBA which set out the case for more limited but clearly defined and measurable 'design restraints' (RIBA, 1995 – see Fig. 3.1). The report alluded to many of the well-established concerns of architects that:

- Design control is conceived to be primarily concerned with aesthetics (external appearance), hence the term 'aesthetic control' is favoured
- As currently administered, aesthetic control impedes the quality of building design, by denying designers appropriate latitude in which to design – (stifles expression)
- Quality design can only be achieved by the use of good designers, able to exercise choice within given, reasonable, limited and measurable restraints
- Officers and planning committees are guilty of imposing personal taste and opinion (undue power given to those untrained in design)
- The result is design of a poor quality, governed by the lowest common denominator of taste and opinion (design is subjective)
- Design control as currently exercised wastes time and resources and leads to often acrimonious and inconclusive exchanges on matters of taste
- The planning appeals system does not provide an adequate safeguard against such abuse because of the time scale, risk and expense involved
- Safety, environmental and construction standards should be confirmed as exclusively the preserve of building regulations and not of planning regulations
- Consideration given to schemes currently excludes the most important players, the applicant and architect (architectural training confers special status in aesthetic judgements).

Unlike architects, whose opposition to design control is often a reaction against the deep-rooted public – and therefore planning committee – suspicion of modern design (Moro, 1958), the grievances of developers tend to focus on the procedural aspects of controlling design, rather than on controlling design per se. In particular, concerns focus on a perceived tendency for councillors to ignore the advice of officers, so rendering pre-application discussions useless; on local authority delays and indecision; on the authorities' disregard for the financial implications of planning requirements or for the saleability of developments and preferences of potential purchasers; on the rigidity of some planning standards, particularly those for highways; and on the tendency for design policies to stray from legitimate planning grounds established in government guidance (DoE and HRF, 1976).

The grievances of architects and developers are based to some extent on legitimate concerns resulting from shortcomings in the system. This is inevitable because, whatever the context, there will always be limitations to what any design control system can achieve. In the end the system as it stands is largely reactive, being dependent on the client and his/her aspirations, vision and resources to deliver quality, his/her 'civic responsibility' as the DoE has entitled it (Gummer, 1994a, p. 8), without which any system would be hard pressed to guarantee anything other than mediocrity.

Despite this, the true value of the system might best be measured in terms of what remains unseen and, more particularly, in terms of what the system prevents rather than what it allows. This view is perpetuated by the fact that developers rarely operate in a free market situation, more often one of monopoly (CPRE, 1995, p. 3), in which the pressure to maximise profit by reducing quality is intense. Thus, the need for the essential checks and balances provided by design control is justified, while those who advocate complete reliance on civic responsibility, the workings of the market, and professional expertise, to some extent place faith beyond reason. Effectively, they wish to deny the public the voice in design matters provided by the planning system and reject the undoubted strong public support for design control as testified by the spread of conservation areas across the country (Punter, 1990b, pp. 9–13). The disastrous results of withdrawing the essential crutch provided by design control – no matter how imperfect – are plain to see in areas of the world subject to the high development pressures commensurate with western living but without the balance provided by design control (parts of the United States, Middle East and Far East). In the UK, the London Docklands 'non-plan' (non-urban design) Isle of Dogs provides a case in point (Carmona, 1991, pp. 133–6)

With this in mind, the case for control has been made in equally strident terms to the case against:

- Design control prevents 'outrages' and stops much 'bad' building
- Design control raises the standard of much development by ensuring that more thought goes into its design
- Design control encourages the architect to stand up to his client who may often want only the cheapest building to sell on to another user
- Design control is democratic (in a manner of speaking) because it incorporates the view of the public, which might otherwise be ignored

- Design control is accountable because decisions are made by elected representatives
- Design control provides a necessary bridge between lay and professional tastes
- Architecture is the most public of arts, and it is often the local populace rather than the client who are required to live with the building.

(Punter and Carmona, 1997).

To these can be added the facts that:

- Most development in the UK is not designed by trained architects, and consequently the general standard of design fluctuates from mediocre to poor
- The design agenda has widened from a standards-based approach and from a primary concern with controlling external appearance to broader urban design and environmental concerns such as safety, comfort, convenience and sustainability, so giving it a new and valuable legitimacy.

Urban design – current guidance (England and Wales)

The primary instruments of government advice on aspects of urban design are widely spread across a number of sources: in primary legislation, across a wide range of PPGs and Circulars, and in a number of other government publications (see Tables 3.1–3.3). In March 1992 a new framework for controlling design was effectively established by the introduction of Annexe A to PPG1. This indicated that development plans – supplemented where appropriate by guidance for particular areas or sites – are the most appropriate means by which planning authorities should pursue their design objectives, and for the first time that '... the appearance of a proposed development and its relationship to its surroundings are material considerations ...' in determining planning applications. However, PPG1 Annex A went on to warn that good design is primarily the responsibility of designers and their clients, and that the subjective nature of aesthetic judgements should make authorities wary of trying to '... impose their taste on applicants ... simply because they believe it to be superior' (DoE, 1992a, paras. A1–A3).

The historic inconsistencies apparent in central government's approach to design control were therefore still apparent, on the one hand, proclaiming that the control of design is a legitimate role for planning authorities while on the other, warning that design interference is most definitely not. Nevertheless, a deeper reading of the guidance suggested an important new direction for control, one which received further backing in later government statements – a new emphasis on urban rather than architectural design. To illustrate this new direction, the Secretary of State in his preface to the Quality in Town and Country, Urban Design Campaign publication stated that 'Too much of our national debate about development focuses on architecture but ignores urban design. As a result, too much of that debate revolves around a handful of one-off landmark buildings which, by their nature, will never be repeated' (DoE, 1995b).

This is an approach supported by recent research into design policies in local plans (Punter and Carmona, 1997). This research argues that, outside of environmentally sensitive areas, planning authorities will be more able to influence the quality of the built environment if they concentrate on defining and controlling those urban design qualities which give character and quality to the public realm and which determine the most equitable use of public space. Such an approach is also less likely to stir the wrath of architects because it gives them a freer hand in architectural design.

If seen in this regard, government guidance gave authorities more scope to actively pursue quality, contextually appropriate, urban design. Since 1992 this was strengthened by the fact that most of the design principles raised in PPG1, Annex A, as legitimate for control were urban-design related – character, setting, appearance and treatment of spaces, landscape design (hard and soft), scale, density, height, massing, layout, and access (DoE, 1992a paras. A1–A6), while most of those which are considered to be non-legitimate concerns largely relate to matters of detailed design. This emphasis on urban issues is now confirmed in advice spread across government guidance (see Tables 3.2, 3.3) and includes a range of 'planning/design process' concerns of particular relevance to design control (see Table 3.4) and to the creation of a full hierarchy of design guidance.

The most compelling evidence of a sea-change in government's approach to urban design, however, came in 1997, with the publication of new design advice in the form of a (revised) PPG1 (DoE, 1997). In this the value of prioritising urban design was explicitly recognised, alongside a general re-emphasis on the importance of design as a material consideration in planning decisions, and a dramatic extension in the range of design issues considered appropriate for local authority consideration (see Tables 3.2–3.4).

Table 3.2 Legitimate design control concerns (normal areas)

Issue covered in guidance	Material status	Advisory status
access	*PPG3, PPG6, PPG1*	*DB32*
active frontages	*PPG6*	*PPG13*
biodiversity	*TCI, RE*	
building design	*PPG1*	*PPG6*
building line	*PPG6*	
bulk	*TCI, PPG7*	
car park design	*PPG6*	
character of place	*PPG3, PPG6, PPG1, RE, PPG7*	*DB32, SoS*
colour	*PPG7*	
compactness	*PPG1*	
context	*PPG3, TCI, PPG6, PPG1, RE, PPG7*	*DPG, SoS*
crime prevention	*PPG6, PPG1, Circ' 5/94*	*DB32, PPG13*
daylight	*CL*	*SDS*
defensible territory	*Circ' 5/94*	
density	*PPG3, PPG13, PPG1, PPG7*	*DB32*
disabled access	*PPG1*	*PPG6, Circ' 11/95*
enclosure		*SDS*
energy efficiency	*PPG12, PPG3*	*SDS*
environmental quality	*PPG3, PPG1*	
external appearance	*PPG1, PPG7*	
eyesores	*PPG7*	
good design (everywhere)	*PPG1*	
height	*PPG3, PPG1*	
house size (if proven need)	*PPG3*	*DB32*
house type (if proven need)	*PPG3*	*PPG12, DB32, SoS*
housing design	*PPG3, PPG12, Circ'5/94, TCI*	
interest (visual)	*PGG6*	
landscape character	*PPG7, RE*	
landscape design	*PPG3, PPG6, PPG1, Circ' 36/78, Circ' 11/95, PPG7*	*Circ' 5/94*
landscape, hard and soft		*Circ' 11/95 (DoE, 1995d)*
landscape integration	*PPG7*	
landsape management		*Circ' 11/95*
landscape value townscape	*PPG1*	
landscape works/materials	*Circ' 11/95*	
layout	*PPG3, PPG1, Circ' 5/94*	*SDS, DB32*
local distinctiveness	*PPG6, PPG1, PPG7*	
local style (rural areas)	*RE*	
massing	*PPG3, PPG1, PPG7*	*SoS*
materials	*PPG1, PPG7, RE*	
materials (sensitive locations)	*PPG3, TCI*	
mixed use	*PPG7, PPG13, PPG6, PPG1*	*Circ' 5/94, QTC, SoS*
neighbourhood impact	*PPG1*	
open space	*PPG3*	*DB32*
orientation	*Circ' 5/94*	*PPG12*
out-of-centre development design	*PPG6*	
overlooking	*PPG1, CL*	*SDS*
overshadowing	*PPG3, CL*	*SDS*
parking	*PPG3, PPG13, PPG6*	*DB32*
passive supervision	*Circ' 5/94*	
patterns of movement/activity	*PPG1*	
paving	*PPG6*	
perception of place	*PPG1d, RE, PPG7*	*SoS*
privacy	*PPG1*	*SDS*
public/urban space	*PPG1*	*PPG6*
quality of life and public health	*PPG12*	
quality of public domain	*PPG1*	
regional building traditions	*PPG7*	*PPG1*
relation to other buildings	*PPG3, PPG1, TCI, PPG7*	

Table 3.2 Continued

Issue covered in guidance	Material status	Advisory status
relation to parks/open spaces/waterways	*PPG1*	
residential amenity	*PPG3, PPG12, TCI*	
road and footpath design	*PPG1, PPG13, PPG7*	*DB32*
road hierarchy		*DB32*
road safety	PPG13	*DB32*
scale	*PPG3, PPG1, PPG7*	
settlement pattern	*PPG3, PPG7, PPG1*	*QTC, SoS*
shopfront design		*PPG6*
siting	*PPG3, PPG1, Circ' 5/94, PPG7*	
size	*PPG7*	
space between buildings	*PPG3, PPG1*	*SoS*
spatial design	*PPG1, PPG7, PPG13*	
street frontage	*PPG6*	*PPG, 13*
street furniture/signs	*PPG6*	*Circ' 11/95*
streets and squares	*PPG1*	
sunlight		*SDS*
sustainable design	*PPG1*	
sustainable development	*PPG12, PPG6, PPG1, RE, PPG7, PPG13*	*QTC, SoS*
textures	*PPG7*	
town cramming	*PPG3, PPG12, TCI*	*PPG7*
traditional building styles		*PPG7*
traffic calming	*PPG13*	
urban design	*PPG6, PPG1*	
urban villages		*PPG1*
variety	*PPG6, PPG1*	*Circ' 5/94, PPG13*
views & vistas	*PPG1, Circ'11/95, PPG7*	*DB32, SoS*
vitality (in urban locations)	*PPG17, PPG6, PPG1*	*PPG13*

Legend Tables 3.2–3.4

- *CL*   *Protected in Common Law*
- *DB32*   *Design Bulletin 32*
- *DPG*   *Development Plans: A Good Practice Guide*
- *SDG*   *Supplementary Design Guidance*
- *QTC*   *Quality in Town and Country*
- *RE*   *Rural England (White Paper)*
- *SDS*   *Site Layout Planning for Daylight and Sunlight*
- *SoS*   *Secretary of State Speech 12.12.94*
- *TCI*   *This Common Inheritence (White Paper)*
- *SPG*   *Supplementary Planning Guidance*

NB: The Tables 3.2–3.4 are differentiated to illustate those issues which have material status given by government guidance as legitimate areas for design control from those which have advisory status only (due to the specific wording of the guidance or because of the status of the medium of guidance itself). Tables compiled July 1997.

Table 3.3 Non-legitimate design control concerns

Issue covered in guidance	Material status	Advisory status
detailed design (unless sensitive context)	*PPG3, PPG1*	*SoS*
disabled access	*PPG3*	
functional requirements within a development	*PPG3*	
internal space standards	*PPG3*	
garages (provision or not)	*PPG3*	
gardens (size)	*PPG3*	
house type mix	*PPG3*	
location on plot (rigid formulae)	*PPG3*	
materials (in non-sensitive locations)	*PPG3*	

Table 3.3 Continued

Issue covered in guidance	Material status	Advisory status
outlook	*CL*	
rigid formulae (for house location)		*PPG3*
style	*PPG3, PPG1*	*SoS*
taste	*PPG1, PPG1, Circ' 11/95*	

Table 3.4 Legitimate design control processes

Process covered in guidance	Material status	Advisory status
appraisal valuable	*PPG7*	*DPG*
area design guides supported	*PPG1*	
avoid stifling originality/innovation	*PPG1*	
briefs on layout and design of residential roads and footpaths supported	*DB32*	
briefs to aim for unified development		*TCI*
briefs to identify goals/problems/opportunities		*TCI*
briefs to identify site characteristics and appropriate materials in sensitive areas	*PPG3*	
civic responsibility	*PPG1*	*SoS*
countryside design summaries/village design statements useful		*PPG7*
cross reference policy to briefs/SDG	*PPG1*	
decision-making criteria in plan policy not in SPG	*PPG12*	*DPG*
decisions need policy/SDG support	*PPG1*	
demonstrate regard to policy/SDG	*PPG1*	
demonstrate regard to good design	*PPG1*	
depart from policy for exceptional schemes	*PPG1*	
design briefs supported	*PPG6, PPG1*	*DPG, SoS*
design expectations to be in plan	*PPG6, PPG1*	
economic viability	*PPG7*	
encourage good design in policy/SDG	*PPG1*	
encourage innovation	*PPG1*	*QTC, SoS*
good design the aim of all		*PPG1*
landscape character analysis valuable	*PPG7*	
landscape implementation	*Circ' 11/95*	
level of detail down to local decision	*PPG12*	
no refusal if consistent with policy	*PPG1*	
over-detail and over-prescription in policy	*PPG6, PPG1*	*PPG3*
phasing of development	*PPG1*	*Circ' 11/95*
phasing of landscape	*Circ' 11/95*	
planning conditions/obligations useful for design	*Circ' 11/95*	*PPG1*
planning conditions/obligations (comply with)	*PPG1*	
policy based on appraisal of context	*PPG1*	
pre-application consultation		*PPG1*
presentation, importance of	*PPG1*	
public user consultation on design policy/SDG	*PPG1*	*PPG6*
reject poor designs	*PPG1*	
SDG on layout of residential areas supported		*DB32*
SDG on materials and lighting		*PPG1*
SDG on shopfront design		*PPG6*
SDG supported	*PPG1*	
secure public acceptance through design		*PPG1, PPG3, PPG7*
show proposals in context	*PPG1*	
SPG is a material consideration		*DB32*

Table 3.4 Continued

Process covered in guidance	Material status	Advisory status
SPG and briefs useful, particularly when cross-referenced to policy	*PPG12, PPG6*	*TCI, SoS*
standards on the design of residential roads and footpaths supported		*DB32*
standards need flexibility	*PPG13*	*PPG1*
survey of principal physical characteristics	*PPG12*	
urban design analysis		*PPG6*
written statements of design principle	*PPG1*	

The note begins by bringing design and mixed use to the fore alongside sustainability as 'three themes which underpin the Government's approach to the planning system' (para. 3) – a clear U-turn when compared against the 'hands-off' approach of the 1980s, encapsulated in the much reviled Circular 22/80 'Development Control: Policy and Practice' (DoE, 1980). In a subsequent five paragraphs (paras. 8–12) the new urban design creed of mixed use receives a major endorsement, reflecting themes developed in the various Quality in Town and Country documents. The guidance effectively accepted the current orthodoxy that single-use zoning is both divisive and anti-social leading to unwelcome homogenisation in the environment (Gummer, 1994, pp.8–9).

This advice, along with eight design-specific paragraphs (paras. 13–20), and seven paragraphs in a new Annex A to the note (paras. A1–A7) represents a clear move forward from the design advice contained within the 1992 guidance. Together they give a new priority to urban design, whilst at the same time strongly endorsing the planning system's legitimate interest in the design of buildings. In particular the role of urban and building design in preserving the character and quality of context was emphasised, with specific mention of public spaces, streets, vistas and sense of place. A characteristically brief and inadequate reminder that hard and soft landscape should also be considered as an integral part of urban design is also included.

The conversion – although dramatic – remained partial, however, with the old preconceptions remaining that design control is to some extent subjective and that a concern for detailed design might be considered as interference. Nevertheless, these concerns were toned down considerably from the 1992 guidance, taking the form of a warning that planning authorities 'should not attempt to impose a particular architectural taste or style arbitrarily' and 'should not concern themselves with matters of detailed design except where such matters have a significant effect on the character or quality of the

area, including neighbouring buildings' (para. 18). This wording largely incorporated paragraph A3 of the earlier guidance, but significantly the key phrase 'aesthetic judgements are to some extent subjective' was omitted. This continued a dilution of the 'subjectivity' argument which began with the 1992 note, which itself had watered down the earlier guidance in Circulars 22/80 and 31/85 both of which had stated that 'Planning Authorities should recognise that aesthetics is an extremely subjective matter' (DoE, 1980, para. 19).

At the heart of the new guidance lay a difficult balance, one which warned against control of detail and imposition of unnecessary taste while promoting a concern for local distinctiveness, supported in plan policy and supplementary guidance that has been subject to public consultation (paras. 17–18). In the case of the latter the note even offered the examples of local or regional building traditions and materials as important concerns of local distinctiveness – both major departures for government advice (para. A1.). To some extent the contradiction was clear and left the guidance trying to square an impossible circle. Nevertheless, the support for local distinctiveness is a valuable new policy direction which was presaged by the DoE, following determined lobbying from a number of conservation/amenity groups, including the CPRE and the Countryside Commission. It is just this concern for erosion of local distinctiveness, in urban design and architectural terms, which over the years spawned so many design guides from concerned planning authorities and, in response, such a determined fight against perceived design interference from development and design interests.

So by analysing government guidance, and by reading into the Quality in Town and Country rhetoric we can begin to see a clear and legitimate role for urban design in planning practice. This constitutes a new agenda, moving away from the traditional conflation of design with aesthetics, yet recognising the value of local tradition and character.

The need for a theoretical conceptualisation of urban design

The absence of any clear definition of design in government policy has been one of the key problems faced by planning authorities. Consequently, policies and guidance frequently fail to cover key areas, contain an inadequate range of considerations to ensure appropriate design control, and display a continuing bias towards architectural or external appearance issues at the expense of broader urban design concerns (Punter and Carmona, 1997). To avoid this, any new guidance from local authorities will need to be based on, and reflect the full range of urban design concerns established in urban design theory.

Interestingly, and for the first time, the DoE attempted to define urban design as part of its Urban Design Campaign, in so doing accepting that quality design consists of more than just buildings and that it is the underlying pattern of buildings rather than the buildings themselves that stands the test of time (DoE, 1995b, p.2). In an amended form the definition was incorporated into the (revised) PPG1 of 1997, further strengthening its urban design emphasis. Urban design is taken to mean:

> ... the relationship between different buildings; the relationship between buildings and the streets, squares, parks, waterways and other spaces which make up the public domain; the nature of the public domain itself; the relationship of one part of a village, town or city with other parts; and the patterns of movement and activity which are thereby established: in short, the complex relationships between all the elements of built and unbuilt space (DoE, 1996, para. 12).

This definition explicitly recognises the multi-layered nature of the discipline, its spatial, functional, morphological, and contexual/visual dimensions, and to some extent even its social dimension, through reference to the public domain and to the patterns of movement and activity. What is missing is recognition of the important perceptual dimension, following removal of the phrase, 'the interplay between our evolving environment of buildings and the values, expectations and resources of people', from the earlier Urban Design Campaign definition (DoE, 1995, para. 2). Nevertheless, it potentially provides a starting point for more comprehensive government guidance on urban design.

In the UK, planning practice has until recently been dominated by the visual and contextual conceptualisations of the 'townscape' and conservation movements (external appearance, street scene, building height, views, etc.) and by the functional issues derived from a concern for residential amenity (privacy, sunlight, layout, density, etc.). Recent research has revealed, however, that local plans – and therefore, presumably, also planning practice – are beginning to reflect social and sustainable issues, particularly a concern for accessibility and security; for the quality of public space; and for energy efficiency and ecological preservation (Punter et al., 1996, paras. 6.2.1–6.7.4).

Taking these new concerns, together with the more traditional issues addressed in planning guidance – and in the light of the writings of other theorists and practitioners (see Chapter 1) – planning authorities might develop their own urban design framework within which the various conceptualisations of urban design can be accommodated. Using such a framework, authorities might structure the many urban design concepts currently found in government guidance and in use in local plans and supplementary design guidance into a logical and useable form, a form underpinned and informed by the local political, economic and environmental circumstances (see Table 3.5).

The importance of appraisal to underpin policy and guidance

Such an approach to structuring policy and guidance merely provides a framework, as each locality is inevitably subject to its own unique set of qualities, opportunities and threats, against which to direct local authority action. Furthermore, urban design operates at many different spatial scales of operation and over different time frames.

As a consequence, urban design needs to be seen as part of an ongoing process, rather than as a one-stop answer to specific problems. Moughtin suggests that there are four stages in this process – analysis, synthesis, appraisal and decision-making (Moughtin, 1992, p. 19). These stages are neither independent nor necessarily sequential, but are instead part of an integrated, cyclical and iterative process in which the nature of urban design as an activity is reflected. Furthermore, decisions made about urban design inform, and are in turn informed by, those made about town planning above and building design below. At the heart of this lies the value and importance of appraisal (analysis) – as both the start and end of the process – setting the

Table 3.5 Structuring of design considerations into a conceptual urban design framework

Spatial	Morphological	Contextual	Visual	Perceptual	Social	Functional	Sustainable

Design issues listed as legitimate design concerns in government guidance (from Table 3.2)

Spatial	Morphological	Contextual	Visual	Perceptual	Social	Functional	Sustainable
open space	building lines	character	amenity	defensibility	access	daylight	biodiversity
road hierarchy	density	conservation	appearance	distinctiveness	active frontages	footpaths	energy efficiency
settlement pattern	layout	context	building traditions	enclosure	activity patterns	house size	landscaping
town cramming	street pattern	environmental quality	bulk	place	crime	house type	orientation
		height	colour	variety	mixed use	infrastructure	sunlight
		landscape	development size		play space	layout	sustainable design
		materials	eyesores		public health	overlooking	trees
		neighbourh'd impact	interest		public space	overshadowing	
		relation to other b'lgs	local style		quality of life	parking	
		siting	massing		supervision	privacy	
		streetscape	scale		vitality	road design	
		views	texture			road safety	
		vistas					

Design issues listed as non-legitimate design concerns in government guidance (from Table 3.3)

Spatial	Morphological	Contextual	Visual	Perceptual	Social	Functional	Sustainable
		location on plot	detailed design		disabled access	garden size	
		outlook	style			space formulae	

Other relevant design concerns not explicitly covered in government guidance

Spatial	Morphological	Contextual	Visual	Perceptual	Social	Functional	Sustainable
capital web	block size	boundaries	balance	appropriateness	community	infrastruture	ecology
compact form	connectivity	building groups	corners	gateways	facilities	lighting	economic viability
districts	edges	contrast	focal points	human scale	minority needs	servicing	environment capacity
neighbourhoods	grain	plot size	form	identity	personalisation	SLOAP	microclimate
public transport	incremental design	unity	harmony	image	public/private	traffic calming	road dominance
topography	morphology		landmarks	legibility	public realm		robustness
	nodes		proportion	sensual experience	social cohesion		site capacity
	permeability		rhythm		social equity		structure planting
	space network		roofscape				
	spatial proportions		solid v void				
			townscape				
			vertical v horizontal				

Design considerations appear under one approach only, although in reality many fit into more than one of the categories identified. This emphasises the interrelated, and interdependent nature of urban design theory and of the urban design considerations identified.

initial parameters from which guidance and policy are drawn, and feeding back into and reflecting the experience of implementation.

Conservation area statements frequently provide the most developed examples of appraisal from local authorities in the UK, reflecting not only the increased scope for intervention in these areas, but also the encouragement given by English Heritage for the production of such statements (English Heritage, 1993). It is important, however, that authorities seek to ensure that development everywhere (not just in conservation areas) responds to the different character of context by clearly defining the key contextual factors to be considered. This advice is implicit in the wording of PPG12 (DoE, 1992c, paras. 4.1–4.3), and is made explicit in the revised PPG1, which required authorities to base policies on a proper assessment of the character of surrounding built and natural environment and in PPG6, which encourages authorities to undertake urban design analyses to provide a framework for development plan policy and for guiding the preparation of development briefs (DoE, 1997a, para. A1, DoE, 1996, para. 2.33).

The aim must be to isolate those area characteristics which are particularly worthy of protection and to develop design principles and considerations which will ensure that development respects these qualities. However, it is equally important to identify the potential for improvement in areas of average or poor quality and to consider the opportunities for new development or environmental enhancement to upgrade such areas. In this way authorities can aim to counter disadvantage and make a significant contribution to regeneration. Poor-quality environments should not represent an invitation to poor-quality development.

Like policy and guidance, such appraisal might adopt a similar urban design structure to that already discussed, with appropriate criteria (depending on context and policy objectives) taken for analysis from Table 3.5, combined with a basic SWOT (strengths, weaknesses, opportunities, threats) analysis (Table 3.6). It is likely, however, that each context and study will require the adoption of its own unique approach in order to:

- Seek out any coherent patterns
- Understand a place's equilibrium
- Discover its unique character
- Develop concepts based upon understanding of the place's distinctive characteristics (Lynch and Hack, 1984)

Only by adopting such a clear structure can appraisal move beyond the merely descriptive to the analytical

and prescriptive guidance necessary to put into place appropriately robust policy. Furthermore, such appraisal should be readily accessible to the public and based on thorough and ongoing public consultation, if the resultant policy and guidance are to benefit from broad public support. Ultimately, though, if development control is truly to influence a general improvement in the quality of design, it will be an investment in appraisal that makes this possible. Recent research clearly identified the lack of such appraisal as one of the key weaknesses in policy formulation. For this reason, respect for context through an investment in appraisal features foremost among recommendations for ensuring best practice from local authorities on the writing of design policies in development plans (Punter and Carmona, 1997).

The value of a full hierarchy of design guidance for effective implementation

Essential to the successful operation of any design control regime is the need for a comprehensive hierarchy of design guidance of a type more common on the Continent or in the USA than in Britain. Such coverage ensures that national and strategic principles are backed up by consistent, contextually relevant coverage in statutory local plans, by design guidance outside the plan expanding on and complementing the policy within, and by design frameworks and briefs for individual sites proactively putting those principles into practice. In reality the development plan has only recently taken over from other forms of supplementary design guidance as the primary instrument of design advice in many localities in the UK, reflecting the primacy now given to plan policy in the new plan-led system. Formerly, the popularity and faith placed in design guides in the wake of the *Essex Design Guide* (Essex County Council, 1973), had spawned a rash of similar guidance up and down the country. Until the 1990s this guidance constituted the main source of design advice in many authorities, in an era when design policy in local plans was frequently sketchy at best.

In 1990 the important status of design guidance prepared and adopted in this way received an unexpected boost in the appeal courts. The case Tarmac Homes (Essex) Ltd v S.o.S and Epping Forest D.C. (15/6/90) confirmed that failure to comply with advice contained in design guides – in this case the Essex guide – could be a legitimate justification for the rejection of housing schemes (Holt, 1988, pp. 71–185). This helps to justify the continuing importance placed by many authorities on a variety of supplementary planning instruments for controlling design.

Table 3.6 Structure for appraisal

	Strengths	Weaknesses	Opportunities	Threats
Spatial	Do distinctive district/neighbourhood boundaries exist, if so where? Is the topography a positive character-giving asset. Will developments fit into the existing capital web? What quality open spaces exist?	Where does the spatial pattern breakdown? Do no-mans lands exist between adjoining districts? What topographical restraints are apparent? Is the road hierarchy a uniting or divisive factor? Any public transport?	What opportunities are there to add to the network of open space? What opportunities exist for large-scale interventions that enhance the existing spatial form/capital web? Can the existing spatial form be repaired?	What high-impact threats lie over the horizon i.e. new roads, developments, business closures? Is town cramming a problem? Is urban sprawl a problem? Is public transport viable in the long term?
Morphological	Is the morphological form distinctive? Which morphological elements give character – street pattern/blocks/edges/nodes/building line? Is the historical grain intact and is permeability good – pedestrians/cars/cycles?	Which spaces lack definition/enclosure? Where does route connectivity break down? Where has the urban grain been lost/ignored? Have standardised layouts been imposed? Are density targets too rigid?	Do opportunities exist to enhance connectivity? Can a distinctive network of spaces be formed? What opportunities exist to reimpose/establish a legible urban form/grain? Can permeability be enhanced?	Are incremental developments damaging morphological form i.e. plot/block amalgamations? Do comprehensive redevelopments constitute any threat? Is built density increasing or decreasing?
Contextual	Where is landscape setting especially important? Which characteristics most clearly define the context? Do any important building groups exist? Is unity or diversity the defining characteristic?	Which areas possess no defining character? Where does environmental quality break down? Do buildings gel together in distinctive groups, if not, why not? Which areas require further (increased) protection?	What opportunities exist to enhance existing or open up new views and vistas? Do opportunities exist for high buildings? Is conservation policy appropriate (CAs, LBs)? Do opportunities exist to define context anew?	Is landscape character being eroded? Is increasing building height a problem? Which existing contexts are under threat – incrementally or comprehensively? Are traditional boundary treatments being replaced?
Visual	What townscape qualities can be identified? Which traditional materials are used in which areas, what colours predominate? Do local styles exist, what are their key qualities? Is roofscape an important element (a fifth elevation)?	Does scale tend towards the inhuman? Do wider amenity concerns impact on areas? Are buildings visually interesting from different views and distances? Are corners given due emphasis?	Do opportunities exist to establish new landmarks or focal points? What opportunities exist to remove eyesores? How can existing townscape be enhanced? Do opportunities exist to encourage modern design?	Do any large-scale developments threaten the townscape character? Are important skylines under threat? Do plot ratios result in an increasing building bulk? Do new building technologies pose a threat?
Perceptual	Which areas possess a distinctive sense of place and impart a clear image and why? Which areas are clearly legible and what qualities contribute to this? Is the prevailing scale human in nature?	Which areas suffer from a lack of clear identity? Are any areas threatening in character and if so why? Do parts of the town/city suffer from a poor image, and is this related to design factors? Is monotony a problem?	Can potential gateways be identified to enhance district/settlement identity? Can an increase in visual and social variety be used to enhance sense of place? Do possibilities exist to reinforce existing sense of place and legibility?	Is local distinctiveness being undermined? Are standardised and corporate designs a problem, and where should such design be resisted? Do particular land uses contribute to sense of place? Are they under threat?
Social	Which design factors contribute most strongly to improving quality of life? Which areas exhibit a strong and cohesive community spirit? Identify important gathering places, what qualities make them so?	Which areas suffer from a high incidence of crime, is this due to design factors? Do women feel excluded/intimidated in some areas? Where are the needs of the disabled not adequately catered for? Why is this? Is play space adequate?	Identify opportunities for mixing uses. What design opportunities exist to cater for minority needs and improve social cohesion? Do opportunities exist for improving accessibility and providing public space?	Where is vitality being undermined and how? Does personalisation represent a threat. What forms can be encouraged? Is there any noticeable trend to privatising the public realm? Do problems affect health?

Table 3.6 Continued

	Strengths	Weaknesses	Opportunities	Threats
Functional	Which potential expansion areas are well linked to existing infrastructure? Which housing types have been used particularly successfully and why? What principles can be identified for successful road design/integration?	Identify any space left over after planning (SLOAP), what can be done with it? Under what circumstances have standards-based approaches failed? In what circumstances has road design been allowed to dominate urban form?	Do opportunities exist for traffic calming? Can more flexible space standards and functional criteria be identified for development forms? What opportunities exist to better utilise existing infrastructure?	Does the need for adequate servicing pose any threat? Does demand for parking represent a threat? Does town cramming threaten basic amenity? In which areas does road safety pose a real or potential problem?
Sustainable	Which development forms are most energy-efficient? Identify any ecologically valuable sites. Appraise indigenous vegetation, is it appropriate for use in development? Which trees are worthy of preservation?	How do microclimatic factors impact on development strategies? Are any potential development areas poorly served by public transport? Where has landscaping been treated as an after-thought, and why?	Do opportunities exist to fully integrate natural and built environmental concerns? What opportunities exist for green sites/buildings? Which principles guarantee robust development forms – adaptability and resilience?	Which areas are in danger of exceeding their natural environmental capacity? Are street trees ageing? Are enough brownfield sites available for development? Which developments encourage car use?

Note: The questions in Table 3.6 are indicative only, they neither represent the full range of concerns, nor will they necessarily be appropriate in the light of local circumstances.

Various organising frameworks have been developed to examine and classify supplementary design guidance. Chapman and Larkham have classified guidance in the form of a 'cascade', according to its level of operation (national to site-specific), its role in decision-making – appraisal, encouragement, guidance, control and its degree of prescription (Chapman and Larkham, 1993, pp. 33-35). Murray and Willie on the other hand have classified design guidance according to its relative scale of operation – district, neighbourhood, street, site etc. (Murray and Willie, 1991, p. 22). Both frameworks represent useful synopses of the relationships between the different forms of design guidance in the hierarchy. However, neither includes the full range of guidance currently in use, and so they fail to illustrate the potential range of tools available to planning authorities in controlling design.

In fact an eighteen-level classification of guidance types can be identified, as illustrated in Table 3.7, incorporating guidance across four distinct spatial levels – national, strategic, district/city-wide and area/site-specific. Such a hierarchy incorporates design advice from central government, strategic and local authorities, and even from developers themselves, with each classification of guidance possessing the potential to further design objectives. However, it would be likely that few areas would be subject to more than eight of the guidance types.

Fundamental to the successful operation of such a hierarchy is the need for a development plan to act as an umbrella and coordinating framework for any supplementary design guidance or design briefs which in turn elucidate and expand on the advice contained within the plan. These supplementary forms of guidance have a vital role to play in policy implementation by relating policies to neighbourhood strategies or to specific sites, and by calling attention to key problems associated with particular types of development. Such guidance provides an important source of advice to unskilled designers and should ensure a more efficient control process for all concerned. Furthermore, while central government insists on keeping development plans thin and accessible to all, other sources of advice on design issues are inevitable and indeed desirable if authorities are to move beyond the overarching design objectives contained within the plan.

Recent and extensive research has fully examined existing practice in the formulation, presentation and implementation of design policies in British local plans (Punter et al., 1996), making comprehensive recommendations on best practice in design policy writing (Punter and Carmona, 1997). At the heart of this research lies the clear recommendation that urban design policies embracing a fully developed conceptualisation of urban design, such as that discussed above, should represent the cornerstone of substantive design policies. Urban design recommendations from this research include those outlined in Table 3.8.

Comprehensive urban design policies thus represent the keystone in the hierarchy, effectively imple-

Table 3.7 The hierarchy of urban design guidance

Guidance	Role and utility
National planning guidance	
1 **Primary legislation** (planning acts)	Provides the statutory basis for planning and conservation, and therefore also for development and design control.
2 **Government guidance** (PPGs) (NPPGs in Scotland)	Sets out and elucidates government policy on planning matters, including design control and a new stress on urban design. Lays down the limits of design as a material consideration, thus limiting local choice. Such guidance is a paramount material consideration, but remains general and flexible in nature, requiring interpretation in the light of local circumstances.
3 **Government advice** (Circulars) (PANs in Scotland) (Design bulletins)	Gives government advice on more detailed and technical design concerns such as crime or road layout. Criticism levelled over tendency to encourage copycat solutions, and lack of interpretation in the light of local circumstances e.g. DB32. Can be used successfully to illustrate good practice e.g. PAN44 (SO, 1994b).
Strategic planning guidance	
4 **Regional guidance** (RPGs)	Establishes broad regional emphasis on environment/design/conservation in the light of competing claims on resources (economic, social etc.). Tendency to ignore design as a detailed concern, and not a strategic issue, until recent guidance e.g. RPG3 (DoE, 1995b)
5 **Structure plan/ UDP Part 1 policy**	Provides an important opportunity (usually missed) to set out a spatial design/environmental framework to guide local plan policies, and ensure consistent emphasis across districts.
6 **Landscape character assessment**	Ensures emphasis is given to landscape concerns and helps ensure proper regard is had to natural design issues as well as to those concerning the built environment. Such appraisals are of maximum value if able to inform policy (prescriptive rather than descriptive).
7 **County design guidance**	Influential over the years, particularly for residential development e.g. Essex, Cheshire, Kent, Sussex guides. Ensures a consistent approach to design across districts. Tend to focus on county matters such as road hierarchy and broad vernacular, but opportunity to establish broad urban design principles e.g. Essex. General at best, and no substitute for district policy.
District or city-wide guidance	
8 **Local plan/ UDP Part 2 Policy**	Provides the most potent tool in the planning authorities' armoury, benefiting from the full force of section 54A. Should be used to lay down a contextually relevant framework for design control, prioritising urban and landscape over architectural concerns. Closely scrutinised by central government to prevent over-prescription (see Punter et al., 1996).
9 **Development control guidelines** (in plan)	Used by authorities to place standards and guidance in the plan e.g. the London boroughs' development standards appendices, but status unclear. Well suited to those key rules of thumb construed to be too detailed for policy, but which constitute an important basis for control e.g. space around dwelling criteria. Tend to be quantitative rather than qualitative.
10 **Design guides** (SDG)	A material consideration, which should relate clearly to plan policy and through which design advice can be elucidated and disseminated. Well suited to single design issues, or to different development types and contexts. Can encourage copycat solutions and suffer from a lack of weight. Nevertheless,they possess great under-utilised potential to develop urban design policy.
11 **Design standards**	Largely relate to residential amenity considerations (health and safety concerns). Such quantitative measures rarely secure good design by themselves and need to be operated flexibly and with skill, alongside other urban form policy to avoid over-regimented solutions.
12 **Design strategy** (usually for established contexts)	Give spatial expression to urban design policy, and provide a mechanism through which detailed briefs and frameworks can be generated e.g. the Birmingham Urban Design Study (Tibbalds et al., 1990). A proactive form of guidance, best suited to expressing broad urban design issues. They represent a major investment of resources in urban design and require an agreed vision of future form.
13 **Landscape strategy**	Focus on managing and enhancing, as well as protecting landscape (urban and rural). Such strategies help integrate natural and built environment concerns, ensuring a more sustainable approach to urban design concerns (e.g. Bath C.C., 1993). Require a great skills investment.
Area- or site-specific guidance	
14 **Area appraisal** (Design appraisal) (CA assessments)	Although resource-intensive, such appraisal should form an essential part of the design policy writing process, ensuring that proper regard is given to the visual, social, functional and environmental context (e.g. Dacorum B.C. 1995). It is vital to make appraisal prescriptive rather than descriptive, and to publish it alongside the plan as a material consideration.
15 **Design codes** (usually for new build)	Area-related (but not site-specific) urban design codes or principles, usually used to structure areas of comprehensive development over long periods,but without two-dimensional masterplan. Can borrow cues from surrounding context or define anew, but no certainty over eventual form. Require long-term will to implement (e.g. Hulme Regeneration Ltd., 1994).
16 **Development frameworks**	Proactive approach to encouraging an appropriate two/three dimensional form (capital web) on large, long-term sites. Maximum value if placed in plan and used to coordinate individual briefs. Allows flexibility for designers to design with a coordinated controlling framework.
17 **Design briefs**	Proactive, readily adaptable, resource-efficient guidance, well suited to defining the urban design, development and planning (not architectural) requirements of individual sites. Can be used to aid policy implementation, consultation, marketing and to lever planning gain. In practice often ignored and lacking design content, but nevertheless material considerations, capable of ensuring the best possible use of land and promoting design quality.
18 **Master plans**	Three-dimensional vision of future form (allowing some architectural freedom within limits of defined form). Maximise certainty, but minimise flexibility. Rarely used by local authorities as too resource-intensive and considered too prescriptive.

Table 3.8 Writing of urban design policies in local plans (see Punter et al., 1994 for further recommendations)

Recommendations for urban design policy (normal areas)

General urban design policies

Urban design policies should be given priority in order to emphasise that design policies concern more than external appearance, but encompass the visual, social, functional and environmental context as well.
A comprehensive urban design policy spelling out the full range of design considerations in a locality is important as the cornerstone of all design policies.

Spatial form

Authorities should begin by developing a clear conception of the future spatial structure in their areas.

Townscape policies

Policies to prevent overdevelopment are also critical, and these need to embrace density, height, massing, daylight and sunlight, and cross-relate to townscape, views and high buildings policies. If plot ratio controls are used these need to be carefully tailored to the locality and to other design considerations. They need to be flexibly interpreted to allow development to accord with its context. The pursuit of a human scale in development can be strengthened by respecting the grain of the locality and to other design considerations. They need to be flexibly interpreted to allow development to accord with its context.
The pursuit of a human scale in development can be strengthened by respecting the grain of the locality and by controlling building bulk.
Townscape policies are recommended to ensure development has an appropriate relationship with its surroundings. Views and skyline protection policies may be an important part of such policies.

Public realm policies

Particular emphasis should be placed on public realm policies to complement the more traditional scale and townscape policies. These will include policies to encourage the vitality of streets through active frontages, mixed-use schemes, and the creation of attractive spaces.
Layout policies should seek to develop well-defined public and semi-public space and to achieve a sense of place through the creative use of the site's qualities.
Access considerations need to emphasise the value of permeability and easy access for the elderly, women and children as well as for the disabled, and need to be underwritten by a concern for surveillance, visibility and safety.
Attention should be paid to the management and modification of space that will have high-quality design as a primary object. Public art policies will play a valuable role in this regard.

Alternative approaches

Both conventional townscape and public realm policies can usefully be complemented by context-specific policies, particularly for environmentally sensitive areas, by policies which differentiate according to the scale of development (large scale, infill etc.), and by policies addressing the special design problems created by different types of development (industrial, residential etc.).

Sustainable policies

Landscape policies at both the micro and macro scales should complement built environment considerations, and consider open space provision, green landscape and hard landscape concerns.
A broader environmental view of urban design needs to be adopted, integrating built form and natural environment considerations, and embracing issues of sustainability.

---

menting government guidance from above and forming a framework for the more detailed supplementary guidance below. Scepticism over the true value of supplementary design guidance, briefs and appraisal, however, continues to exist in some quarters (Gummer, 1994, p.15), particularly when considered alongside the resource implications involved in its preparation, implementation and review. Recent research into design policies in local plans (Punter et al., 1996) revealed that authorities generally have a strong faith in the utility of supplementary design guidance, especially when it is closely related to plan policy and made the subject of public consultation. This faith is demonstrated by, firstly, the high priority given by many authorities to the preparation of such guidance as part of an ongoing programme as and when time and resources permit and, secondly, by the substantial body of supplementary guidance already in use by the majority of authorities.

These findings have generally been confirmed by other studies examining the utility of supplementary design guidance. The Time for Design study, for example, revealed that 55 per cent of authorities believed guidance to have a 'moderate' or 'considerable' effect in improving applications, 75 per cent thought guidance had a 'significant' effect in improving the operation of development control and 54 per cent rated guidance as having a 'significant' effect when dealing with appeals. The general feeling appeared to be that guidance was most effective as a back-up to pre-application negotiations and in providing a consistent approach to design within planning departments, as well as as an educative tool leading to a gradual improvement in the public's perception of good design. The research concluded that the production of design guidance was the most successful type of initiative in achieving the aims of the experiment – to improve the quality of design (DoE, 1991, pp.39–40 and p. 9).

A later study also concluded that the attitudes of local authority planning departments towards design guidance and its potential benefits are generally positive, although legislative advice and resource constraints seemed to be inhibiting factors. Other inhibiting factors revealed were: that authorities frequently failed to make the relationship between plan policy and design guidance clear; and that adopted design policies and published design guides represent only a small proportion of the amount of design guidance available, much of which is provided on an informal, advisory or ad hoc basis (Chapman and Larkham, 1993, p. 36). This practice flies in the face of advice given in PPG 12 that the use of informal or 'bottom drawer' policies is '... unsatisfactory and incompatible with the requirements of ...' a plan-led system (DoE, 1992b, para. 3.20). It also fails to gain advantage from the potential benefits of a fully integrated hierarchy.

Good practice pointers can be drawn from this work for the preparation of supplementary design guidance in order to maximise its effectiveness. They include:

- The need to make the relationship between policy and guidance explicit
- The need to publish all design guidance and any informal policies
- The need to tie guidance preparation into a fully informed overview or assessment of priority rather than as knee-jerk reactions to topical issues

- The need to target guidance to the perceived audience, be that applicants, the public or inspectors (in minority languages if necessary)
- The need to avoid unnecessary description and over-prescription
- The need for appropriate methodologies to inform area appraisals and assessments
- The encouragement of guidance to reflect wider urban design priorities and not always detailed design concerns
- The need to make design briefs as attractive and easy to use as design guidance usually is
- The need to update or disregard the large quantity of obviously outdated guidance still in use (after Chapman and Larkham, 1993, pp. 23–5).

To these can be added one more suggestion made in this and in the earlier DoE study:

- That there is considerable scope for standardised guidance particularly in non-contentious areas, to be formulated on a national or regional basis. Typical subjects might include crime prevention, mobility provision for people with disabilities, and so forth (DoE, 1991, p. 8, and Chapman and Larkham, 1993, p. 36).

A last major study also backs the largely positive view of supplementary guidance. This work carried out for the Royal Fine Art Commission (RFAC, 1990) falls into the long tradition of support from the RFAC for the general value of design control (House of Commons, 1985). Amongst other recommendations, it suggests that government should: 'Encourage planning authorities to draw up local design guidelines ... and then use them as a checklist, not a straitjacket', either supplementing or as part of the local plan itself (RFAC, 1990, p. 34). Such a system of design guidelines is already used both in the United States (Portland, San Francisco) and in Continental Europe (Paris, Siena, Bologna). These guidelines, the study argues, could potentially be developed here as a method of reducing subjectivity and increasing contextual compatibility.

Although addressing the problem from a very different perspective, this approach has much in common with a design constraints approach based on nationally defined standard guidelines now supported by the RIBA (see above and RIBA, 1995). The crucial and telling difference is, however, that in the RFAC's proposals such guidelines would be locally rather than nationally determined and consequently contextually based, democratically derived and most likely more effective too.

The potential of local authorities

Urban design and planning practice is a potentially vast subject which a chapter of this nature can only begin to address. Nevertheless a number of key issues have been raised:

- The ever expanding agenda of urban design
- The widespread acceptance of urban design as appropriate for local authority consideration
- The incontrovertible case for urban design as appropriate for control
- The need for new government guidance on urban design
- The need for a theoretical conceptualisation of urban design to underpin policy
- The over-riding importance of appraisal
- The value of a full hierarchy of design guidance
- The role of design policy in local plans in acting as an umbrella for other guidance
- The widely accepted utility of supplementary design guidance and design briefs.

Of course, the role of local authorities in urban design can and should represent much more than their role in controlling design. Indeed, authorities have the potential to influence urban quality through a much wider range of their statutory functions: for example, through urban management and maintenance, town centre management, conservation work, land use allocation (zoning), urban regeneration and transport planning, through education, culture, image-building and promotion, and above all by being proactive about facilitating development and urban quality. For this reason it is useful to examine briefly a successful strategy where the key elements discussed above have come together – alongside other proactive approaches and a widespread will to create a better urban realm – to facilitate a dramatic transformation in Glasgow city centre[1].

Glasgow city centre – 'Miles better'

The regeneration strategy employed in Glasgow[2] has been well documented (Galloway and Evans, 1991; Hallyburton and Dally, 1992). Once known as the 'Workshop of the World', and the second city of the British Empire, in the postwar period Glasgow suf-

fered a dramatic decline. This was induced by a decline in the traditional heavy industrial workbase of the city and associated job losses, accompanied by a deterioration in the physical fabric of the city itself, in part – at least – due to the utopian planning policies of the post-war reconstruction. Recently, however, Glasgow has been enjoying something of a revival, brought about by a keenly targeted regeneration strategy, directed at improving both the image and quality of the environment within the commercial city centre.

This has been done in the hope that an improved image for Glasgow's highly visible centre will in turn act as a catalyst for a wider regeneration, thereby moving the whole of Glasgow towards a new prosperity (Hallyburton and Dally, 1992, p. 11). Hence, Glasgow's well known 'Glasgow's Miles Better' campaign of the early 1980s (being used again now) and a host of more recent high profile initiatives, including the 1988 Garden Festival, the 1990 City of Culture, and the successful bid in 1994 to host the City of Architecture and Design, 1999. All of these initiatives have one thing in common – an emphasis on design. This has been a common theme of the regeneration strategy throughout, a theme developed and implemented in planning terms through a number of key documents and reports (see Table 3.9).

The Potential for Glasgow City Centre and the Glasgow Central Area Local Plan

The inclusion of Gordon Cullen in the commissioning of *The Potential for Glasgow City Centre* (Cullen and McKinsey, 1984) by the then Scottish Development Agency (SDA) and Glasgow City Council showed an obvious faith in the value of urban design as an integral part of the solution to Glasgow's regeneration. Through an extensive appraisal, from which Cullen distilled the essential character of the city centre and its local culture, an urban design strategy for the centre was born (see Figure 3.2). The essential strategy was one 'of implosion'; or in other words, by concentrating the essence of 'Glasgow' within the core axis of Buchanan Street in order to create a 'spark' that could ignite the physical regeneration process' (Galloway and Evans, 1991, p. 13).

[1] Scottish planning advice is laid down by the Scottish Office Environment Department, in the form of National Planning Policy Guidelines (NPPGs) and Planning Advice Notes (PANs). The primary guidance on design is given in NPPG1 (SO, 1994a, pp. 22–3), which although not quite as restrictive as the 1992 PPG1 Annex A in England and Wales, is broadly similar in scope and content. More positive advice on design is given in a number of the PANs, particularly in PAN44 (SO, 1994b).

[2] An extended version of the Glasgow case study is included, alongside others, as part of Carmona M. (1996) 'Controlling Urban Design – Part 2: 'Realizing the Potential' *Journal of Urban Design*, Vol.1, No. 2, pp. 79–200.

Table 3.9 Glasgow – Key urban design documents and reports

Key themes and appraisal	Urban design controls

The Potential for Glasgow City Centre, 1984

- Urban design seen as a key element in wider regeneration
- Extensive appraisal utilised to distil character
- Robust strategy based on 'implosion', concentrating the essence of Glasgow within a core axis, thus creating a spark to ignite the physical regeneration process

- Walled city approach adopted (M8 and Clyde boundary)
- Gateways emphasised
- Axis on Buchanan Street (poles at ends and central focus)
- Linkages east and west – Merchant City/Blythswood New Town
- 'String of pearls' (spaces and events) along the Clyde.

Glasgow Central Area Local Plan, 1990

- Urban quality highlighted as the objective (to aim for a positive and attractive image)
- Largely conservationist stance
- Set of character areas defined (with their own character, identity, issues and opportunities)
- Robust urban design policy base established (urban design prioritised over architectural concerns)
- Firm basis for establishing city centre design frameworks and briefs e.g. the 'Merchant City Policy and Development Framework'
- Opportunity sheets further detail development and environmental opportunities (one for each character area)

- Cullen's spatial strategy developed
- Mixing of uses encouraged (continuing successful reintroduction of residential uses into city centre)
- Strong morphological conservation and density controls (grid iron pattern, buildings lines, containment)
- Concern for visual and contextual environment (skyline, building height, amenity, materials, shopfronts, adverts, public art, elevational proportioning)
- Social concerns considered (quality of public space, accessibility, disabled access)
- Sustainability issues considered (landscaping, tree planting, balanced transport strategy – restraining car use)

Glasgow City Centre and the Clyde, Continuing the Renaissance, 1990

- Key aim to encourage implementation of much of the earlier strategy and policy framework
- In-depth analysis of the city (historic fabric, pedestrian accessibility, neighbourhood structure, open space, land uses, visitor attractions and institutions, linkages, focal points, and spatial sequences – rooms)
- Analysis used to support flagship projects such as creating a 'Great Street' out of Buchanan Street

- Spatial strategy further developed
- Three broad urban design themes developed: greening/energy conservation, street improvements, city approaches and skylines.

Glasgow City Centre Public Realm, Strategy and Guidelines, 1995

- Addresses minutiae and broader principles of public space
- Appraisal of city townscape and character further developed (the contribution of the city's distinctive geometric morphology – the street grid, the spatial proportions of streets – the street hierarchy, the use and perception of the city centre by pedestrians, key destinations and open spaces are evaluated and opportunities for adding value and enhancing linkages to those key features, the role of the city's neighbourhoods in giving character and identity, transport issues – pedestrian/vehicular conflicts)
- 3-part prescriptive framework to encourage implementation
- Identifies a number of key demonstration projects

- Ordering framework established for the city's streets and spaces ('principal streets and spaces', 'major streets and spaces', 'minor streets and spaces' – defined according to function and prominence)
- Detailed design guidelines laid down for skilled interpretation by designers, to reduce street clutter and encourage boldness, simplicity, style and elegance in the streetscape (management and maintenance – including sustainability and security, surfaces, soft landscape, street furniture, signing, lighting, water, public art and climate)

Glasgow City Centre Millennium Plan, 1995

- Aims to bring into balance the different forms of traffic using the city centre, in favour of pedestrians, cyclists and public transport
- Through establishing readily measurable targets
- To be implemented in part by taking forward the key projects identified in the public realm strategy

- Aims to improve access into the city centre (particularly for the disabled)
- To enhance the quality, visual appearance, and vitality of the city's streets
- To control traffic to a level compatible with the environmental capacity of the city centre

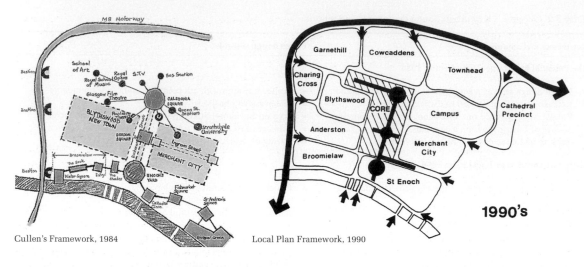

Cullen's Framework, 1984   Local Plan Framework, 1990

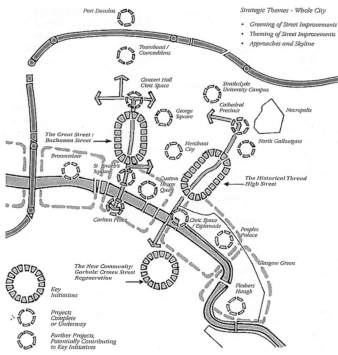

Gillespies' Framework, 1990 and 1995

Figure 3.2 Glasgow's evolving urban design framework.

Thus, a 'walled city' approach was envisaged, with the M8 along with the Clyde forming the dominant boundary to the historic city core, through which a number of distinct gateways would be emphasised. Inside this cordon a main axis was envisaged, centred on Buchanan Street, with two 'poles' at each end, and with a central focus, through which linkages could be made to a newly enhanced Merchant City to the east, and Blythswood New Town to the west, as well as to a linked 'string of pearls' (spaces and events) along the Clyde. It was hoped that this, together with the nine-part economic strategy for the city, would lay the basis for Glasgow's economic future (*Architects' Journal*, 1984, p. 47). If nothing else, it was to provide a robust spatial strategy and a generally high conceptual standard for the plethora of guidance which followed.

The real value of Cullen's work becomes apparent when examined alongside the Glasgow Central Area Local Plan (Glasgow City Council, 1990), the first draft of which was being written at the same time as the strategy. More than a little cross-fertilisation of ideas between the two is apparent (see Figure 3.2). The plan took a conservationist stance and looked at the city centre not as a collection of land uses, but rather as a set of meanings – depending on who the user was – and as a set of smaller character areas (Galloway and Evans, 1991, p. 13). As well as defining the broad strategy of rehabilitation within the existing fabric the plan gives specific encouragement to the mixing of uses (particularly to continuing the successful reintroduction of residential uses into the central area), and establishes a robust set of urban design controls, through which innovative new development can flourish (see Table 3.10).

Beyond the plan's obvious utility in establishing a robust urban design policy base, prioritising urban design over architectural concerns, it also provides a firm basis for establishing the authorities' city centre design frameworks and briefs. The *Merchant City Policy and Development Framework* (Glasgow City Council, 1991) for example builds on the character area principle laid down in the plan by suggesting a detailed planning framework for the area (character area No.10 in the plan), relating the plan policies to this unique context. Finally, a series of twelve loose-leaf opportunity sheets further detail development and environmental opportunities (one for each of the character areas) and potentially have a clear relationship to the production of briefs – many of which have been produced. Thus, a strongly hierarchical approach to design was established, with plan policy building on thoroughgoing design appraisal, implemented through detailed development frameworks and site-specific design and development briefs.

Glasgow city centre and the Clyde – Continuing the Renaissance

At least in part due to the urban strategy, the 1980s are considered to have been a successful time for Glasgow, with the city's external and self-images in particular benefiting from a major boost. In the early 1990s, however, the tide turned, reflecting the fortunes of the wider economy, bringing to a virtual halt the series of successful – in urban design and regeneration terms – projects which had been transforming parts of the city centre, particularly in the Merchant City and on the Buchanan Street axis. Within this context and to ensure that the city did not rest on the laurels of its earlier successes, the city council began the process of updating the local plan in the light of the new circumstances. At the same time the SDA appointed Gillespies to update the earlier strategy, to – as the title confirmed – 'Continue the Renaissance' (Gillespies, 1990).

Working hand in hand with the city planning department, Gillespies developed the new strategy as a logical continuation of the earlier work. As in that work, the involvement of Gordon Cullen ensured the further development of the urban design framework alongside a wider regeneration strategy. The study analysed the city in greater depth than the earlier work in terms of its historic fabric, pedestrian accessibility, neighbourhood and open space structure, land uses, visitor attractions and institutions, linkages, focal points and spatial sequences (rooms) (see Table 3.8). In so doing, it established a physical framework within which to consider existing and proposed projects and through which to integrate the river once more fully into the heart of the city centre (Gillespies, 1990, pp. 69–70).

To implement the framework the study goes on to identify a range of existing and new opportunities through which to realise the broad strategy and elevate Glasgow into the ranks of the great European cities. These key projects are complemented by four principal initiatives, of which Cullen's plan for the creation of a 'Great Street' out of Buchanan Street, to act as a new central axis for the city takes priority. Finally, a number of broad urban design themes are briefly established – greening/energy conservation; street improvements; and city approaches and skyline. Thus, the strategy further developed the existing theoretical and spatial framework for the city, incorporating sustainable, social and visual conceptualisations of urban design, to add to the strategy's overall contextual imperative. In addition, the attempt to make the framework real through the use of focused, proactive projects and proposals effectively turned theory into practice.

Glasgow City Centre Public Realm, Strategy and Guidelines and the Glasgow City Centre Millennium Plan

By 1995 although a noticeable and much-admired improvement had taken place in the appearance of the city's buildings, it was generally accepted that the quality of the public spaces lagged far behind. Although these issues had been addressed in the previous reports, they lacked detail (being more concerned with the strategic rather than detailed aspects of urban

Table 3.10 Glasgow Central Area Local Plan, Urban Design Policies, 1990

Urban design policy 1	Any new development within the central area will comply with the following urban design criteria: • Retention of the grid iron street pattern • Continuity of traditional building lines • Continuity of street containment • Respect for the traditional elevational proportioning.
Urban design policy 2	Any new development, except housing, will normally conform to a maximum plot ratio of 3.5:1. Relaxation of this policy will only be considered if a definite urban design benefit is apparent.
Urban design policy 3	To facilitate improved servicing in rear lanes, any new building line should be established 3.05 metres from the centre line of the lane.
Urban design policy 4	Any proposal for new development will take into account the following criteria when determining an appropriate building height: • The average height of surrounding buildings • The impact of the proposal on the skyline There will, therefore, be a general presumption against high rise development within the central area, with the exception of those areas defined in Map 8 where high buildings may be acceptable in principle subject to appropriate design and their effect on the skyline.
Urban design policy 5	Any development, apart from those of a minor nature, will include a 'percentage for art' in its capital budget, for new artwork which should become part of the publicly visible or accessible areas of the development. In this respect the following rates are appropriate: – 1/2% for projects up to £500 000 – 1% for projects up to £20 million – Projects over £20 million will be negotiated on an individual basis.
Urban design policy 6	The materials used in new buildings, and in alterations to existing buildings, should be of the highest possible quality in terms of type, texture, durability etc (see also conservation policy 6)
Urban design policy 7	Applications for planning permission shall be accompanied by sufficient detail to allow the proposal to be considered. Drawings shall show adjacent buildings in the context of the overall street block and in certain cases A 1:500 Model may be required.
Urban design policy 8	Shopfronts and their signage shall be designed in sympathy with the buildings of which they form part and with their surroundings, and in accordance with the shopfront design guide prepared by the director of planning. Every opportunity will be taken to encourage the display of well designed and well made signs on commercial premises so as to provide additional colour, interest and life to the central area, particularly after dark.
Urban design policy 9	Advertising hoardings and signage will not generally be permitted in sensitive locations, in particular where it would obscure architectural detail. Advertising signage may, however, be acceptable if well designed and formulated with respect for the scale and character of the building on which it is to be displayed; providing it does not detract from the surrounding area and is not out of scale with existing permanent development. Where signage is proposed to be illuminated it should also have an acceptable appearance during daylight hours.
Urban design policy 10	Advertising hoardings will not generally be permitted in the following areas: • The central conservation area, as defined in map 7 • The principal routes into and out of the central area, as defined in map 8 • The existing traditional housing areas and proposed housing areas, as defined in map 4. Outside of these areas, well designed advertising hoardings may be acceptable and will be judged on their merits. Where building operations are taking, or about to take place; temporary displays on site hoardings may also be acceptable subject to certain conditions.
Urban design policy 11	In all new and refurbished developments, appropriate disabled access arrangements shall be incorporated to the standards provided in the 'access for disabled people – design guidance notes' available from the Director of Planning.
Urban design policy 12	A programme of strategic urban landscaping will be promoted in the central area, and the following opportunities will be pursued: • A framework of boulevard tree planting in the Cowcaddens and Townhead areas • The strengthening of existing motorway planting, where appropriate • Formal tree planting at motorway entry and exit points and at other gateways into the central area.
Urban design policy 13	Pedestrian precincts and public spaces within the city centre will be the subject of a consistent design treatment, the principal elements of which shall be very high quality natural surfacing materials, large urban trees at strategic locations and essential street furniture. This approach will be applied to the following existing precincts and squares: • Buchanan Street (South) • Argyle Street (East) • Sauchiehall Street (East)

Table 3.10 Continued

• Gordon Street (East)
• St Enoch Square
• George Square
and the following proposed precincts and squares:
• Buchanan Street (North)
• Gordon Street (West)
• Argyle Street (West)
• John Street (North)
• Dixon Street
• Stockwell Square
• Royal Exchange Square
• Nelson Mandela Place
All as defined in map 8.
The main priorities in this improvement programme will be:
• The Buchanan Street, St. Enoch Square and Dixon Street axis;
• The Royal Exchange Square and Gordon Street axis
• George Square

Source: Glasgow City Council, 1990

design), and anyway needed coordination in a single coherent document (Gillespies, 1990, p. 1). The main substance of the Public Realm Strategy develops the analysis of the city's inherent character and townscape contained in the 1990 report (see Table 3.9).

The main contribution of the report, however, comes not in its analysis, most of which already existed in one form or another in the earlier reports, but in its translation of analysis into a three-part prescriptive framework. First, an ordering principle is established for the city's streets and spaces, in the recognition that it would not be financially possible (or appropriate) to propose the high-quality treatment of all streets in the centre. Thus 'principal streets and spaces', 'major streets and spaces' and 'minor streets and spaces' are defined according to function and prominence, with appropriate treatments for each. Secondly, a series of design objectives and detailed design guidelines are established for application to the public realm – '... the streets, spaces and lanes which make up the cohesive, pleasant, safe, attractive and exciting matrix of a great city' (Gillespies, 1995, p. 39). The guidelines aim to lay down appropriate ground rules for skilled interpretation by designers, to reduce street clutter and encourage boldness, simplicity, style and elegance in the streetscape. They address in turn: management and maintenance (including sustainability and security); surfaces; soft landscape; street furniture; signing; lighting; water; public art; and climate (including use of shelters). Finally, a number of demonstration projects are identified as highly visible demonstrations of how the strategy and guidelines might work in practice. Tied in with the Millennium Plan (Strathclyde Regional Council, 1995), the projects are selected to benefit considerable numbers of people and to reinforce major focal points in the city, while effectively acting as dry runs for more ambitious projects in the future.

Finally, the Glasgow City Centre Millennium Plan (a complementary and still developing initiative) aims to create an environment in the city centre commensurate with those of the leading cities in an expanding Europe. In its terms '... a city centre that is vibrant, attractive and effective for all those people who live, work, study, shop and relax in it' (Strathclyde Regional Council, 1995, p. 1). The first document to result from the initiative, a consultative Transport Strategy aims to develop a more sustainable city by bringing into better balance the different forms of traffic in the city centre (see Table 3.8), in favour of pedestrians, cyclists and public transport; to improve access into the centre, particularly for those with disabilities; to enhance the quality, visual appearance and vitality of the city's streets and spaces; and to control traffic to a level within the environmental capacity of the city centre and in so doing reduce pollution. In order to achieve these broad aims a number of readily measurable targets are established and strategies outlined for giving pedestrians and cyclists a better deal, for promoting public transport and for accommodating essential vehicle access only. The document concludes by mapping out the next five years up to the new millennium with projects ranging from the ambitious to the utilitarian.

Revised City Centre Local Plan – Glasgow: Into the Future

The key documents and reports examined above quite clearly place urban design and environmental quality more generally as a top priority in planning the regeneration of Glasgow. This priority is rarely seen in the planning strategies of other British cities badly hit by the new post-industrial climate in the UK (Punter et al., 1997 paras. 5.2.3–5.2.4). One of the key factors in the success of Glasgow has been the willingness of the profusion of different bodies representing the different interests of the city to work together for the greater good of the whole while promoting 'good design' at all levels and through a variety of means and agencies.

This partnership approach is clearly reflected in working drafts of the Glasgow Central Area Local Plan (Glasgow City Council, 1996), which is under revision. In this the Millennium Plan and the Public Realm Strategy are adopted through policy to ensure that a consistent approach to design quality is taken throughout all agencies and throughout the city centre. The revised policies build on these documents and on the 1990 plan, adding important new policies aimed at preserving the character of the city's river frontage, civic squares and pedestrian areas, emphasising corner sites and the value and individuality of the 'identity areas', facilitating increased permeability and promising a new lighting strategy for the city centre.

Conclusion: urban design renaissance?

Glasgow's experience is now being emulated by many other UK and European cities including Birmingham, Manchester and Dublin (Gillespies, 1990, p. 8), and is widely seen as a model for others to follow. Of course, Glasgow, like many cities, still has a long way to go in urban design and wider regeneration terms. Some commentators, including McKinseys the co-authors of the original 1984 report, have argued that for truly sustainable improvements to be felt the limited geographic focus of the various reports could be counterproductive in the future; they favour instead a wider spread of resources, to ensure that the benefits of the first ten years are not solely restricted to the core area (Hallyburton and Dally, 1992, p. 37). Others have argued the case for a more wide-ranging urban design framework, to encompass a concern for the overall city form and spatial structure (not just that of the city centre) and to include its most disadvantaged communities in the outlying estates (Frey, 1994, pp. 6–7). Nevertheless, with a robust urban design framework in place for the city centre, based upon thorough and ongoing appraisal, ranging from spatial to the detailed urban design concerns, and represented across the full range of design guidance, the city centre at least illustrates some of the best UK planning practice in urban design.

To conclude, a number of distinct action points can be drawn out from the Glasgow case study which help to illustrate the earlier discussion and confirm good practice for practitioners, politicians, developers, designers, and students alike:

- Prioritise urban design whether managing growth or decline
- Structure urban design policy and guidance using a fully conceptualised urban design framework, integrating both natural and built environment concerns
- Value appraisal and design-related consultation as the only means to legitimise fully urban design policy and control
- Develop a comprehensive hierarchy of guidance, ensuring that each level of the hierarchy is well related to those above and below, and directed towards the same agreed ends and corporate vision;
- Be prescriptive, not merely descriptive, in policy and guidance
- Create a climate for good urban design, recognising the limitations of purely negative controls, the value of guidance and positive advice, the importance of patronage of design skills, the limitations imposed by cost and functional constraints, and the need to respect designers and their philosophies
- Ensure any actions are seen as part of a long-term programme and not as one-off gestures – investing time, resources and expertise in urban design is essential
- Continually update, monitor and review any strategy, guidance or policies to respond to changing circumstances and pressures (environmental, economic and social)
- Be proactive and promotional rather than reactive and complacent. More specifically, encourage cooperation between the private and public sectors for the benefit of both and rely on more than negative controls to improve environmental quality
- Encourage a partnership approach in the cause of urban quality between different public bodies and between different departments within the same body – particularly between planning and transportation departments
- Above all, note that development plan policies on urban design, refined in the light of local experience and context and backed by a full hierarchy of design guidance, have potentially the pivotal role to play in improving urban design quality and urban design planning practice

With the acceptance by central government in the UK of the pivotal importance of urban design in delivering environmental quality (DoE 1994a, para. 2, DoE 1997a, paras. 13–14, 1996, para. 13), the opportunity now exists – perhaps as never before – to usher in a renaissance in the control of design through the planning system. It is hoped that the opportunity will be seized and that government policy will permanently reflect and encourage the best in UK planning practice – represented here by Glasgow – instead of always the lowest common denominator of reactionary detachment from the design control debate and abstinence from urban design prescription (Gummer, 1995, pp. 7–8).

It has been argued that in order to achieve this a four-part framework for control might be adopted, incorporating: a concern for urban design over building design; a wide-ranging conceptualisation of urban design theory as a basis for control; a rigorous approach to urban design appraisal; and based on the above, a full hierarchy of design policy and guidance at the national, strategic, district-wide and site-specific scales. In Glasgow, such a strategy has been adopted alongside a focused and integrated partnership approach to urban quality. Glasgow therefore helps to illustrate one possible direction for other UK authorities, whose design strategies are less advanced, to follow, if a renaissance in the treatment of urban design through the planning system is truly to be secured.

4 Conservation in the built environment

Sandra Manley and Richard Guise

The urban context

Most urban design activity takes place within existing urban environments and involves the revitalisation of buildings and areas through a combination of renovation and new development. The urban designer, therefore, is called upon to exercise informed judgement to identify the areas to be retained and enhanced and those that should be redeveloped.

Judgement can be made at a number of levels. First, in terms of convenience of layout; availability of open space and daylight, ease of vehicular and pedestrian access and the type and mix of existing accommodation. Secondly, in terms of condition; the cost of building repair and alteration to comply with the provision of facilities and upgrading to meet current building regulations, health and safety standards, fire precautions and access for people with disabilities, must be balanced with the financial return on the sale or rent of the property. The third level in this process concerns the exercise of aesthetic and cultural judgement. This involves deciding whether the building or area under consideration has sufficient 'special' character to merit its retention or enhancement. Moreover, if the building or area is altered or alternative uses are introduced, are those changes sympathetic or are they likely to compromise the integrity of the building or area? Ultimately, can we justify those aesthetic and cultural decisions in terms of policy and will they withstand rigorous examination at planning appeals?

These considerations, which are central to the management of change in valued urban environments, are the basis of conservation: with a body of knowledge complementary to and overlapping urban design. Within the British context conservation has been accepted as an integral part of town planning legislation, although seemingly at one remove, due to its perceived specialist and detailed focus. Nevertheless, it is within the town planning context that both strategic conservation policy and the detailed negotiations regarding individual alterations take place.

This chapter therefore contains three components, (i) an historical background, (ii) a commentary on present-day conservation area criteria and policy and (iii) a consideration of individual listed buildings in relation to urban design. Factors such as European comparisons, appropriate use of historic buildings, tourism, paving and current infill policy will also feature within this context.

1. The emergence of the conservation movement

The development of the concept

The concept of conservation is a relatively recent one and its emergence as a key element of the planning system can be linked to the increasing pace of widespread development and redevelopment in towns and cities and the burgeoning outward pressure on the fringe of settlements. The preservation of individual buildings and structures had been enshrined in Ancient Monuments Legislation since the late nineteenth century, mainly as a result of the effective campaigning of William Morris, who founded the Society for the Protection of Ancient Buildings in 1877. This was the first national group to press for the sensitive repair of historic buildings in the face of overenthusiastic and ill-considered restoration. These ideas were endorsed and explained by Morris's contemporary John Ruskin, in the *Lamp of Memory*, part of the *Seven Lamps of*

Architecture (Ruskin, 1849). However, the totality of the historic environment was still at risk of destruction or inappropriate change. From the standpoint of today, when conservation is an accepted concept in urban development, it seems unthinkable that Elm Hill, the picture postcard street in Norwich was threatened by a slum clearance order in the 1920s and in the 1930s the London squares were being drastically redeveloped by overblown neo-Georgian offices and apartments. Historic cities, such as Bath and Chester, were also at the mercy of developers and highway engineers even in the late 1960s. Earlier commentators in the interwar period such as Clough Williams Ellis (Williams Ellis, 1928, 1938) and Thomas Sharp (1940) looked forward to the forthcoming town and country planning legislation as a means of ameliorating the impacts of large-scale developments on the character of towns and villages. This concern and the sense of loss was reflected in the growth of the amenity movement, which had so much influence on the direction of the British approach to conservation.

Postwar conservation awareness

Postwar planning legislation could claim some success in saving many historic buildings, through the process of including historic buildings on a statutory List of Buildings of Special Architectural or Historic Interest which gave a measure of protection. Green belt policies, introduced at the same time, prevented some of the worst effects associated with the coalescence of neighbouring urban areas and suburban sprawl along arterial roads. However, the march of postwar reconstruction, underpinned by Comprehensive Development Areas, resulted in the loss of many of the tight-knit, attractive townscapes that had escaped the Blitz. Successive postwar governments strove to create modern town centres conveniently laid out to meet land use and traffic requirements unencumbered by the legacy of the past. This 'progressive', rational approach contrasted with much of European practice, where cities such as Warsaw (see Figure 4.2), Lubeck and St. Malo, were faithfully rebuilding their war-damaged centres in an effort to re-establish national pride and identity.

The initial euphoria of the 1950s and the confidence that the wholesale reconstruction would yield good results, quickly dissolved as the criticisms by commentators such as Ian Nairn (1955), who drew attention to the lack of identity and placelessness of town centres and suburban areas, were widely endorsed by the public. A second wave of amenity groups, many of which were formed in local areas to protect relatively modest townscapes, grew up at the same time as their umbrella organisation, the Civic Trust, which was established in 1957.

The thrust of the argument advanced by the Civic Trust was that the legislation was only effective in protecting individual buildings of merit and did not safeguard the totality of the street scene. The implication

Figure 4.1   Elm Hill, Norwich: a valued townscape today, but threatened with clearance in the 1920s (Richard Guise)

Figure 4.2   The Old City, Warsaw: left, the city as virtually obliterated by war damage; right, the same scene faithfully rebuilt in the 1950s as a symbol of national identity. (Richard Guise)

of this was that the legislation should take into account the need to protect whole areas of the urban landscape. This idea was raised in Gordon Cullen's book, *Townscape* (1961) which was particularly influential because it drew attention to the importance of the spaces between buildings and the contribution of groups of buildings that were not necessarily of architectural or historic interest, to the enclosure and definition of urban spaces. Both Cullen (1961) and Lynch (1960) provided a language by which people could describe and assess the values and experience of these areas. Although these authors can be criticised for the personal and aesthetic quality of their vision, this language has endured and continues to play its part in the identification and evaluation of conservation areas.

The role of the Civic Trust

In the early 1960s, the Civic Trust promoted the idea of area-based conservation through its award scheme for new buildings which had been successfully integrated into the street scene and through its demonstration enhancement schemes such as Magdalen Street in Norwich (see Figure 4.3). Ten years after the establishment of the Trust the President, Duncan Sandys, successfully steered the Civic Amenities Act through Parliament. The Act established the designation of

conservation areas as a measure designed to preserve and enhance areas of special architectural or historic interest. The 1967 Act was considerably strengthened by subsequent planning legislation, notably in 1972 and 1974, which is now embodied in the consolidating measure, The Town and Country Planning (Listed Buildings and Conservation Areas) Act 1990.

Preservation or conservation?

The use of the term 'conservation' within the legislation was a deliberate choice and was intended to reflect the dynamic rather than static nature of the approach to the protection of the historic environment. If the word 'preservation' had been used, it could have implied that buildings and areas should be retained in their original state, regardless of the need to adapt to changing circumstances in order to ensure their survival without massive government aid. Conservation is officially defined quite narrowly and perhaps unfortunately as 'preservation and enhancement.' The opportunity to redefine conservation to reflect a wider view of the concept was available when the legislation was consolidated in 1990. This wider view could have addressed the need to manage change sensitively within the historic environment to ensure the retention of this finite resource in a way which

Figure 4.3 Magdalen Street, Norwich: used as a testbed for facelift schemes by the Civic Trust in the early 1960s. (Richard Guise)

does not compromise its integrity, while guaranteeing its economic well being.

The organisational framework

The incremental growth of the conservation movement over the past 150 years has resulted in a complex framework of governmental and non-governmental agencies which have responsibility for or influence on the activity of conservation. This complex relationship is illustrated in Figure 4.4.

At the international level UNESCO has the responsibility of preparing a register of World Heritage Sites. Although inclusion in the list affords no additional protection, it does draw attention to the importance of the particular site within the world community. The current list includes the Pyramids of Egypt, the city of Venice and the works of Antonio Gaudí in Barcelona. By January 1995 there were 15 sites in England including Stonehenge, the city of Bath, Ironbridge Gorge and the Palace of Westminster. The European Union, through Directorate General X, administers grants for outstanding conservation schemes in member states. Schemes such as the enhancement of College Green in Bristol to provide a more appropriate setting for the cathedral received money from this source.

Recent reorganisation of central government departments has split the responsibilities for conservation at national level between two departments and one agency, which can cause confusion about roles and responsibilities. This is compounded by the different administrative arrangements in England, Scotland, Wales and Northern Ireland, although the arrangements are broadly similar and the organisations have parallel responsibilities. In England, the Department of Culture, Media and Sport (DCMS) has central responsibility for the Schedule of Ancient Monuments and the compilation of the Lists of Buildings of Special Architectural or Historic Interest. Government advice in the form of circulars and planning policy guidance notes normally originates in the DCMS, but is often issued jointly with the Department of the Environment (DoE). The DCMS is also responsible for overseeing the funding bodies who administer grants and loans for historic buildings, such as the Architectural Heritage Fund and the National Heritage Memorial Fund. The DoE deals with all appeals in respect of development in conservation areas and consideration of Listed Building Consents. The agency English Heritage provides detailed advice on conservation areas and listed buildings as well as maintaining and presenting the historic properties in its care, of which there are about 400. These bodies also administer Conservation Area Partnerships which are established with local authorities to fund schemes for the enhancement of conservation areas.

This plethora of bodies offering advice, information and funding is further complicated by the quasi-official status of the old established national amenity societies. These bodies, such as The Ancient Monuments Society and the Society for the Protection of Ancient Buildings,

opment pressure will often be of historic interest in both their street patterns and townscape. The fact that virtually all the City of Westminster and most of the commercial core of Bristol are included within designated conservation areas illustrates the need to reconcile modern developments with conservation interests.

The continuing growth in the number of conservation areas and the extent of the area now covered by designations has prompted critics, such as Morton (1991) and the development industry in general to question whether too many areas have been designated. The argument is advanced that the sheer number of designations and marginal quality of some areas has 'devalued the currency' and reduced the 'special importance' of the earlier designations. The consequence of designating a large number of areas could

Figure 4.5   Bath: The Royal Crescent. The whole of the eighteenth-century city is a conservation area. (Richard Guise)

Figure 4.6   Burford: one of many of the Cotswold market towns in which materials and scale exert a unifying influence. (Richard Guise)

Figure 4.7 Letchworth: the first garden city, circa 1904: significant as a social and economic experiment as well as for its low-density arts and crafts architecture. (Richard Guise)

be that resources, both human and financial, could be spread too thinly. A further question which might be raised regarding the designation of conservation areas and the efficacy of the process of designation as a means of protection, is that if designation is to have real meaning, the controls over new development should be more extensive to include development that currently does not require formal planning permission. The powers under Article 4 of the Town and Country Planning (General Permitted Development) Order (1995) have recently been extended to enable a local authority to restrict development in relation to dwellings in conservation areas using a simpler procedure (Article 4 (2)). In cases where these directions are 'backed up by a clear assessment of the area's architectural and historic interest, where the importance to that special interest of the features in question is established, where the local planning authority can demonstrate support for the direction' it is possible to control the removal of particular features. This will make it possible, for example, to prevent the loss of original windows, doors, quoins, parapets, stonework or other features. However, it could be argued that such controls should be applicable as a matter of course when designating an area.

Extending control over building operations is only part of the issue. It is argued below and belatedly recognised in PPG 15 (DoE and DNH, 1994) that character is also defined by a 'particular mix of uses'

The current use classes defined by the Town and Country Planning (Use Classes) Order 1987, are drawn too crudely and do not protect uses from pressure from other higher-value uses. This can result in the loss of activities characteristic of an area. The Birmingham Jewellery Quarter, for example, is suffering the loss of small workshop industries in the face of competition from retail and office units.

Of course, the contrary view of the designation process is that during a time of scarce resources it may not be regarded as morally right to spend money on preserving historic buildings and conservation areas. This view might be supported for different reasons by those who regard conservation controls as an unreasonable impediment to the normal process of decline, demolition and redevelopment and assert that conservation might inhibit investment. This view, however, should be considered alongside the evidence which has indicated that listed buildings and properties within conservation areas have performed well in investment terms as compared with new developments during the recent period of economic recession (Cullen and Hunter, 1994). Using conservation as a means of regenerating run-down areas has also proved successful in some areas, not least because the controls themselves lend a degree of stability to the area and can reassure nervous investors.

Arguments against designation will, however often, be put forward by prospective developers and boundary lines will be questioned. All this points to a need for the conservation planner to be able to justify and explain his/her decisions and for those decisions to be based on a sound appraisal of the area.

Defining character and appearance To decide on the eligibility of an area for conservation designation, it is necessary to examine in some depth the meaning of certain key phrases within the legislation. Defining character and appearance is critical. At a superficial level this may seem to be an easy task and yet making the distinction between character and appearance can be difficult, especially as 'character', as implied by the definition, has more than purely a visual or spatial dimension, as is illustrated diagrammatically in Figure 4.8.

'Character' is that quality which emanates from the fusion of topography and built form, geology and traditional building materials, street patterns, and the grain and boundaries which reflect past ownerships. An area's character is experienced through its townscape; a network of spaces, both modest and grand, intimate or exposed, revealing views to landmarks or glimpses to secluded alleys and courts. The pattern of uses and activities is crucial to defining the character of an area and yet this is not always given sufficient emphasis. This includes a consideration of the legacy of past uses as detected in place names, building types and the original identity of certain districts and their transparency in the public realm. It follows from this that character is also a sensory experience involving the experience of sounds and smells as well as sight. Perhaps a place can only gain real character with the passage of time; when people have been able to alter and adapt it, when it has weathered and gathered the patina of age and when people have evolved their own images of that distinctive place in their minds.

Consideration should also be given to the meaning of 'appearance.' Obviously, this relates to the visual

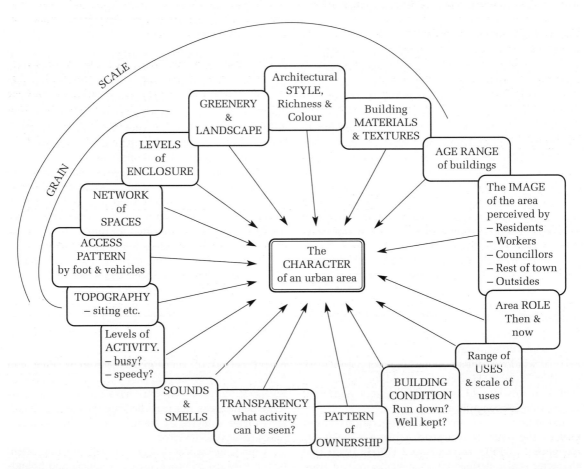

Figure 4.8 What is character? (Manley and Guise)

qualities of the area: the style and proportions of the buildings, their colour and materials, the attractiveness of the relationships between buildings and spaces, trees and landscaping, the design of street furniture, signs and floorscape. In a word it is the unique combination of these and many other factors which contribute to the visual delight of an area.

Architectural or historic interest It is likely that some individual buildings within a conservation area will be of sufficient architectural interest to merit being listed. However, most will be modest buildings which nevertheless contribute to the interest of the streetscape or reflect vernacular building patterns. The historic interest of areas usually derives from their interest in terms of industrial archaeology or their significance in terms of planning or social history. The naval dockyard of Chatham or the model village of Bournville fall into these categories. Some of these designations will be of national importance whereas other areas may be also worthy of protection because of their local significance.

Conducting Character Appraisals It has already been explained that the process of designation as a conservation area is a simple one, but this does not absolve the local authority from undertaking this duty in a serious and rigorous manner. To do this effectively, the preparation of a Character Appraisal is an essential element of the process, although surprisingly it is not required by the legislation. However, the appraisal

comes into its own to support the choice of the area's boundary and the judgements made regarding developments in conservation areas, particularly when these become the subject of appeals. Additionally, bids for Conservation Area Partnership funding from English Heritage must be accompanied by a statement to explain the national significance of the area's quality and to justify the design decisions within that context. Finally, statements can support Article 4 directions made under the Town and Country Planning (General Permitted Development) Order 1995 to restrict permitted development rights within conservation areas. Directions might include the removal of the normal rights to extend or alter property when the authority can claim that such alterations would damage the character of the area.

A character appraisal is likely to contain a number of component parts as indicated in Figure 4.8 above, and in Table 4.1 below. An effective appraisal should be carried out with the involvement of the local community, and draw on local knowledge and expertise as a way of endorsing its content and gaining public support for the aims of conservation.

Where do we draw the line? A conservation area is defined by a boundary drawn on a map. Within that boundary the local authority is conveying the message that protection is the name of this urban game; that change will be qualitative rather than quantitative; that the environment is a premium one – 'better' than

Table 4.1 Suggested contents of a character appraisal

Component	Content
Aims, terms of reference	Context and issues facing the conservation area. Identification of conservation area boundary, listed buildings, tree preservation orders, etc.
Evolution of the area	Sequence of maps identifying significant events, periods, changes in ownership and economy which have shaped the growth and character of the town
Townscape	Setting, skyline, approaches, landmarks, views, edges, structure, hierarchy of spaces, plots, streets, scale, density, details
Sub-areas	Small areas of individual character identified by predominant uses, forms, enclosure, soft landscape etc..
Local building traditions	Vernacular building types, forms, siting and materials, paving traditions – prominent architecture styles
Activities, uses and linkages	Patterns and types of activity/uses. Times and levels of activity. Links between uses. Influence of past uses. Transparency
Images and associations	How is the area perceived by people living, working and visiting it? Sensory experience: sounds, smells etc.
SWOT	Strengths, Weaknesses, Opportunities, Threats
Suggested strategy for action	Amendments to conservation area boundary. Key infill site guidance. Buildings at risk. Opportunities for enhancement

the outside. These messages are likely to have market implications; property values tend to rise and higher-value uses can displace the existing, sometimes lower-value ones, which, paradoxically, are often the uses which give the area its unique character. This is the much-discussed process of gentrification. It can be a damaging process, particularly if the original occupiers of property are displaced. It is sometimes inevitable as existing uses may be virtually obsolete and subject to decay. It can, however, be beneficial such as when a totally derelict or investment-starved area is 'discovered' and regenerated. To some extent the cyclic process of decline, renewal and subsequent decay is part of the ecology of the city and conservation must work within this process.

In order to define the precise position of the boundary of the proposed area it will be necessary to interpret present-day and historic maps. Examining a sequence of historic maps, particularly with the assistance of an urban archaeologist, makes it possible to determine market places, lines of long-removed town walls, encroachments on market places, burgage plots, and church precincts. Later Georgian improvements, Victorian bye-law developments, and developments that have been influenced by the Garden City movement can also be identified.

Inevitably, given the pattern of development and rebuilding in most towns, environmental quality is not homogeneous. There will be pockets of poor-quality or inappropriate development in an area of generally good-quality townscape. A conservation area, however, should not look like a piece of Gruyère cheese with a patchwork of holes in it; it must have a coherence and be easy to comprehend. Therefore inappropriate development is likely to be included, as long as it is in the minority in the built-up area. It is necessary to balance the danger of diluting or debasing the quality of this special area with pragmatic consideration. Indeed, it can be argued that to include some poorer-quality areas can help to stimulate enhancement and improvement can take place at a future date. A similar dilemma exists where the townscape on one side of a road is obviously of different quality from that of the other, possibly because more recent stereotyped suburban development has taken place. Normally, it would be preferable to draw the line to include the properties on both sides of the street as both sides contribute to the quality of the street scene. However, in this case it would be advisable to draw the boundary line on the back edge of the footpath abutting the inappropriate buildings. This conveys the message that the street is considered as far as possible as a totality and that subsequently some improvement may be made to the boundary fronting the street.

Deciding on an appropriate line is therefore a question of careful judgement and it will be necessary to balance the arguments carefully, particularly in situations where there may be political considerations or public pressures for a particular choice of boundary. Developers have recognised the scope to challenge the suitability of boundary lines and ultimate decisions must be soundly based on conservation arguments and capable of justification.

How large should a conservation area be?   Some areas such as the city of Bath or the Settle–Carlisle railway line are massive in extent, others are quite small; perhaps encompassing the buildings fronting a square or churchyard. The touchstone should be homogeneity of character, even if that character is defined by a certain variety. For instance, an area should not contain a set of unrelated and diverse characteristics to the extent that it cannot be described as having an overall character which can be subdivided into a network of related areas of individual identity. Hence a market town is an entity in its own right, yet that entity contains related components: a bustling market place, a quiet green church precinct, main approach streets and back lanes. It may also be characterised by Georgian improvements and enhancements and could be framed by its countryside setting which affords valued panoramas of its skyline. This may all be one designated area. However, outlying or different townscapes less related to that whole might be better defined on their own as separate conservation areas.

Figure 4.9 which indicates the conservation area for Bridgwater in Somerset, illustrates some of the considerations taken in drawing a particular boundary. It would have been possible to have defined the dock and associated waterfronts as a separate conservation area. Indeed they were designated separately in 1972 and 1977, but were later amalgamated to achieve continuity of administration in the waterfront.

Design control in conservation areas

Applicants for planning permission for development in conservation areas are required to submit detailed proposals and cannot expect to gain planning permission or Conservation Area Consent on the basis of an outline submission. This reflects the fact that it is not only the basic principle of whether development of a particular type is acceptable, but the precise detail of the way in which it is related to the site and its context that has to be considered. Thus the conservation planner, for example, in looking at an edge-of-town housing scheme, will be concerned about matters such as the relationship

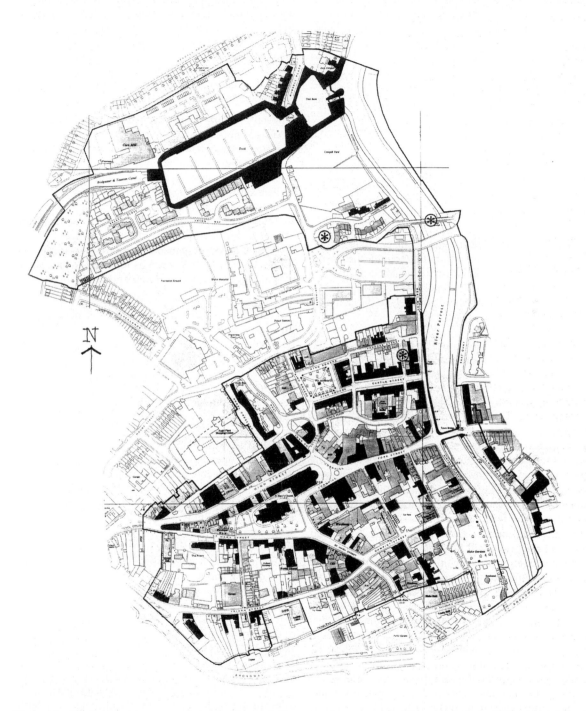

Figure 4.9   The Bridgwater conservation area. The original conservation area covered the town centre and quayside. A later conservation area was designated to protect the canal basin. Finally, the two areas were linked to safeguard the waterfront. The listed buildings are shown in black. (Manley and Guise; produced with permission by Sedgemoor District Council © Crown copyright)

of the new development to the street scene, the foot-print and form of the buildings and their relationship to each other. The quality of the spaces between the build-ings, the rooflines and window–wall relationships, the type and quality of materials to be used and how they reflect local traditions will also be important. These factors will be much more significant than, for example, the precise number of houses on the site. This creates tensions between the intentions of the volume house builder and those of the planner. The standard house types produced by developers, with their characteristic square plan and detached layouts are rarely appropriate in conservation areas. In villages and small town loca-tions, where pressure for development of estate housing is particularly concentrated, a wide-frontage, lower-profile, informal terrace is likely to be more reflective of local building traditions than the typical 'executive' house. Bearing in mind the large number of such situa-tions in this country and the cultural significance of the village and small market town, it should be possible for the creative developer to generate appropriate house types which would contribute positively to the character of these conservation areas.

Infill in conservation areas   The need to consider the relationship of new developments with the existing form and grain of the conservation area is even more challenging in relation to infill sites. These are usually gaps within a continuous street frontage, corner sites or backland areas behind frontage development. The problem in many situations of this type is one of trying to assimilate a potentially large bulk into a smaller-scale context. This might typically be a large office building or a new town-centre shopping development; every-thing about these buildings is potentially damaging to the fabric of the townscape. The sheer width of a single building where the frontage may originally have com-prised many narrow-fronted buildings built and adapted over time will be difficult to assimilate. The structure required in many of these cases is a wide-span multi-storey frame construction, often with a flat roof that is likely to conflict with the existing complex and diverse roof structures of an historic area. Space requirements of modern shops or offices may also dic-tate a planning grid with rigid right-angular changes in the direction of the building's footprint, which bear no relationship to the more subtle changes of direction in building form typical of a traditional street frontage.

Pressure to accept larger-scale developments in his-toric contexts is particularly difficult to resist when many towns must compete to maintain their vitality and economic viability in the face of competition from out-of-town centres, shopping malls and business parks. The conservation officer's lone voice against

these pressures may not be heard unless it can be underpinned by reasoned argument. More work needs to be done on studies to determine the capacity of his-toric towns in terms of acceptable levels of develop-ment which can be absorbed into the fabric without destroying the essential characteristics that originally led to designation as a conservation area. Such a study would determine such matters as:

- View corridors to protected skylines and landmarks
- Height policies which can be varied or uniform to reflect view corridors and topography, e.g. the city of Salisbury's 12m height restriction to maintain the dominance of the cathedral spire
- Perceived ridgelines from street level, i.e. the princi-ple of higher buildings to the rear of sites.
- Maximum and minimum bay widths to maintain the vertical rhythm of a typical High Street
- Pitched roof requirements to govern the scale of new development, break down its bulk and to accommo-date water tanks, plant rooms and lift motor rooms.

The results of such a study could form the basis of con-trol mechanisms, perhaps in the form of design briefs for specific sites or more general building codes which have been useful elsewhere to govern street-level percep-tion of buildings. Codes might perhaps focus on entrances in terms of location, legibility and accessibil-ity; corners, which can act as pivotal points in the town-scape; or gable end treatment. A code of this type could, for example, stipulate that gable ends should not be blank but that opportunities should be taken to include oriel windows, entrances or decoration. Codes could also specify that only active street frontages would be applicable in certain specified areas in order to avoid blank frontages, or car parks at street level. The sum effect of such an approach should help to ensure that buildings will be able to shoehorn them-selves into the urban fabric without disrupting the char-acter of conservation areas. It is essential to concentrate on the major decisions if this is to be achieved, rather than on the more superficial matters such as style, colour and materials, for although these matters are important they are not of strategic significance. It is at this level of aesthetic decision-making that planners and urban designers have most to offer: this should therefore be the essential thrust of their interventions in relation to design in conservation areas. With this strategic view in mind Table 4.2 gives a suggested approach to infill decision-making which is particularly appropriate to historic contexts although the basic essentials are transferable to other situations. The theme of this table is an emphasis on the choice of approaches to infill design, each of which may be appropriate in certain circumstances. For example, a

Table 4.2 A suggested approach to infill decision-making

Infill design options	Characteristics	Context	Comment
Retain façade	Original building gutted, façade retained and tied back to new structure. New structure must relate to existing storey heights on façade.	This option adopted when the façade is recognised as the most important feature of the building, or is crucial to the street scene.	Too often an expedient to maximise site value yet retain familiar façade. Purists (conservationists and modernists) concerned at loss of integrity. Often stability problems during conversion.
Copy existing or adjacent	Either on vacant site, or a rebuild of existing unstable building. Adjacent building/s copied in bay widths storey heights, fenestration, materials, jointing decoration.	Usually most appropriate in a unified townscape composition, e.g. unfinished Georgian Square; otherwise when a listed building is demolished and required to be replaced.	Deceptively easy option, but requires great attention to detail, supervision and workmanship. Materials (natural) may be very expensive. How is the effect of age to be achieved? Is it appropriate to do this?
'Rational'/objective parameters	Basic briefing by planners regarding the new building envelope: includes massing layout, scale, views, heights, skyline, proportions, building lines, fenestration, materials etc.	Appropriate in most typical street scenes where maintenance of scale is important, but style could be varied.	A 'cool' measurable approach which can be well articulated and defended (at appeal by LA). Can result in lifeless conformity – good solutions depend on good architect – LA negotiation.
Neutral/deferential	Requirements regarding the overall effect of the building, e.g. balanced proportions and regular window/wall relationships. Recessive, low-contrast colours.	An approach devised to set off the quality of its (varied) neighbours.	Could be monotonous if overused in same street. Could also produce cliché-ridden designs 'acceptable' in conservation areas eg. false mansards, or reflective glass.
Context-expressive	An eclectic approach drawn from an analysis of and response to the character style and use of the street or area. Light-hearted. Often post-modern in style.	Usually in an area of varied and rich character, not especially of 'High' Architecture but mixed use, adapted areas.	At best it is both scholarly and witty in its references and adaption of motifs. Relies on choice of good architect. At worst can be glib and can look tatty/outdated in short time.
Bold contrast/structure-expressive	A modernist/high-tech approach: an expression and celebration of late 20th century technology and building function.	Appropriate: (a) in confined sites as one-off jewel-like contrast (b) in larger cleared or run-down areas where a statement of change and confidence is needed.	Appropriate if scale is right. Should be 'friendly' at street level (transparent, accessible). Could be dull or overassertive if not well designed. What effect if repeated in same street?

direct copy of existing buildings or a bold high-tech approach might each produce a good scheme, provided the design had integrity. To design with integrity is to design with sensitivity to the surroundings and with scholarship. Questions of scale and massing of the form of the building must be considered as a first level or strategic decision. Once this essential point is established attention can be given to detailed aspects.

Design of the space between buildings   A major task of conservation work is the identification and implementation of schemes for the enhancement of conservation areas. The majority of these involve the improvement of the public realm and include the restriction and calming of motor traffic and the removal of street 'clutter' such as piecemeal and inappropriate street furniture. Unfortunately, many paving schemes have resulted in the same depressingly stereotyped solution, using a limited range of materials and street furniture. This is characterised by widespread use of red brick paviours laid in herringbone pattern, concrete paving slabs in natural grey in 400mm × 400mm units or others coloured and moulded in 'natural riven' finishes. Many of these solutions are unconvincing, subject to fading and have a short shelf-life for reinstatement (see Figure 4.10).

English Heritage, in their conditions for entering into agreements with local authorities for Conservation Area Partnership schemes which involve paving, are now insisting that the floorscape traditions are understood by designers and are respected in the choice of materials. This means learning from the remnants of paving which are present in the area and using natural and traditional materials wherever appropriate. Good paving schemes can convey confidence to neglected areas or streets and be a spur to shopkeepers and other business people to carry out other improvements to the area (see Figure 4.11).

Design of shopfronts   A common complaint voiced by many who are interested in the character of historic houses is that every High Street tends to look the same as it represents the outlet of a wide range of national and international multiple chain stores. Shop fascias with standard colours and logos all at a standard size tend to be fitted to buildings, irrespective of their design, proportions, window patterns or materials. Moreover, the multiples have not been the only ones responsible for this erosion of character. Many of the smaller independent traders have used shopfitters who have fitted silver-finish anodised aluminium frames and internally-lit acrylic fascias regardless of the building in which they are placed.

Figure 4.10   Inappropriate paving scheme? Wall-to-wall swirls of brick paviours and busy street furniture change the character of this High Street. (Richard Guise)

After over a decade of pressure from conservation officers and shopfront design guidance, however, the situation shows signs of improvement. The larger multiples who use top designers have shown flexibility by developing a range of applications of their standard logos and at times have dispensed with illuminated fascias, altered the size of the logos and used graphics applied to or incorporated within the plate glass shopfront. Independent shopkeepers often respond to advice to retain existing older shopfronts and use good sign writers to restore and paint the fascia. To some extent, however, shopfront design advice has become stereotyped. All too often the only conservation advice seems to be to encourage retailers to adopt a diluted Victorian design, using plywood fascias and thin beadings to give a mildly reproduction effect. There are certainly valuable lessons to be learned from Victorian and Edwardian shopfronts – the satisfactory position-

Figure 4.11   The Market Place, Wells: a restrained repaving scheme of 1995 which enhances the setting of the surrounding historic buildings. The former tarmacked area has been replaced by York stone. (Richard Guise)

ing and proportion of the fascia, the graceful framing of plate glass windows and the need for a stallriser of about half a metre to protect the base of the shopfront from the worst of the weather and impact damage, and now as a deterrent to the recent phenomenon of ram raiding. There are also valuable lessons to be learned from the best contemporary shopfront design in terms of graphics, lighting and overall concept. The main concern for the conservation planner is to ensure that the shopfront design respects the character of the building in which it is located. In particular it is important to maintain the rhythm of the original plot widths, especially if the shop extends across more than the width of one plot; the fascia and window pattern should reflect these original bay patterns. It is also important that the top of the fascia is located below the sill of the first-floor window. Some historic buildings, such as former banks or houses are often converted to shops. In these cases the provision of a fascia may be inappropriate and lettering might be fixed directly to the building or to the window with an effect that allows for the legitimate desire of the owner to advertise the business activity without compromising the integrity of the building.

The dangers of 'heritage' design   The concept of 'heritage' has had some unfortunate consequences which have been contrary to the aims of conservation. Heritage, as Hewison (1987) argued, can imply the simplistic, sanitised presentation of our past – through some of the many heritage centres that have grown up since the 1980s, through the marketing of some refurbishment schemes and through an approach to restoration which seeks to apply an instant ageing effect through the use of reproduction materials and artefacts. Indeed, to some degree the battles fought against over restoration in the late nineteenth century are being repeated at the turn of the millennium, Conservation should be aiming to reveal the story of the development of a building or area 'warts and all' through the honest differentiation between new additions, alterations, repairs and the original. The heritage approach, however, can lead to the application of reproduction street furniture (pseudo-Victorian lamp posts and seats), the use of inappropriate graphics (ye olde signs), aged natural-effect concrete products (riven stone-effect paving slabs, roof tiles or walling materials), which seek to harmonise with the original but only succeed in belittling it. The effect can be compounded by over-cleaning of the historic building which can obliterate the patina of age which gives the building its rootedness in time.

The planner, urban designer or conservation officer will often have to persuade the overenthusiastic developer or council member who feels that the heritage approach is sympathetic to the aims of conservation, that a more restrained philosophy is likely to be more appropriate in the long term (Hewison,1987).

Figure 4.12   Windsor: is the marketing of 'heritage' eroding the character of historic places? (Richard Guise)

3. Listed buildings policy and practice

Comparisons and context

Virtually all developed countries and many countries in the developing world possess a system of protecting monuments and buildings considered significant to their culture and heritage. The system usually consists of identifying and scheduling the buildings and protecting them through legislation to prevent their demolition. In some cases state funds exist to administer grant aid for their protection; the state may also own and maintain these buildings. However, in most cases the buildings are in private or corporate ownership.

The British system of Ancient Monuments and Listed Building protection dates from 1882 and 1947 respectively. Although the system is more recent than that in France or Sweden, for instance, it is true to say that the number of listed buildings and conservation areas is greater in Britain than in most other countries. The total number of listed buildings currently stands at over 450,000 and the number continues to rise. Buildings which are included on the list are classified into two main groups. Grade I buildings, which make up only 2 per cent of the total, are exceptional buildings such as Blenheim Palace or Stourhead, all of which have a national importance (see Figure 4.13). Grade II buildings, which make up about 94 per cent of listed buildings are of special interest, but some are distinguished as Grade II* because of their particular importance. All buildings built before 1700 which survive in anything like their original condition are included on the list and the majority of buildings built between 1700 and 1840. Later buildings of the period 1840–1914 may be included on the list because they are of particular quality and in order to ensure that the principal works of the major architects are represented. More recent buildings will only be selected if they are of definite quality and character. No buildings less than ten years old are listed and only exceptional examples will be listed that are less than 30 years old. The criteria for selection of buildings are indicated in PPG 15 but in view of the recent decision to open up the process to public debate it is probably appropriate to reconsider the criteria

In Britain many listed buildings and conservation areas are modest in terms of national significance, being special in a more regional context. Their significance is likely to be more for their townscape contribution, their embodiment of an early example of a structural type (see Figure 4.14), a new use, or a particular style, rather than their links with a historical event or personality. Thus, for example, early uses of cast iron or reinforced concrete may be important, or early examples of the new uses emerging during the Industrial Revolution – machine houses, railway stations or department stores. Similarly, Art Nouveau architecture (rare in Britain) and early Modern Movement buildings as well as, say, the works of original and notable architects such as Nicholas Hawksmoor, John Soane, Philip Webb or Charles Holden are likely candidates for listing. It is clear that to assess potential buildings for protection it is necessary to have a detailed knowledge of the history of

Figure 4.13   Kingsweston House, Bristol: a Grade 1 listed building designed by Vanburgh circa 1710, but mothballed since being vacated as a police training centre. It is now essential to find a sympathetic new use for the building. (Richard Guise)

Figure 4.14   Albert Dock, Liverpool: threatened with total clearance in the 1970s it is now the largest complex of Grade 1 listed buildings in England and Wales. (Richard Guise)

architecture, British social history and an understanding of structural types and building materials.

The first lists were compiled by a handful of inspectors who had no powers to enter private buildings.

Consequently, a large proportion of the obviously important buildings were included in the early (1940s–1950s) lists, but many significant omissions became apparent. Changes in taste and perceived threats have meant that Victorian and vernacular architecture has been included to a greater degree in later lists.

Because the early inspectors were so few and faced the Herculean task of compiling lists from scratch, it is not surprising that buildings which appeared unpromising externally, but which possessed very interesting interiors, were passed by. Typical examples of this would be the apparently everyday eighteenth century town house perhaps much altered by later work. It was not always appreciated that earlier, fifteenth or sixteenth century town houses were often refronted in the eighteenth century. Eighteenth century householders and builders were not averse to completely remodelling the facade of their house to conform to the latest classical style, as set out in the many Pattern Books published at that time (see Figure 4.15). Thus skin-deep facades were erected onto earlier buildings and the 'old-fashioned' gable end was dis-

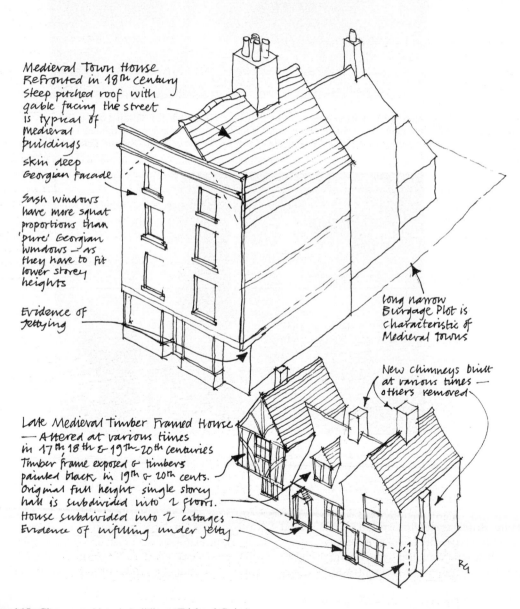

Figure 4.15   Changes to historic buildings. (Richard Guise)

guised by a high parapet and simple facade of sash windows. Examples abound in virtually every market town, notably in Shrewsbury and Gloucester. Often the regularity of a classical front was compromised by the demands of the existing lower storey heights, or the shape of the steep pitched roof behind the facade. This is always a clue to the existence of refronting. Later evidence has often revealed medieval wall paintings or Jacobean plaster ceilings behind these apparently unexceptional fronts.

Recently, the effort has been focused on including more postwar buildings on the list. In 1995 the Secretary of State for National Heritage invited the public to contribute to the debate about which buildings were to be included on the revised list under the rolling '30-year rule', whereby any building built over 30 years ago could be considered for listing. This even resulted in a special feature in the London Evening Standard – almost unprecedented for a conservation issue – and hundreds of comments were received by the Secretary of State for National Heritage. The final decision to include buildings such as New Zealand House and Centre Point in London, Coventry Station and the Sheldon Bush Shot Tower in Bristol (see Figure 4.16) was greeted with both enthusiasm and outrage. However, it does seem to indicate that the public do care about listed buildings and want to make a contribution to the discussions.

The problem posed by postwar buildings is that, with the possible exception of the Royal Festival Hall and Coventry Cathedral, they are generally unloved. The modernism of the 1960s was often quite deliberately 'brutal' but the 'honest' uncompromising expression of concrete revealed when the timber shuttering was removed was rarely popular with the public. This direct expression of structure, combined as it was with the asymmetrical form derived from the function of the building, was intended to produce aesthetically acceptable buildings. These intentionally stark buildings might have been more widely accepted if they had been more successful in functional terms. However, the spectre of the failing flat roof, leaking joints, poor performance of new materials, inadequate thermal insulation and lack of response to the needs of the user in so many cases, has given us an inheritance of alienation from and mistrust of modern architecture. This general mistrust perhaps blinds us to examples of good modern architecture which has functioned well, remains attractive and is worthy of preservation.

Finding new uses for vacant listed buildings   The dilemma of the Brynmawr case, in South Wales, where it has proved impossible to find a new use for a listed Modern Movement factory complex seems to illustrate the problems surrounding listing. Buildings have to 'earn their keep'; they have to be put to a new use if their original use has become obsolete. Almost invariably the new use requires some adaptation and extension of the building. The question is to what extent do these adaptations and extensions retain the essential

Figure 4.16   Sheldon Bush Shot Tower Bristol: built in 1960s, this unique concrete structure and distinctive local landmark has recently been added to the list. (Richard Guise)

character of the building which justified its listing? The answer is to find suitable new uses. This search may take some time and in the meantime the building is 'at risk'. The risks are that the building will deteriorate when vacant as essential maintenance is not carried out. Also, the building while vacant can be broken into while vacant and be subject to vandalism, illegal occupation and fire damage. Each local authority is encouraged by English Heritage and the equivalent bodies to compile a Buildings at Risk Register in order to identify vulnerable listed buildings and bring them to the attention of the market.

Sometimes a trust might be established to save a building and to offer it for sale after sensitive conversion. The Landmark Trust, founded in 1965, has done worthwhile work in saving very 'difficult' buildings such as martello towers, follies, stations and remote farm buildings which have been imaginatively reused as holiday homes. The result is that the building is saved in a virtually authentic state and it earns its keep by being let throughout the year as an interesting holiday destination. Most buildings, however, must face considerable adaptation to accommodate new uses, though there are limits to the appropriateness of the use which must be taken into account to avoid damaging the integrity of the building.

Criteria for decision-making for alterations to listed buildings It is important to recognise that the protection offered by the listing of the building covers the whole building: its entire exterior and interior and any fixtures. It also covers the curtilage of the building and any buildings or boundary walls within that curtilage. Figure 4.18 explains this in principle, but, inevitably, as every building is different there will be differences of interpretation.

The challenge for the decision-making rests in deciding whether alterations or extensions to listed buildings are acceptable and result in the retention of a building which is worthy of its status as a listed building after the works are complete.

English Heritage and the Society for the Protection of Ancient Buildings have developed principles for sensitive conversion of historic buildings which should act as guidelines for conservationists and developers. First, be conservative: retain as much of the original character of the building as possible. Secondly, make the alterations reversible. For instance, can new subdivisions, for both floors and walls, be demountable; can restoration techniques be reversed if treatments are found to be destructive or better techniques are developed in the future? Thirdly, a clear distinction should be made between the original work and new work. The building should reflect the fact that it has been

Figure 4.17   The Black Castle, Bristol: a substantial folly of circa 1765, reused as a restaurant in 1994. Its neighbours have belittled its status as a Grade II* listed building. Its setting, in a sea of black tarmac, compromises its integrity. (Richard Guise)

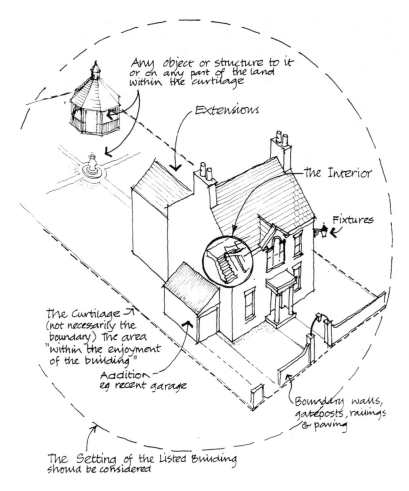

Any object or structure to it or on any part of the land within the curtilage

Extensions

the Interior

Fixtures

the Curtilage (not necessarily the boundary) The area "within the enjoyment of the building"

Addition eg recent garage

Boundary walls, gateposts, railings & paving

The Setting of the Listed Building should be considered

Figure 4.18   What is listed? (Richard Guise)

adapted at various times and new work should not try to match the old in a seamless way, by reproduction or by artificially ageing new materials. It is better to be sensitive in the design of new work in order not to clash or compete, but to be 'honest' in reflecting the changing story of the building.

There are many considerations which may be useful when appraising the suitability of proposals which involve the alteration and extension of a listed building. There is not space to consider them within this chapter as they require the exercise of careful judgement in the matters of setting, prioritising elevations, the design of new work, detailed elevational design, roofs, walls and openings and interior design. Suffice it to say that the architect or surveyor should bear in mind the issues and principles discussed earlier in this chapter.

Conclusions

In conclusion it is worth reflecting on whether the British philosophy of conservation, with its rather pragmatic approach, is achieving its objectives. The area-based approach with its emphasis on local areas and buildings of importance has the advantage of recognising locally valued environments and the totality of buildings and townscapes. However, this has the potential in national terms of devaluing the cultural significance of the more important areas and buildings and spreading limited resources ever more thinly. The essential requirement of each building and area to be commercially or economically viable has led in many cases to almost unacceptable compromise in conversion work and unscholarly replication. The contradiction between the decision to designate a conservation area to protect its character and yet to allow the erosion of this character through permitted development rights and insufficient protection of floorscape surfaces has to be addressed if the credibility of conservation areas is to be maintained. The thin veneer of 'heritage' design of new buildings, alterations, materials, street furniture, shopfronts, and paving is unconvincing and will not stand the test of time.

If the essential meaning of conservation is revisited, it becomes clear that there is no place for a superficial approach. Instead the wise use of existing spatial and cultural resources has more in common with the aims of sustainable development, a principle which is likely to guide urban design decision-making in the new millennium. Indeed, it can be argued that the historic city in many ways is a model for a sustainable city. Its survival is a testimony to the fact that a city which has a critical mass of mixed uses in close proximity has sufficient adaptability to regenerate itself. The pre-industrial city embodies an optimal density which both facilitates convenient interaction and mix of use and in the best cases allows for gardens, ground-floor front doors, public spaces and access to the countryside. The fabric of the historic city is human in scale in that distances and building heights are easily reached on foot. Finally, and arguably most significantly, the historic city is the product of its relationship with its site in terms of topography, shelter, nodal points of routes, local economy and resources and building materials.

This chapter has attempted to demonstrate that urban designers need to gain an understanding of the lessons that the inherited built environment can teach us regarding the creation of valued environments. They also need the sensitivity and skills to manage change in a way which will integrate new development with the existing urban form and foster continued renewal and vitality.

5 Urban design and regeneration

Marion Roberts

The prominence of regeneration policy

Urban regeneration has occupied a dominant position in North American and Western European policy initiatives over the last two decades. Concern about the decline of inner cities, about unemployment, about harsh and inhumane urban landscapes has led to a succession of initiatives and approaches, each rapidly replacing the last. Urban design considerations have been significant in the formulation of many of these initiatives, although the extent to which each initiative can be said to have a consciously formed design content varies enormously.

In response to this variation this chapter considers definitions of urban design with regard to urban regeneration. It is suggested that the concept of regeneration has moved from a physical definition, albeit with visionary overtones, to a more complex set of propositions which integrate social, cultural and economic goals. Nevertheless, it is argued that urban design has an important role within regeneration schemes, not least because a consciousness of urban design practices and principles can ensure that a scheme has a degree of quality, which may be absent from a purely economic or socially oriented rationale.

Whilst the aim of urban regeneration activities is to make a positive intervention into the fortunes of a city, the degree to which they achieve that goal has been the subject of considerable debate. The failings of property-market-led urban regeneration have been investigated by many authors (Bianchini et al., 1992) and are particularly applicable to 'flagship' interventions where a landmark building or set of buildings have been provided. Gains in terms of the diffusion of benefit to all members of society have sometimes proved illusory. Consideration of the design content of regeneration proposals has generally been more limited and it is the intention of this chapter to explore this aspect of regeneration more fully.

It is interesting to speculate that an emphasis on the aesthetic dimension of new schemes, an emphasis which in Britain in the mid-1990s has been led by central government in its concern for 'quality', will produce a convergence between urban design and urban regeneration. Certainly, urban regeneration initiatives provide a significant source of employment for urban designers and it seems likely that this will continue.

The main body of the chapter is concerned with examining the benefits and dilemmas arising in urban design schemes which form part of urban regeneration initiatives. A range of international examples will be referred to, mostly from Europe, but also some from the USA. The selection of interventions has been necessarily biased in favour of the author's own knowledge and experience. Readers are urged to see the examples as illustrations, rather than as a comment on a unique event, for it is suggested that the observations made are applicable to a range of schemes world-wide. It should be noted, though, that both urban design and urban regeneration may take different forms in different countries due to variations in government, economic and administrative arrangements.

Definitions and context

Urban regeneration is a term that has a multiplicity of meanings; at present it encompasses the creation of new jobs, the construction of new buildings, community support, the restructuring of a city or a neighbourhood in physical terms and cultural interventions. This list is not exhaustive and other initiatives may come under the umbrella heading 'regeneration'.

In terms of the built environment, regeneration initiatives have a long history. Even Pope Sixtus Vth's restructuring of Rome in order to attract a greater number of international pilgrims could be termed 'regeneration'. This example is not as preposterous as it might seem as it invokes the religious connotations which were inherent in the original meaning of the term. In the seventeenth century regeneration meant reconstituting or reviving on a 'higher' spiritual or perceptual level (Shorter Oxford English Dictionary). This dual notion of reordering and improving is helpful and use of it will be made later in the chapter. In more recent times the slum clearance measures of the nineteenth and twentieth centuries constituted the most obvious early examples of urban regeneration. For example, in London, these included driving New Oxford Street through notorious slums or 'rookeries' as an early public health measure, an action which drove out the indigenous inhabitants as well as bringing in light, air and through traffic (Stedman-Jones, 1971). Later, in the interwar period of the next century inner-city housing developments were built to house slum dwellers on the site of their existing houses. Examples of this type of renewal still survive, of which Ossulston Street in Somers Town near Euston Station in London provides a fine architectural example. These efforts at urban renewal were motivated mainly by concerns for public health; in consequence the resulting urban renewal was often mean-spirited, despite the occasional heroic scheme, in terms of creating a better future.

The Second World War changed attitudes towards urban renewal as plans for reconstruction were part of the war effort. Reconstruction was seen as a moral crusade, against what Beveridge described in his wartime report as the five giants: idleness, want, ignorance, homelessness and sickness. It was also seen as a physical process, in which architecture and planning came to the fore: 'If the war could be "planned", why not the peace?' (Cullingworth, 1975, p. 1)

Unfortunately, the reconstruction programmes of the 1940s, '50s and '60s were built in the style of International Modernism. Although the plans were often made with the best of intentions, the combination of what Ravetz (1980) has termed 'clean sweep planning' with the worst effects of modernism, such as a sense of placelessness, car-domination and the use of concrete, turned public and professional attitudes against this style of masterplanning. Whole centres of cities and districts underwent radical change and whilst some of the early initiatives such as the Lansbury district in the East End of London had a human scale and a range of social facilities, the seeming inhumanity of huge high-rise housing developments as in the Gorbals in Glasgow fuelled the disillusionment of the 1970s.

Furthermore, the process of carrying out these major programmes of urban renewal also caused much hardship and discontent. 'Planning blight' occurred as perfectly good houses and shops were vandalised while they stood empty, waiting for a large parcel of land to be assembled for demolition. 'Decanting' or the removal of tenants from their unsatisfactory homes whilst new ones were being built also caused problems; once the original inhabitants had left an area, it often was impossible for them to return because of the long delay between demolition and completion of the new scheme. This also meant that it was difficult to consult people about the future shape of an area because the future tenants or inhabitants would be unknown when the plans were drawn up.

Disillusionment with physical planning and comprehensive redevelopment was often given expression by community groups, whose opposition both to the brutal redevelopment programmes produced by local authorities of whatever political hue and to Conservative administrations who had reduced expenditure for local authorities, created a climate for regeneration, rehabilitation and revitalisation rather than wholesale renewal.

This stance formed an uneasy congruence with the anti-statist mood of the Conservative government which was elected in 1979. Although the crisis of poverty, a poor environment and unemployment were still strong in urban areas, government policies moved towards property-led development and a rhetoric of 'rolling back the State'.

The need for urban regeneration itself had not abated. The reasons for this lay in an economic restructuring within the western hemisphere in which the traditional heavy industries of the nineteenth century, such as ship-building and steel production, had declined and economic activity had transferred to the tertiary or service sector. This restructuring of production had left many areas within cities which were formerly occupied by infrastructure such as railway goods yards and dockyards, or by manufacturing plant, vacant and derelict. Whole areas were left devoid of their major source of employment, causing social stresses and secondary economic decline as the shops and services which had been supported by an employed population were no longer able to survive. Economic restructuring had been brought about by changes to the world economy. An increasing mobility of investment capital and deregulation of the financial markets meant that local economies were no longer bounded by regions or even nation states. Cities were competing against each other for inward investment and were offering concessions and inducements to attract businesses and industry, tourists and a skilled labour force (Harvey, 1989).

To counteract the effects of decline new measures were introduced, such as Urban Development Corporations. Although these areas were purposely 'freed' from conventional planning controls (but not, as has been noted, 'freed' from subsidies), it is interesting that this freedom from design controls was not universally popular with developers. When the developers, Olympia and York, decided to invest in the Canary Wharf development in London's Docklands, they made it a condition that there was a physical masterplan. This meant that the development was controlled in a design sense, as had been their previous largest development at Battery Park City in New York (Edwards, 1992).

Criticisms of the piecemeal and property-led nature of urban regeneration projects increased throughout the 1980s. Urban unrest and racial conflict was still an issue which erupted, periodically, into disturbances on the streets. In 1991, in response to these pressures, the government initiated City Challenge, which was a programme which invited local authorities to put together bids with the private sector for specific regeneration proposals within their areas. City Challenge was quickly superseded by the Single Regeneration Budget Challenge Fund, whereby government abolished the system of grants which it had given under the previous Urban Programme and invited local authorities and the private sector to make bids for money for regeneration projects which combined different types of regeneration, physical, economic, social and cultural.

These new types of regeneration proposals contrasted greatly with the earlier, postwar schemes for urban renewal. There was a greater commitment to preservation of the historical fabric and a recognition of the importance of preserving key buildings and spaces. Community involvement was recognised as having a real part to play. Criticisms of monofunctional development on the one hand and of 'excessive' state involvement on the other meant that public–private partnerships were required by central government in their approval for schemes. Expectations of the quality of regeneration pro-

grammes were also raised. Physical renewal was no longer sufficient but other outputs were also intended, such as an increase in employment, reduction in poverty and social exclusion, the provision of community facilities and training schemes.

A further factor was the increasing recognition of the importance of the arts, culture and entertainment industries. Whilst cultural strategies had been relatively commonplace in Western Europe (Bianchini and Parkinson, 1993), it was not until the last half of the 1980s that their significance was fully appreciated in Britain. It was realised that projects such as opera houses and concert halls could be perceived as providing economic benefits by creating jobs associated with their administration and promotion and in associated venues such as cafés, restaurants and bars. Cultural interventions were then, generators of economic growth rather than the by-product of it. This change of attitude is also discussed in Chapter 7, in connection with public art. The manner in which 'heritage' sites and buildings could assist in regeneration by drawing in visitors and creating jobs also became more widely accepted.

This change of attitude did not occur in isolation. Experiences from North America, Australia and Europe also informed a different approach. Public–private partnerships, the techniques of commercial revitalisation, the establishment of new areas as part of the 'urban spectacle' (Harvey, 1989) – each of these had precedents abroad.

This very brief account of urban renewal and urban regeneration in Britain has highlighted a move from physically-led urban renewal to a more integrative approach. It has also demonstrated that 'regeneration' has different shades of meaning, from simple 'renewal' to a more imaginative interpretation as a renaissance or rebirth with a higher sense of order. It has also demonstrated that the practice of regeneration is evolving. Lessons are still being learnt about what to do and how to do it. In this sense, the process is as important as the product.

Although there has been a shift away from seeing regeneration as a purely physical process, urban design is still an important component of many regeneration projects. Whilst physical changes cannot deliver social and economic changes automatically, design changes can make a large impact in terms of providing a new image for a city or an area, forging new connections, introducing new uses, releasing creativity and providing continuity within the context of the new. In the next section the ways in which urban design schemes can deliver these benefits will be considered in more depth.

Key elements of urban design and regeneration

Strategic interventions: Examples

Over the last decade many regeneration schemes have attempted to raise the profile of a city by introducing new prestige buildings with an accompanying fanfare of publicity. Whilst this move towards 'civic booster-ism' or 'flagship' development involves design in the sense of architectural design, it does not invoke any of the issues or concerns which this volume would consider to be part of urban design. Often a design intervention such as a new opera house is described as design-led regeneration even though the actual proposal is for only one individual piece of architecture. It is both important and useful to distinguish between projects conceived as 'big architecture' and those which are conceived as urban design strategies.

The Grands Projets, Paris   The Grands Projets in Paris fall into the category of flagship developments rather than coordinated interventions into the urban structure. The Grands Projets are major architectural projects, mostly based on cultural activities, which were built predominantly during President Mitterand's period of administration. Taken together, they may be read as a strong symbol of the cultural revival of the city and of the international importance of Paris within Europe (Buard, Lebhar and Le Guay, 1989). Only a few of them involve urban design in the formal sense in terms of forming a part of the city's pattern of spaces. One or two are simply buildings, for example the Opera House in the Place de la Bastille. Most famously, one of the earliest of the Projets, Piano and Rogers' Centre Pompidou does form an addition to the city's spaces in the form of the lively square in front of it, although the building itself provides a major intrusion in terms of height, scale and mass into the surrounding urban tissue. The Grands Projets did have an underlying strategy, in the sense that more were concentrated in the impoverished east of Paris, rather than in the more affluent west.

The 'Museumsufer', Frankfurt   In a similar vein, Frankfurt's Museum Quarter also consists of a series of unrelated buildings, some exquisitely designed by highly talented and renowned contemporary international architects. Frankfurt is one of Germany's most economically successful cities. However, it had suffered from a poor image in terms of its city centre, due in part to an undeserved reputation for a high crime rate and also because it had taken twenty years to build a metro system so that the city's streets were constantly being disturbed by construction. To counteract this, Frankfurt successfully pursued a cultural strategy, spending 10 per cent of its budget on cultural facilities and activities. Whilst the strategy involves events such as festivals and training, one of its most permanent expressions is the 'Museumsufer', a series of refurbished villas adjoining the River Main, in which six new museums have been inserted. Three more museums and galleries have also been built in the city centre across the river.

Figure 5.1 Schirn Art Gallery 1985 Frankfurt, Architects Bangert Jansen Scholtz Schultes. (Marion Roberts)

The 'Museumsufer' does not only offer educational possibilities. Its establishment was regarded as a way in which to enhance the image of the city on an international stage and to attract tourists (Kunzmann and Lang, 1994). Perhaps this threefold ambition on the part of the policy makers has led to a certain dissonance in the programme as a whole. Each individual building and collection has much to recommend it, for example the Schirn Art Gallery (see Figure 5.1) provides a number of public uses and facilities as well as housing and shops and forms a link between the cathedral and the old town square. Despite their defender's claims (Burdett, 1991) for them as a showcase for the process of modernism, others have suggested that the museums, taken as an urban ensemble, leave much to be desired. Most of the museums are situated within ten minutes' walk of each other but bear no mutual relation in terms of stylistic concerns, urban spaces or even programmatic content. As the critic David Dunster observed, they are a random collection of architectural set-pieces '... pragmatic undertakings ... impossibly under-theorised' (Dunster, 1989, p. 36).

Barcelona   Whilst Paris has been more successful than Frankfurt at remaking its image as a world city, neither of them has created a new order within the city. For an example of how an urban design strategy can literally revitalise the structure and image of an entire city, it is worthwhile turning to Barcelona.

Barcelona provides an example of a city whose public realm has been extensively restructured in a comparatively short space of time. One of the most interesting aspects of this transformation is that instead of proceeding from the general to the particular, that is from the masterplan to local intervention, it has been implemented in reverse order, that is, from a series of local interventions to a coherent transformation (Buchanan, 1992).

As the regional capital of Catalonia, Barcelona received less investment than might have been expected in terms of its position as Spain's second city during the years of General Franco's presidency, probably due to its history as a centre of resistance during the Spanish Civil War. The city had grown up around a medieval core, centred around the contemporary Ramblas. The Ramblas forms the most lively street within the city and is crowded even in the evening, with flower stalls, walkers, street entertainers and cages of small but beautiful animals for sale, providing an urban spectacle. For political reasons the city had been confined within its walls until the seventeenth century and this has contributed to the liveliness of the medieval quarter.

In the nineteenth the walls were torn down and the city extended by at least twice its original area. The plan for this expansion, known as the Example (Eixample), was originated by the city engineer, Cerdà. Cerdà's plan was for a strongly geometric grid, based on a square perimeter block of 110m. In the 1960s and 1970s the city expanded again, but this time in a more haphazard way and the areas of the existing city became crammed and congested.

The reintroduction of democracy into Spanish political life following the death of Franco in 1976 released an enormous energy and regional pride. This was skilfully orchestrated by the city's officials and politicians. The programme started with an extensive programme for small, local public space projects which were intended to 'monumentalise' the fabric of the city. This programme for 160 squares included collaboration between artists and architects. The 'physical imposition of formal dignity' was intended to promote social cohesion and to spread throughout the city, through the strategic location of sites for the parks (Bohigas, 1987, p. 12). It is interesting that, although the logic of the choice of sites for the parks and open spaces was not immediately obvious to the visitor in the past two decades, they are now slowly being connected up.

Barcelona's successful bid for the Olympic Games permitted a larger scale of intervention. Not only did the Games promise to draw in outside investment, it also meant that both central and regional government were obliged to support the necessary improvements to the city's infrastructure.

The sewage and rainwater collection systems had been unable to cope with its postwar urban expansion. Because of Barcelona's situation in a 'bowl' surrounded by mountains, rainwater ran off the hills periodically flooding the streets. Major improvements of both sewage and surface water systems were made in the 1980s, not only protecting public health but also enhancing the city's image for tourism.

The planning of the Olympic sites was particularly skilful in political terms. Rather than concentrating the Games facilities in one area, sites were identified in key areas for the city's revitalisation and at radial points around the city's periphery. The main stadia were situated at the hill of Montjuic, on which buildings for the 1929 exhibition had already been built. The Olympic village itself was located on a redundant industrial and goods yard area which separated the eastern portion of the city from the Mediterranean. Other facilities were located in the hills above the city, such as the velodrome at the Val d'Hebron. Barcelona at this time suffered from severe traffic congestion. In their choice of Olympic sites, each of which had its own impeccable

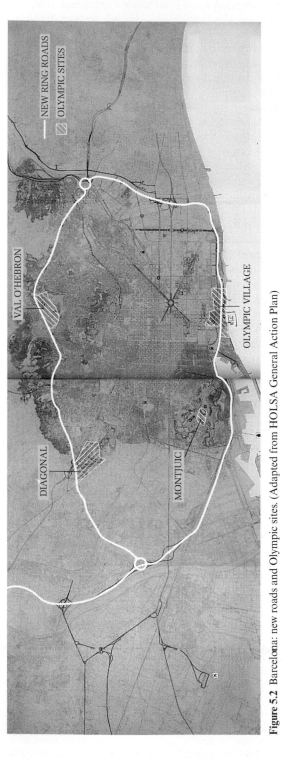

Figure 5.2 Barcelona: new roads and Olympic sites. (Adapted from HOLSA General Action Plan)

logic, the city managers were able to justify the improvement and extension of the coast ring road (Ronda de Mar) and the construction of a second ring road (Ronda de Muntanya), which joined each other and the Olympic sites to form a complete orbital motorway around the city, thereby easing traffic congestion within the city and easing the way to further economic prosperity (HOLSA, 1992). Furthermore, the Spanish Ministry of Public Works and the regional government were persuaded to put funds into the infrastructure projects, thereby relieving the Olympic company and the city of the much of the burden.

The transformation of Barcelona through its squares programme and its Olympic and infrastructure facilities has been breathtaking. Although new construction has dwindled since the Olympics, the boost which has been given to the city's cultural and artistic life has been considerable. It is now held up as an example to be emulated (Fisher and Rogers, 1992: Starkmann, 1993) and because of its startling success other references will be made to it throughout this chapter and this book.

Re-positioning

In the previous section it was demonstrated that strategic urban design interventions can assist in changing the entire image of a city. The competition between cities has become particularly intense and urban design strategies can play a part in changing the position of cities within a country or a region. The construction of a new transport hub, Euralille, in the French town of Lille provides an example of this kind of repositioning. The example of Euralille is particu-

Figure 5.3 Moll del la Fusta: innovative methods of dealing with the demands of traffic and pedestrians. (Marion Roberts)

larly interesting as it offers an example of the integration of a development outside the town centre as a means for regenerating the conurbation itself.

Euralille The creation of Euralille might at first seem to be an example of 'big architecture' – given that the chosen master planner, Rem Koolhaas and his Office of Metropolitan Architecture is a key exponent of that genre (Latham, 1995). It might also be classified as an example of urban renewal rather than regeneration in that nearly all of the buildings and spaces are new. Its interest in urban design terms lies in its explicit location at an international transport interchange and in its development as a multi-use centre as a catalyst for growth. Furthermore, the design of the project was the subject of detailed attention with a 'quality circle' of outside experts giving advice on a monthly basis (Newman and Thornley, 1996).

The development is situated at the interchange of two TGV routes, the regional rail network, a major highway and a short metro link into the existing town centre. This complex project which comprises the railway stations and interchanges, a World Trade Centre, a hotel, a shopping centre, a conference/exhibition centre, an urban park and offices is ordered and integrated by Koolhaas's masterplan. Whilst the pedestrian environment is rather unfriendly, giving a somewhat windy walk from the new international station into centre of Lille itself, the integration of the transport elements is particularly adroit. In commercial terms, the development seems to be offering success, with the new modern shopping centre complementing rather than competing with the existing town centre.

Economic and physical growth has occurred at other transport nodes or infrastructure sub-centres within major cities and conurbations, with perhaps the most vivid example being London's Heathrow airport. The importance of Euralille is that it is the most contemporary example of such a sub-centre in which growth has been planned and in which design considerations have played such a major role. Ironically, the design input, in this author's view, has produced some spectacularly ugly buildings which reproduce the most unfriendly, inhuman aspects of modernism, and Loew (1995) also casts doubt over the quality of the spaces. It would have been interesting to see the result had a different architectural and urban design treatment been employed. Nevertheless, it seems probable that the construction of such sub-centres at major transport interchanges may offer a more valuable prescription for the future regeneration of cities than the reconstruction of urban quarters (Roberts et al., 1996).

Community involvement

Colqhoun (1994) has underlined the importance of the support of the local population to a successful regeneration. This might mean political support, where local politics is operating at a grass-roots level, or it might include different, more informal structures. Rob Cowan's chapter in this book discusses community participation in urban design in a wider context and readers who wish to know more about this aspect of regeneration should turn to Chapter 12.

In the context of this chapter, it is important to note that community involvement in urban design

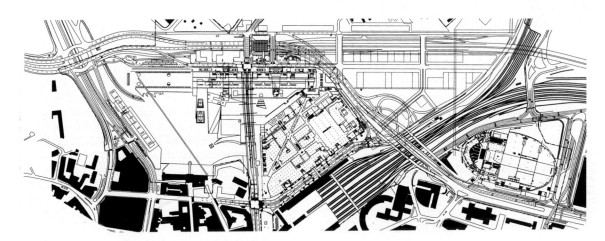

Figure 5.4 Ground floor plan Euralille: masterplan Rem Koolhaas & OMA Architects, Euralille. (Euralille)

Figure 5.5 Euralille showing Euralille shopping centre and Crédit Lyonnais building, architect Christian de Potzamparc. (Marion Roberts)

strategies is not purely a matter of professionals 'consulting' the lay public, but sometimes may form the starting point for the initiative itself. This is often the case where a local area is under threat, as happened at both Covent Garden in London, where the whole market area was under threat of demolition by the Greater London Council in the 1960s and 1970s and in the Temple Bar area of Dublin where much of the area was due to be redeveloped for a transportation centre (Quillinan and Wentges, 1996). In both cases the area was saved and has since flourished.

Community involvement is also critical to the evolution of a project, in terms of information and education as well as consultation. The Crown Street Regeneration Project in Glasgow provides an instance where this aspect of the process has been taken particularly seriously, with even primary school children being encouraged to put forward their ideas.

Mixed development and mixed finance

Further ingredients of successful regeneration, which are part and parcel of the process of urban design are the inclusion of mixed sources of finance and a mixture of uses. Jane Jacobs (1984) first commented on the importance of these two elements (see Chapter 2 for a discussion of Jacobs' ideas) and they were again taken up in Alcock et al's *Responsive Environments* (1985). Their significance in design terms is that a mixture of uses ensures twenty-four hour surveillance of spaces and pedestrian densities, thereby enhancing a feeling of safety. It also encourages vitality in a district both visually and functionally. Definitions of mixed use vary widely (Coupland, 1996), but in the sense in which it is used here, a relatively fine-grained distribution of uses throughout an area is implied.

A mixture of finance means that building plots are developed separately, with different styles of architecture and different priorities. This ensures a visual variety and also means that if problems are encountered with one major player in an initiative, then the entire scheme is not in jeopardy. In housing terms it also implies either a mixture of tenures or a mix of landlords which in itself may ensure a variety of types of tenant.

It is interesting to note that even Euralille, which appears visually as a monolithic development, was reliant on a mixture of funding sources for its construction and management. Newman and Thornley (1996) point out that Euralille is a mixture of smaller projects, financed by private investors, controlled, in design terms, by a masterplan produced by the public sector, and coordinated by a public sector-controlled management agency. The pattern of a design framework being produced by the public sector, or a public sector-led agency is becoming more common with regeneration schemes, as this model permits a measure of freedom for private investors while securing the coherence and quality of the whole scheme. This model has been pursued at Temple Bar in Dublin, where a public–private partnership, Temple Bar Properties Ltd, was set up with the involvement of local businesses to manage the regeneration process.

Continuity

Whilst the purpose of regeneration is not the preservation of the past, as in conservation schemes, continuity is an important part of a successful regeneration scheme as Colqhoun (1994) points out. The purpose of making some physical links with the past is to increase a sense of identity, of individual points of reference and of what the Italian theorist Aldo Rossi (1989) calls 'the collective memory'. Rossi contends that the collective memory of a city lies in its monuments and important buildings, the pattern of its streets, layout and topography. Continuity lies in the reuse of some or all of these.

The importance of the retention of key landmarks was brought home to this author on a recent trip to Manchester. Riding on a coach up Regent Road in the Urban Development Corporation area of Salford Quays, the only way in which the site of my late grandmother's hardware shop could be identified was by reference to a gasometer. This provided the sole reminder of the former 'Coronation Street' style terraces which have since been replaced by grass-fringed pavilions which apparently accommodate computer companies.

The manner in which key buildings and spaces have been kept in regeneration schemes has ranged from the reverential to the superficial. The North American developer Rouse first used the concept of a dramatic conversion in the transformation of Boston's Faneuil Hall Market Place and adjacent Quincy Market into a 'festival marketplace', a new species of shopping mall with specialist shops, barrows and street performers. This was followed by a similar transformation of a former chocolate factory in Ghirardelli square in San Francisco by Lawrence Halprin in 1964 and became a formula which was widely copied (Ellin, 1996).

In a more thoughtful vein the Power of Place project in Los Angeles has used public art to make the continuities between past and present. This has been done through the medium of streetscape projects, plaques, paving schemes and other imaginative interventions to celebrate the 'buried histories' of ethnic minority groups and notable individuals (Hayden, 1995; Miles, 1996).

Another way in which continuity may be evoked is through the interpretation of past urban forms to provide new models for contemporary life. The architects CZWG have done this in their master plan for the Crown Street Regeneration Project in Glasgow. The Crown Street Regeneration Project is located on a 40-acre site in the Gorbals, once one of Glasgow's monstrous slum districts. The slum tenements were demolished in the postwar years and were replaced by modernist housing estates. The project lies on the site of the notorious Hutchesontown 'E', the fifth phase in the development, whose slab blocks were so damp that the local community successfully campaigned to have them demolished in 1987 (Galloway, 1993).

The project was set up in 1990 and had the aim of renewing the area both in terms of community and quality of life. To this end a public–private partnership with a strong element of community involvement was set up. A mixed development was proposed. The masterplan for the area was put out to competition and this was won by CZWG architects. Their scheme is interesting in that it keeps the Glaswegian vocabulary of streets and blocks and even uses a 'deformed' version of the Glasgow grid which had previously run across the site. These forms have been flexibly reinterpreted so that the blocks are no longer as strictly orthogonal as in nineteenth-century Glasgow and incorporate curves and crescents. Large areas of communal open space are enclosed by the blocks, accessible only to the tenants and residents living adjacent.

RESIDENTIAL BOULEVARDS

VIEW DOWN BOULEVARD

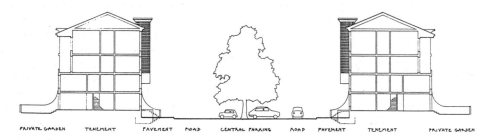

PRIVATE GARDEN   TENEMENT   PAVEMENT   ROAD   CENTRAL PARKING   ROAD   PAVEMENT   TENEMENT   PRIVATE GARDEN

SECTION THROUGH BOULEVARD

FAMILIES IN TENEMENTS

Where parking is in the street, more than half of a tenement building can be family housing. The arrangement is on ground and first floor, 4 maisonettes with 3 bedrooms upstairs and one with 4 bedrooms. Two must

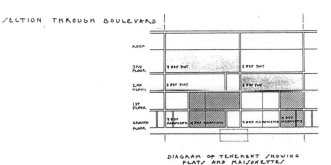

DIAGRAM OF TENEMENT SHOWING
FLATS AND MAISONETTES

Figure 5.6 Residential boulevards, Crown Street Regeneration Project Report by CZWG Architects. (CZWG Architects)

The traditional Glasgow tenement has been reinvented, such that the height and grain of the blocks has a distinct urbanity, yet current living patterns have been incorporated so that the streets have now become boulevards with trees and car parking. The blocks accommodate a variety of dwelling forms, with maisonettes on the first two floors with their own front door and front and back garden and one-, two-, or three-bedroom flats accessed by a separate communal stairway above. The architecture of the blocks is modern in style and different architect/developer teams are responsible for different development parcels.

The preservation of routes, rather than buildings, adds more than historical meanings to a place. It actively integrates the old and the new, creating new meanings and new combinations. This observation leads on to the next major element of an urban design scheme, that of linkages.

Integration

The production of an urban design strategy provides the opportunity for reaffirming and remodelling routes or links across an urban fabric. Physical links do not only provide material access by pedestrians or public transport or cars, but they can also, almost literally, extend horizons. This may apply to people who live in a place and may see ways of getting out in terms of access to employment or other attractions that the city may offer, or it may apply to people being able to move into an area easily, thereby integrating the district into the urban fabric as a whole.

Birmingham   The regeneration of the city centre of Birmingham provides a fine example of the way in which reforming the pedestrian network can play a key role in the transformation of the whole city. Birmingham emerged from the 1960s and 1970s scarred by the excesses of modernism in architecture and town planning. Although a vital economic centre for its region, the city was characterised by brutal concrete high-rise buildings, 'bland architecture' (Evans, 1994), an ugly and disorientating road system and a hostile set of external public spaces, such as the infamous 'Bull-Ring'.

The specific impetus for a reappraisal of the city centre was sparked by the victory of conservationists in preserving the nineteenth-century central post office. A further rationale was also provided by a realisation that the failings in its environmental quality might adversely affect the city in terms of its future potential as a retail and commercial centre. In 1988 the city council held a series of conferences and commissioned an urban design study of its inner area. This study (LDR/HLN Consultancy, 1988) was ground-breaking in that it identified the manner in which the pedestrian experience of the city could be ameliorated through attention to sensory elements and through the provision of a series of interlinked spaces which joined main pedestrian flows from car parks on the edge of the inner area to a new heart.

The new spaces drew on the strengths of Birmingham's Victorian architecture and its winning of European Regional Development Funding for a new international convention centre. The spaces were cleverly linked by a pedestrian overbridge over an arterial road and by using the public but indoor spaces of both the convention centre and the main municipal library. A food court was created within the former library space.

Simultaneous with the transformation of Birmingham's civic spaces was a further study carried out by the late Francis Tibbalds. This *City Centre Design Strategy* (Tibbalds et al., 1990) drew on previous studies and symposia and suggested ways in which the definable districts or areas might be enhanced. Drawing on Kevin Lynch's ideas, it was proposed that the 'legibility' of the city be made clearer by a greater definition of the street and the city's topography and by reinforcing the benevolent and distinguishing characteristics of individual districts. It was also proposed that Birmingham's canals be improved and put to greater use as walkways.

Much of both studies has been implemented. A further extension of the city centre's pedestrian pattern of spaces has been extended over the canal to the new Brindley Place development, which incorporates an important civic square. Over a comparatively short space of time the image and ambience of Birmingham's city centre and outlying districts has been totally altered. This has provided a context for Birmingham's cultural renaissance, which leads on to the next benefit which an urban design strategy may assist, a release of creativity.

Creativity

Many successful regeneration schemes have been characterised by a release of creative potential, in the form of public art, the construction of cultural buildings, a profusion of 'designer' night-clubs, bars and cafés and a burgeoning of the arts and cultural industries. An urban design strategy does not guarantee that such a 'renaissance' will occur and some would argue that over-controlled development acts against it (O'Connor, and Wyne, 1996), by designing out the cheap spaces and

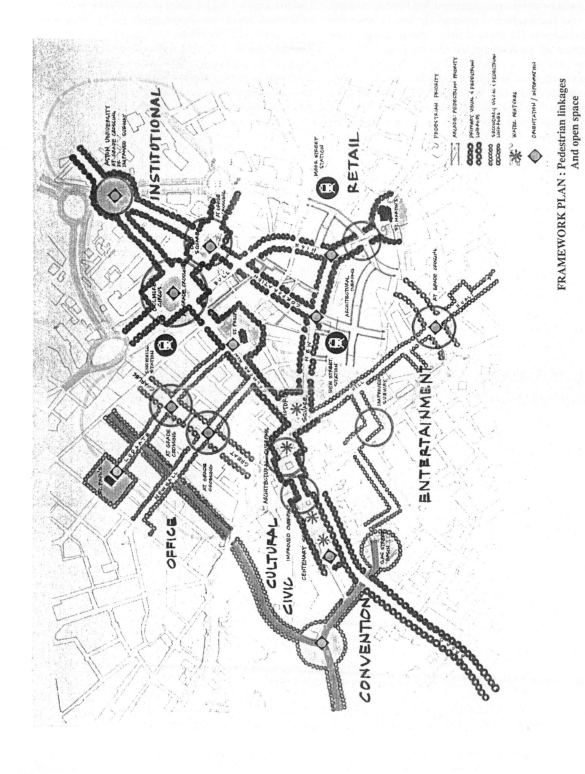

Figure 5.7 Pedestrian linkages, Birmingham city centre. (Adapted from Framework Plan, LDR/HLN Consultancy and City of Birmingham 1988)

places where artists and young people might meet, work and enjoy themselves. Nevertheless, there is some evidence that a well-managed urban design scheme can contribute to the creative activities in an area.

Temple Bar, Dublin   The area of Temple Bar in Dublin provides a shining example of such a happy congruence. The Temple Bar area of Dublin lies in the centre of the city, close to the shopping area of Grafton Street, historic Trinity College and Dublin Castle and borders the River Liffey. In the late 1980s it was an attractive but run-down area, with a street pattern and buildings dating mainly from the seventeenth and eighteenth centuries. As has been previously recounted, it had suffered from urban blight for many years as the state bus company wished to redevelop it as a transport interchange. Paradoxically, the decline in property values had led to a growth in the type of lively, creative enterprises which thrive on low rents and short leases. These included artists' galleries, rehearsal and recording studios, restaurants and pubs and clubs, book shops and other cultural and media activities. These uses augmented the existing historical uses of printers, cutlery shops and 'seedy hotels' (Montgomery, 1995).

Cultural planning formed the basis of the regeneration strategy. This meant that rather than wholesale redevelopment or rebuilding, improvements were made to individual properties through tax incentives to businesses. A development plan which positively promoted mixed uses was adopted, with vertical zoning such that ground floors were reserved for uses which generated interaction and street activity, such as bars, shops and cafés, whereas offices and studios were encouraged to use the first and second floors, with residential uses on the upper floors. 'Cultural animation' also helped to enliven the area with programmes of events and festivals.

The public realm was given great importance with an urban design framework competition which was held in 1991. The winning proposal included the creation of an east–west route, three new squares and a curved street and increasing the north–south routes through the area with a new bridge across the Liffey. A Percent for Art scheme is in force and temporary and permanent installations have been included in public spaces and buildings. In the first phase of regeneration cultural projects which have been completed include: the Irish Film Centre, a new art gallery, a children's cultural centre, a print gallery and studios, a photographer's gallery, a photography archive, a Viking heritage centre, a school of photography, a school of acting, a centre for the applied arts and a multi-media centre (Montgomery, 1995). Each

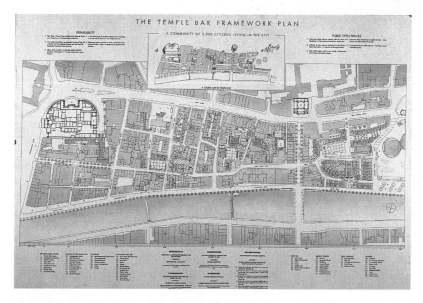

Figure 5.8 Framework plan, Temple Bar Dublin by Group 91 Architects. (Group 91 Architects and Temple Bar Properties Ltd)

employs a variety of architectural styles; each makes its own relationship with the fabric of the area.

As well as these major cultural interventions, many of which are funded by the Irish government, there are a number of associated bars, clubs, shops, restaurants, galleries and workshops which have enlivened the streets. The meaning of this creativity is not just about urban space, or the cultural industries, or urban renewal. The liveliness and quality of the area has been summed up by Declan McGonagle in his essay 'On Reading Temple Bar': 'The "art" in Temple Bar lies in the relationships between individual buildings, the total environment, social space and the attendant public transactions within the city. Since these have to do with the reintegration of culture with social interaction, they cannot be judged in aesthetic terms alone' (McGonagle, 1996, p. 52). The overall success of Temple Bar suggests that regeneration in the sense of the creation of a new 'higher' order is achievable, given the right approach and propitious circumstances. In the next section more difficult aspects of urban design and regeneration will be discussed, some of which may be a product of a scheme's commercial or economic 'success'.

Dilemmas

Contextualism

In the preceding section it has been argued that effective design strategies include a measure of control which ensures coherence and quality throughout a scheme and also permits a degree of continuity between past and present. The balance of these ingredients, which might be termed contextualism, produce the same controversies as those Matthew Carmona considers in his chapter on design control. The difference is that, in the context of a regeneration scheme, the control under discussion might only apply to a limited geographical area.

Berlin   The redevelopment of the Dorotheenstadt and Friedrichstadt area of Berlin provides an illustration of the type of issues which might arise around contextualism. In this example the unification of Germany following the destruction of the Berlin Wall in 1989 has offered the city of Berlin an enormous challenge. Berlin is to become again the capital, but in doing so it has not only to represent the national aspirations of a new Germany but also to repair the scars of the past.

In immediate urban terms the problems are severe. Much of the city centre adjacent to the Wall was left undeveloped after being cleared of bomb damage. This included one of the major urban focal points after the First World War, the Potsdamer Platz. Similarly, key sites adjacent to the bombed centre of the Third Reich, the Reichstag, were left vacant. Altogether, several hundred hectares of land were available. There is also a severe imbalance in physical terms between the intensity of retailing and commercial activities in the western half of the city, which generates a good deal of traffic, light and pedestrian movement and the mainly housing, industrial and administrative uses in the centre of the eastern half, which yields a rather deserted, grey environment. Interestingly, both portions have a similar mix of grand nineteenth-century perimeter blocks and modernist built form.

The Dorotheenstadt and Friedrichstadt areas form the part of the city which was most closely identified with the centre of prewar Berlin. They contain the monumental avenue of Unter den Linden, the university, Spree Island, the royal library, the Opera House and the two former important squares, Leipziger Platz and Potsdamer Platz.

Debate about the physical form which Berlin's redevelopment should take has been heated. The opportunity existed both to learn from past mistakes in other European cities and to profit from an intense interest amongst private developers. Fundamental to the guiding principles which the director of construction and housing has tried to impose has been that of 'critical reconstruction'. The idea of critical reconstruction was developed from the IBA Exhibition in Berlin in the 1980s, in which several demonstration projects were completed which combined elements of the nineteenth-century block form with an innovative architectural approach. It is also important to mention that the reconstruction of Berlin has been the subject of much public debate, both within the media and more formally, through the Stadtforum Berlin, a committee of experts, social groups and politicians which advises the senator for city development and the protection of the environment (Frick, 1995).

'Critical reconstruction' favours mixed use within the context of specialised districts in order to allow new uses and economic patterns. It also sets out the following rules:

- The historic street network and associated frontage lines of streets and squares should be respected or restored
- A maximum permissible height is 22m at the eaves or 30m at the ridge
- 20 per cent of the gross floor area is to be used for housing

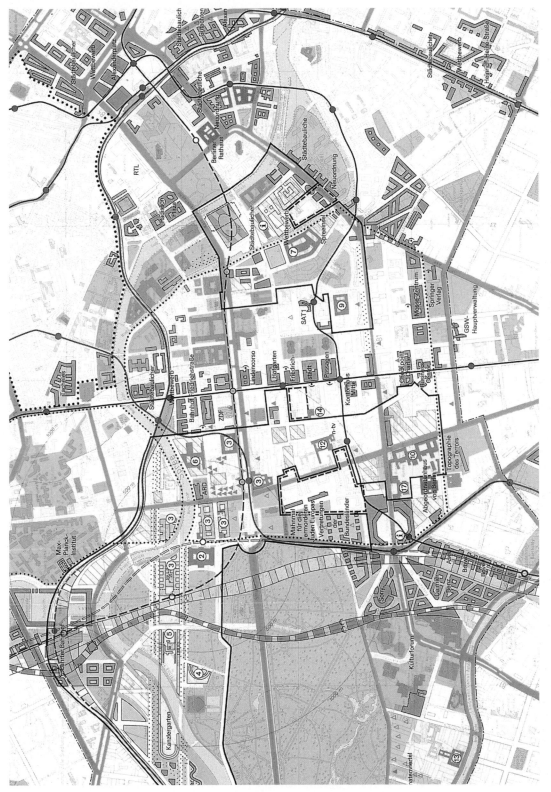

Figure 5.9 Plan of Berlin, showing existing and proposed blocks. (Adapted from Die Planung für Berlin als Bundeshauptstadt, Bürgermeister von Berlin)

- Densities are not prescribed but the plot ratio would normally be 5:1
- Development of one building per historic plot would be encouraged. The maximum permissible plot to be in one ownership would be one block.

As the director of construction and housing ruefully admits, 'critical reconstruction' was easier to demand than to implement. Major problems and barriers occurred, with ownerships being concentrated in few hands, the requirements of traffic preventing the narrowing of streets and a previous history of large-scale project competitions between 1989 and 1991. This has meant that where new blocks are to be constructed within the context of the city's existing grid pattern, 'critical reconstruction' has been able to operate. Where development has occurred within a relatively unrestrained context, as at the Potsdamer Platz–Leipziger Platz complex, the resolution has all but broken down. Despite a human-scaled masterplan by Hilmer and Sattler, the desires of developers for semi-public shopping malls, an increase in the vertical scale of development and the aerobatics of the internationally renowned team of architects who designed each block, have stultified and monumentalised the entire proposal. Sadly, it is difficult to imagine that this important square will be restored as the 'heart' of the city. However in the rest of the Dorotheenstadt and Friedrichstadt, where the original block form is more intact, Frick reports that, 'Remarkably, the rules are nevertheless being adhered to' (Frick, 1995, p. 437)

He speculates that this might either be because the architects and planners agree with the ideas, or because agreement is the fastest way of obtaining planning and building permission. This controversy over redevelopment has extended not only to developers, but to some architects, such as Daniel Libeskind, who are concerned about a sterile, bland uniformity becoming the norm (Billingham, 1996) and to preservationists who are concerned about the reinstatement of historical decoration. At the time of going to press, political control in the city has changed; it remains to be seen how this will affect the overall thrust of development.

Berlin is redeveloping in the hope of revitalising its economy to capital city proportions. It is too early to tell whether this will be achieved. In other regeneration schemes, economic objectives have been achieved and the pressures which this causes can undermine the achievements of the scheme as a whole.

Authenticity

The up-grading of an area causes land and property values to rise, which in turn affects the type of people who can afford to live and work there and the businesses which are able to locate there. The subject of gentrification in the housing market has occupied many commentators and some, such as Zukin (1993), have pointed to the importance of design and cultural factors in the process.

Covent Garden   Covent Garden Piazza has an important place in British urban design history as it was laid out as London's first prototypical square in the early 1630s. Its fortunes changed over the centuries in terms of its fashionable status and in the early nineteenth century a fruit and vegetable market was constructed in the square itself. As has already been recounted, the area was saved from redevelopment in the 1970s and the market buildings restored as a 'festival market place' by the Greater London Council.

The liveliness of the community's struggle and the existence of relatively cheap space also meant that avant-garde uses and activities could flourish, such as wholefood shops, ecological organisations, bookshops, theatres and craft and designers' workshops. As the area became known for these specialist uses, it attracted a lively cast of street entertainers and became a honey pot for visitors and tourists.

Gradually, as property prices have risen, the nature of the area has subtly changed. It has become less of a local area, with shops run by struggling artists and crafts people and has attracted national and international finance. The warehouses, which, in an intermediate phase, were occupied by designers and craft makers, are now mainly given over to retail and office uses. There is no trace of the area's earlier use apart from the still-functioning community association. The overwhelming commercial success of Covent Garden in attracting people throughout the day and evening has caused it to become overcrowded to the extent that strategies are now being considered to attract people away from the area into other parts of London.

In the space of two decades Covent Garden has changed from being a local quarter in which a resident population lived and worked, and which attracted visitors only to its Opera House, church and early-morning pubs, to a destination for international tourism. Its character is maintained by the built form and the continued existence of the more up-market specialist shops, craft workshops and theatre. There is still a resident population, but they must be swamped by the daily tide of visitors. The regeneration of Covent Garden may be considered to have been a success in the sense of economic prosperity and building preservation, but it has been at the expense of the commercialisation and commodification of the area.

Figure 5.10 Covent Garden: a transformation – but for whom? (Bill Erickson)

Covent Garden's revitalisation was, however, an early example of a regeneration programme and it is to be hoped that much has been learnt from it.

This type of process has been echoed in other schemes across the globe. The term 'Disneyfication' has been coined to describe the manner in which places have been made to look as if they were old, combined with a rampant commercialism to attract investment (Cuthbert, 1996). The challenge for urban design in regeneration then, is not only to secure the success of an initiative in economic and social terms, but also to secure its cultural authenticity, in terms of the meanings and values of the new order created.

Concluding comments

This chapter has highlighted the role which urban design can play in regeneration schemes. Whilst recognising that the thrust of regeneration policies, in Britain at least, has shifted to emphasising social and economic objectives as well as physical, the discussion has demonstrated the way in which urban design can assist in the renaissance of a district and even of an entire urban area to produce an improved order in urban space, a restructuring which provides a significant improvement on the past, if not a wholesale transformation for the better.

Many of the components of effective regeneration coincide with the hallmarks of urban design theory and practice. Mixed development, a mixture of finance, community involvement, the integration of past and present in buildings, visual references and linkages, the integration of new and existing, a release of creativity: these all constitute elements of sound urban design thinking as well as considered regeneration proposals. It is suggested that urban design has more to offer regeneration than simple 'design' ; a series of fragmented interventions, however striking, is not a substitute for a coherent, thought-through strategy.

The urban processes and pressures which affect our cities are obviously equally pressing for urban regeneration schemes. The chapter has highlighted two particular pressures which are currently causing controversy and concern. The first is the extent to which new insertions should be contextual whilst allowing individual developers and architects freedom. The second is connected to commercial success: as a district increases in prosperity, it becomes prey to gentrification in terms the type of people and businesses it attracts, thereby potentially exacerbating social divisions. Rising property prices may also force out the local businesses which once gave it its distinct identity and the district can become overtaken as an outlet for national and international commodities.

The dilemmas posed by contextual design will inevitably form part of a public debate. In a democratic society this type of debate about the future shape and appearance of our urban areas is to be welcomed. The problems raised by gentrification, globalisation and loss of authenticity in our environment are complex, but here again the urban designer can play a part in articulating the specificity of place.

The urban designer has much then to contribute to regeneration initiatives. 'Design' should not be seen as 'the icing on the cake', the gloss which might be given to a prestigious project, or as an afterthought. Urban design principles and practice lie at the heart of sound physical interventions for regeneration and as such, need to be incorporated at an early stage.

6 Landscape and urban design

Ian H. Thompson

Design comparisons

What is the difference between urban design and landscape architecture? A glib answer would be that the former is done by urban designers, generally with a background in town planning or architecture, while the latter is done by landscape architects, who belong to a distinct profession with its own educational requirements for qualification and practice. Another possible – but potentially misleading – reply would be to say that landscape architects are primarily concerned with the open spaces within towns and cities, particularly those which are vegetated, whereas urban designers are principally interested in built form and development processes. But this would underestimate the extent to which the activities of landscape architects and urban designers can overlap. A landscape architect is quite likely to be asked to design a hard-paved courtyard within a new office development. An urban designer might seek to promote the planting of street trees, or the creation of a new park or square. Landscape architects and urban designers often work in collaboration, bringing complementary perceptions and skills into the design process.

Of course there are many things that landscape architects do which lie outside the scope of this book. For example, they often work in the countryside, rather than the town. They may be called upon to design country parks or forests, or to advise on the routeing of new roads or power lines. They work alongside civil engineers to reclaim derelict industrial sites, quarries and opencast coal mines, and they are frequently asked to advise on the impact upon the landscape of new developments. In towns and cities,

however, landscape architects and urban designers are united by a concern for the quality of urban life and by the belief that this can be enhanced by positive interventions in the public realm.

In this chapter we will consider why vegetation and open spaces are so important in our urban areas. We will consider the sorts of greenspaces that may be found, paying special attention to those which have been provided through conscious design interventions, either as components in commercial developments or as publicly provided amenities. In particular we will consider the problems involved in managing our legacy of Victorian parks and suggest strategies for addressing them. Finally, we will look at the way in which design philosophies which have arisen from considerations of the landscape have had a powerful influence upon urban design. Therefore the first section will look at 'vegetation', the second at 'open space', followed by a discussion of 'parks' and lastly we will bring the components together within the urban context of 'the City Beautiful'.

1. The benefits of vegetation

For the landscape architect it is axiomatic – people need plants. There is evidence enough to support this intuition. There are over 10 million keen gardeners in Britain, making gardening one of the most popular leisure-time activities in the country. Innumerable inner-city window-boxes and back-yard arcadias prove that this enthusiasm is not confined to the suburbs. More academic support is provided by the qualitative studies carried out by Burgess and Harrison (1988) for the

Greenwich Open Space Project. Their main finding was that their subjects had an intense desire for contact with nature. When asked about the kinds of open spaces they preferred, these city dwellers responded much more favourably to an ancient oak woodland than they did to an area of closely mown urban common. There would seem to be a deep psychological need for contact with vegetation. A study by Ulrich (1983) has demonstrated that postoperative patients recover more quickly, and need fewer analgesics, if they convalesce in a ward which has a view of trees. If trees can help to restore health to the sick, is it not possible that they may also have a role in preventative medicine? Anyone who has gone for a walk in the park to relieve the stresses of the day might agree that this is so.

Sociology and environmental psychology now seem to be providing the justification for the landscape architect's long-held belief in the efficacy of urban planting. The designer also understands that there can

be many aesthetic and functional benefits from using plants in cities. Trees and shrubs can, for example, be used as a kind of green architecture. They can perform many of the same spatial roles as bricks or masonry: they can demarcate boundaries, enclose spaces, direct circulation and channel views. They can be used to ameliorate an unfavourable micro-climate, providing shelter from wind and rain or shade from strong sunlight. A hedge will often provide better shelter than a wall because it is semi-permeable and does not create the sort of turbulence effects associated with more solid barriers. Planting can create privacy and seclusion, and can be used to screen unattractive features of the urban scene like storage areas, refuse skips, loading bays or car parks.

Trees and shrubs can act as a foil to architecture or sculpture, the soft and nebulous qualities of foliage providing a welcome contrast to the rigidity and hardness of built structures. They are also affected by changes in season and climate, varying throughout the year in ways which can be aesthetically pleasing – autumn tints and ice-encrusted branches – while serving to reconnect urban humanity with the great cyclical processes of nature. As natural forms, intermediate in size between a building and the human figure, trees can often help to humanise the scale of large developments.

To this catalogue of psychological, aesthetic and functional benefits we can also add ecological advantages. The large city can be a harsh environment. On average the temperature in a city will be 2°C higher than in the surrounding countryside, the so-called 'heat-island' effect caused by the concentration of artificial heat sources and the absorption of the sun's energy by hard materials. Buildings reduce the influence of cooling breezes while increasing local air turbulence. The air in cities is also likely to be fifty times as dusty as country air and also more polluted by traffic fumes. Although cities often have higher rainfall than the surrounding countryside, a by-product of this heat-island effect, the rain runs off quickly into sewers and does not replenish the groundwater. The combination of these effects makes urban areas comparatively arid.

Urban planting can mitigate some of these effects. Areas of grass or shrubs – or 'soft landscape' as they are sometimes called – can impede run off and aid groundwater replenishment through improved percolation. If storm water can be directed into ponds within the urban area, rather than immediately directed into drains, wildlife habitats can be created. Vegetation can decrease air turbulence, filter dust particles, and, if carefully sited, direct cooling and cleansing breezes.

Figure 6.1 Walkers in Highbury Fields, London. (Bill Erickson)

Difficult though city conditions may be, the publication in 1978 of W G Teagle's *The Endless Village* showed how wildlife could adapt to city conditions and reported the results of an extensive survey in the Birmingham area. The warmer conditions make cities attractive to birds for roosting and overwintering. Blackbird, magpie, crow, jay, blue tit, wagtail and starling are among the species that have adapted to urban living. Among mammals, foxes, grey squirrels, hedgehogs and bats have all become successful city dwellers. The view that the city is devoid of wildlife has given way to the realisation that built-up areas have their own urban ecology.

In terms of wildlife value it is seldom the manicured parks and recreation grounds that produce the interesting flora, for the nutrient levels are generally too high and the maintenance regimes are designed to prevent natural succession. Conversely, on old coal tips, areas of alkali waste or demolition rubble, one is quite likely to find lime-loving plants which are more usually found on chalk or limestone grasslands. Compacted sites which become waterlogged may support rushes and foxtails.

It is often the neglected, derelict sites which are most interesting from the point of view of nature conservation. This raises interesting questions about values and aesthetics. Do people prefer to have wild areas near their homes, or do they demand that their open spaces should look tidy and well-managed? The work by Burgess and her colleagues gives some support to the nature conservation lobby, but qualifies this by stressing that natural landscapes must appear to be managed landscapes, and that people's sense of security depends upon the presence of professional staff such as rangers or community workers.

Positive action to enhance the opportunities for wildlife in the city can be taken through the planning, design and management of open spaces. City conditions shatter the mosaic of habitats – woodland, heathland, wetland and grassland – that previously existed. Only fragments of these habitats persist, and often these are too small to support a wide variety of species. An important concept is that of the 'wildlife corridor', a linear arrangement of greenspace which allows species to penetrate the urban fabric, linking larger tracts of open land together and possibly to the surrounding countryside. Fortunately, linear parks and vegetated cycle-paths, developed primarily to meet human requirements, may also function as wildlife corridors. If it is not possible to create continuous corridors, a second-best option is the creation of 'stepping-stones' for wildlife within the urban matrix.

What kinds of vegetation are suitable?

Although a new ecological aesthetic is being forged, native plant material is not yet the automatic choice for all situations. In more formal parks, squares and boulevards, horticultural aesthetics still hold sway. Landscape architects have been criticised for choosing plants from a very narrow palette – for relying upon well-tried favourites like *berberis* and *cotoneaster* in all situations. Even if the Latin names are unfamiliar, you would recognise the plants – they are the reliably hardy low-growing shrubs and groundcovers often found in street planters or around supermarket car parks. This unadventurous approach satisfies neither the gardener's appetite for unusual and interesting species, nor the conservationist's demand for indigenous planting which will be of greater value to wildlife. As things stand, however, the landscape architect often has only one chance to get the planting right, and it is perhaps understandable if this leads to cautious specifying. No one wants to spend money – often public money – on planting that will fail within a year and have to be removed.

When planting trees in urban situations it is very important to consider the ultimate dimensions that a particular species might attain. Limes (*Tilia spp.*), for example, are excellent large trees for an avenue or large square, but will rapidly outgrow the typical urban garden. Smaller trees like rowans and whitebeams (*Sorbus spp.*), and some of the maples (*Acer spp.*) are frequently recommended for street planting, but flowering trees, like cherries (*Prunus spp.*), are often regarded as too suburban and kitch for city centre planting.

Poplars (*Populus spp.*) and willows (*Salix spp.*) have a bad reputation as thirsty trees with invasive root systems that can block drains and sometimes damage foundations. They are particularly problematic when growing on shrinkable clay soils, found primarily in south-east England. During periods of drought such soils are prone to dry out, causing cracking in buildings. Old poplars also have an unwelcome habit of dropping their branches on unsuspecting passers-by. Other trees to be wary of include the much-loved horse-chestnut (*Aesculus hippocastanum*), if only because small boys are fond of throwing bricks and other missiles into its branches to dislodge conkers (but note that *Aesculus 'Baumannii'* is a cultivar which does not have conkers so avoids this fate). Most limes are inhabited by hosts of aphids which produce an unpleasantly sticky substance which can make a mess of parked cars. For street or car park planting designers choose Caucasian lime (*Tilia euchlora*) which does not have this drawback.

The list of native trees and shrubs for ecological planting is not too long to memorise, limitation of choice being one of the main reasons why designers often resort to exotics. A simplified list of the commoner British trees would include alder, ash, beech, birch, elm, field maple, holly, hornbeam, larch, lime, rowan, oak, poplar, scots pine, whitebeam, willow, wild cherry and yew. Note that some familiar trees, like sycamore, horse chestnut and plane, are not included because, strictly speaking, they are introductions. The most common native shrub species are blackthorn, broom, dog rose, elder, goat willow, hawthorn, hazel, gorse and guelder rose. In general native trees and bushes support much greater numbers of insect species than the introductions: the oak, for example, is associated with 284 species, whereas the sycamore supports only 15. On the other hand, sycamores will grow in many tough urban conditions that other trees might not withstand, and while they host fewer insect species, those they do support, they support in profusion, providing a rich food source for birds. Similarly the *buddleia* – the so-called 'Butterfly bush' – is non-native, but, as its name suggests, it can be a worthwhile addition to planting plans designed to encourage wildlife.

Like the choice of species, both the style and the method of planting depend upon the context. When planting tree belts to provide shelter, to give spatial structure to a new park, or to create new habitats, the landscape architect may employ techniques derived from forestry practice, using large numbers of young trees planted in notches or small pits. For more formal planting, including street planting, larger trees are used. In nursery parlance these are 'standards', 'heavy standards' or 'extra heavy standards' – the heftier the specification, the greater the girth of the trunk and the higher the price. The principal drawback of this larger material is that it does not always respond well to being moved and, as a consequence, may grow badly – or even die. Nevertheless, where an immediate effect of size and maturity is called for, it is sometimes worth taking a risk and using the biggest nursery stock of all – 'semi-mature' trees. Special techniques must be used to prepare such trees for transplanting.

Forestry-type planting is less likely to suffer from the attentions of vandals than amenity planting of the 'lollipop' type. Where the latter is called for, the designer must balance the requirement for a young, adaptable tree against the need for a robust one that cannot be casually broken. Generally, it is the more formally patterned plantings, like avenues or circles, that are likely to attract the vandals.

2. The need for open space

If it is axiomatic that people need plants, it would also seem to be self-evident that people need open space,

but how much do they need? In 1925 the National Playing Fields Association laid down a target of ten acres of open space for every 1,000 people, of which 90 per cent was to be for active recreation, while 10 per cent was to be 'ornamental'. In terms of managed recreational space, this target has never been reached. A report prepared by Harrison, Burgess and colleagues (1995) for English Nature recommends that a network of 2-hectare spaces arranged so that every dwelling is within 280 metres of a greenspace should be the pragmatic target for planners and designers. This, they argue, would ensure reasonable levels of biodiversity and accessibility if the design and management were good.

Open space statistics say nothing about the qualities of the places in question. David Nicholson-Lord (1987) takes issue with the whole notion of 'open space', which he considers to be a bland bureaucratic invention. Real spaces have hills and streams and woods. Unfortunately, much of the land shaded green on municipal maps is 'urban prairie' or 'ecological desert' – an expanse of closely mown grass which may have some use as an informal football pitch or a dog toilet, but which makes little contribution to the scenic qualities of the neighbourhood and gives little support to wildlife.

Designed open space in the development process

Some of the most important open spaces in our towns and cities are not the product of conscious planning or design. These are the areas of common grazing, like the Town Moor in Newcastle upon Tyne or Wimbledon Common in south London, which are irreplaceable assets that should be protected through the planning process, but too often prove vulnerable to a process of attrition.

If the common represents undesigned open space, the Georgian square is its antithesis. Rather than being protected remnants of a more rural scene, these are architecturally conceived amenities, created in the course of speculative development. Such spaces can be found in Glasgow, Edinburgh, Cheltenham, Bath and London's West End. Many cannot be classed as truly public, since they are often private amenities for the benefit of the residents of the surrounding houses who alone enjoy rights of access.

For the urban designer, the speculative developments of Georgian England offer an interesting precedent. Landscape design played a key role in such capitalist ventures as Edinburgh's New Town (1766) or Bath's Circus (1729) and Royal Crescent (1767), see Figure 4.5. The terrace of houses facing an area of greenspace was an urban interpretation of the country house standing within its landscaped park. The most celebrated example of this approach is John Nash's Regent's Park in London (designed between 1811–1826).

There is undoubtedly a strong connection between property values and an outlook upon parkland or over water. The geographer, Jay Appleton, has suggested that a deep-seated psychological mechanism, a remnant from our evolution as a species, lies behind such preferences. In order to catch prey and to avoid predators it was necessary to see without being seen. We still favour landscapes which afford both opportunities for prospect and for refuge.

Whatever the deep psychological roots of our landscape preferences, the history of urban development has demonstrated time and time again that the most successful and well-loved additions to our cities have incorporated designed open space. Haussmann's plan for Paris in the mid-nineteenth century, with its parks, squares and boulevards, was perhaps the greatest public works project in history. Haussmann was assisted by an engineer and landscape designer named Adolph Alphand.

In North America, Alphand's contemporary, Frederick Law Olmsted (who, incidentally, was the first person to adopt the title 'landscape architect') was able to persuade New York's city fathers that it was worthwhile setting aside 843 acres (340 ha) of prime commercial land in the centre of Manhattan to create a public park (1857). The property prices in the streets and avenues that surround the park testify to his foresight. Olmsted also laid out the garden suburb of Riverside in Chicago (1869) and initiated a system of linked public parks, the 'Emerald Necklace', in Boston (1880).

Similarly, Beverley Hills (1914) in Los Angeles is one of the most profitable real estate ventures in history, but it might not have been so successful if the landscape architect, Wilber Cook, had not been engaged to develop an infrastructure of tree-lined boulevards, parks, squares and golf courses. Indeed, the site was an unpromisingly arid hillside, and Cook had to build an aqueduct and establish a nursery in order to effect his transformation.

This tradition has continued into the twentieth century. Recent developments like London's Broadgate, West Ferry Circus and Cabot Square at Canary Wharf, or New York's Battery Park City, have sought to incorporate landscape elements to add value to speculative developments, both in terms of amenity and commerce.

Victorian parks and the social imperative

If we owe some of our most important open spaces to the enlightened self interest of capitalist developers, there is an equally powerful tradition of socially motivated greenspace provision. While it is probably an over-statement to say that every land-speculator or greedy mill-boss of Victorian England was matched by a philanthropist or social reformer, there were certainly enough people of good will around to ensure that most towns and cities of the Industrial Revolution were plentifully supplied with new public parks.

There was a strong element of paternalism and social control in the movement for public parks. When the Select Committee on Public Walks presented its report to parliament in 1833, parks were seen as a way of keeping the urban population out of public houses. Parks, it was argued, would improve the morals and the health of the working classes, and might thereby head off social unrest. The earliest parks were created at a time when local government was just evolving and town planning, as we now understand it, did not exist.

According to the landscape historian, Hazel Conway, the earliest of the new municipal parks was Preston's Moor Park, created in 1833 by the council-promoted enclosure of the Town Moor. Derby can claim the first purpose-designed public park – the Arboretum – laid out by J.C. Loudon, and given to the city by the wealthy manufacturer, Joseph Strutt, in 1840. As its name suggests, this was meant to be an edifying collection of trees, with no species appearing more than once, and each having a label against it to educate visitors. Loudon had been taught by Jeremy Bentham and, in addition to being the leading landscape gardener of his day, was concerned with social issues like education, town planning, housing improvement and clean air.

As a result of the local government reforms of 1835, municipal corporations were set up in the industrial areas. For these new bodies, the establishment of a public park was an outward symbol of civic responsibility and pride, as well as a way of pleasing the masses. Some of the new parks, like those in Hull and Halifax, were even known as People's Parks. The parks were certainly popular. When Joseph Paxton's Birkenhead Park was completed in 1847, 10,000 people flocked to the opening celebrations. It was partly in response to heavy usage that the first trip rails and 'keep off the grass' signs first appeared, but it was not long before behaviour was heavily circumscribed with bye-laws.

It is interesting to note that Birkenhead Park provided Olmsted with the direct inspiration for New York's Central Park. The American landscape architect visited twice, in 1850 and 1859, and was inspired to emulate this vision across the Atlantic. Paxton meanwhile went on to become the foremost British designer of his day, laying out Kelvingrove Park (1854) and Queen's Park (1862) in Glasgow, both developed in conjunction with housing, Crystal Palace Park in London (1856), the People's Park in Halifax (1857), Baxter Park in Dundee (1863) and the Public Park in Dunfermline (1866).

From the outset there were conflicting demands placed upon public parks. Principally, they were supposed to be pleasure grounds for passive recreation, to be strolled through and enjoyed as a sequence of spaces and views. They had, after all, been modelled on the country house landscapes of William Kent, 'Capability' Brown and others of the English Landscape School. At the same time, they rapidly became horticultural showpieces, where the Victorian enthusiasm for bedding displays and other exuberant demonstrations of human dominion over the plant kingdom could be given full expression.

A third requirement was that they should be recreation grounds. Sports facilities were seldom features of the earliest parks, but they were often added in response to public demand. When Olmsted visited Birkenhead Park he noted that land had been set aside for cricket and archery. Today the park also contains football pitches, bowling greens, a cycle track and tennis courts. Olmsted said on several occasions that he thought of Central Park as primarily a work of art. Fortunately, it is large enough and diverse enough to absorb a multitude of visitors and activities without too much detriment, but there will always be a conflict between the park as an object for aesthetic contemplation and as a facility for active recreation. Imagine how out of place a ragged game of football would look in a painting by Constable.

The problem of neglected parks

Although politicians periodically promise to return British society to a golden age of social cohesiveness and civic virtue, most commentators would agree that the Victorian parks, which were once an expression of civil rectitude, have been neglected and in decline for decades.

In part this is because they are seen as anachronisms in an age when entertainment can be delivered to homes through a cable or a satellite dish, when rising car ownership has made the real countryside more accessible for city dwellers, and cheap air flights have put warmer climates and more dramatic landscapes within the reach of many. However, it is also the result of a general squeeze upon public spending which has reduced levels of maintenance, and a political dogma which has insisted that all services should be subject to competitive tendering. Uniformed park-keepers were the first victims of the cuts, then, in the interests of economy, the gardening staff were reorganised, so that rather than teams being based within each park, gardeners are now dispatched from a central depot. As a result, levels of supervision and care have declined. Meanwhile, the physical fabric of the parks has continued to decline, while the original Victorian plantings have passed from maturity into a moribund condition.

Three strategies for parks renewal

There are three ways in which this decline could be arrested:

The nature strategy   This involves admitting that the Victorian park has outlived its usefulness, whilst recognising that people value open space and wildlife in cities. Ecologically inspired management practices can replace the intensive procedures required to maintain formal landscapes. Grass can be cut less often to allow flower-rich meadows to develop, other areas can be allowed to develop scrub vegetation and ultimately to become woodland through natural succession. Where the emphasis was once upon expensive displays of horticultural prowess, the new initiative can be towards the creation of diverse habitats. Rangers can replace park-keepers.

All of this has been tried, but often as a result of financial necessity rather than any positive vision. Many of our older parks have areas in which nature is allowed to go its own way. However, it is certainly a mistake to see this strategy as an exercise in cost-cutting. Parks cannot just be abandoned to nature; to maximise their ecological value they need to be managed positively, and for people to feel confident and secure when visiting them, this management needs to be evident in the form of facilities and staff.

While new parks may be created along ecological lines, it is difficult to see a nature conservation strategy playing more than a secondary role in the future management of our historic parks. Such a strategy would bring the values of nature conservation into collision with those of historical conservation, and it is also arguable that, for the present anyway, the public is not ready to accept the looser, more ragged, less controlled landscape aesthetics that would ensue. Parks, as Hilary Taylor (1994) has pointed out, are metaphors for social order.

The Heritage Strategy   Thanks to the National Lottery Heritage Fund this seems to be the dominant thinking of the moment. Many public parks are listed in the English Heritage Register of Parks and Gardens of Historic Interest, and there is a lobby for historic landscapes to be afforded the same kind of statutory protection that is given to listed buildings. While Lottery funding may be welcomed as the source of capital needed to restore run-down parks to their former glories, it does not provide any help with their on-going maintenance, which must be met from revenue. There is a danger that the downward spiral will start again.

The heritage strategy is a sound option for prestigious parks close to town or city centres. As well as being physically central, they are also at the heart of notions of civic pride, and, as Crouch (1994) has observed, they are often utilised in marketing and tourism strategies. It is less likely to be a viable strategy for parks in housing areas remote from the civic centre. Here, notions of ownership, in the sense of a shared culture and a sense of belonging, become crucial. For Crouch, this is best exemplified by the way in which allotment-holders value their plots, and he asks whether a similar sense of attachment could not be generated by local parks if local communities could become more involved in their design and management. Rather than opting for a backward-looking 'heritage' solution, with connotations of a packaged commodity, this approach would build upon the idea of a shared local history.

The Strategy of Urbanism   This is the hardest of the three strategies to describe, partly because it is so at odds with the traditional British view of what a park should be. It is exemplified by Bernard Tschumi's masterplan for the Parc de la Villette in Paris. This contemporary park was developed on the site of a former abattoir and cattle market following a design competition in 1982. The competition brief was uncompromisingly innovative. La Villette was to be a park for the twenty-first century. The organisers recognised that the traditional parks in Paris were failing to fulfil the urban and cultural role they had once played. Rather than being asked to recreate countryside or a garden in the city, the entrants were called upon to devise a new form of functioning cultural space, which would be actively used both by day and at night.

Tschumi, a Swiss-born Deconstructionist architect, turned his back on both the romantic naturalism of the English Landscape school and the symmetrical formality of the French garden. Instead he developed a design based upon clashing geometries. A rigid grid

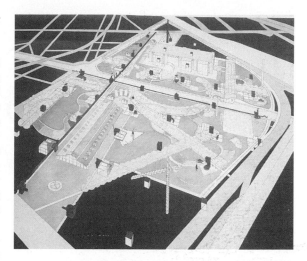

Figure 6.2 Parc de la Villette, aerial view 1985. (Tschumi, 1987) *Cinégram Folie: Le Parc de la Villette*, Princeton Architectural Press)

of *'folies'* was laid down across the site. Each of these was based upon a 10m red steel cube; some were developed as functional structures such as cafés or play features, others were built into the structure of larger buildings. Superimposed upon this grid was a path system, consisting of both straight axes and a sinuous ribbon called the *promenade cinématique*, and a spatial structure based on simple geometrical figures like the square and triangle. In choosing to disperse many of the requirements of the competition programme into the grid of *folies*, rather than concentrating them in a small number of larger buildings, Tschumi claims to have created not a park, but the 'largest discontinuous building in the world'.

Similarly in Barcelona, as a major element in that city's resurgence during the 1980s, a series of urban parks has been developed which explore new ways of urban living rather than seeking to ape nature or traditional gardens. Parks such as the Parc de l'Estacio del Nord, which features a ceramic mound by the land artist Beverley Pepper, and the Parc del Clot, in which elements of the site's former use as a railway yard have been imaginatively combined with drifts of planting and crisp architectural details, are celebrations of city life rather than a retreat from it. This strategy is easier to apply in the creation of wholly new parks than in the 'retro-fitting' of traditional parks.

It is hard to say which of these three broad strategies will become dominant as we enter the new century. After a decade or more of dabbling with ecological ideas, there is currently a swing towards the heritage strategy. Whether the conservative British will

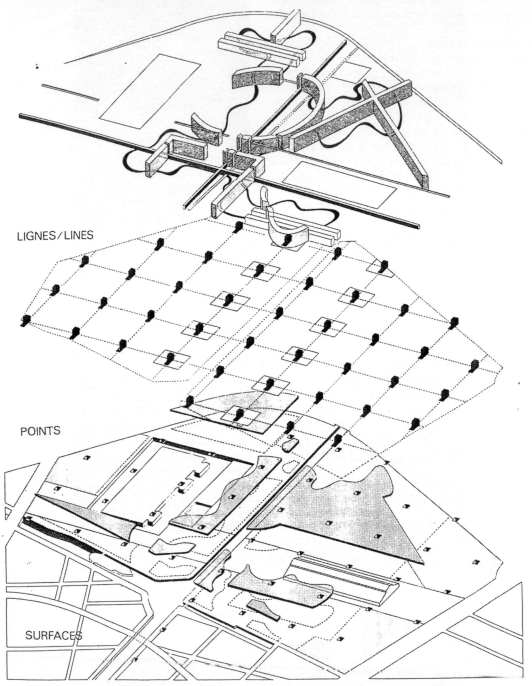

LIGNES/LINES

POINTS

SURFACES

THE SUPERIMPOSITION OF THE THREE SYSTEMS (POINTS, LINES, SURFACES) CREATES THE PARK AS IT GEN-
ERATES A SERIES OF CALCULATED TENSIONS WHICH REINFORCE THE DYNAMISM OF THE PLACE. EACH OF
THE THREE SYSTEMS DISPLAYS ITS OWN LOGIC AND INDEPENDENCE

Figure 6.3 Parc de la Villette, points, lines and planes. (Tschumi, 1987) *Cinégram Folie: Le Parc de la Villette*, Princeton Architectural Press)

Figure 6.4 A view of the Parc de la Villette, Paris showing one of Tschumi's folies. (Ian H. Thompson)

Figure 6.5 Parc del Clot, Barcelona. (Ian H. Thompson)

ever produce parks as vibrant and adventurous as those in Paris or Barcelona is certainly open to doubt.

3. The City Beautiful and the Garden City

Landscape issues are not confined to the open spaces within urban areas; often the whole form of an urban area is influenced by ideas derived from landscape design. Landscape considerations have been very close to the heart of two enormously influential town planning doctrines – the City Beautiful and the Garden City.

The City Beautiful Movement, whose prophet was the Chicago-based architect, Daniel Hudson Burnham (1845–1912) took its inspiration from Haussmann's reconstruction of Paris, and from L' Enfant's masterplan for Washington (1791), itself inspired by Le Notre's grand designs for the gardens at Versailles. The formal landscape at Versailles, with its huge vistas and axes focused upon the palace of Louis XIV, the Sun King, was the perfect expression of absolutist royal power. It is ironic that it should have appealed so strongly to Thomas Jefferson as the prototype for the capital of a fledgling democracy. There was surely an element of keeping up with the European Joneses about this, and this same inferiority complex made it easy for Burnham to recruit the leaders of the emerging commercial cities of the American Midwest to his monumental visions. His main achievement was the Chicago Plan of 1909 which superimposed a scheme of classical civic order on the existing grid-iron, but he was also responsible for the completion of L' Enfant's Washington Plan (1901–22) and for a new civic centre for Cleveland, Ohio (1902).

The language of City Beautiful design is one of civic prestige and ostensible power. The Lutyens–Baker plan for New Delhi, the capital of British India (1913), is a City Beautiful design, as were other colonial schemes for Lusaka, Nairobi and Kampala. It is also not surprising, considering the movement's tyrannical antecedents, that Mussolini's (fortunately compromised) plans for Rome and Speer's grandiose but unbuilt vision for Berlin were direct descendants of Burnham's Chicago Plan.

The Garden City movement was altogether gentler and more humanistic. It too had its prophet, the shorthand writer turned town-planner and social visionary, Ebenezer Howard (1850–1928). Born in London, Howard emigrated to America at the age of twenty-one and spent some years in Chicago, which at that time was known as the Garden City. Peter Hall (1988) suggests that Howard must also have been influenced during this period by the construction of Olmsted's garden suburb of Riverside just outside the city.

Returning to London, Howard was able to synthesise a variety of progressive ideals. In 1898 he published *Tomorrow: A Peaceful Path to Real Reform*, which was reissued in 1902 under the title *Garden Cities of Tomorrow*, in which he analysed the benefits and disadvantages of both rural and urban living. Towns offered social opportunities, places of amusement and better wages, but were also blighted by poor housing conditions, foul air, high rents, fogs, droughts and murky skies. The countryside was often sentimentalised as a place of beauty, fresh air, abundant clean water and bright sunshine, but this image disregarded the lack of social interaction, public spirit and opportunity in rural areas. Howard advocated the creation of a new kind of settlement, the garden city, in which

the best of town and country would be combined. Here the beauty of nature, accessible parks and fields, clean air and pure water, bright homes and gardens, would be combined with high wages, social opportunity and all the possibilities resulting from enterprise and cooperation.

Howard was not just a theorist. He was also instrumental in the formation of the Garden City Pioneer Company in 1903 which purchased a site at Letchworth, 34 miles from London, and set about turning his vision into reality. In 1919 a second garden city was begun at Welwyn, also in Hertfordshire. In a watered-down form, Garden City ideals influenced Raymond Unwin and Barry Parker's Hampstead Garden Suburb (1907) (and similar suburbs in Ealing, Leicester, Cardiff and Stoke). Diluted still further, turn-of-the-century arcadian visions were translated into the sprawling suburbs of the inter-war speculative builders, which were vilified by modernist architects and planners as 'a kind of scum churning against the walls of the city' (from Observation No. 20, CIAM Meeting, Marseille, August 1933).

Attitudes towards suburbia have softened a good deal recently. Where suburbs sprawl for mile upon mile, they are still pilloried for their monotony and for consuming countryside, but commentators have also recognised that suburbia has been an undeniably popular, stable and successful form of development. It is also fair to say that in Britain the transition between the city centre and surrounding residential areas has rarely been as abrupt as that found in American cities where a business district of skyscrapers stands out from an ocean of low-rise housing. For a balanced appraisal of this still contentious subject see *Dunroamin' – the Suburban Semi and its Enemies* (Oliver, 1981).

While no true garden cities were built between the wars, the ideal lived on in satellite towns like Parker's Wythenshawe outside Manchester (1930), and it was an influence upon the postwar New Town movement. The development of an extensive structure of greenspace was central to the planning of most of the new towns, particularly those developed in the 1960s. In Warrington in particular techniques of ecological planting and management were pioneered and these have had a far-reaching effect on the way that landscape architects think.

Although no new towns have been designated since the early 1970s, the Garden City ideal lives on. There are periodically calls for more new settlements, particularly around London, but in many ways the creation of Howard's ideal town-country is now beginning to happen inside the old conurbations, as the old industries depart to be replaced by city farms, nature parks and other varieties of urban green. It may be that instead of new towns we are learning to make Garden Villages within the city.

As we approach the twenty-first century the Arcadian vision of a life for human beings which is in tune with natural processes is every bit as strong as it was in Ebenezer Howard's heyday. Indeed, the rise of the science of ecology has deepened our understanding of this vulnerable relationship, and prompted the development of new forms of ethical thinking which emphasise humanity's responsibility for planetary welfare. Landscape architects, who for many years have been primarily concerned with questions of amenity and aesthetics, are now giving much thought to questions of sustainability. The ways in which landscape design can contribute to this environmental ideal are manifold, ranging from the design of landforms and shelter planting to reduce the energy demands of buildings to the design of biomass plantations to supply energy or of reed bed filtration systems to treat sewage. The most interesting challenge for the new millennium will be the need to develop new aesthetics to complement the new environmentally-friendly technologies. It will be an exciting time to be in practice.

7 Art in the public realm

Marion Roberts

Expanding interest

Public art has seen a renaissance in the last fifteen years in Great Britain (Arts Council, 1989). The definition of public art is contested (Selwood, 1992) but Malcolm Miles (1996) offers some useful explanations. He suggests that public art in urban spaces can take the form of art placed outdoors as a monument, as in, say, the traditional figure of a man on a horse. Alternatively, it is sometimes conceived as works which might normally be shown in an art gallery 'expanding' onto the street and sometimes this idea is used for temporary shows in an urban area. Sometimes the term is used to describe the integration of works of art and craft in urban design and this might take the form of artist-designed benches, lighting and other street furniture, art works applied to buildings as in gates, murals, friezes and stained glass, or a more integrated conception of landscaping, buildings and art. Finally, the term is also applied to artists who wish to make interventions in public issues. An example of this was the American artist Jenny Holzer's collection of one-line aphorisms, such as 'Housing is a Human Right', which were printed as commercial fliers and pasted up around Manhattan in 1976 (Steinman, 1995).

Great Britain has not been a leader in the field of public art; other countries in Western Europe and most notably, the USA, have enjoyed a similar, if not greater flourishing. This chapter will review the context for the provision of public art in terms of its recent history as it relates to urban design. Many works of public art have been provided in non-urban places such as in sculpture parks, green spaces and nature trails. The work of organisations such as Common Ground has been pioneering in introducing art works both into the rural and urban landscapes and in treating the one as a continuum of the other (Clifford, 1993). This chapter will concentrate on art works in urban areas since this forms the main focus of urban design effort.

The motivations of public-and-private sector providers of public art will then be reviewed, since ultimately the types and number of works which adorn urban areas will depend on the ability and desire of those who are prepared to pay for them. The chapter will then briefly consider the nature of public art itself in terms of some of the controversies which have been raised around the meaning of the term 'public'. It will be suggested that in discussing the impact of works of art in urban space three major factors should be included: the provider, the site and the audience. A discussion will then be framed in terms of examples of work which relate strongly to each of these factors.

The review of public art in this chapter is limited by considerations of space and tends to be focused on urban space rather than buildings. A further factor which is regarded as important in the achievement of thoroughly considered projects is the process by which they are made, in terms of the working relations between the parties involved. As such, this set of relationships, which is closely allied to contract law and procedures, lies outside the scope of this chapter.

The background context

The rise of modernism in architecture and planning expelled works of decorative art and craft from the fabric and substance of buildings (Banham, 1960). Modernist artists and sculptors continued to collabo-

Figure 7.1 Head of a Man, River Thames, London 1992. (Lisa Harty, Artangel)

rate with architects, producing exhibitions, such as the 'This is Tomorrow' exhibition in 1956 (Cork in Rosenberg, 1992), working alongside architects and planners, as in Victor Pasmore's work at Peterlee New Town, and creating works of art allied to specific famous buildings. While there were some noteworthy successes, for example, Graham Sutherland's work in Basil Spence's Coventry Cathedral or the Naum Gabo sculpture acquired for St Thomas's Hospital in London, the inclusion of art in the urban environment was generally less felicitous.

The art critic, Richard Cork, has suggested that works of sculpture and modern art were included in the uncompromising urban landscapes of the immediate postwar years as a way of softening the impact of the harsh concrete surfaces and the brutal road schemes which typified the era. In this, he suggests, these works were unsuccessful. They tended to look as though they had been 'parachuted' in and were left stranded: '... The works looked raw and uncomfortable, dumped in locations that remained inimical to their presence. More frequently than not, they were rewarded with indifference, bewilderment or outright anger by those obliged to pass them in the street' (Cork, 1991, p.132).

Public art remained in this impasse, in Britain at least, until the work of aspiring young artists in the community arts movement opened up new possibilities. A generation of young artists, thwarted by the limited opportunities provided by the gallery system of art commissioning, almost literally took to the streets. By working with local communities, producing murals

and other forms of artistic output, they were able both to revivify and enhance a neighbourhood, to engage with local residents at a political or community level and to find a showcase for their creative activities (Miles, 1991). Culturally aware and ambitious local authorities, such as the London Borough of Lewisham learnt from these lessons and incorporated an artist, John Maine, in their team for a remodelled Lewisham, Lewisham 2000 (Heath, 1992).

It was but a short step in conceptual terms from realising the impact that public art could make on community development to considering public art production as a component of urban regeneration. The commercial possibilities of such local action in terms of urban regeneration were soon grasped. During the 1980s, as Bianchini et al., (1993) has noted, the ethos for government funding for the arts moved from a position of 'art is good for you' to 'art is good for business'. This change of perception was influenced by reports such as Myerscough's (1988) *The Economic Importance of the Arts* which set out evidence to support the argument that the 'cultural industries', that is the arts, films, media, were generators of economic wealth and an important part of the economy.

The notion that the provision of works of art might benefit business directly and indirectly was supported by examples at a local level such as Blackness and Smethwick, where artists worked with local shopkeepers and businessmen to revitalise their run-down neighbourhoods (Miles, 1991; Selwood, 1995). At a larger, international scale the inclusion of major programmes of public art at the privately developed

Battery Park City and Broadgate complexes in New York and London demonstrated the efficacy for business of such provision.

Government sponsorship of the arts tended to emphasise potential financial benefits and encouraged the involvement of private business through sponsorship schemes and agencies such as ABSA, the Association for Business Sponsorship of the Arts.

The Arts Council had funded the provision of works of art outside the gallery since its inception in 1946. However, it considerably raised the profile of public art in 1988 when a 'Percent for Art' steering group was set up under its auspices. 'Percent for Art' was an idea that had been pioneered in the USA and Western Europe since the end of World War II. The concept behind the idea was that developers of major construction projects, be they from the private sector, a public body or a partnership between the two, would set aside a percentage of the construction costs for the provision of works of art. This idea has been adopted as mandatory by some states in the USA and is also exercised at a national level for certain types of public works in some Western European countries (Shaw, 1991).

The 'Percent for Art' steering group wanted British local authorities to adopt a mandatory 'Percent for Art' policy for projects with a value in excess of £3million. Legal advice deterred them from this, as such a requirement could not have been upheld within planning law. Instead, the Arts Council launched a campaign which urged local authorities to adopt a voluntary 'Percent for Art' policy in their development plans and to use such a policy for their own developments and developments built on their own land.

By the end of the 1980s, the provision of public art was gaining ground, both in policy terms and in actual provision. Many potential sponsors of public art were, however, constrained by their lack of artistic knowledge. Local authorities and property developers alike had little experience of commissioning art. This prompted the growth of a number of charitable agencies, who responded to this gap in knowledge by offering specialised commissioning and promotional services. By 1993 there were twenty such agencies (Selwood, 1995), some offering specialised services such as commissioning temporary works only. The agencies themselves have done much to promote public art, through publications, and events (Public Art Commissions Agency, 1991) and through the medium of a voluntary association, the Public Art Forum.

It is against this context of enthusiasm and voluntarism that public bodies and the property market are being encouraged to provide and promote public art.

In the next section their motivations for doing so will be examined more closely.

Public art and the property market

It is relatively commonplace nowadays to find examples of art and craft works in privately-funded developments. Shopping malls frequently embrace sculpture and indeed some shopping complexes such as Covent Garden in London include performance artists. The headquarters buildings of major companies also provide sites for works in their grounds and foyers. Famous examples of these include the work of the sculptor Elizabeth Frink for WH Smith at Swindon and Henry Moore at the Time-Life Building in central London. This last example recently caused some controversy when the owners wished to move the sculpture from the building and Westminster City Council raised legal objections, arguing that the sculpture was listed along with the building and should therefore be preserved in place.

Research carried out by the University of Westminster investigated the commercial benefits of public art to the property market. Initial interviews with selected property companies revealed that the primary motivation for the provision of public art was financial; in only one case did a developer suggest an environmental as well as a commercial incentive. The representatives of property companies were opposed to the notion that public art could be used like a mascot, or a badge to be simply applied to a building, rather they emphasised that public art should be considered as part of a total 'package' of quality.

More detailed interviews with the fundholders and investors in speculative office developments gave a further insight into the type of benefits which the provision of works of art in the public and semi-public spaces around buildings could provide. Fundholders and investors saw public art as adding identity to a development and thereby giving it an 'edge', in terms of the market, over neighbouring, similar developments.

Although opinion amongst fundholders was not unanimously in favour of the provision of public art, a typical comment of those who were proactive was: 'We want to be doing our bit for the environment ... art can make a building distinctive and give it a feature and if that means the tenant comes to you instead of next door, it must be worthwhile'.

Surveys of occupiers of office buildings which had been provided with public art provided evidence of satisfaction. Sixty-two per cent of those interviewed

Figure 7.2 'St George and the Dragon', sculptor Michael Sandle 1987, commissioned by the Public Art Development Trust at 1–3 Dorset Rise. (Unknown)

example, which owns a small development in St James' in central London (itself an icon of the Modern Movement in architecture designed by Alison and Peter Smithson), regularly holds temporary displays of public art in its piazza.

The support which private companies and the property industry give to public art needs to be placed in context, however. The same piece of research by the University of Westminster team found, from a survey of local authorities, that the ratio of publicly-funded works to privately-funded was in the region of 3:1. Although this figure should be treated with caution as only 42 per cent of planning authorities in England and Wales responded to the survey, and two of these had 'too many works of public art in their areas to count', it does nevertheless suggest that the private sector could come a long way in matching the public sector in patronage. This patronage and its development into public policy will be examined more closely in the next section.

thought that the contribution which the works of art made to their building's image was significant. Eighty per cent had no adverse comments to make about the art works. On the basis of this and other evidence the University of Westminster team concluded that the provision of public art could yield commercial benefits to the property market in terms of facilitating letting and thereby reducing risk.

The team also found evidence for art being provided in new areas of commercial developments. The Sainsbury chain of supermarkets, for example, has experimented with public art in some of their new developments. On a more industrial note, one of the largest freight distribution centres, Magna Park at Lutterworth, also includes some art works. While the property industry has tended to commission the more traditional media for public art, in particular permanent sculptures, there has been some experimentation with other media and art forms. *The Economist*, for

Figure 7.3 'Luce di Nara' by Igor Mitoraj, 1991. Temporary display at *The Economist* Building, London. (The Economist)

Public patronage and public policies towards public art

Of course it is not only local authorities who are public providers of public art. Institutions such as hospitals, schools, universities and new towns have had a distinguished history of commissioning and acquisition (Rosenberg, 1992). Other types of public body, such as transport authorities, have also been leading providers.

Interviews with public providers and their responses to questionnaires have yielded some information about the attitudes of such bodies towards commissioning. A University of Westminster questionnaire which was sent to planning authorities in England and Wales found that the most commonly cited reason for their sponsorship of public art was to foster civic pride, followed by the promotion of local artists. Interestingly, other types of material considerations, such as the use of public art as a form of planning gain, was mentioned by only 27 per cent of respondents. However, economic and social regeneration were mentioned by local authorities as additional reasons for provision. It is possible, given the number of regeneration schemes which have successfully incorporated public art since the survey was carried out (see for example Temple Bar in Chapter 5 of this volume), that this motivation might have grown in importance.

The motivations of local authorities differ then from those of investment funds and developers. Case study evidence from quasi-public bodies such as transport authorities suggest that their motivations lie somewhere between the commercialism of the property market and more altruistic aspirations towards civic embellishment. Health authorities and schools obviously have different motivations; their purposes are more closely related to their healing and educational functions.

The launch of the Arts Council 'Percent for Art' initiative in 1988 sought to raise awareness amongst local authorities and Urban Development Corporations of public art and to encourage them to adopt 'Percent for Art' as their policy. Despite legal restrictions on the use of 'Percent for Art' as a general policy, local authorities and UDCs are empowered to impose a 'Percent for Art' clause for land which they own themselves and some have taken advantage of this.

Since 1990 there have been a number of surveys of local authorities to ascertain the extent of their policies towards public art. The most recent, Griggs' (1995) survey of London boroughs, found that 81 per cent of respondents had policies which promoted public art. Selwood's (1995) earlier survey of three regions, found that 48 per cent of authorities responding had policies to promote public art and a further 14 per cent were in the process of developing one. Roberts, Marsh and Salter's (1993) survey of local planning authorities in England and Wales concluded that on average 70 per cent of local authorities in urban areas had policies to encourage the provision of public art and that this was likely to increase. Selwood's survey confirmed the urban bias of authorities with policies. The relatively recent adoption of policies means that their impact is likely to be felt more keenly in the future.

Although the majority of urban local authorities have recently adopted policies towards public art, the extent of implementation of those policies is fragmented. Selwood, in her survey, found that 32 per cent of her respondent authorities had not implemented the policy. Griggs also found that a high proportion of London boroughs had not been able to implement their policies. The reasons which were given for this were lack of finances, the recession in the property market and a lack of specialist expertise. Griggs also found that the majority of London local authorities did not have any structured set of procedures for dealing with the commissioning or approval of public art installations. This lack of expertise will be considered further below, where the mechanisms for commissioning public art will be discussed.

Implementation of public art provision

The specialist nature of the art world has meant that many institutions who wish to commission works of art have little knowledge about how to approach the task. To fill this gap, a number of specialist agencies have set themselves up over the last two decades. These public art commissioning agencies provide specialist expertise in finding artists, setting up competitions, helping with consultation and managing contracts.

Commissioning agencies have also evolved a certain degree of specialisation. Artangel for example, only commissions temporary works of a challenging nature. It commissioned the sculptor Rachel Whiteread's work 'House' in the East End of London in 1993, which attracted a great deal of controversy. Other agencies tend to work in particular geographical regions, but deal with a variety of artistic output; to provide a further example, the Cardiff Bay Art Trust commissions community art and temporary features as well as more conventional site-specific work.

Whilst commissioning agencies have without doubt played an important role in bringing public art to the forefront of public consciousness, there have been some criticisms of their operation. Dunlop (1995), in her case studies of public art in transport systems found criticisms levelled at a major commissioning agency by one of its corporate clients. The criticism was that of keeping commissions to a closed group of artists, thereby restricting the range of choice and innovation. This may be an inherent danger in relying on a range of experts whose activities may, ironically, act in opposition to the potential for populism and democracy within public art.

Some local authorities and UDCs have preferred a different route to implementation and have appointed specialist arts officers. The numbers of such officers vary all the time as funding flows change and individuals follow different career trajectories. The number has never been large and seems to vary between 10 and 20 in the country as a whole. Whilst individual officers can achieve a great deal – for example Robin Campbell has facilitated the commissioning of over 100 works in Swansea alone, the reliance on an individual's skills and abilities has an inherent instability in the absence of agreed procedures and criteria.

The recent decision of the Arts Council to demand 'the involvement of artists and craftspeople as an integral part of capital schemes' submitted to it for funding by the National Lottery has increased the quantity of work for artists working in the public sphere (Arts Council for England, 1996, p. 7). Furthermore, the Arts Council also encourages the other Lottery distributors to encourage the involvement of artists in their projects, mentioning heritage and sport in particular. In assessing its own schemes the Arts Council considers the process by which the artist collaborates in the project, encouraging an integrated approach rather than an add-on or afterthought. This funding through the Lottery is obviously on a scheme-by-scheme basis and relies on the inventiveness of the applicants, rather than a commissioning policy for a geographical area. Its importance lies in the number and scale of the commissions which it is likely to produce, which promises to be larger than anything experienced hitherto in England.

The implementation of public art policies is in an early stage of its development. Some considerations for good practices and structures to achieve them will be considered in the ensuing sections. Before turning to this, it is necessary to look at the criticisms which the renaissance of interest in public art has aroused.

Critisisms of public art

The increased quantity of art works in public places has not met with universal approbation over the last decade. Criticism has been voiced within the pages of quality newspapers, by academics and by artists and architects. Comment has focused on the desirability of public art, its nature and its quality.

Some writers are not convinced that there is a necessity for artworks to embellish the public sphere in a widespread manner. The conjunction of mediocre works of art and poorly-designed buildings has led to particularly scornful attacks. The architect Sir Norman Foster famously described such pieces as 'lipstick on the face of a gorilla' (Dormer, 1992). The architecture critic, Peter Dormer, has been especially scathing in his attacks, suggesting that much recently installed public art is superfluous. Furthermore, the vandalism to which many works have been subjected, also suggests a lack of empathy on the part of the general public. The American critic, Patricia Phillips, points out that the goals of public art have been reduced to those of amenity, embellishment or camouflage, and that even these modest aims are rarely satisfied. She goes on to comment: ' ... there is a growing feeling of – well, why bother? Indeed, an enterprise that emerged with such idealism now feels like a lost opportunity' (Phillips, 1988, p. 93)

Part of the problem for or with public art, revolves around its relationship to conventional or gallery art. Indeed, there is a confusion in terms of reference, with some commentators referring to 'art in public places' and others to 'public art'. This confusion is further compounded over definitions of public art: does it include street furniture, works of landscape, environmental improvements? The answer to these questions seems to be 'Yes', in terms of practice, but this then begs the question, is it art? If 'It is art', who then is the arbiter of taste in its installation? Should it be the provider, the artist, the public or the planning authority, if involved in planning permission?

If the term 'art' raises philosophical questions, then the concept of 'public' is equally problematic. It is now becoming a commonplace that public space is being eroded (Punter, 1990b), with increasing privatisation in the form of shopping malls, car parks and other forms of management and control. Furthermore, the notion of a generalised, homogenous public has been shattered by the emergence of the politics of identity and a realisation that gender, sexual orientation and ethnicity are as powerful points for allegiance as geographical locality (Massey, 1992). The audience for public art may consist then of a number of publics, rather than a public or 'the community'. Add to this the attack which an individualised, free-market ethos has made on the rhetoric of public, civic values and it may be seen that definitions of the 'public' are not simple.

The critic, Patsy Phillips, described the creative possibilities of public art as society changes and transforms itself:

> Public art is about the free field, the play of creative vision. The point is not just to produce another thing for people to admire, but to create opportunities, situations that enable viewers to look back at the world with unique perspectives and clear angles of vision. This image embraces the instrumentality, intimacy and criticality of public art. Public life cannot be decreed, but has to be constantly reinvented' (in Holman, ed. (1994), p. 11).

Dunlop (1995) has suggested that a lack of engagement with these difficulties by artists and providers has led to a blandness and mediocrity in works of public art. She argues that public art is a different art form to gallery art because it is site-specific, it is imbued with the intentions of the provider and the audience is actively involved in constructing its meanings. By this she means that within the world of the gallery, the space is deliberately neutral – normally it is a white box and is designed not to interfere with contemplation of the work of art. The audience in an art gallery is also self-selected in that people have to actively choose to go to a gallery. Public art relates directly to its site and its audience; when people walk through, use or overlook, the space is readily provided. Some of them may not choose, or want to, even look at an art work, let alone to reflect on its meaning. Dunlop argues that if public art is to succeed, then it must have a relationship to its site and audience and the intentions in its provision need to be clear.

These points of distinction between private and public art production, the provider, the site and the audience, provide a useful set of categories with which to examine the potential and failings of contemporary public art practice. In the next section specific examples of public art 'interventions' are discussed with regard to these three categories. This is not to imply that in each of the examples, the commissioners did not give thought to the other two categories: rather, the works have been chosen to illuminate the importance of these factors in the equation. The examples also illustrate the importance of political will and enabling organisations which facilitate 'public art'as well as the role of physical factors such as 'site', and cultural factors such as audience response and theatrical setting in creating memorable interventions.

Public art interventions: providers

Democracy: Barcelona

The city of Barcelona offers an example of a place where the provider of public art, the Ajuntament or municipality of Barcelona, expressly wished to give the city a new identity, both in the eyes of its inhabitants and of visitors from outside. Barcelona is Spain's second city and, in the period following the Second World War, suffered from political neglect during the regime of President Franco. This is not to say that the city declined, rather it expanded in a haphazard and unplanned way during the 1950s and 1960s.

The first democratically controlled city council was elected in 1979 after Franco's death. The municipality was constrained by a lack of finance and could only make small interventions into the urban fabric. Its first programme which ran from 1980 to 1987 was for the insertion of over 100 parks, piazzas and public spaces within the fabric of the city. Its object was to insert new spaces, new 'tissue', at strategic points into the body of the city in order to provoke and focus regeneration.

The programme was extraordinary in its eclecticism. Teams of artists worked with sculptors to produce a widely varying range of spaces. The architectural and artistic language or styles employed ran from the traditional to the modernist, producing an exciting variety of experiences. In many cases the sculptors employed were asked to cooperate with the architects in order to integrate the space and to create a new kind of monumentality in the city. The art critic Robert Hughes points out that intellectuals in Catalonia wanted to avoid the type of empty or grandiose official statements that had characterised so much of previous Spanish postwar projects. Instead, new ways of attaching place and meaning within the context of the modern city were explored.

The results, it has to be admitted, were uneven (Sola-Morales, 1992). Too often the sculpture appears as an afterthought, simply filling a space. This is particularly poignant in the case of a large piece by Barcelona's most famous modern artist, Joan Miró, 'Woman and Bird', in the Parc de l'Escorxador. This large abstract work seems unrelated to the formal composition of its setting and its meaning, to the foreign visitor at least, is unclear.

A more happy cooperation seems to have occurred between artist and architect in the Parc de l'Estacio del Nord (Arriola, 1994).

Figure 7.4 El Parc de L'Estacio del Nord: Architects Andreu Arriola, Carme Fiol, and Enric Pericas (municipal architects). Sculptor: Beverly Pepper. (Marion Roberts)

Here Beverly Pepper's sculpture, 'Fallen Sky', rises out of the grass of the park and appears like a dragon submerged in the ground. The shape of the sculpture and its construction out of ceramic tiles recalls Miró's own work and that of Barcelona's most famous architect, Gaudí. It is difficult to tell where the landscape of the park ends and the sculpture stops. Indeed it is striking that Ian Thompson has also singled out this park for mention (see Chapter 6).

It seems invidious to discuss only two of the spaces and artworks, where so many are represented. Nevertheless, in the absence of space to discuss the detail of the programme, there are two further general points to be made. The first is that the programme, although experimental, did not extend to using new media for art works such as electronic displays or temporary works. The second is that the sites chosen appeared not to have any strategic relation to each other. Indeed, the city's own maps and guides to the spaces were produced so that they could be found easily. This situation is now changing as the city has started to link the spaces and the logic of their choice is becoming more apparent.

The second stage in Barcelona's strategy involved the creation of entirely new pieces of infrastructure such as two new roads which ring the city (for a fuller discussion of this strategy see Chapter 5). These interventions formed part of the Olympic programme for the city. Here too, sculptures were deployed to humanise and mark the space. Barcelona's success in attracting the Olympic Games to the city in 1992 provides an acclamation for its urban design and artistic strategy.

Civic pride: Birmingham

The publicity which Barcelona's strategy generated attracted followers. Birmingham, which is England's second city, also deployed an artistic programme to complement its urban design strategy, both of which were part of a process of regeneration (see Chapter 5 for a discussion of the urban design strategy). In common with Barcelona, Birmingham also needed to reassert its civic pride, much battered after its visually disastrous redevelopment of the 1950s and 1960s. A springboard for the programme came from the construction of the National Convention Centre, where one of the conditions of the grant from the European Development Fund was that a percentage of its costs be spent on artworks. Rather than spend the money on works which would only be seen within the convention centre, the council decided to include works leading up to the centre, in Centenary Square itself. They were aided in their task by a well-established commissioning agency, the Public Arts Commissioning Agency.

Whilst the art in the square attracted a great deal of critical acclaim (Bianchini et al., 1991), it was not an unqualified success. One of the sculptures, by Birmingham born artist Raymond Mason, a fibreglass work which was meant to depict the people of Birmingham's forward march of progress, attracted a great deal of criticism and even a campaign by a local newspaper to have it removed (Selwood, 1995). This prompted the council's officers to be more cautious in their commissioning of work for their next major space, Victoria Square. Here the artist, Dhruva Mistry, was requested to work in traditional materials such as stone and brass.

Figure 7.5 Victoria Square, Birmingham, 'The River' by Dhruva Mistry, 1993. (Marion Roberts)

Birmingham's motivation was twofold. On the one hand the council wanted to create a different image for Birmingham, one that its citizens could be proud of and on the other, it wanted to revitalise the economy. It appears to have been successful in achieving both these aims (Wright, 1995), although some have questioned who the recipients of its inward investment are (Loftman and Nevin, 1993).

Public art interventions: site

Permanent: Swansea

Public art, it has been argued earlier in this chapter, is public in the sense in which it relates strongly to the site. In this context, the term 'site' is taken to mean anywhere in which the work is placed. Conventionally, this might mean an urban square or civic space, as in the examples discussed above. It could also encompass a variety of other public spaces, such as parks, streets, bus stops (although not bus shelters which are owned by the transport company), motorways and bridges. Semi-public spaces may also be included, such as shopping malls, transport systems, the foyers of large buildings and concourses of bus and rail stations. The facades of buildings, although they are privately owned, may form the 'walls' of a public space and therefore may be used for display, decoration or projection. An artist may use several 'sites' for one 'piece' of art work, as in the Jenny Holzer fliers mentioned at the beginning, of which 35 were displayed in various locations in Manhattan.

As such, much is demanded of the artists in terms of establishing a connection which goes beyond their immediate aesthetic or philosophical concerns. The artworks in Swansea's Maritime Quarter provide a fine example of works which are closely related to the site, both in immediate and universal terms.

Swansea's Maritime Quarter is a docklands regeneration scheme, comprising the conservation of some fine dock buildings as a museum and theatre, the construction of a marina and a mixed development of housing, retail premises and a hotel. The design of the quarter consists of a fine ground plan of linked squares and spaces and housing constructed to a design brief. Whilst the architecture of the quarter tends to the banal, the quarter itself is distinguished by some seventy works of art which run through it, employing a variety of means of expression.

Swansea is characterised by its position in Wales, set in a beautiful bay surrounded by hills, with a rich industrial history of mining, manufacture and seafaring. The town's cultural history is also significant, since it is the birthplace of Wales' and arguably England's most famous modern poet, Dylan Thomas. The artworks in the Maritime Quarter, 80 per cent of which were made by local artists, draw on and celebrate this heritage. There is an interesting mix of styles, from naturalistic sculptures of Dylan Thomas, to bas relief panels depicting an eccentric local doctor, to abstract sculptures commemorating nautical and maritime themes. Often the materials relate to Swansea's past, as in the use of copper in the Lighthouse Tower, which recalls Swansea's mining history (Swansea City Council, 1993).

The Welsh critic, Hourahane, regards Swansea's Public Art and Enhancement programme in the Maritime Quarter as successful because of the way it combines the intricate and the poetic, local and universal themes. The relation to site is both straightforward and subtle: Welshness is invoked by direct representation of local figures and by a more indirect use of materials and themes. Whilst the use of nautical and astronomical references is specific to the site, it is also universal.

Although the definition of art is wide in Swansea and encompasses relief carvings, pavilions, decorations, inscriptions, sun dials and a host of other forms, it is nevertheless permanent. The relationship which an artist makes with the site need not take the form of permanent artworks, rather it can be an event which explores the potentiality of the site in a manner which is just as valid.

Temporary: Southwark, London

In the creation of temporary installations, the boundaries between different forms of artistic expression may

Figures 7.6 and 7.7 Lighthouse Tower by Robert Coneybear, 1987, Maritime Quarter, Swansea. (Marion Roberts)

merge or dissolve. Indeed the term installation is used because the artwork itself is an event which may incorporate a number of elements and a multi-media presentation. The divisions between theatre, visual art and music become notional. Robert Wilson's recent installation, at Clink Street Vaults in London's Southwark, combined a theatrical use of space with sound and light provided by Hans Peter Kuhn and production design by Michael Howells. Robert Wilson is well-known on mainland Europe for his theatrical and operatic events and direction and he frequently collaborates with Hans Peter Kuhn. This installation, which was commissioned by the temporary arts commissioning agency Artangel, made use of the huge Piranesian spaces of the railway arches between London Bridge and Cannon Street stations, on the site of a former medieval prison, a space which is owned by Railtrack and often used for 'raves'.

The installation was entitled 'HG' and presented the audience with an enigma. In the first set of spaces the visitor was presented with an empty room, a Victorian room in which a half-eaten meal was set out on a table, there was a smell of oranges and spices on the air and a newspaper set the date at 1895. Thereafter, the visitor was set on a path through the cavernous vaults, in which the huge spaces were animated by different tableaux, illusions and sensations. These explored the themes of time and space: in one a mummy lay on the floor, a handful of petals on its face; in another a series of hospital beds, crisply made up with white sheets, were surrounded by buckets of blood and a Medical Officer of Health's report left on a table set the date at 1919, while a piano tinkled in the distance; in another time's golden arrows flew towards a classical colonnade against an azure sky. In one room a distant figure moved, barely perceptibly, out of the gloom, to slowly reveal himself as a performance artist, in another a grille revealed a view of a rainforest, complete with attendant animal noises and birdsong. These descriptions only cover part of the experience, which had more than 20 separate environments.

The installation proved popular and attracted approximately 20,000 visitors over its month's showing. Critical response varied enormously, as the event was widely reviewed. *The Observer* was dismissive and compared it to the film *Heaven's Gate*, 'an over-extended epic' (Feaver, 1995, p. 14). Other critics were more favourable and took away a more contemplative impression. Richard Dorment in the *Daily Telegraph* made connections between the installation, the site and the human condition:

> What Wilson is doing in this piece, I think, is using the medieval prison as a metaphor for our own

imprisonment in the present. Like [HG] Well's time machine, it is the imagination that sets us free. By telling us stories, artists and writers ... release us from the dark and narrow present in which we are otherwise doomed to live (Dorment, 1995, p. 11)

Robert Wilson deliberately eschews the narrative form in his work, that is, he does not expect it to tell a story. He expects his audience to find their own meanings, their own stories, in the events which he stages. In HG the vaults themselves formed a strong part of the event and in the words of one critic turned 'architecture into an actor' (Greenberg, 1995). In his approach, of rejecting the one simple story or message, Wilson is adopting a post-modern attitude, which recognises the multiplicities and varying nature of the audience which might engage with his work. This means that different groups of people might take it in different ways: some for example, may enjoy the sensory experience, whilst others would enjoy the detective puzzle of tracking down the meaning of the historical 'clues' left through the sets. The notion that different types or groups of people will have a different 'take' or perception of a piece of art work is a common preoccupation of much contemporary public art.

Public art interventions: audience

Monument : Hamburg

Works of art are not merely objects, for use or decoration. If they are to survive at all in a transcendent sense then a relationship with the audience is required. In a gallery the terms of that relationship are clear: the audience is invited to look, stop and see but generally not to touch, a catalogue or other interpretive device is available to explain the work and finally, if the viewer responds favourably, then an item of memorabilia such as a postcard may be purchased.

In the public sphere the opportunities open to the observer are both more open and more challenging. Participants may touch, climb on and even vandalise the installation. It is also more difficult to provide interpretative material if the work goes beyond traditional expectations.

Some of the most successful pieces of public art which have made a striking relationship with the audience have been temporary. For example, Conrad Atkinson's ironic posters on the Newcastle Metro and the London Underground challenged values in the art world through a manipulation of advertising conventions. Other artists have preferred to take a stronger political stance and have regarded the process of making a relationship with their audience as the 'art'

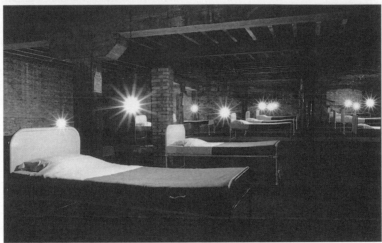

Figures 7.8 and 7.9 Scenes from 'HG', an installation in Clink Street Vaults, Southwark, by Robert Wilson, Hans Peter Kuhn and Michael Howells, 12 September – 15 October 1995. (Artangel)

in itself, whilst tackling difficult topics such as AIDS or domestic violence. This approach has been particularly strong in North America and the artist and critic Suzanne Lacey has suggested that this makes up a movement of 'new genre' public art (Lacey, 1995).

Outside of this movement, but tackling many of the same issues an interesting example of a deeper engagement with the public is provided by Jochen and Esther Gerz's 'Monument Against Fascism War and Violence – and for Peace and Human Rights'. This piece is paradoxical because it is both monolithic and ephemeral, it is permanent but was once a series of temporary events.

The artists were invited by the city of Hamburg to create this monument in 1986. They rejected the site proposed by the city, which was a leafy, dappled park, and instead chose an ugly shopping mall in a suburb, populated mainly by Turkish immigrants and German manual workers. The monument in a sense was an anti-monument, raised to remind Germans not of past victories, but of past crimes and to commemorate the invisible victims of the Holocaust. The 'monument' consisted of a 12 metre high aluminium column which was covered with a thin sheet of lead. The column was suspended over a shaft with a chamber on top, equal in depth to its own height. A plaque invited observers in seven different languages to add their signatures to those of the artists and to remain vigilant against injustice. As the column filled with signatures, it was to be lowered gradually into the chamber, until, eventually, it was completely covered. The plaque concludes: 'In the end, it is only we ourselves who can rise up against injustice' (Young, 1992, p. 58)

After the monument was first unveiled the reactions of the public surprised even the artists. The monument did indeed become full of signatures, but also was almost attacked by scribble, graffiti and some racist slogans and even swastikas. Although opinions varied in the town as to its worth, the local newspaper pointed out that this was closer to the truth of society than the rows upon rows of neat signatures that the artists had originally imagined. As Jochen Gerz commented in 1993 at the time at which the column was finally lowered into its chamber:

The monument's ugliness is the ugliness of human beings, but it may also be the same ugliness that has

given 20th-century art a certain credibility. It is something you cannot make peace with. It's a knife in the wound that will not close. If we can organize mass murder in the name of our culture, then perhaps we can survive with a knife in the wound, too' (Gerz and Shalev-Gerz, 1994, p. 24)

As the column filled up, at each one and a half metres, a ceremony was held with leading dignitaries in the town and it was lowered into a 12 metre deep shaft topped by a chamber. The column has now completely disappeared and a series of photographs of its progress into the ground remain as an ironic reminder of this anti-memorial. Observers can view part of the column through a transparent panel set in the side of the raised chamber on which a plaque explains the monument.

The Gerz's anti-monument provides a highly interactive instance of the depth of demands and meanings which public art can engage in. However, it is also a reminder that artworks can and do challenge and engage with 'public' values and definitions – not simply through their location but through their form and meaning. The most valuable works of public art are those which can operate at all three levels: to meet the provider's intentions, to resonate with the site and to create an engagement with the diverse publics who come across them.

Concluding comments

Public art is not a new phenomenon. This chapter has charted how its demise in the early part of this century through the rise of modernism in architecture and planning has contributed to changing its function from commemoration and decoration to more diverse ends. These objectives incorporate traditional motives such as the enhancement of the public realm and the creation of a sense of pride of place as well as more recent aspirations such as economic regeneration. There is some evidence to suggest that the inclusion of artworks in the public or semi-public realms assists in the creation of identity and therefore facilitates more commercial objectives.

Initiatives by the Arts Council and local authorities have put into place a series of policies in Britain to encourage the provision of public art. These have not been fully implemented as yet because of the recession in the property market. The authorities which have adopted the most advanced policies have also developed strategies for implementation and in some instances, have set up public–private Arts Trusts to act as advisors and commissioning agencies. The National

Figure 7.10 The monument being written upon. ' Das Mahnmal gegen Faschismus' Hamburg, by Esther and Jochen Gerz, 1986.

Lottery now seems to be the most intensive source of funds for public art and may increase considerably the number of works available to the public.

The scene is set then for a proliferation of public art in the near future. Urban designers would be advised, however, not to embrace the notion of the use of art installations as space fillers or means of decoration, but to think critically about why and how the proposed works are provided, sited, received and maintained. In this endeavour consideration of the provider's intentions, the resonance of the site and the reception of the audience over the period of the proposed work's life is necessary. In this the designer should collaborate and cooperate with the artist at the earliest stage possible. Planners and designers need not be afraid of public art policies: at their most creative they can achieve every politicians' dream and outlive their providers, as permanent installations and as events forming part of the collective memory of the contemporary city.

III USER REQUIREMENTS AND RESPONSES

---

8 Design for movement

Hugh Barton

Introduction

Back to basics

This chapter is entitled 'design for movement' rather than 'design for transport' for a quite particular reason. 'Transport' is often taken – especially by the Department of Transport – as referring to motorised transport. Walking is not considered a means of transport. Since in the context of local design walking is central, we use the more general term 'movement'. Movement (or transport) is, furthermore, not usually undertaken for its own sake (though of course you may choose just to 'go for a walk' or 'go for a spin'). It is usually undertaken to *get* somewhere. It is about getting to places where activities occur – working, schooling, shopping, meeting friends, going to the park, going to the dentist. So it is about *access,* it is trying to ensure a good level of *accessibility.*

This point may seem obvious, but it has potentially radical implications. The tradition of the recent past has been to design for *mobility* not *accessibility.* Mobility is about allowing people and goods to be mobile, increasing traffic speeds, reducing congestion. Designing for mobility has meant, in practice, road improvements, 'free-flow' traffic management, and settlements dominated by motor traffic. For some this can mean a *decline* in accessibility, for example, housing estates are often designed around the car in a way that actively deters walking, cycling and public transport. With fewer people on the streets local facilities cease to be viable and access to facilities is reduced. By contrast, design for accessibility means ensuring there is a real choice of types (modes) of transport to suit different needs, and that facilities are as convenient and as local as possible.

Provision for movement is not purely functional, however. While elements of design such as road widths, sight lines, gradients and curbs have important access/safety implications, they also impact on the aesthetics of the environment. Movement should be a delight. Where the pedestrian environment is attractive and feels safe, people walk more. The roads, paths and squares that allow movement are the *main* ingredient of the public realm and therefore a key expression of urban art and culture.

Transport also has a critical impact on environmental pollution. Growing car dependence is itself dependant on increasing energy use. The burning of fuel in internal combustion engines leads to emissions which are damaging to the health of people locally and to the health of the global ecosystem. Current trends are not sustainable, and design for movement must aim to provide an increase in accessibility while cutting back on transport-related emissions.

Structure of the chapter

The chapter is divided into three main parts. Part 1 first examines the goals of designing for movement, concentrating on accessibility and sustainability, then outlines the basic principles of a sustainable design strategy and evaluates current practice in the light of that. Part 2 moves from analysis to prescription, and sets out guidelines for design for public transport, pedestrians, cyclists and vehicular traffic. Part 3 continues with prescription, but shifting focus onto the integration of land use and movement at the local level. Particular themes are access to facilities, the future High Street, and patterns of density.

The material in Parts 2 and 3 is largely derived from *Sustainable Settlements*: *A Guide for Planners,*

Designers and Developers (1995), by Hugh Barton, Geoff Davis and Richard Guise.

PART 1: GOALS AND STRATEGIES

Planning for access

Access for whom?

If design for movement is concerned with ensuring a good level of accessibility, then it is important to understand access for *whom,* to *what,* and by what *means* (or mode). It is important to distinguish between households that have access to a car and those which do not. Two thirds of households now have a car, and the proportion with two or more cars has risen to about 23 per cent. Car ownership levels are very strongly related to household income (see Table 8.1), but are also related to the structure of the built environment. Low-income households are much more likely to own a vehicle in low-density rural areas than in the inner city where journeys are shorter and public transport is available (Hillman and Whalley, 1983).

Our love affair with the motor car must not be allowed to blind us to the interests of non-drivers, including not only non-car owners but people in car-owning households who cannot drive or have no access to the family car when someone else is using it. A check list of groups with specific needs could include:

- Parents with babies/toddlers (often in a buggy or pram)
- Children
- Adolescents
- Adult carers without access to a car
- Workers before/after work and at lunch times
- Elderly without access to a car
- Infirm/disabled.

Many of these groups have been marginalised by the urban design fashions of the past decades. Children's access, for example, has been sidelined to the extent that their behaviour has changed dramatically. One study, comparing the results of children's independent mobility in 1970 and 1990 found a substantial reduction in parental 'licences' for children of any age to go out on their own. The research showed that in 1971 43 per cent of 7-year olds were allowed to cross the street on their own, but by 1990 this had fallen to 29 per cent. Equivalently, the use of bikes fell from 67 per cent in 1971 to 25 per cent in 1990 (Hillman et al., (1991). Such declining levels of freedom – the result of real and perceived dangers – have not been observed by comparable studies in Germany (ibid).

From the designer's perspective proper consideration for specific needs means a focus, in detail, on safety, a sense of security, and local provision so that trips (especially by foot) can be kept short. The operational needs of pushchairs, wheelchairs, trikes and bikes are paramount.

Access to what?

The purposes of trips vary greatly with age and gender. It is salutary to note that, except for men in the 30–59 age bracket, the most important reason for travel (judged by distance) is not commuting but leisure activity (Table 8.2 and Table 8.3). Quality of life can be dramatically affected by the ability to make 'non-essential' trips to friends, social, and leisure facilities easily and cheaply. However, the key purposes in

Table 8.1 Car ownership (by real household income equivalent[1] 1992/94)

	No car	One car	Two cars	Three or more cars	All households
Lowest quintile	68	29	3	–	100
Second quintile	55	39	5	1	100
Third quintile	23	54	20	3	100
Fourth quintile	12	55	27	5	100
Highest quintile	6	45	41	8	100
Total	33	44	20	3	100

[1] The real equivalent income measure adjusts household income to take account of the size and composition of the household as well as inflation over the survey period.

Source: National Travel Survey 1992/94 (as in *Transport Statistics for Great Britain*, DoT 1995a)

relation to the capacity of the transport system are commuting and school trips, which create the morning and evening peaks of demand.

The designer needs to be aware of the degree to which accessibility can be affected by the degree of segregation or clustering of activities. The viability of local facilities, for example, can be enhanced by associating an optional trip end – such as a shop or library – with an obligatory trip end – such as a school. Despite high car use most trips are still local, with almost a third of less than a mile, and three-quarters of less than 5 miles (DoT, *National Travel Survey,* 1995b). But the trend towards longer trips is being reinforced by land use change.

Access by what means?

In terms of total mileage travelled, car use predominates, accounting for 80 per cent of the total (DoT, 1995b). But in terms of *number* of trips car/van use accounts for 55 per cent and walking accounts for

Table 8.2 Distance travelled per person per year in Great Britain: by age and purpose, 1991–93 (miles)

| | | 16–29 | | 30–59 | | | |
	Under 16	Males	Females	Males	Females	60 and over	All persons
Commuting	29	2,285	1,420	3,173	1,045	214	1,199
Business	6	1,165	337	2,253	367	176	676
Education	429	410	266	46	46	6	171
Escort education	49	22	40	85	144	13	64
Shopping	394	593	801	810	1,052	796	747
Other personal business	656	813	654	1,160	929	549	797
Social/entertainment	1,472	2,578	2,295	2,115	1,901	1,238	1,803
Holiday/other	816	855	866	930	942	949	900
All purposes	3,851	8,722	6,679	10,573	6,427	3,942	6,357

1 Excludes all journeys under one mile

Source: *National Travel Survey* (DoT, 1995)

Table 8.3 Journey and distance per person per year by distance and main[1] mode: 1991/93 (miles)

| | Journey per person per year (miles) | | | | | | | All lengths | Distance per person per year |
	<1	1–2	2–5	5–10	10–25	25–50	50<		
Walk	249	48	11					309	180
Bicycle	5	6	5	1				19	38
Car driver	27	65	127	78	53	14	7	372	2989
Car passenger	18	40	74	43	29	9	6	220	1945
Motorcycle	–	1	2	1	1			5	38
Other private	1	5	11	8	7	2		36	433
Bus (local)	4	15	32	13	3			67	269
Rail	–	–	3	4	7	2	2	17	389
Taxi	1	3	4	1				10	36
All modes	307	183	269	151	101	28	18	1057	6317

[1] The main mode is that used for the longest part of the journey

Source: National Travel Survey (DoT, 1995b)

30 per cent. For short trips (under 1 mile) walking predominates, with 81 per cent. Though this is declining as second car ownership becomes more widespread, a recent survey from Oxford Brookes University showed that 93 per cent of trips under half-a-mile were still walking (Hedicar and Curtis, 1995).

The propensity to walk and cycle is affected by local planning and design. The simple existence of local facilities encourages a proportion of local walking trips (Coombes, Farthing, and Winter, 1994). The quality of pedestrian and cycling provision is a significant factor (Ecotec, 1993). Fear of accidents and fear of violent or intimidating behaviour, may mean that people go walking less than they otherwise would. The dramatic reduction in children walking to school is an example of this. Busy roads cause community severance, cutting people off from each other. Neighbourliness of residents in a street is inversely related to the amount of traffic. So in a number of ways the lack of safety on the streets is affecting social cohesion.

It is salutary to note that reliance on non-motorised modes varies widely between different European cities. Whereas in the typical British city walking and cycling jointly account for about 35 per cent of trips, in Dutch cities it can be in the 60–65 per cent range (e.g. Groningen, Delft) with car reliance of course commensurately lower.

In conclusion, the key to planning for accessibility is to recognise the needs of the transport poor (those without access to a car) as well as the transport rich. There is a diversity of needs and that calls for a diversity of provision. Traveller *choice* is of the essence. Design should not rest on the assumption that everyone now goes by car, or that everyone wants to use the same route. On the contrary, design should attempt to open up the options that are available to people, with special attention given to those who are inherently less mobile. This means trying to ensure that a wide range of work, business, educational, social and leisure needs can be satisfied with short trip lengths, that there is the opportunity and encouragement to walk or cycle, and that public transport is viable. The environment should be *permeable*, with alternative routes and alternative modes available between any two destinations.

Planning for a sustainable environment

The emphasis on non-motorised movement which is clearly desirable from the social viewpoint is reinforced when considering the impact of traffic on the environment. There is a growing recognition that the apparently inevitable growth in traffic, with its concomitant growth

in pollution, danger, congestion and environmental degradation, cannot be allowed to continue. The government itself articulated this concern in its 1990 White Paper, *This Common Inheritance*, while at the same time – ironically – promoting a view of future traffic growth based purely on past (unsustainable) trends (see Figure 8.1).

The environmental consequences of such trends have been spelt out in detail by the Royal Commission on Environmental Pollution (1994). In its conclusions it states (p. 233)

> At present pollutants from vehicles are the prime cause of poor air quality that damages health, plants, and the fabric of buildings. Noise from vehicles and aircraft is a major source of stress and dissatisfaction, notable in towns but now intruding into many tranquil areas. Construction of new roads to accommodate traffic is destroying irreplaceable landscapes and features of our cultural heritage. The present generation's cavalier and constantly increasing use of non-renewable resources like oil may well foreclose options for future generations. This is doubly irresponsible in view of the risks of global warming ... In our view the transport system must already be regarded as unsustainable ... and will become progressively more so if present trends continue.

The trends in relation to the key indicator of CO_2 emissions (associated with climate change) are particularly worrying, with transport's contribution remorselessly growing (Figure 8.2). The Commission recommends that the transport CO_2 target should be to reduce emissions in 2020 to no more than 80 per cent of the 1990 level. To do this, it suggests, will require a concerted strategy embracing fiscal measures, vehicle design, and land use/transport planning aimed at reducing the need to travel, especially by car.

The government has responded to these concerns at a number of levels. At the broad policy level it gave a commitment on climate change at the 1992 Earth Summit in Rio. At the more detailed level it modified planning guidance notes quite extensively in the period 1992–95. The most significant pointer to altered attitudes is Planning Policy Guidance Note 13 on Transport (DoE/DoT, 1994). PPG13 puts reducing the need to travel and reducing car dependence at the top of its agenda. However, the programme of transport investment, managed by the Department of Transport, still does not fully reflect these altered priorities.

Objectives for sustainable transport

In conclusion, the review of social and environmental issues related to transport has shown that the two

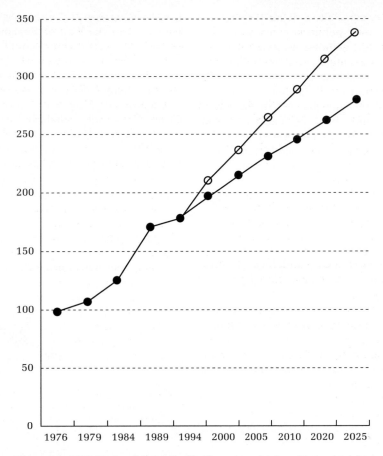

Figure 8.1 1989 National Road Traffic Forecasts – high and low rebased to 1994 (1976 = 100). (*Local Transport Today*, 12 October 1995)

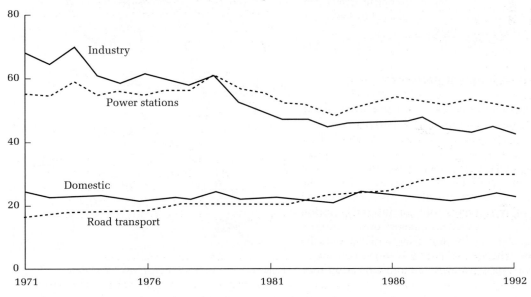

Figure 8.2 Carbon dioxide emissions by source. (*Social Trends* 25, HMSO, 1995 and National Enviornmental Tehnology Centre)

perspectives are compatible. Solving the pressing problems of transport pollution can also help to solve the recognised inequities in access to transport. The two priorities are mutually reinforcing. A radical sustainable strategy could therefore win support from quite a broad constituency. In the long run the economic benefits are also arguable, in that the current high-pollution, resource-intensive road-based strategy is not robust. Settlements geared heavily to motor use at the expense of other modes are exposed to diseconomies should fuel prices rise in the future because of scarcity or carbon tax. And a settlement that provides real transport options for its inhabitants also facilitates economic activity.

To summarise, objectives for sustainable transport could be as follows:

- Reduce levels of pollution – both local pollution that poses health problems and global pollution that threatens climate
- Improve access quality of the transport system for transport need groups rather than improve mobility for motor traffic
- Provide for increased modal choice for travellers
- Reduce the need for travel by encouraging local facility provision and local jobs
- Create an attractive convenient, safe pedestrian environment
- Reduce reliance on the car, and reduce its perceived attractiveness vis-à-vis other modes.

These goals imply a paradigm shift in thinking, reversing long-standing social and development trends. The scale of the shift required can be gauged by looking at current development patterns.

Current development patterns

Sadly, most new development is actively reinforcing car dependence. The dominant pattern is one of land use segregation, dispersal and a relatively hostile environment for pedestrians. Bristol North Fringe, the biggest development zone in South West England, encapsulates this approach. While the decision to encourage growth in this zone, accessed by M5/M4 motorways and an intercity station (Parkway) giving excellent connections, is entirely defensible, the distribution of activities across the zone is not. The map (Figure 8.3) shows how major commercial, residential, retail and education uses

have been segregated. The biggest trip generator, the University of the West of England, is isolated from residential areas which could provide student accommodation, and from shopping/leisure facilities. The average distance students have to travel is 4 miles and only 1 per cent make the journey on foot. The major shopping centre in the North Fringe at Cribbs Causeway is similarly cut off from potential residential hinterlands and viable public transport routes. 98 per cent of people drive to shop there. Even where development has been plan-led throughout, as in Bradley Stoke, the principle of land use apartheid is applied, increasing journey lengths, and the transport framework is devised on the assumption of car use predominating, with the pedestrian/bike network geared 114argely to recreational rather than daily functional use, and public transport considered only as an afterthought.

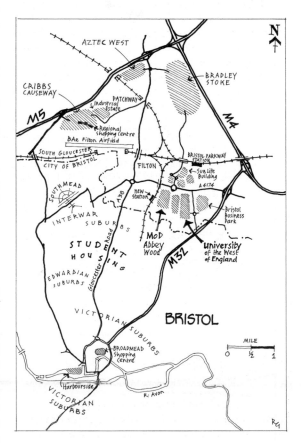

Figure 8.3 Bristol North Fringe. (Richard Guise)

Attitude surveys of Bradley Stoke residents show a high level of dissatisfaction with the area in terms of access to facilities (Winter et al., 1993). Study of the detailed layout (Figure 8.4) shows how poor detailed design has contributed to this low level of access by:

- *Indirect pedestrian routes* which increase distances (often, for shorter trips, by several times) and thus deter walking and increase car dependence. This is partly the result of the ghetto mentality of new housing development, in which each developer creates a private residential enclave, lacking direct connection with neighbouring zones. There is thus a lack of *permeability*, and the viability of local services is reduced.
- *A hostile pedestrian environment*: given the ghetto approach, pedestrians are obliged to use the main roads to gain access to other parts of the development. The main roads are designed for faster (and therefore more dangerous) traffic, and impose noise and fumes on pedestrians or cyclists. The houses do not face onto the road. Rather traffic is funnelled along between the 6-foot brick back garden walls. Not only does this make for a less than pleasant back garden, but, more seriously, removes the 'eyes on the street'. The street becomes a potentially isolating and hostile environment, when it should be unifying focus of community activity.
- *Bus stops in 'dead' streets:* bus services have been provided in Bradley Stoke, thanks to subsidy from Avon County Council, though they offer a limited range of destinations. However, they are inevitably located in the street environment described above, and poorly related to other facilities (e.g. shops, schools) which could permit multi-purpose walking trips. A journey to the bus stop becomes a special trip, with no opportunity for 'popping into the shop' on the way. The viability of both bus and shopping facilities suffers in consequence.

Bradley Stoke and the North Fringe as a whole typify an unsustainable approach to movement. Parts 2 and 3 of the chapter set out a more sustainable approach.

PART 2 : SUSTAINABLE MOVEMENT STRATEGIES

Given the prevailing car-based design practices, it is perhaps surprising that there is a fair degree of consensus over what a more sustainable transport strategy might involve.

- Extend pedestrianisation and create a dense network of footways linking all the main activities and public transport facilities, ensuring safety, directness, ease of use for the less mobile, and an attractive, secure pedestrian environment.
- Provide a network of convenient cycle routes and a safer cycling environment, both by reducing the speed of traffic on multi-purpose roads and by dedicated facilities.
- Increase the provision and effectiveness of public transport services, giving general priority over other traffic and access to the heart of areas of high demand, ensuring good interchange between different services and with pedestrian/cycling networks.
- Extend traffic-calmed areas and reduce overall capacity, ensuring a slow but steady pace of traffic, thus improving conditions for other road users and deterring car use.
- Constrain car use through restricted parking provision at all main traffic generators in centre, suburbs and out-of-town.

The critical feature of this strategy is that each element of it is mutually reinforcing: carrots and sticks are used to wean car users from dependence on their vehicles. A high-quality public transport system (e.g. light rail, tram or superbus) is complemented by enhancement of the pedestrian environment and reinforced by reduced capacity for other vehicles and high parking charges. Cities that have adopted such a strategy in a wholehearted way can demonstrate significant growth in energy-efficient modes and decline of in-city car use.

Freiburg, in the Rhine rift valley, illustrates the implementation of the strategy. The city, with population of 175,000 and quite high car ownership, is a main tourist centre for the Black Forest. It embarked on a scheme for the progressive pedestrianisation of its mediaeval core in the 1950s. Through the gradual process of renewal rear servicing has been provided for many of the central area businesses and the public realm is dedicated to people on foot. The network of bike and pedestrian ways extending out from the centre now is so good that well over half the total shopping trips are walking or cycling. At the same time the attractiveness of public transport has been turned round. From a low point in the early 1980s public transport use increased rapidly as a result of improvements to the tram system and ticketing arrangements. The trams now serve over 60 per cent of the residential areas and 70 per cent of job locations and the routes are helping to shape development decisions. The Environmental Travel Card, introduced in 1984, offers a very cheap monthly option and the promotion has explicitly played on people's fears of the destruc-

Figure 8.4 Bradley Stoke – typical housing layout. (Adapted from OS plan © Crown copyright)

tion of the Black Forest by acid rain, itself partly caused by the traffic of Freiburg. By a combination of good public transport (a 5-minute service on main routes) and high parking charges a significant modal shift has occurred from car to bus and tram.

In addition, much of the city is subject to traffic calming, with 30 km/hour being the typical speed limit in residential areas. Whereas cars are visibly 'tamed', public transport vehicles have special privileges, for instance, access across the central area.

Although the supression of car use might have been expected to damage the competitive position of the city, the opposite has in fact been the case. Pedestrian activity, and central area rents have risen disproportionately, reflecting the enhanced quality of the historic environment (TEST, 1987).

While the strategy can be made to work in towns, in the rural areas it fails because of low densities, long distances, and consequent very heavy car dependence (Hillman and Whalley, 1983). In some situations constraints on car use *in-town* can simply lead to more traffic *out-of-town* (MVA Consultancy, 1991). This is particularly the case where park-and-ride schemes on the urban fringe encourage suburban and exurban car use (Mills, 1994). Recent guidance suggests such park-and-ride schemes should be outlawed (Barton et al., 1995).

In the context, then, of a coherent and committed overall strategy we can turn to more detailed consideration of good practice, mode by mode.

Public transport

The structure of public transport provision in a privatised system is not a matter purely for the private operators. When setting out a development brief for an area the planner can effectively influence the viability of public transport by the disposition of roads, footways and land uses. The operators should be brought into the consulting process as early as possible. The overall pattern of development can then be designed so that a good level of public transport accessibility is afforded to all parts of the development with the minimum number of routes. The points where routes meet or cross (nodes) then become the locations for jobs and services.

Achieving the most effective public transport configuration should be given pre-eminence in the design process and closely specified by any development brief. Different land uses should then be 'hung' on the public transport network. The network becomes a starting point, not an afterthought. At the outset, therefore, of the design process, the following questions need to be asked:

- What is the current pattern of public transport provision and use?
- Which routes potentially offer direct connections to important destinations?
- How can the viability of existing/potential routes be reinforced?
- Can a strong mixed-use focus for services be created on site?
- Can services be concentrated on to a few high-quality public transport corridors which still reach all homes/businesses?

Figure 8.5 illustrates some of the key principles of public transport planning at the scale of an urban sector. Where possible catchment zones should take a linear form, so that the minimum number of routes can serve the maximum population and thus provide a good quality of service economically. Limited lateral movement has to apply to other road vehicles as well as to buses and trams, so that there is no distance advantage in using the private car.

The public transport spine is given meaning by major trip generators along the route. It should provide a direct service between points of primary attraction (magnets). Where there is likely to be conflict between public transport and other road users, and congestion could delay services and impair reliability, then priority measures at junctions, and bus-only lanes on the spine, may be necessary.

The relationship of housing to the public transport route is critical. Essentially, the objective of maximising access to stops means using nearby land as intensively as is feasible, with the higher-density housing, and housing providing for households with below-average car ownership, being closest to stops.

All significant development should be within easy walking distance of a good (or potentially good) public transport service. The general guideline distance is 400m. Achieving this is considered critical – the 'bottom line' of sustainable development – and in the case of medium or large developments should not be negotiable. This standard is backed by government in Circular 82/73 (DoE, 1973) and by the Confederation of British Road Passenger Transport (Addenbrooke, 1981), as well as being widely employed in Europe.

Ideally, pedestrian routes to public transport stops should be direct, with a maximum route deflection of 15–20 per cent from any location. In practice they are often very indirect, in both lattice/grid and cul-de-sac layouts, and in this situation the radius of a theoretical circular catchment area can often be reduced from 400m to 300m. The *quality* of the pedestrian access is also an important influence (Ecotec, 1993). The routes

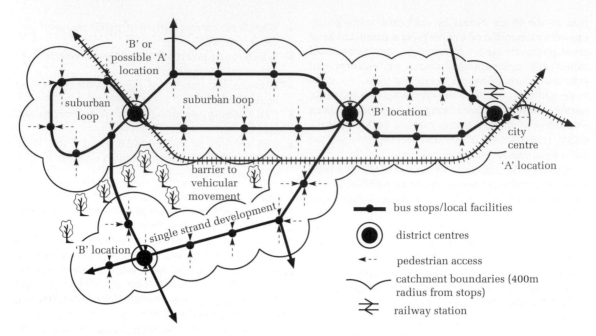

Figure 8.5 Principles of public transport planning. (Barton et al. (1995) *Sustainable Settlements: a Guide for Planners, Designers and Developers*, UWE/Local Government Managers Board)

should be convenient, safe and attractive, avoiding physical/psychological barriers such as main roads, subways and overbridges, associated with traffic intimidation, delay and, maybe, the fear of assault.

Planning for the pedestrian

Walking is the most ubiquitous form of movement, open to almost everybody. Many motorised trips involve a walk at one end. And walking, like cycling, involves no direct expenditure on fuel and can be a healthy and pleasurable, aesthetic and physical experience. Yet the pedestrian environment in many urban areas is increasingly hostile – and this is being exacerbated by the car-oriented nature of much modern development.

Walking is the most important mode in terms of number of trips or part-trips (though not of course distance). Walking constitutes the majority of trips for non-car owners, women and children. Even quite modest changes in walking habits will therefore have an impact on overall energy use. At distances of less than 0.5km the vast majority walk, but at a distance of 1km, while *non-car users* generally walk, most *car users* rely on their vehicles.

Some of the basic principles of pedestrian planning are that:

- Every development should have convenient and prominent pedestrian access points in terms of signage, lighting and gradients.
- The local pattern of footpaths/pavements should allow easy permeability: a choice of routes filtering through an area.
- Routes from houses to local facilities, especially shops, schools and bus stops, should be as direct and pleasant as possible, avoiding steep slopes or steps/kerbs where possible.
- Longer-distance walks (to the centre, or for recreation) should be facilitated by a strategic network, dovetailing where possible with the green 'open space network'.
- Safety from traffic should be improved by effective traffic calming.
- A feeling of security can be helped by appropriate detailed design and footpaths that are effectively policed by nearby residents – 'eyes on the street'.

There is a tension between the conventions of cul-de-sac housing layouts, with alley links often blocked to reduce danger and escape routes, and the need for a dense network of routes giving good 'permeability' and maximum access of any place to any other. The answer lies partly in good layout, ensuring any links between cul-de-sacs are easily policed by residents and avoiding threatening features such as blind corners or thick shrubbery on the pathway. But also the answer lies in creating neighbourhoods where walking is the natural and pleasurable means of access between activities, indeed becomes a social activity in its own right. Thus the number of people on the streets and paths itself provides security.

A development brief can specify the way the local network should link seamlessly into networks in surrounding areas, identifying key desire lines from suburbs to services, jobs and leisure activities. The main routes should radiate out from local centres/bus stops, with design quality assessed in terms of minimal deflection from the straight line routes, the variety and attractiveness of the potential walk experience, and the absence of points of intimidation or severance.

The attractiveness of pedestrian routes can be enhanced by making good use of:

- Traditional or historic footpaths, especially those with local names
- Landmark features (e.g. mature trees) which enhance local identity
- Existing and proposed planting areas, e.g. hedges, streams, shelter belts
- Views
- Microclimatic conditions such as orientation to the south and shelter from winds (pedestrians prefer to walk in the sun, cyclists prefer low wind speeds).

It is sometimes assumed that pedestrians and cyclists are so mobile that almost any surface, gradient or width of path will suffice. Streets have been so thoroughly orientated to the needs of vehicle traffic that even the remaining refuge of the pedestrian, the footpath, is undermined by proliferating traffic signs and parked vehicles. The challenge for sustainable design is to create streets that contain vehicles, and are wholly safe and enjoyable for energy-efficient modes of movement – including the movement of people with prams, small children, the elderly and those with impaired vision or mobility.

Planning for the cyclist

While walking and public transport are complementary modes of transport, the position of cycling is rather more equivocal. The principal motorised alternative for many cyclists is not the car, but the bus. An increase in bike use is liable to be at the expense of the bus, and expensive buses oblige people to get on their bikes. Conversely, the bike is available to many people at low cost, is innately energy-efficient, and can provide benefits in terms of health and fitness. Most journeys in the UK are short enough to be cycled. The concept of 'bike and ride', where cycle parks are provided at railstations, is one way of making bikes and public transport complementary, and reinforcing a public transport strategy.

The average length of journey by bicycle according to some recent research is about 3km with a *maximum* regular trip of no more than 16km (10 miles). The threshold beyond which cycling will *generally* not be used as the mode of travel lies around 5km (3 miles).

By comparison with the bus and (in town centres at least) the car, the bike offers a door-to-door service. The pattern of cycling desire lines is disparate, reflecting a myriad different trip ends. In that context the provision of one cycle route (along a disused railway, for example) is of marginal relevance. Cyclists typically (except for recreation) choose the shortest and easiest route. Normally, that means using the local road network, and it is therefore the quality of the road network rather than special routes, which is paramount. In this context bike priority measures and traffic calming are important.

The network principles incorporated in the cycle planning in Delft (Netherlands) involve a hierarchy of routes, from 'sub-district' with a grid of 100–150m related to individual house groupings or streets, to district with a grid of 200–300m, and 'city' with a grid of 400–600m. Trip lengths of 0.5km, 1–1.5km, and 2–3km correspond to sub-district, district, and city networks. Obstructions can cause detours of 800–1200m, which may amount to 30–50 per cent of the journey length, according to the Delft planners, so a main priority for transport investment is to overcome obstructions (e.g. by providing a new railway crossing point), thus reducing journey length and time.

Criteria for network design

- *Access*: Are general purpose streets (giving access to homes and facilities) bicycle friendly, with the traffic 'calmed'? Direct access to homes and facilities is a particular advantage of the bike. Cyclists' behaviour is relatively anarchistic, and they will take the route that provides direct access. In conventional layouts this is normally the road. Segregated routes are desirable in some situations but are no substitute for roads that are safe to cycle.
- *Continuity*: Are main bike routes as continuous as possible, with few stops? Cyclists prefer to conserve

their momentum, to minimise effort, and are therefore reluctant to stop – even at junctions, where most accidents occur. An effective network is created by optimising continuity. Conversely, fragmented stretches of cycle path can actually increase overall dangers, so the process of implementation should allow for safe intermediate phases.

- *Safety*: Are separate lanes or paths provided where there is a potential conflict with motor-traffic? The design of junctions requires paying particular attention. eighty per cent of accidents occur at or near junctions; yet most involve cycles travelling straight ahead, indicating that motor vehicles are often at fault.
- *Directness*: Are routes direct? As a rule of thumb, cyclists will not accept a diversion of more than 10 per cent of their journey distance. Segregated routes are sometimes impractical since the direct route in existing urban areas is via the main road. In new developments, priorities can be reversed, allowing cyclists and pedestrians the shortest route.
- *Comfort*: Are routes comfortable, with attention given to the gradients and surfaces? The design of adjacent buildings and landscaping can also contribute towards an optimum microclimate for cycling.
- *Amenity*: Are routes attractive, interesting and well-maintained? They should also be clean, and free from heavy fumes, extreme noise, and the turbulence caused by speeding traffic (especially HGVs).
- *Bike parks*: Are routes linked to conveniently located bike parks or secure workplace sheds that protect from theft and rain? Use of bikes by commuters is significantly affected by trip-end provision e.g. at local authority offices.
- *Interchange*: Planning Policy Guidance note 13 (DoE, 1994b) gives particularly direct guidance on this. Is there '... provision of secure cycle parking at public transport interchanges, including railway stations and park and ride facilities, to increase opportunities to use cycles in combination with public transport and car sharing'?

Planning for traffic

Planning for traffic is put last in this sequence for the perverse reason that it is normally placed first by designers and thus dominates the pattern of development. But if sustainable development is the goal then the needs of public transport, pedestrians and cyclists should come first, and car access should be made to fit, rather than the other way round.

In the light of this, there are some key general principles of good planning and design:

- The capacity of the road system should not normally be increased by any means (road/junction improvement, traffic management or new construction) unless justified as essential for serving new or intensified development.
- Changes to the road system should be judged not by the potential time-savings to car users (as current DoT assessment requires) but by their capacity to improve the quality of the environment for residents/shoppers/pedestrians/cyclists, and to facilitate public transport operation.
- In existing urban areas road capacity for ordinary traffic may be reduced, as a side-effect of positive planning for other modes – e.g. by widening pavements, in areas of high use, by safeguarding continuity and safety for pedestrians and cyclists, or by inserting bus priority measures or tram lines.
- Traffic management in urban areas should be aimed not at speeding up traffic (with consequent increased danger/intimidation to other road users), *nor* at slowing traffic right down (with resulting stop/start conditions, increased energy use and emissions) but rather at achieving a modest but steady pace.

The idea of traffic calming is not to adopt punitive measures against the car but to civilise it, reduce its environmental impact, and, by capacity restraint, gently deter its use. Appropriate speed limits can be built into the design:

inner urban areas	20 mph
residential areas	20 mph
shopping streets	20 mph
suburban areas (with the exceptions above)	30 mph
rural areas, except dual carriageways	50 mph

Speeds can be policed by design – road widths, curvature sightlines and rough surfaces (but not on bike lanes). Road humps and platforms are awkward for buses unless very gentle, and can waste energy on braking and acceleration.

Where there are viable alternatives to the car, then car restraint is appropriate through limits on the amount of parking space. Parking controls need to be carefully devised to reinforce other transport and land use policies without causing undesirable side effects for residents or penalising car use where essential. The Dutch policy of 'the right business in the right place' grades the level of parking provision (10 per cent, 20 per cent or 50 per cent of theoretical demand) in line with the availability of alternative modes of access. Where, say, public transport is likely to be upgraded in the future, temporary parking provision is permitted. These rules apply as much to suburban or exurban as city centre locations. The implications for the release of land from car parking blight are considerable. Government guidance provides significant backing for this whole approach (DoE, DoT, 1994, PPG13, para. 4.6).

The road hierarchy needs to be easily legible and afford reasonably direct access from any place to any other place (i.e. a good level of permeability) for all road users, with low route deflection which adds to trip length and fuel use. However, some route deflection is acceptable where pedestrians, cyclists and buses are given the advantage of a more direct route.

Many recent housing developments employ a 'tree' structure of access, with only one main entry to the site, which makes for excessive extra mileage. Figure 8.6 shows this hierarchy of roads, which produces high vehicle-flows towards the entrance. Dwellings located on the Access Road 'A4' suffer significantly more air and noise pollution, and risk of accident, than those within the cul-de-sac. The access road may also be a relatively hostile environment for pedestrians and cyclists.

Design Bulletin 32 (DoE, 1977) suggests a *network* alternative, with an increase in the number of access points (related to density and the location of external attractions) so that peak vehicle flows can be kept to a minimum. Traffic is distributed more evenly throughout the layout.

The consequences for pedestrian and cycle movement are significant. *Shared surfaces* can be used more generally and routes tend to be more direct, with higher amenity and safety. The plan is potentially more coherent and legible on the ground. The roads may be narrower, taking up less land and constructed to a lower specification, therefore using fewer natural resources. Furthermore, loops and circuits are better for service vehicles (e.g. milk delivery) and reduce the problems of nuisance caused by reversing and turning vehicles. 'Weak links' allow service vehicles and emergency services to travel along the short segregated cycle and pathways which break up the traffic grid. Discontinuity would otherwise be a nuisance, and reduce the quality of the environment.

PART 3: DESIGNING THE LAND USE/MOVEMENT PATTERN

If the main purpose of movement is to get to places, then it follows that the location of those places is at least as important a factor in achieving accessibility as the quality of transport provision. As noted earlier, government now belatedly accepts the truism that transport and land use planning are interrelated, and PPG13 sets out principles of integrated land use/transport planning. These principles may broadly be summarised as follows (Barton et al., 1995):

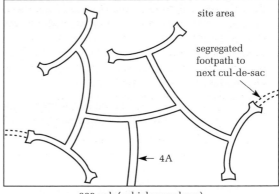

320 vph (vehicles per hour)

Culs-de-sac (adapted from DoE NI, 1988, Layout of housing roads: Design Guide)

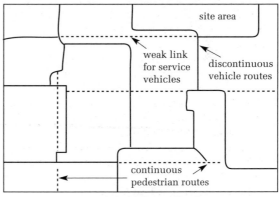

40 vph (vehicles per hour)

After DB32: a network or grid arrangement, with many more vehicular entrances to the site than in the first diagram.

Figure 8.6 Tree and network patterns of residential road access. (Barton et al. (1995) *Sustainable Settlements: a Guide for Planners, Designers and Developers*, UWE/Local Government Managers Board)

- Maximise the job and service autonomy of each small town or area of a city, localising the provision of facilities where possible.
- Plan compact rather than dispersed settlements, with growth areas selected for their public transport accessibility, and intensification of urban use encouraged where this would not result in loss of valued open space.
- Cluster jobs and facilities closely together in mixed-use centres at local, district or city scales according to their likely catchments.

- Plan housing within easy walking distance of local facilities and public transport stops, with higher-density development closer to services.
- Design layouts that maximise the permeability of the urban environment, especially by foot and bike, and increase the level of street activity.

Every new greenfield or brownfield development can be used either to reinforce the car-dependent trend of the past, or shift the pattern towards one which has the potential to be more sustainable.

Local facility catchments and accessibility

The starting point is the spatial relationship between housing and local facilities. It is self-evident that the monoculture, single-use character of postwar housing estates has failed, but the reasons for this are only partly to do with design. Increased wealth and mobility, and changing commercial practice, have led to the decline (and sometimes the eclipse) of local services. The economic unit size of provision has altered. So while the goal of a more localised, mixed-use style of development is clear, it is profoundly difficult to achieve.

In an increasingly privatised economy it is often not possible or appropriate to define specific catchments for specific services. The principle of consumer choice and the fact of mobility means that local people may not in any case choose to use local facilities. The population necessary to support a given quality of service is tending to increase as a result. Changing patterns of service provision and of retailing often lead to increased unit size of facility, with the same result – poorer accessibility at the local level. Nevertheless, some sections of the population remain highly dependent on local facilities and 'planning for sustainability' means trying to ensure everyone has the opportunity to use local facilities and preferably a choice of local facilities.

Traditional approaches to catchment areas, as in the new towns, equated catchment areas with neighbourhoods and 'environmental areas' (where through traffic is excluded). The problem with this approach is its inflexibility, its inability to adapt to changing economic conditions and social needs. It also offers limited choice to residents in any particular neighbourhood. Table 8.4 and Figure 8.7 illustrate the difficulty of identifying one specific catchment. It may well be that the traditional High Streets offer more flexibility and a better level of access.

Table 8.4 illustrates facility provision within the context of a township of 30,000 people, which is assumed here as distinct from the rest of the urban areas. The catchments are taken from the ranges shown in Figure

Table 8.4 Possible local facility catchments

Facility	Population range
Primary school	2,500–4,500
Secondary school	7,000–15,000
Doctor's surgery	2,500–3,000
Public house	5,000–7,000
Corner shop	2,000–5,000
Local shopping centre	5,000–10,000
Post office	5,000–10,000
Health centres (4 doctors)	9,000–12,000
Library	12,000–30,000
Church	9,000 minimum
Community centre	7,000–15,000
Youth club	7,000–11,000
Sports centre	25,000–40,000
Superstore/district centre	25,000–40,000

CAUTION: this list is indicative only, and based on city-scale not small towns. Catchments may vary from place to place and over time.

Sources: Coombes, Farthing and Winter (1992–94); Greater London Council (1965); Milton Keynes Development Corporation (1992)

8.7 . The principle is to ensure a good level of provision with some variety of unit size, allowing for operational flexibility and consumer choice. For example, within the township there could be (in this illustration) a choice between a larger or a smaller secondary school. Most parents will choose the closest, but some will be drawn by a particular kind of school. Note that facilities could be clustered at the township scale, but that there are not set neighbourhoods within the township, rather a pattern of overlapping catchments.

This policy of good varied provision contrasts with current norms for greenfield development, and implies the need to incorporate better standards in local plans and implement them through planning agreements where possible. There is a gradation of standard access distances which are desirable, depending on the user, the use, and the catchment requirements. The spiral diagram, Figure 8.8, suggests a *range* of standards which may be adapted to local traditions or circumstances. The standards involve awkward judgements balancing different criteria. Partly for this reason a *range* is shown, with the 80 per cent level representing the desirable standard, and the 100 per cent level perhaps being more realistic. The principle is that all new housing (on brownfield or greenfield sites) should be accessible to a full range of facilities in order to minimise journey length, facilitate walking and cycling, and increase accessibility.

The provision of local facilities is a high priority for people moving into new estates, and the lack of

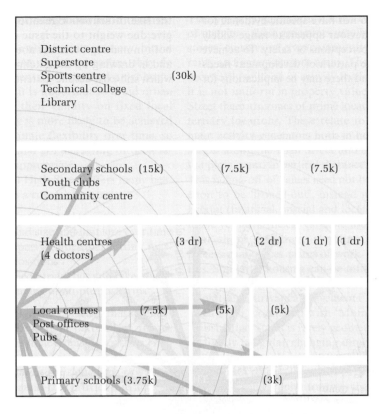

Figure 8.7 Facilities within a new township of 30,000 people (illustrative) – a good level of provision but with flexibility of unit size is important. (Barton et al. (1995) *Sustainable Settlements: a Guide for Planners, Designers and Developers*, UWE/Local Government Managers Board)

them is a very common cause of complaint (Coombes et al., 1994). Local provision encourages local trips, with a high proportion of these by foot or public transport (Ecotec, 1993). Clustering provides an opportunity for multi-purpose trips and close association between uses reinforces their viability. Clustering also increases the proportion using public transport rather than private car (Cervero, 1989).

Such standards do not imply that people will necessarily use their nearest facility, but it gives them the *opportunity* to choose local. In higher-density urban areas overlapping catchments mean that local choice is further increased. The identification of specific standards risks being arbitrary. The justifications for a selection of suggested standards are given below:

- *Allotments* should ideally be within 200m of every home except in low-density areas. The full energy-saving value of allotments is only realisable if the

trips to and from them are by foot, and organic wastes from the home are composted. 200m is taken as the maximum convenient barrow distance. This implies a pattern of allotment provision radically different from at present.
- *Primary school* should be within 400m of most homes, and 600m of all urban homes. Within distances of 400m, walking the children to school is the norm, but there is increasing resort to the car as distances increase beyond that. The standard can only be achieved, at reasonable densities, if primary schools are very evenly distributed and have good, direct access from all directions. The quality of pedestrian access (e.g. safety and aesthetics) is a material factor in some people's decision whether to walk or not.
- *Secondary school* should be within 1500m of every home. For distances up to around 1500m there is still a substantial proportion of non-motorised

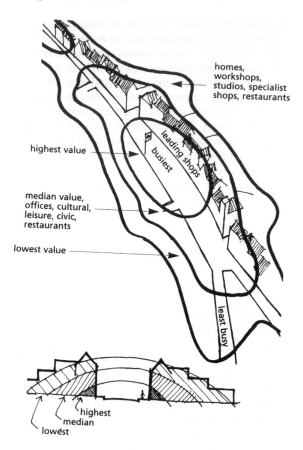

homes,
workshops,
studios, specialist
shops, restaurants

leading shops
busiest

highest value

median value,
offices, cultural,
leisure, civic,
restaurants

lowest value

least busy

highest
median
lowest

Figure 8.10 Typical High Street diagrammatic values/uses contours. (Barton et al. (1995) *Sustainable Settlements: a Guide for Planners, Designers and Developers*, UWE/Local Government Managers Board)

pollution and hazards to pedestrian movement. Thus the trend towards the bypassing of town centres and their subsequent pedestrianisation may be welcomed, with the caveat that a tolerable level of traffic with a reason to be in the High Street – buses, delivery vehicles, parking for disabled people, even a certain amount of casual parking helps to maintain the vitality of the place and should help to reduce the necessity of service yards and access roads which can be costly and space-hungry.

Thus the local High Street, and the principal bus routes that run along its length and link to the wider world, provides the focus for design. The grain of development is provided by local pedestrian routes linking housing, High Street and open spaces. Priority throughout is given to people living, working and playing in the area, and to the quality of their immedi-

ate environment in terms of convenience, conviviality, security, health, beauty and diversity.

Density patterns

The planning of density may provide a key to achieving a coherent solution. Density can be measured in terms of residential population per hectare, workers per hectare or visitors/clients/shoppers per hectare, and also in related development densities such as dwellings per hectare or square metres of office per plot. From the viewpoint of transport energy use all these are measures of use intensity and proclivity to generate trips. While clearly higher use intensity is generally asociated with employment and retailing use, it can be that a block of flats or town houses generates more person trips per hectare than industrial or warehousing development. Use intensity, defined as a measure of trip generation, is therefore the significant factor.

Old towns and city sectors frequently exhibit a basic pattern of density contours grading down by distance from the town centre or radial High Streets. The core area may be eighteenth or nineteenth century, at quite high densities, surrounded by medium-density Edwardian housing, in turn giving way to lower-density interwar and postwar development. Thus the areas most accessible to buses, shops and pubs have the highest population density, sometimes also equated with lowest car-ownership levels. This pattern has major advantages in terms of minimising average trip lengths, increasing the number of walking trips, and bulwarking the viability of local services.

While the main thrust of postwar policy has been to wind down linear centres (no shops on main roads), and to modify the clarity of the density gradient, the traditional form is still there, awaiting resurrection. While change in existing built-up areas is often slow, there can be flurries of development activity which could, in principle, be harnessed to reinforce the density gradient, if there were clear intensity zonings in local plans. Flats, shops and local offices would be restricted to the inner zone, while lower-intensity uses would be encouraged on the fringes (see Table 8.5). In each zone there is a mix of uses. Clearly, such zones should be defined so they respond to distinctive local conditions and reflect the need for a varied and aesthetically satisfying environment.

Such linear concentration along main public transport routes could be complemented by the 'parkway' or 'greenspace' network, providing for recreation and water management and acting as the lungs of the urban area.

Table 8.5 Levels of use intensity

Levels of intensity	Examples of land use
Highest intensity Town centre activities	offices over 200 sq m superstores comparison retailers multi-screen cinemas central library
Higher intensity Local High Streets	small offices local shops pubs, cafés, flats community centres
Medium intensity Close to public transport, shops, and High Street	terraced housings workshops playgrounds
Low intensity Mainly open space	playing fields parks small-holdings woodland

Source: Barton et al. (1995)

The same principles could be extended to suburban development zones. Figure 8.11 illustrates one way the variation of use intensity can be applied to a greenfield town expansion scheme. Linear bands served by a public transport loop, provide attractive and varied living environments, centred on bustling mixed-use High Streets, close to a network of greenspaces for recreation. The form is compact. It could be designed to permit further extension without distorting the basic principles.

- Public transport provides the spine and structure for the settlement – one very effective route serves the whole 'loop' population of 20,000 people.
- Facilities and higher-intensity housing are concentrated at intervals in local 'High Streets' along the public transport spine.
- Everyone lives within 400m of the public transport service and walking distance of some local facilities. A wider choice of facilities is available one or two stops away.
- The town centre is at the crossing of the public transport routes. It is also accessible by foot or bike via the open space network.
- Densities grade down away from the core, thus giving varied living environments and a range of housing, while maximising accessibility.
- The main roads are kept peripheral to the development, so as to attract car traffic away from the High Streets and serve Category C sites well.
- The multi-function open space network threads through the development. All dwellings are within 400 metres of extensive open space.

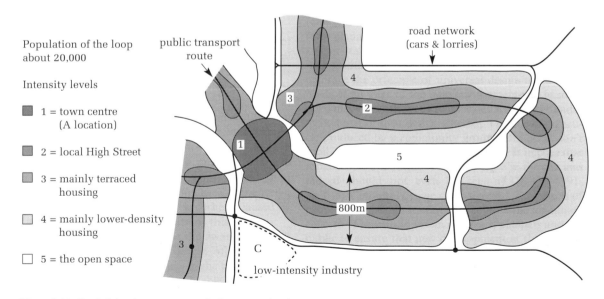

Figure 8.11 Graded density patterns applied to a new development zone.

Who are the users of the built environment?

One of the key themes of this book is to look at the question of urban design from the bottom-up, 'user' perspective, as well as from the 'provider', top-down, professional perspective. People with disabilities, as will be explained, constitute a major section of users, and thus of citizens.

The cartoon drawn by Hellman, reproduced as Figure 9.1, sums up very effectively the way in which many people with disabilities view the environment in which they live. The steps symbolise all the barriers which restrict the opportunities of people who experience some kind of impairment from achieving their potential and participating fully in mainstream community life. However, one of the disadvantages of the Hellman cartoon is that the image portrayed in the drawing is of a wheelchair user. This is the popular stereotype of a person with a disability, although wheelchair users probably constitute about 4 per cent of the total population of disabled people. In fact, the population of disabled people is far from being a homogeneous group; a wide variety of different impairments affect mobility, including sensory impairments, respiratory disorders, arthritis, heart conditions, learning difficulties and the general effects of the ageing process.

The task of attempting to quantify the numbers of people who have different types of disability and classifying the nature and degree of the impairment which they experience, is fraught with difficulty for a number of reasons. First, many people with disabilities object in principle to what Oliver (1993) has described as 'the sterile barriers of head counting'. This is almost certainly because the gathering of such information is associated with able-bodied people acting as the gatekeepers of benefits and other resources. Many people with disabilities are also disinclined to declare to officials that they have an impairment, partly through fear of social stigma or discrimination, and partly because they are subject to pressures which encourage them to deny their disability (French, 1993).

Hidden impairments, such as epilepsy, heart disease, asthma and other respiratory disorders are also less likely to be included on the official OPCS registers and yet many of these impairments can affect personal mobility. Even official estimates for the number of disabled people in the UK population vary between 6.1 million and 9.3 million (OPCS, 1988a). The Royal National Institute for the Deaf estimated in 1989 that 7.5 million people in the UK have experienced hearing loss; this amounts to 17 per cent of the total population. Royal National Institute for the Blind estimates indicate that in 1987 there were 959,000 people registered blind and a further 740,000 with a sight disability. Official figures and those quoted by voluntary groups must be treated with caution as an indicator of the per-

Figure 9.1 Louis Hellman

centage of the population who would benefit from a more accessible environment as there are no completely reliable statistics and the figures are likely to be underestimates. However, some trends are recognisable. The proportion of people over 55 in the population currently stands at 17 per cent of the total and this is likely to rise to 19 per cent by 2025. It is well known that the prevalence of disability increases with age, although many elderly people would not contemplate being considered as disabled. People are living longer and the generation who have experienced high levels of personal mobility are approaching retirement age. If this group, pregnant women, small children, and people who have a temporary mobility impairment are added to the list of people who need a barrier-free environment, it might be wondered why the consideration of ensuring good access is considered to be a minority interest. The fact is that everyone benefits from better access, so justifying provision on the grounds that a certain percentage of the population would benefit is not particularly helpful.

It is preferable to adopt a universal approach to design. In towns and cities improved accessibility is also likely to encourage greater pedestrian activity. In the current climate of increased acceptance of the need to encourage people to make fewer trips by private motor vehicle, the argument for improving the accessibility, safety and convenience of streets is particularly pertinent. It might be possible to increase the percentage of pedestrian trips, thus reducing dangerous and unpleasant vehicle exhaust emissions, if the pedestrian environment was made more attractive and convenient to all users. This is also likely to encourage the essential vitality recognised as a critical aspect of ensuring that towns and the central areas of cities remain economically viable in the face of competition from out-of-town centres. Although accessibility is only one of the Health Check Indicators suggested (URBED, 1994) as a measure of the vitality and viability of town centres, its inclusion and the reference to ensuring access for all is significant. Creating accessible streets can therefore be seen to be part of a wider agenda for a more sustainable future focused on the civilised town or city centre, rather than as a direct benefit dispensed to a minority, 'special needs' group.

Creating accessible environments is nevertheless also about improving the quality of life for people who have experienced severe limitations on their activity through the disabling nature of the built environment. To illustrate this point it is worth quoting an example of how gaining access to the city can have a direct affect on an individual's life. After much discussion the Manchester Metro was made accessible to wheelchair users by the arrangement of platforms and the design

of entrances. Although it is far from perfect as an example of good access, it undoubtedly affected the quality of life for one young wheelchair user interviewed as part of a research project (Manley, 1996). She remarked, 'You have no idea how much fun I have choosing my own clothes instead of listening to the well-meaning advice of parents or friends and what's more the sales assistant has to talk to me if I'm alone, instead of talking over my head to whoever is with me.'

Models of disability

What role does the town planner have in attempting to make the environment more accessible to all users? It is not simply a matter of adding a few ramps at the entrances to buildings – a much more radical reconsideration is necessary that recognises that the design of

Figure 9.2 The Manchester Metro: accessible to disabled people through the arrangement of platforms. (Sandra Manley)

development in both urban and rural areas must embrace the need to design universally. The precise nature of the role of town planning and urban design in contributing to this aim depends to a great extent on the 'model' of disability that is adopted: the medical, the charitable, or the social model (Swain et al., 1993).

The *medical model* tends to see disabled people as 'sufferers' from an illness of a long-term nature which is normally set within the confines of the hospital or institution. Such people are unlikely to impinge upon the community or the built environment 'outside'. However, in recent years, the policy of care in the community, albeit unsupported by adequate financial investment and support, has precipitated the need for the built environment to be made more accessible to a wider range of disabled people. A second view of disability is the *charity model* in which there appears to be little or no role for state intervention. The image is one of pity, embarrassment and dependency – an image that has been sharply rejected by people with disabilities who do not wish to be dependent on the good will of the 'able-bodied' population.

This contrasts sharply with the *social model* of disability which is based on the premise that people with disabilities have human rights. The emphasis is shifted towards seeing society's attitudes and thus the design of the built environment as disabling, and 'making' people disabled. According to this model town planners have a major role to play. Disability groups argue that people should be able to gain access to buildings, streets and spaces as workers, shoppers, theatre goers, students or in any other capacity without fuss, and with no special assistance. More fundamentally, it is argued that the whole structure of cities, employment, education and society needs rethinking. For example, dezoning of cities, the provision of accessible public transport, greater frequency of local centres, shops and employment, and changes in the internal design of all types of buildings are advocated (Imrie, 1996). Disabled people simply want to be themselves, good or bad, without having to pre-plan before trying to go out.

Implications of the social model for the built environment

The social model of disability has been widely welcomed by many groups of disabled people, mainly because it recognises that society creates the disabling environment and not the medical condition alone. Accepting the social view of disability implies agreement that equal opportunities and the removal of dis-

criminatory practices are equal rights issues. This view has gathered momentum in recent years in what has been described (Driedger, 1989) as a 'world wide awakening' of the community of disabled people. The campaign style adopted has become much more vociferous than hitherto, almost certainly because people with disabilities have recently become more visible, have taken a greater share in the responsibility for the campaign and ceased to rely on able-bodied well-wishers to orchestrate protests and lobby governments.

This awakening has already had implications for how built environment professionals perceive disability, particularly in relation to access rights, which have become higher on the political agenda. Gaining knowledge and expertise in this aspect of the design of the environment will become even more relevant to planners and urban designers who may be directly involved in design schemes or be responsible for making judgements about the quality of a proposed development scheme produced by others. Wider knowledge of the social model of inequality by the built environment professions should, with time, lead to a different 'cultural attitude' towards planning for disability and presumably greater regulation and enforcement power through the planning system.

The inaccessible nature of the built environment is, of course, only one aspect of the disabling social environment which prevents many people from gaining access to education, goods, services, transport and, most significantly, employment. However, even if it were possible to remove all other barriers to equal opportunity, including changing attitudes to people with disabilities, the inaccessible nature of cities, towns, buildings and streets would continue to be an absolute and inescapable physical barrier for many people. Consequently, to pursue a policy of equal rights which would effectively allow everyone an opportunity to reach their full potential and obtain the best possible quality of life, requires that the built environment should be planned to be barrier-free. Providing access is therefore primarily a question of human rights.

This argument may not convince everyone. However, economic considerations alone make it desirable to enable as many people as possible to support themselves by obtaining employment and living in the community rather than in state-provided accommodation. Similarly, the economic benefits of ensuring that everyone has access to goods and services has already been recognised by some retailers, such as Boots and B & Q, who are making concerted efforts to make their existing premises more accessible. The question of whether the community and the development industry can bear the cost of improved access, almost inevitably emerges in

Figure 9.3 A barrier-free environment can benefit all age groups. (Sandra Manley)

any debate on the issue. It is often argued that it is too expensive. Yet, it is worth noting that studies in the USA have demonstrated that the inclusion of accessibility features in new site construction totals less than one per cent of the construction costs and usually less than one half of one per cent. Authorities from around the world reporting to the UN have agreed that if accessibility is considered at the outset of the design, the costs are negligible (Wilkoff and Abed, 1994). Alteration costs to bring existing buildings up to new standards are, of course, more difficult to determine, and currently requirements are not retrospective. The costs involved in alterations depend on the local circumstances of the case, but in many instances it is possible to incorporate access improvements into a refurbishment programme when the costs are likely to be a negligible part of the total. It has long been argued, however, that in order to make real progress towards the creation of a barrier-free environment there is a need for legislation to change people's actions as well as their feelings. Reliance on an approach based on changing attitudes is not the answer.

Legislative change

This section and the following one consider the means available to increase access from the perspective of planning practice. While aspects of the legislation and controls are touched upon in passing in this account,

there is much more that is of relevance to the whole debate about the powers to increase access and the role of the planner, architect and urban designer in this process. Therefore the legislation and related Building Regulations, PPGs (Planning Policy Guidance Notes) and other controls have been set out more fully in Appendix I. In particular the 'problems' of the Building Regulations and their current failure to address certain aspects of access to buildings is explained in more detail in a longer section within Appendix III. There is, in fact, as stated in Chapter 1, considerable debate about the extent to which urban design does, or should include a concern with individual building design, architecture, and external and internal construction details. Many disabled people would undoubtedly say from personal experience that access to individual buildings and the way in which they relate to the spaces and streets around them is an essential aspect of achieving a high-quality built environment that is accessible to all. In practice, many planners, as part of their assessment of planning applications, will be called upon to comment on the design of buildings from all points of view. It is important that planners bring to the design process an understanding of the social consequences of design as well as considering aesthetic impacts. This is likely to reduce the perception of the planner as one who 'interferes' in the architects' sphere of expertise by commenting only on aspects of the external appearance of buildings or building style.

Notwithstanding the debate about the precise nature of the role of planner and urban designer, it is evident that the nature of the legislative code is inevitably highly influential as a factor in achieving good access provisions at the scale of individual buildings and at the city-wide scale. After many years and a series of relatively weak previous pieces of legislation, campaigns in the UK have led to the first tentative steps at anti-discrimination legislation in the passing of the Disability Discrimination Act (1995). Although this legislation does not proceed anywhere near as far as the parallel legislation in the USA, Australia and Canada, it does represent a considerable step towards equal rights, compared with the previous legislation. The campaign to obtain a more effective anti-discrimination code continues (Rights Now, 1996) and it is likely that it will eventually lead to legislation of a similar type to that now in place in respect of sexual and racial discrimination, particularly bearing in mind acceptance of the rights argument by both the European Union and the United Nations.

The 1995 Act does, however, relate mainly to employment, although section 21 deals with the provision of goods and services, and actually mentions removing physical barriers. This is somewhat undermined by subsequent paragraphs, which water down the requirements, by talking more vaguely about 'alternatives' and 'reasonable expenditure'. The Act was apparently modelled to some extent upon the American civil rights approach to such legislation, but by the time it had gone through parliament it was seriously 'disabled' itself by attacks and stalling techniques. However, the Act must be welcomed to some extent, even though it has been widely criticised. It does at least give some recognition to the need to secure equal rights for people with disabilities and further changes may be secured in the near future.

However, recognising that there is a rights-based case for securing a more accessible environment in the widest sense is only the starting point of provision. Implementing this policy is dependent to a great extent on the nature of the legislative framework to support the basic intention of securing equal rights.

In relation to the built environment there have been previous attempts at legislation, but these have been mainly focused on gaining access to individual buildings and have not addressed wider considerations associated with the design of the public realm or the town or city as a whole. In particular, the passing of the Chronically Sick and Disabled Persons Act in 1970 required that access to certain public buildings should be made available for disabled people if this was 'practicable and reasonable'. The implication of this statement is that provision was regarded almost as an optional, desirable feature, but not necessarily essential. For the designer of a building the message conveyed by the legislative requirements in many cases resulted in access provisions which were not integral to the design of the building, but treated as an add-on extra. The worst examples of this approach produced ugly, ramped entrances which were often inconveniently placed for the user and had an institutionalised appearance. In many cases it led to separate and special arrangements for access, such as a requirement to enter a building through a back entrance, or in a manner which involved more inconvenience and effort for the person with disabilities than for the able-bodied.

The split of responsibilities between the planning system and the Building Regulations has not been particularly helpful as a mechanism for securing an integrated approach to access. The emphasis of the control mechanism on individual accessibility to particular

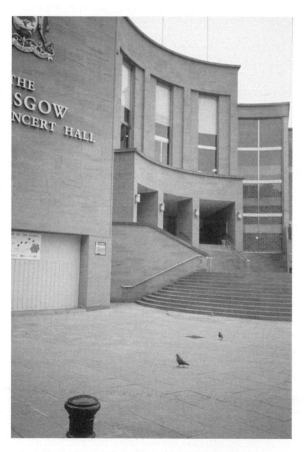

Figure 9.4 Glasgow Concert Hall: disabled people are informed by a poorly positioned sign that access can be gained via an alternative entrance. (Sandra Manley)

buildings and the control of access at this very local spatial level has also tended to give less weight to the importance of ensuring that the spaces between buildings, streets, squares, parks and every part of the public realm are accessible, which is obviously a key concern for urban designers. To the disabled person the fact that a ramped entrance has been provided to the local post office does not mean much, if the High Street itself is inaccessible. However, given the system's weaknesses, it is possible for local authorities to use the powers that they have available in a constructive way. The next section of the chapter will examine these powers and how they are used by local authorities.

Development control and planning practice

In considering applications for planning permission to develop land the local planning authority has a statutory duty under section 76 of the Town and Country Planning Act 1990 Act to draw the attention of developers to the requirements of the Chronically Sick and Disabled Persons Act 1970. This notionally should ensure that new buildings to which members of the public have access are made accessible, although the incorporation of the let-out clause in The Chronically Sick and Disabled Persons Act (as described above) does not make this a very effective mechanism. The legislation falls short of requiring the local planning authority to exert its powers to ensure compliance with access requirements. Recent government advice (PPG1, 1997a) takes a more positive view of the scope of planning authorities in securing an accessible environment than previous guidance. For the first time it is mentioned that improved access will be beneficial to everyone, not just those with disabilities. This must be taken into account within the developement control and development plan processes. It also makes it clear that the Building Regulations are the correct mechanism for securing access to individual buildings and the planning system should not be used to duplicate or exceed these requirements. Nevertheless, planning authorities do have the power to refuse applications for planning permission if access is not adequately provided and some have made use of this power and been successful in subsequent planning appeals. Undoubtedly, considerable improvements to design schemes are made through the day-to-day process of negotiation with developers, and planning obligations under Section 106 of the Town and Country Planning Act have also been used to secure better access arrangements. This section of the Act allows an authority, subject to certain constraints set down by government circular (*Planning and Compensation Act 1991:*

Planning Obligations, Circular 16/91 and 1/97), to regulate the development or obtain contributions from the developer that could not be required by a normal planning condition. Some agreements of this type have resulted in more spacious lifts in shopping centres, provision of accessible bus services and other improvements.

Scope does exist within the planning and development control system to improve access to new buildings, to buildings that are being altered and to the spaces between buildings, although that scope is limited by the tendency to concentrate on the building rather than on the broader issues. Many planning authorities are content to leave access issues solely to the consideration of building control staff at the stage of submission of detailed applications for approval under the Building Regulations. Local authorities who wish to pursue the aim of achieving better access at the planning stage of the development, when it is more likely that the designer can be encouraged to take a universal approach to the design of the building, are likely to be more successful if the development plan has specific statements and policies that make these requirements clear to the developer.

All local planning authorities have a statutory duty to prepare a development plan for their areas to act as a general statement of their policies and provide a basis for the consideration of applications for planning permission. The incorporation of Section 54A into the 1990 Act in 1991 has increased the status of the development plan as a decision-making tool, because local planning authorities must now determine planning applications in accordance with the plan, unless material considerations indicate otherwise. It follows from this, that an authority with a strong commitment to achieving a barrier-free environment in the widest sense of this definition, would need to incorporate access policies in its development plan as part of an overall strategy for urban design in their area.

Studies have found (Imrie and Wells, 1993; Manley, 1995) that the way in which local authorities have utilised the opportunities available within the existing statutory planning system varies in different parts of the country. Authorities have been categorised (Manley, 1995) into three main groups.

Low priority   Authorities in this group demonstrate little or no commitment to the issue and are even dilatory in pursuing their statutory duties. They regard access as a matter of 'special needs' for a small minority of the population.

Minimum statutory powers   These authorities are likely to fulfil the minimum statutory requirements, but do not pursue the idea of barrier-free environments. They tend to regard access as a technical issue concerned with gaining access to individual buildings. This approach is unlikely to include policy at the level of the district-wide plan and may give little or no consideration to means of improving the spaces between buildings.

Rights-based approach   These local authorities are much more proactive and pursue the objective of achieving barrier-free environments as a universal need. They are more likely to have accepted that access is a basic human right and one which cannot be denied without prejudicing the quality of life of many people.

It is evident from the research carried out that the majority of local authorities in England and Wales fall into the second category: the pursuance of access issues largely as an administrative or technical task. This approach retains undesirable overtones of the able-bodied professional prescribing and dispensing provision as a charitable act to the less fortunate. The authorities which fall into the third group, pursuing a more proactive approach, are predominantly situated in the London area, the metropolitan districts, and other city locations. These authorities are taking a 'bottom-up' approach to the development of policy and are attempting to influence public opinion and ultimately government policy by their actions. In some cases authorities have met resistance from central government and have been required to amend or 'water down' policies which have strayed too close to being a back door method of achieving a more effective set of building regulations (Frankum, 1992). Rural authorities, even those with large elderly populations, who are more likely to have mobility problems, are unlikely to have adopted a proactive approach. Considerable scope exists for improvements in these areas, particularly in the field of raising the awareness of local authority staff and councillors to the need to consider access issues as a key aspect of their work.

From the study of local authorities a checklist of matters which might be considered as essential elements of a proactive approach has been devised. It could be used to find out how a particular planning authority's approach compares with this list with a view to lobbying for change. Alternatively, it might prove useful to a local authority wishing to judge its own performance against a set of criteria. It is produced in the form of recommendations for good practice. Clearly, to be completely effective, policies for achieving a barrier-free environment need to be part of an overall strategy for design in the area which forms part of the development plan. The list neverthe-

less gives some suggestions for good practice in relation to policy-making for a barrier-free environment. Although it could be argued that the design of individual buildings is a matter for public control at the stage of consideration of Building Regulations applications and is not therefore of interest at the planning stage, it is often too late for the planner to convince designers to approach their design from the point of view of universal access at this late stage in the design process. The following guidelines in the checklist can therefore only be effective if they are linked to a commitment to ensure that each designer of individual buildings has universal design in mind and takes opportunities to link the new development to the existing pattern of streets and spaces.

Checklist for policy makers

1   *Appoint an access officer* to act as a catalyst for action within the authority. The access officer should have a reasonable time allocation for undertaking tasks, some status within the organisation and should, if possible, be a disabled person or have some experience of coping with an inaccessible built environment.

2   *Include access policies* in the development plan as part of a wider urban design strategy. Incorporate access policies as an integral part of the planning and urban design framework for the area. The range of topics covered should be comprehensive, including access to housing, leisure, transport and the public realm.

3   *Consult people with disabilities* on policy decisions. Encourage the formation of access groups and committees. Set a committee of the council with specific responsibility for access or equal opportunity issues.

4   *Check applications for compliance* Check all planning applications and Building Regulations applications to ensure that new development is as accessible as possible and meets current legislative requirements as a minimum. Refuse applications where necessary and be prepared to fight planning appeals. Use planning obligations to secure better access in new developments.

5   *Produce design guides* for developers to assist in the dissemination of good practice. Ensure that site-specific guidance in the form of planning or development briefs or urban design statements includes access requirements.

6   *Raise awareness of disability issues* for staff throughout the authority, for developers who habit-

ually work in the area and for the public as a whole by a combination of staff training, auditing, awareness days and other appropriate methods.

7 *Produce action plans* Conduct building audits and prepare programmes of works to improve access to public buildings. Allocate a percentage of the annual budget for necessary works to such buildings. Conduct access audits in the public realm as a basis for action plans to improve the quality of the pedestrian environment by making public spaces safer, cleaner, more aesthetically pleasing and more accessible.

Design in the public realm – the role of the planning system

It is important to recognise that ensuring that access is provided to individual buildings is only part of the role and responsibility of local authorities, even though the legislation is focused in this way. The spaces between buildings, streets and spaces, squares and parks also need to be barrier-free if people with disabilities are to achieve greater freedom of movement. Bearing in mind that urban design has a strong focus on the design of the public realm, this aspect of design for barrier-free environments will form the main substance of the remainder of this chapter.

One of the key difficulties in attempting to create a more accessible public realm relates to the lack of overall control of the organisations which shape it, many of which may have little or no interest in ensuring barrier-free streets. Local authorities, in their role as the highway authority, may be the most influential force in shaping the public realm, but the actions of statutory undertakers, utility companies and developers may all be involved. The diversity of the arrangements for the provision of utilities and the privatisation of some of the key statutory undertakers, such as gas, electricity, water and telephone, has made control over the design of the public realm even more difficult than hitherto. In theory, legislation is in place to control the standard of work carried out to lay cables and other services, but, in practice, local authorities do not have the resources to check street works. The consequence is temporary barriers to movement which are often inadequately marked to warn pedestrians of the obstruction. In some cases poorly-laid paving and other reinstatement works may be permanent and possibly dangerous obstructions to movement. The fact that much of this work can be carried out under the permitted development rights laid down by the Town and Country Planning (General Permitted Development Order) 1995, and thus does not require formal permission, makes it almost impossible for a local authority to exert complete control over the accessibility of streets.

The duties of a local authority under planning control in relation to providing barrier-free environments are currently limited in scope, but this does not absolve the authority from responsibility. Although the legisla-

Figure 9.5 Temporary barriers to movement are hazardous but the effects of street works may become permanent if paving is poorly reinstated. (Sandra Manley)

tive framework may be flawed, it is important to be aware that much can be achieved by persuasion as well as using legislation. The preparation of urban design schemes for key areas of the town or city can include consideration of ways of improving the quality of the pedestrian environments. One way of raising public awareness of the need for barrier-free design for both buildings and streets is through the conduct of access audits. If effectively organised and managed audits can:

- Raise awareness of the existence of barriers to movement
- Raise awareness of the way in which barriers affect people with different types of mobility impairment
- Give an appreciation of the importance of detailed design considerations which may appear trivial, but can render a building or street inaccessible
- Provide a basis for the production of a prioritised action plan designed to remove barriers based on a rolling programme of works
- Provide valuable information for people with impairments by identifying accessible and inaccessible routes, spaces and buildings
- Contribute to the development of policies and strategies designed to improve access
- Provide concrete evidence of the existence of barriers and make it possible to compare performance over time and between different buildings or areas, thus providing ammunition for those who are mounting campaigns for the removal of barriers.

Building audits

The conduct of access audits has tended to focus on the assessment of access to particular buildings. Since 1993 local authorities have been required by the Audit Commission, as part of the Citizens' Charter legislation, to determine the degree of accessibility of the buildings in their control. The intention of this requirement is to enable citizens to answer the question 'How easy is it for disabled people to use council buildings?' and to make comparisons of performance.

In response to this requirement, and with the intention of ensuring consistency of approach, The Access Committee for England (1992a and b) produced a checklist of matters to investigate, based primarily on the content of the Building Regulations. The Centre for Accessible Environments (Fearns, 1993) have also produced a useful audit kit which suggests ways of producing an action plan for barrier removal as part of the outcome of the audit process. This approach is a useful one which could be linked to the normal

maintenance budget for the building, so that low-cost solutions, such as improving colour contrast to aid visually impaired people, could be implemented under the normal maintenance regime.

Audits of the public realm

Conducting access audits of the public realm seems to have been less well developed than the audit of individual buildings. Early work by Norwich City Council in the 1960s identified barriers to movement in great detail and provided a useful source of information for disabled people. Possibly the impetus for the continuation of the audit process as a technique was given a low priority as the need to accommodate the ever increasing volume of road traffic became one of the dominant considerations of almost every local authority. Walking as an activity and as a means of gaining access to buildings, goods and services seemed to become a minority interest at that time. More recently there has been an increased awareness of the need to encourage walking, cycling and easy access to public transport. Indeed, local authorities are now being exhorted by central government (PPG13, 1994) to consider the encouragement of means of transport other than the private motor vehicle as an essential element of the move towards more sustainable towns and cities. If the encouragement of walking is to be successful, it is of course essential for the public realm to be safe, pleasant and above all accessible to everyone.

Conducting an audit of the public realm

Some local authorities, such as the former Avon County Council, centred on the city of Bristol, have commenced the development of a systematic pedestrian policy which is linked to the idea of making the city more legible to all users. In the case of Avon, the policy was based on the conduct of access audits by planning and engineering staff and by the involvement of students at the University of the West of England. To act as a basis for systematic recording of information a checklist of matters to be considered was developed in conjunction with local groups representing people with disabilities, as well as other interest groups. A programme of staff training ensured that the auditors would have an understanding of the audit method and its purpose.

Reviving the idea of audits in the public realm may be opposed by some councillors and officials because of the possible costs involved in removing barriers. It

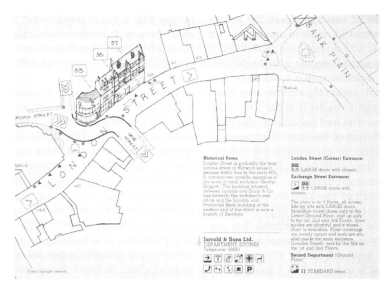

Figure 9.6 Norwich: the results of comprehensive audits of the public realm were made available to people with disabilities long before many local authorities had considered the issue of barrier-free environments at all.

is interesting to note that discussions with disabled people often reveal relatively modest requirements. For example, the removal of high kerbs and their replacement with well designed dropped crossing points can make the difference between being confined to home and being able to visit local shops and facilities. Poorly maintained street surfaces and inadequate street lighting are often mentioned by pedestrians as a major problem and the number of recorded accidents to pedestrians seems to bear out these concerns. It is therefore important to realise that conducting an audit as a means of highlighting the difficulties which may impede pedestrian use does not necessarily mean that major works have to be undertaken.

There are a number of alternative ways of conducting an audit of the public realm. One method, which has been employed successfully with student groups, delegates at short courses and groups of disabled people is to use a simple notation to record obstructions in the public realm.

The audit process, which can be conducted either alone or with colleagues, consists of the following steps:

1 Obtain a scale plan of the area to be studied. If participants are unfamiliar with plans a larger scale is preferable. It may be necessary to explain some mapping conventions.
2 Provide each auditor with coloured marker pens, clipboard, paper, measuring tape and a checklist of matters to note.

Figure 9.7 Students from the University of West of England, Bristol, conducting an access audit. (Sandra Manley)

3 Brief the participants by discussing the content of the checklist. Participants can be invited to add additional matters to be considered and hence gain a sense of ownership of the audit checklist.
4 Divide participants into pairs or small groups and commence the exercise.
5 Return to base. Information can be plotted onto a plan by participants. Discussion of outcome of the process.

Figure 10.2 Public transport systems are still failing to provide vehicles and services which meet women's needs in terms of accessibility and safety. (The London Transport Unit for Disabled Passengers)

organisations concerned with women and planning issues, established the London Women and Planning Group (LWPG). The aim of the group was to provide a support network, an information exchange, and a collective voice, with which to try to influence policy and practice on matters of concern to women in the capital. In July 1990, LWPG organised a one-day conference entitled *'Shaping our Borough – Women and Unitary Development Plans'*. The main themes of housing, shopping, leisure and community facilities, environment, employment and transport were discussed and recommendations were drawn up to try to influence future policies. LWPG has subsequently been monitoring the extent to which London boroughs have included the recommendations from this conference in individual authorities' Unitary Development Plans, and members have been reporting how women-focused policies within UDPs are being enforced through the procedures of planning applications and appeals. Since January 1994, the LWPG has held quarterly London Women and Planning Forum (LWPF) meetings to discuss topical planning issues of concern to women and reports of these meetings have been published as part of Women's Design Service's Broadsheet Series (WDS, BS).

Support for women-focused planning policies has also come from the Royal Town Planning Institute's (RTPI) Equality Panel, which has been active in outlining strategies for benefiting women. In 1989 the RTPI Women's Group produced the report *Planning for Choice and Opportunity*, and in 1995 it issued the Practice Advice Note No. 12: *Planning for Women*, which aimed to '...clarify how policies can unwittingly discriminate against particular groups such as women

and how members of the Institute can use their influence in the public, private and voluntary sectors to promote good planning practice sensitive to the needs of women' (p. 1).

During the 1970s and 1980s, a network of organisations was established throughout Britain, committed to addressing issues of inequality and diversity in the planning and architectural design process. These organisations collectively form the Association of Community Technical Aid Centres (ACTAC). Most technical aid agencies include among their objectives raising awareness of women's issues, and Planning Aid for London (PAL) has been especially active in targeting women in their advisory work. Two agencies deal specifically with women's needs in planning and design: Matrix, a feminist architectural collective and Women's Design Service, a voluntary organisation, which is funded by the London Boroughs Grant Unit to provide information and resources for women on built environment issues. These organisations have been responsible for producing a wide range of analysis, practical advice and design guidance relating to women's use of space.

Many local authorities now have women's, equality, or access officers or units, with responsibility for coordinating and encouraging practices that will benefit women. Local women's groups and community organisations throughout Britain have also led campaigns for more accessible and safer urban environments for women. Examples include: STRIDE, who are campaigning for safe travel for women in Nottingham, and Birmingham for People, who have been working to improve their city centre environment for pedestrians, and who have established their own women's group and Women's Safety Initiative (WSI).

Part of the long-term objectives of many organisations seeking ways to democratise the process of designing the built environment has been to try to increase the numbers of women working at all levels of the planning profession and related fields, such as architecture, landscape architecture, surveying and the construction industry (Greed, 1991; Greed, 1994). There have been several educational initiatives including women-only access and special training courses (WDS BS1, p. 6). Projects and organisations have been set up, such as Women and Manual Trades (WAMT), Women As Role Models (WARM) and Women in Construction Alliance (WICA), to encourage and support women during training and entering and working in male-dominated work environments. The reasoning behind many of these initiatives is that, until the employees of these professions and industries become more representative of the communities in which they are working, they are unlikely to create environments that will accommodate people's varied lifestyles and needs. But as Clara Greed (1994) points out, merely increasing numbers of women in these fields does not necessarily mean that more egalitarian practices and policies will result. Women may have to develop more strategic methods of influencing planning and design policies for women's benefit (LWPF July 1994; WDS BS10). Despite initiatives to correct the balance, the number of women entering manual, technical and design professions so far has remained disappointingly low. There, therefore, appears to remain a strong argument that until there is more effective change in both numbers and policies, so that women's interests are better represented, there is justification for the continuation of women-focused and women-only educational and training initiatives, forums and pressure groups.

Why do women have particular needs of the urban environment?

The reasons as to why women use the built environment differently from men include traditional gender divisions of labour and the fact that women take greater responsibility for caring for children and other people and for household tasks. This can lead to women spending more time at home or in their local communities. Women also may have different travel patterns from men, involving more short trips to take children to school or to go shopping, using cross-town, rather than into-centre routes. Other factors that can impact on women's use of space are that relatively fewer women have access to cars, they have lower average incomes, and they live longer than men, which can result in them changing their requirements of the environment as they grow older (WDS BS9).

However, the legacy of the middle-class Victorian ideal of separating private and public spheres, with men working in the public arena, while women remained at home in the subordinate roles of mother, daughter, wife, is inadequate as a full explanation of women's difference. As Jos Boys (1991) points out in her essay 'Dealing with Difference', this over-emphasis on the history of middle-class housewives and the home/work divide in early feminist social analysis, was developed from the influence of the American Women's Movement's portrayal of white suburban society in the 1960s. It ignores and marginalises the histories of other women, particularly working class, Black and Third World women, whose experiences within British society have often been heroic struggles to establish and secure decent homes for themselves and their families. These women cannot be perceived

as necessarily experiencing home as a prison, where they are suppressed by chauvinist husbands, or crushed by the weight of kitchen gadgetry. Boys argues that neither should the designed environment be regarded simply as a straightforward response by designers to the demands of the dominant culture, but that we need to develop 'a richer history of the built environment as a shifting and contested response by designers to issues not just of gender, but of class, culture and national identity' (Boys, 1991, p. 254).

The built environment does not affect all women identically. Women's experiences of inequality are varied and changes in social circumstances can alter women's experiences through time. While it may be true that in general women's lifestyles mean that they experience the built environment differently from men, certain groups of women, women from Black and minority ethnic communities, older women, lesbians, women with disabilities and women with children, experience and use the environment in ways that require a more individual analysis.

Changing economic patterns have meant that women are entering paid employment in increasing numbers, particularly on a part-time basis, which increases their range of responsibilities and widens their patterns of movement. Some women's lives have significantly broken away from traditional gender roles and some working women may now find that they have more common experiences with their male colleagues than with women in caring and domestic roles. Conversely, women in caring roles may have more in common with men who have taken on caring responsibilities than with women in professional employment. Analysis of the urban environment in terms of gender is useful only when the interaction of other factors such as class, race, age and individual social and economic circumstances are taken into account.

This diversity of women's experience and requirements within the built environment has created a dilemma for built environment professionals seeking to focus attention on issues of concern to women. They must avoid the trap of confirming stereotypes or projecting too homogeneous an image of women, while at the same time continuing to tackle some of the basic issues which undoubtedly continue to affect many women's lives, such as the lack of childcare facilities or the continuing problem of safety in the streets. For example, if one argues that women use the environment differently because their daily patterns of activity are shaped by caring or domestic responsibilities, one is encouraging images of women as domestically based carers. Similarly, if safety is cited as an important issue in planning urban environments for women, because of their fear or experience of being attacked, this may reinforce notions of women as timid victims, rather than focusing on the fears for their personal safety felt by many sections of the population. One strategy to avoid this problem is to work towards developing more humanitarian urban policies rather than regarding women as having 'special needs'.

Women often bear the brunt of poor environments because multiple disadvantages, caused by wider gender inequalities, reduce their ability to choose where they live or work. These disadvantages include: economic dependency on men, low income, disability, cultural or ethnic isolation, lack of training or work opportunities and responsibility for dependents. The 'feminisation of poverty' has become a pressing issue (McDowell, 1992). Those pressing for greater equality for women need to seek to have these issues reclaimed and dealt with by society as a whole. In the meantime, it remains the case that it is most often women who are disadvantaged by having to cope with caring and domestic responsibilities in hostile or inappropriate environments, and it is this reality that has to be addressed.

Residential neighbourhoods

Women tend to spend considerable time in and around their homes because of caring and domestic responsibilities, their lack of access to cars, and work patterns that are often part-time or home-based. So the quality of housing and local neighbourhood is a particularly important determinant of both opportunity and lifestyle for women. However, it is hard to separate issues of urban design from other factors that affect environmental quality, such as those connected to housing density, space standards, allocation policies, local amenities and public consultation strategies.

Studies of housing forms and internal layouts in the architecture of social housing have shown the extent to which these, historically, have been designed to conform to class and gender stereotypes, and prescriptive notions of the nuclear family (Matrix, 1984; Roberts, 1991). Although there appears to be growing awareness on the part of some professionals of the diverse range of household structures in today's society, there is little evidence in the conformist design of most new build housing schemes, that either reflects or allows for cultural differences. Few social housing units are flexible enough to accommodate future expansion or changes within households, or are accessible to people with mobility difficulties, although these factors affect most people in the course of their lives. Also, the recent lowering of space standards within units to increase housing density has resulted in dwellings that are inadequate to accommodate the most basic of family activities, such as sitting down around a table for a meal (Kahn and Sheridan, 1994). This lack of innovation represents a missed opportunity, and accounts of imaginative schemes for cooperative housing in other parts of Europe and the USA (Franck, 1994; Woolley, 1994) have suggested a richer source of models for housing design.

Good residential neighbourhoods for women are those which not only provide appropriate spatial arrangements in individual units, but are also compatible with affordability and the availability of adequate local amenities, such as public transport, schools, health and leisure facilities, shops, and convenient employment and training opportunities. It is usually the close proximity of these amenities that can enable women to manage the multiple roles of caring and earning that they are increasingly undertaking. However, in appraising housing policies within London, women planners have reported that policies relating to affordable housing on the whole appear to be less difficult to include than those policies relating to mixed land-use and space standards (LWPF, January 1994; WDS BS7).

However good the design and planning of residential environments, these are unlikely to be successful in determining a safe and well-functioning neighbourhood, unless the design is supported by a range of social policies that enable social balance and prevent the ghettoising of communities. There have been numerous failures of well-intentioned residential developments in the past, created by housing policies that have concentrated the poorest families in urban areas and housing estates, where there are few employment opportunities and no social or community facilities. Social commentators have already warned of the downward spiralling effect on the whole local environment that can occur through a high concentration of unemployment, deprivation and disadvantage, as witnessed in Benwell, Newcastle (Campbell, 1995; Clarke, 1995). One of the few ways currently open to planning authorities to halt large-scale urban degeneration is to apply for central government funding. Government funding schemes for regeneration are usually conditional on a demonstration of 'partnerships' between the local authorities and other developers with the community. Women tenants have often been prepared to put in many hours of unpaid work as members of project teams, in order to make these partnerships a reality, and in the hope that they can influence the quality and design of their neighbourhoods to better meet the needs of themselves and their families. Myrna Margulies Breitbart and Ellen-J Pader (1995) have described how women's long history of involvement in community and voluntary work, particularly in housing transformation schemes, which has contributed so much to the quality and stability of our society, has rarely received the acknowledgement it deserves. Unfortunately, under the current competitive system for urban funding, if the bids lose, much of the hard work put in by women is wasted, but even winning projects can bring frustration and disappointment when the limitations and deficiencies of available resourcing become apparent. Also, although women's involvement is often taken for granted at lower levels of project organisation, women are often not included or consulted during higher level decision-making on urban design issues (LWPF, April 1995; WDS BS15).

There is currently a great deal of discussion taking place about 'sustainable settlements', based on the concept of economically and ecologically integrated urban arrangements. Sustainable settlements aim to create a mix of use which avoids the need for long journeys to work and thus the necessity for car ownership. Large residential areas would therefore be broken up in favour of mixed use (Blowers, 1993). This is an approach that has been long advocated by the ideals and models for women-friendly housing developments (Hayden, 1980, 1984) as it makes better use of human resources as well as being more environmentally friendly.

Women and town centres

In Britain during the sixties and seventies, ownership of the private car rose dramatically and planning departments' response to the demands of car drivers resulted in many of our town centre areas becoming dominated by the preoccupation to keep traffic moving at all costs. During the seventies, eighties and nineties the convenience of the motorist has been further catered to by planning permission being granted to develop out-of town and edge-of-town shopping centres. This led to the closure of many small retail units in old town centres and the decline of many local shopping areas. These changes have been detrimental to the quality of traditional town centres for the local resident and pedestrian and the situation is only just beginning to be recognised and seriously addressed through government legislation and local planning policy (PPG6, PPG13, DoE, DoT, 1994). Meanwhile, the continuing practice of creating traffic-prioritising 'red routes' through some urban areas is still dividing many local town centres in half.

The main sufferers from traffic-blighted town centres are women. Women travel to town centres more frequently than men because they are mainly responsible for household tasks, such as food and clothes shopping (Bowlby, 1989). As women are less likely to own or have access to cars, they frequently walk to shops or use public transport. A typical shopping trip

Figure 10.3 Housing quality affects women particularly because they spend more time at home and have more caring and domestic responsibilities than men. Here a front garden provides an opportunity for informal socialising. (Sue Cavanagh)

for women, possibly laden down with heavy bags or pushing children in pushchairs, can include being forced down dark and dirty subways or over foot-bridges, along air-polluted, narrow pavements cluttered with street furniture and obstructed by goods and advertising overspilling from shops.

Within shops and other public buildings, space organisation can also be thoughtlessly obstructive for women. There are often unnecessary stairs to entrances and narrow or rotating doors that are treacherous for women with small children, and for people with disabilities. Maternity or children's departments are often located on the upper floors, where women further discover that there are no toilets or baby-changing facilities, and find that the store restaurant does not allow breast-feeding and does not provide highchairs.

Having put up with these inconveniences long enough, some women have worked with planning authorities and other organisations on campaigns to try to improve access and amenities in traditional shopping centres. The We Welcome Small Children Campaign is a national organisation which provides local guides to those shops that provide good access and facilities for children and their carers. In 1988 they joined forces with Women's Design Service and the planning department at Camden Council to produce a publication *Thinking of Small Children – Access Provision and Play* (WDS, 1988), which contained the first guidelines, aimed at planners, architects and managers of town centres, for providing an environment based on the space and circulation requirements of a carer and a double pushchair. This project was inspired by the success of the disability organisations in bringing the space requirements of people with disabilities, especially wheelchair users, to public attention. In 1989 local women and planners in Haringey launched their 'Open Sesame Campaign' which aimed to raise awareness of the access problems of women as carers in the local shopping centre.

The media have generally been sympathetic to campaigns aimed at improving public amenities for carers and children. In 1992, *The Daily Telegraph* launched the Parent Friendly Campaign in conjunction with St Thomas's Hospital, which took up the issue of encouraging large stores, supermarkets and other public buildings to provide adequate customer facilities for children and their carers. The campaign made awards to the best companies and exposed the worst. Campaigns like this have helped to raise public awareness, which, in turn, does seem to have led to a more sympathetic approach by some of the larger retailing companies, supermarkets and shopping centres to providing facilities, such as shoppers' crèches and baby-changing facilities. Some city councils have made an effort to plan better facilities for children and carers. Edinburgh District Council now has a Child-Friendly Officer, and York and Leicester City Councils have initiated child-friendly award schemes.

Although shopping is usually the main activity in a town centre, it is important not to regard town centres simply as retail areas. A good town centre will provide a mixture of public services and facilities for socialising and leisure activities for women, such as libraries, advice centres, health facilities, cinemas, restaurants and cafés. A variety of activities can contribute towards people's safety, particularly after shops have closed. Pedestrianisation of parts of town centres, removing the threat of accidents and the pollution of heavy traffic, is generally regarded favourably by women, providing these areas are well used at night (Comedia, 1991; LWPF, October 1994; WDS, BS12).

In recent years, there has been an increase in the number of covered shopping malls. This has had the effect of isolating and marginalising other public buildings as users of the malls are disinclined to leave the mall to shop or use other facilities elsewhere. The increasingly cartel-like domination of national and international retail companies in the more popular centres has also meant that less affluent, more specialised retailers and service providers are squeezed out. This leads to a lack of variety which can discriminate against shoppers from different minority ethnic groups, and those with low incomes who seek skilled services to mend, rather than replace objects and machinery. In addition, some local authorities have moved their public advice and administration buildings, such as town halls, to locations away from town centres, which has not helped the balance of retail and public services in town centres (LWPF, October 1994; WDS BS12).

One of the main problems with town and shopping centres, identified by women in the GLC *Town Centres and Shopping Attitudes Survey* (1986), and substantiated since by individual local authority surveys, is the lack of appropriate public conveniences. Research undertaken by Women's Design Service in the late 1980s discovered that women have never been consulted about the design of public toilets. Women's main complaints were: there were not enough public conveniences and many existing conveniences were under threat of closure, they were often inconveniently sited down or up flights of stairs and sometimes on traffic islands; internal space in cubicles was insufficient; and conveniences frequently did not have baby-changing facilities. Most women said they avoided using automatic public conveniences, which have been replacing supervised street conveniences, because they were

Figure 10.4 and 10.5 Inconvenient Victorian public conveniences are now being replaced by even less convenient automatic toilets. Neither of these have nappy changing facilities. (Sue Cavanagh)

frightened they would be trapped inside or exposed by the door opening automatically. They also thought automatic conveniences were too small to take children in, and that they were often out of use, or in an unhygienic condition (Cavanagh and Ware, 1990).

There is now an active national campaigning group All Mod Cons, which seeks to improve public convenience provision by making it a statutory requirement for local authorities to provide public conveniences in town centres and other public areas. There have already been improvements to the building regulations (BS 6465) in response to the growing awareness that as women take almost twice as long to use toilets than men they should be provided at a minimum ratio of 2:1 to men's in new facilities (Cavanagh and Ware, 1990). However, the overall decline in the number of public conveniences provided by local authorities continues. Without legislation to ensure that local authorities provide enough well-located, supervised facilities, with good internal space standards and baby-changing facilities available to male and female carers, women will continue to suffer from inadequate toilet facilities in public places.

Planning for women's safety

The importance of design to the issue of women's personal safety in public places has been controversial and much debated. Women's Design Service is one of the organisations that has argued consistently against overstated claims for 'designing out crime' and has stressed the need to address the social and economic causes of sexist, racist, violent and criminal behaviour (Ware, 1988; WDS BS8). The issue is clouded by the fact that most violence towards women takes place in their own homes and by persons known to them, and confused by figures that show most people who are attacked in public are men. Nevertheless, it is important not to allow these facts to become excuses for denying or diminishing the real limitations to women's activities, caused by fears for their personal safety in public places. Such fears are rarely groundless, they are usually based on women's actual previous experiences of violence, harassment and abuse either of themselves, or of people they know. Many incidents are never reported to police and therefore remain hidden from the authorities while influencing women's attitudes (LWPF, April 1994; WDS BS8).

Safety on housing estates and in residential areas can particularly affect women, as has been explained above (Ware, 1988). The lives of certain groups of women can also be particularly affected by safety issues. Black women and women from racial minorities may face the additional threat of racial harassment, lesbians may experience homophobic harassment and assaults, and older women and women with disabilities may feel they are less able to avoid or escape from threatening situations. Women do perceive themselves as being at risk in particular spaces and at specific times of the day. The combinations of certain physical features, such as poor lighting, obscured corners and lack of natural surveillance can offer greater opportunities for abuses of power: violence, harassment, robbery or assault, which are usually directed at women or people perceived as being weaker than the abuser.

Figure 10.6 and 10.7 Environments which prioritise cars often create unsafe routes for women pedestrians, for example, flyovers and subways, which deter women from going out at night. (Sue Cavanagh)

There is some evidence that improvement in the physical environment can, in certain circumstances, lead to decreased incidence of crime and personal attacks. Kate Painter (1988/89) has investigated the effects of improved street lighting in certain areas and found that improved street lighting did result in a significant decrease in women's fear of going out at night. But there is increasing evidence that physical and design solutions alone are usually not enough to solve the problem. In a series of interviews carried out by Gill Valentine (1991), women described how the social relationships within a space, and knowing the groups who controlled that space, can have a greater influence on how safe women feel than the physical design of that space. A Safe Neighbourhoods Unit's report on crime prevention has indicated that it is fear of violence, rather than fear of property crimes, that most concerns people. However, this report also stresses that although most design improvements can play a part in increasing community safety, these need to be accompanied by local initiatives which support families, create better educational opportunities and improve facilities for young people and the wider community (Osborn and Shaftoe, 1995).

The only effective way of dealing with issues concerning women and personal safety is through consultation with local women to develop the most appropriate policies and to determine the most pressing problems. Local knowledge, supplied and incorporated at an early stage in redevelopments, can prevent mistakes that would later endanger local residents and increase maintenance or management costs. One positive strategy is for planners to work in consultation with local women and other agencies and council departments, such as highway departments, to ensure that safety policies are consistent and thoroughly integrated with other policy areas (Pirie, 1993). A good example of the effectiveness of local consultation occurred on a housing estate in Birmingham, where it had been proposed to erect a high wall along a lonely stretch of road as part of a new estate street layout. Women from the local safety group were able to convince the city council planners and engineers to change the plans for a wall to one for railings, which allows better natural surveillance of the street from the adjacent buildings. Railings were subsequently installed.

People usually feel more confident when there are other people around. Bill Hillier has used a technique called 'Configuration Analysis', developed at the University of London, to show how movement correlates negatively with crime incidence. Sealed-off housing estates which have less pedestrian movement

Figure 10.8 Women's Design Service has devised a process of conducting community safety audits, which enable women and young people to express their concerns about the design of their local neighbourhoods, and to put forward suggestions for improvements. (Sue Cavanagh)

are more susceptible to crime and more likely to be sites of crime (Ostler, 1994). This research supports the argument proposed by Jane Jacobs in *The Death and Life of American Cities* back in 1961, that, to make city streets safe, segregated housing developments should be abandoned, and planners should return to more traditional layouts where buildings overlook the street. Some local authority planning policies are already opposing 'fortress' style housing schemes, which are secluded from public thoroughfares and make surrounding areas even less safe (LWPF, April 1994; WDS BS8).

Into the future

Like the popular 1960s myth in Britain about the approaching leisure age, any optimism once felt by feminists that an egalitarian genderless society could be speedily achieved, has now faded. It is now at least ten years since most of the key issues for improving conditions for women in urban environments were identified, and although some progress has been made in getting these issues included in planning policies, there continue to be problems in implementation. Any advance made in one direction often appears to be cancelled out by a decline in public facilities or services elsewhere. For example, there are more baby-changing facilities in supermarkets, but reductions in local government budgets have led to closure of more local authority public toilets. A low-floor accessible bus has been designed and is operating in some suburban areas, but there are fewer conductors to help people onto older-style buses. If more overall improvements are to be achieved in the future, cutbacks which detrimentally affect women's lives will have to be more rigorously resisted.

The urban design issues of concern to women, as I have tried to show, are rarely related to women's biology, but are thrust upon them as a result of their gender role within society. Real advances will depend on women gaining social and economic equality with men in all spheres of life, and on more democratic and egalitarian policy decision processes. In the meantime, the reality of women's everyday experiences needs to be better understood by professionals involved in urban design. Even women professionals sometimes find it hard to appreciate the circumstances many of the poorest women in our society experience, and the frustration they feel from the lack of control or choice they have over many aspects of their lives.

The key to any real future improvements for women in urban planning is to work with women to create and develop the types of communities and places that they want to live in, and to increase the number of women at all levels of policy and decision-making. It also means recognising the limitations of short-term and individual physical design solutions for improving the quality of people's lives, and working towards integrating good-quality design in the environment with long-term strategic planning to equip local communities with sufficient resources to prosper.

11 Planning for crime prevention

Henry Shaftoe

Public perceptions

Carry out a social survey on users' perception of the quality of life in any built environment and crime will almost inevitably figure at the top of the list of concerns. People want to feel safe both at home and in public places. In the light of substantially rising crime rates over the last twenty-five years, the public desire for personal safety and protection from predatory crime has become an overriding precursor to most other urban design and planning considerations. Why have an efficient night-time public transport system if many people are frightened to leave their homes after dark? Why design a new civic square if it is going to be monopolised by threatening gangs of youths and debilitated by vandalism and graffiti?

We clearly need to address the problems of urban crime and insecurity if we are to improve the quality of life in our cities and built environments. But how can we do this? Is this a job solely for the police and the criminal justice system or is there a link between planning and neighbourhood crime? Can good urban design improve community safety? In this chapter we will look at the evidence for and against a link between design and crime and we will then propose some practical measures, where planning and urban design can have a contributory role in the creation of safer communities.

Before we do this we need to define the nature, location and extent of the problem.

Crime and insecurity

Everybody knows what crime is, but we tend to objectify it, creating in our minds a kind of monolithic beast that stalks every corner of our life and environment. In reality crime is at once much more mundane and a much more complex phenomenon. At the mundane level crime is merely a rag-bag of actions (or inactions) that have been defined as offensive by law makers. Yet this is precisely why an understanding of causes and effects becomes so complex. The only common link between drunken brawls outside city centre pubs, shop-lifting, drug-dealing and graffiti-spraying is that they could all be defined as criminal. A measure that can explain and resolve one type of crime problem may have no effect on, or even exacerbate, another type of crime problem.

Some crimes, such as credit card fraud and business corruption have only the most tenuous links to location. But the crimes which are quantitatively (if not qualitatively) the most substantial: burglary, assaults, criminal damage and vehicle crime, are neighbourhood- or location-specific. It is these crimes, therefore, that may be amenable to control via changes in the physical environments where they occur, and we will appraise this hypothesis shortly in this chapter. First, however, we need to clarify three interlinked background issues that can inform our response: fear, levels and the geography of crime.

Fear of crime is currently as big a problem as actual victimisation. Many people (particularly women, the elderly and people from ethnic minorities) live in constant fear for their safety, their anxiety often fuelled by sensationalist media reporting. Although this is a feeling, it has very real consequences as these people avoid using certain areas and impose their own curfews. For example, a crime audit of Nottingham (KPMG, 1990) estimated that £24 million annual turnover was being lost by the city centre retail and leisure sector as a result of people avoiding the area for fear of crime.

The fear of crime is often irrational in terms of victimisation risk – for example elderly people face a much lower risk of being mugged than young males, who tend to be in the wrong place at the wrong time (for example city centres at pub closing time and after football matches). Women are more likely to be attacked at home by someone they know than by a stranger in the street. Of course, it is not just the quantity of risk that affects people differently, but the quality of the likely effect on the potential victim. Young males may brush off an assault as being part of the hurly-burly of macho football culture, whereas a similar level of violence aimed at an elderly woman is likely to have drastic physical and emotional consequences. Fear can also be perfectly realistic, depending on where you are, because levels of crime vary dramatically according to area. Official figures show that you are 14 times more likely to have your home burgled if you live on a run-down urban council estate than if you live in a rural area (Mayhew and Maung, 1992; Mayhew et al., 1994). And risks of robbery can vary dramatically between various locations – even allowing for the (dramatic) differences in population density, you are still 50 times more likely to be mugged in London than you are in mid-Wales. Finally, actual levels of crime have been increasing consistently for many years (Mayhew, ibid) so it is quite understandable that people in general are becoming more fearful. Rather alarmingly, though, in Holland, where the actual level of crime has stabilised over the last few years, the fear of crime has continued to rise.

One of the clear conclusions we can draw from the statistics, is that crime is an overwhelmingly urban phenomenon. Broadly speaking, the larger the conurbation the greater the per capita crime rate. One method of reducing crime might therefore be to disperse the population into small rural centres; but as 80 per cent of Europe's population now lives in urban areas this would be an uphill struggle even if it were politically acceptable. However, there may be other ways that smaller communities can be created within big cities, as we shall see later.

What went wrong?

As we have seen – and probably personally experienced – crime and insecurity have steadily risen in the postwar period. Who is to blame? What has caused this breakdown in law and order. In desperation, politicians and the general public have sought a number of scapegoats,

one of which has been the brutalising quality of many buildings and their surroundings.

A number of planned environments of the last 40 years have produced unforeseen criminogenic side effects. Notable examples of this are single-use area zoning, which has resulted in various parts of conurbations being unoccupied at certain times of the day or week, and traffic/pedestrian segregation schemes (such as Radburn housing layouts and pedestrian subways) which have provided more opportune locations for street crime and offender escape routes. The Radburn was based upon the laudable principle of separating traffic from pedestrians in housing developments. An access road and garaging would be provided down one side of a row of houses, which on the other side would front on to a purely pedestrianised area, characterised by gardens, communal spaces, and footpaths. Unfortunately, this has resulted in making many houses vulnerable to burglaries on one side and car theft on the other! As a result many Radburn estates have been reorientated to turn them back into conventional 'houses on streets'.

How they're trying to put it right

For the last 20 years, in the wake of Oscar Newman's ground breaking work on Defensible Space (Newman, 1973), crime prevention through environmental design (CPETD) has been widely promoted as a cure. Based on the findings from a controlled design improvement programme on a high-crime housing estate in the New York area, Newman proposed a system of 'defensible spaces' designed to encourage householders to supervise, and take on responsibility for the areas in which they live. He distilled this into four key design measures to overcome the failures of existing mass housing provision:

- Territoriality – the subdivision of buildings and grounds into zones of influence to discourage outsiders from entering and encourage residents to defend their areas
- Surveillance – the design of buildings to allow easy observation of the related territory
- Image – the design of public housing to avoid stigma
- Environment – the juxtaposing of public housing projects with safe zones in adjacent areas.

Although he stressed the parallel importance of social issues such as family networks, community development and good housing management in creating and maintaining safer neighbourhoods (Newman, 1974,

Figure 11.1 Radburn-style layout – Gurnos, S Wales. (Henry Shaftoe)

1995), it was Newman's first two commandments that people latched on to. These notions of territoriality and surveillance were further purified by Alice Coleman (1985), a geographer at King's College, London, who, after studying numerous English housing estates, produced a 'design disadvantagement' index against which one could measure and then rectify design faults which were supposedly 'causing' crime and antisocial behaviour. Despite a number of criticisms of such a simplistic design determinist view of crime and its prevention (for example: DoE 1997), this approach has proved to be very attractive; possibly because of its very simplicity – all you have to do is redesign buildings and communal spaces according to a fixed formula and, lo and behold, crime will wither away!

In the wake of these theories about the possibility of designing out crime, a number of guides have been produced for developers (often jointly prepared by local authority planning departments and the police, e.g.: Leicestershire, Wandsworth, Southwark, Portsmouth, Toronto).

Starting in the Southeast of England, the police-sponsored 'Secured by Design' accreditation scheme for new homes has spread rapidly throughout Britain.

If a new house meets the requirements on a police-inspired checklist (which specifies standards of lock fittings, door strengths, window construction etc.) then the building is awarded a 'Secured by Design' endorsement. This is supposed to be an attractive selling point for the property although cynics have dubbed it salvation by bricks. The key reference work upon which this approach is based is the *Police Architectural Liaison Manual of Guidance* (Home Office Crime Prevention Centre, 1994).

There is much common sense in this designing for security approach, but also a danger of overstating its impact and slipping into a design determinist philosophy whereby people are seen as mere automatons whose behaviour is entirely conditioned by the environment they find themselves in. There are examples of well designed environments where crime levels are high (for example Meadowell on Tyneside and Kirkholt in Rochdale) and 'badly' designed environments where the disadvantagement of the surroundings has not manifested itself in high levels of crime (for example Lillington Gardens in Victoria, London and many housing estates in Continental Europe).

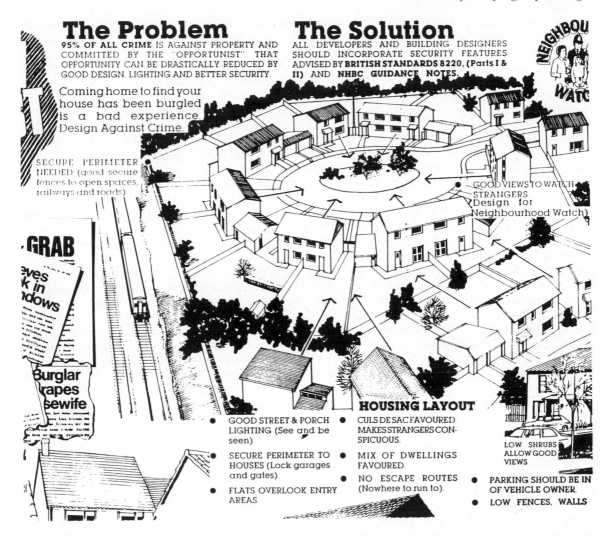

The Problem

95% OF ALL CRIME IS AGAINST PROPERTY AND COMMITTED BY THE "OPPORTUNIST". THAT OPPORTUNITY CAN BE DRASTICALLY REDUCED BY GOOD DESIGN, LIGHTING AND BETTER SECURITY.

Coming home to find your house has been burgled is a bad experience. Design Against Crime.

SECURE PERIMETER NEEDED (Good secure fences to open spaces, railways and roads)

The Solution

ALL DEVELOPERS AND BUILDING DESIGNERS SHOULD INCORPORATE SECURITY FEATURES ADVISED BY **BRITISH STANDARDS 8220, (Parts I & II)** AND **NHBC GUIDANCE NOTES.**

GOOD VIEWS TO WATCH STRANGERS (Design for Neighbourhood Watch)

- GOOD STREET & PORCH LIGHTING (See and be seen).
- SECURE PERIMETER TO HOUSES (Lock garages and gates).
- FLATS OVERLOOK ENTRY AREAS.

HOUSING LAYOUT

- CULS DE SAC FAVOURED. MAKES STRANGERS CONSPICUOUS.
- MIX OF DWELLINGS FAVOURED.
- NO ESCAPE ROUTES (Nowhere to run to).

LOW SHRUBS ALLOW GOOD VIEWS

- PARKING SHOULD BE IN OF VEHICLE OWNER.
- LOW FENCES, WALLS

Figure 11.2 Extract from 'Design Against Crime', City of Portsmouth Planning Department and Hamsphire Constabulary. (City of Portsmouth)

In 1994, for the first time, the government issued guidelines to local authority planning departments on crime prevention (Circular 5/94), and suggested a broader approach to planning out crime than merely security design and layout principles. It stresses the importance of a strategic approach based on the needs and demands of an area as a whole, collaboration with other public service agencies and the recognition of the importance of appropriate management of buildings and open spaces. The Scottish Office proselytised this principle of planning in a broader context for crime prevention in their Planning Advice Note (PAN 46, 1994). They state that

Environmental improvement alone or in conjunction with improved security measures is unlikely to be successful in preventing crime in areas which suffer from profound social and economic distress where fundamental issues such as housing management and maintenance, job creation and community development also require to be addressed. In the regeneration of these areas a wider multi agency approach including planners and the police is required. The same principle applies in areas such as town centres or industrial estates/business parks, where effective liaison arrangements between planning authorities, the police, town centre managers, chambers of commerce, local traders, selling and letting agents can be productive (PAN 46, 1994, p. 9).

Key community safety issues for urban designers and planners

As we have discussed earlier, the problems are not just associated with actual crime, but with fear of crime. Fear can restrict people's activity and use of environments. Fear and actual risk of victimisation do not necessarily correlate. Therefore, depending on the context, we may have to introduce measures that will make people feel safer, reduce actual chances of victimisation, or both. For example, improved street lighting is generally welcomed as a fear reducer but is unlikely to reduce actual crime levels (Ramsay, 1991). Creating fortified environments (such as high boundary walls and solid metal shutters) may reduce the opportunities for crime but may raise levels of fear. In many cases it will be best to encourage increased use of public and communal spaces in the hope that there will be informal social control by the law-abiding majority, rather than to try and exclude people. This approach is sometimes described as crowding out crime.

Social planning is as important as physical planning. It will be necessary to work in collaboration with other professions and users to achieve plans that integrate the social with the physical. It is no good developing a beautiful town-centre plaza if the majority of citizens avoid it because it has been taken over by homeless alcoholics and disaffected youths – usually a sign that there are inadequate activities and support services for marginalised groups in the area. In Coventry city-centre precinct there is a youth arts project which offers more constructive activities for young people than just hanging around in the precinct. In Craigmillar, Edinburgh, residents were consulted over plans to improve a small green in front of their flats. They resisted the proposal to install benches there, because they were worried it would lead to noisy late-night gatherings.

Some environmental measures introduced in one area may displace crime problems to other areas or may prompt different approaches to offending. Similarly, a heightened sense of security generated by the design of one environment (e.g. an enclosed shopping mall) may exacerbate the fear-generators in its surroundings (e.g. pedestrian access routes, car parks and service bays). Kings Lynn central area now has a comprehensive closed circuit television network which has dramatically reduced shop and car thefts, but anecdotal evidence suggests that there has been an increase in burglaries and car crime in the surrounding areas.

As we noted earlier, incidents of crime, per head of population, are much higher in urban areas. An obvious move towards a solution of our crime problems would therefore be to relocate people back into the country. There are clear political and practical obstacles to this, and planning controls on rural development further inhibit this possibility. Given that the majority of people, through destiny or choice, are likely to remain herded together in large conurbations, how can we recreate the village or sense of community, so that people know and support their neighbours and feel they have a stake in their locality? (See example 4 on page 184).

Community control can work in residential areas but in town centres, with transient users, a different approach to the stewardship of the environment is needed. One response has been the appointment of town centre managers who have a cross-boundary remit to look after both local authority and commercial interests in their areas. Town centre managers are able to coordinate (or at least consider) all the factors that can contribute to safety in areas predominantly designed for shopping and entertainment. These factors can range from design and technology (e.g. lighting and CCTV) to deployment of wardens (as in Coventry) or provision of diversionary facilities. An example of the latter can be found at the Dufferin Shopping Mall in Canada, where the manager not only introduced design changes to the communal areas but helped to set up outreach and support services for the disaffected young people and drug users who were frequenting the mall and making it feel unsafe for other customers.

Four examples of how good planning can contribute to safer environments

1 Designing for the optimum mix of uses   Balanced, stable neighbourhoods with a heterogenous mix of demography and activity reduce crime and fear, through informal social control networks and round-the-clock surveillance. This was the approach espoused by Jane Jacobs (1961) who was scathing about the single-use zoning methods adopted by planners. Such zoning means that residential areas can be underused by day and retail areas deserted at night. It is no coincidence that most burglaries are committed during the daytime and commercial break-ins during the night or at weekends. For many years, Norwich city planners have encouraged small city-centre infill sites to be redeveloped with various types of residential accommodation rather than the usual commercial developments. As a result, central Norwich is nowadays well populated at all times with residents who know the area and are aware of what should and should not be happening in it.

Many large council estates with identical family housing types were built in the interwar or immediate postwar period, and a number of these estates, such as Halton Moor in Leeds and Southmead in Bristol have become high-crime areas. This is at least partly to do with the concentrations there of families living in poverty with bored children and disaffected young people. These areas are usually isolated from central social and recreational facilities so some young people make their own (illicit) entertainment or take out their frustration on the built environment.

Commercial/leisure areas with concentrations of pubs and clubs will exponentially increase the risk of certain types of crime or antisocial activity, particularly those which are fuelled by alcohol such as assaults and vandalism. The centre of Newport in South Wales was a drinking and entertainment magnet for people not only from the rest of the city but for many of the outlying villages. There were so many problems of disorder on weekend nights that the council and the police introduced strict controls on the development of further central entertainment facilities and critically reviewed the alcohol licences of existing premises. Ironically, the best approach would probably be to encourage good-quality social and recreational facilities on the outlying estates and villages. This would probably also reduce levels of car theft as late-night revellers would not have to seek motorised transport to get home!

2 Designing and maintaining to give the right psychological signals and cues   A high-quality, cared-for environment will encourage respect for that environment and its users – Newman's (1973) third key factor of image. Conversely, harsh, fortified and neglected environments may reinforce fear and actual risk. Brutal surroundings may provoke brutal behaviour, and there is a risk that increased fortification may just raise the stakes of the force and ingenuity adopted by determined miscreants.

Many modernist housing estates and urban plazas have found themselves in a deteriorating spiral of decline, precipitated in part by the stigmatising visibility of their streaked pre-cast concrete panels and other poor-quality finishes which signal cheap municipal design. Such areas have been gradually abandoned by those with sufficient wealth and influence to move elsewhere, leaving behind the poor, the powerless and the desperate. However, this spiral of physical and social decline can be reversed. Despite general rising levels of theft, robbery and drink-related violence, many banks, shopping centres and pubs have successfully gone against the grain by offering high-quality, welcoming environments in previously unpromising locations (e.g. some pubs in Brixton, South London and Castlemilk, Glasgow). In Haarlem in the Netherlands, as part of a strategy to improve safety and security, the municipality banned further fitting of closed roll-down shutters for shops and offered shopkeepers a subsidy to install see-through ones. At the same time they encouraged more landlords to rent out rooms above shops for residential occupation. The result of these two moves to create a city centre that was more 'transparent', welcoming and lived-in, was a reduction in insecurity and criminal behaviour.

Figure 11.3 This shuttered jeweller's shop in Hereford shows how physical security can look attractive, with a little imagination. (Henry Shaftoe)

Some housing areas have also been transformed, at great expense, by combined physical and social improvements (e.g. Alma Road in Enfield and Moor Lane in Preston, where tower blocks were extensively refurbished internally and externally, surrounding grounds were enclosed and landscaped, and concierges staffed the entrance lobbies on a rota basis; see DoE 1993b, and Osborn and Shaftoe, 1995 for more detail on these and other schemes). In view of the number of radical housing designs that have rapidly declined into unpopular sink estates, it is clear that architects of social housing ought to bite their tongues and provide housing that they can be sure will please their future occupants, rather than designing with a colour feature in the *Architects' Journal* in mind. Sir James Stirling's award-winning futuristic housing development at New Southgate in Runcorn had to be demolished a few years ago, such was its unpopularity. In its place a housing association has built mundane (but well-liked) pitch-roofed brick-clad houses, while the local authority is still paying off the loan on the previous housing!

3 Designing for control of environments by users   This is not just about 'ownership' and surveillance of space, but engaging users/residents in the design and development process so that they have an investment in the end result which they will wish to safeguard. Planners and urban designers may claim they do this as a matter of course through the required consultation mechanisms. However, open consultation sessions and displays of plans will often only attract and engage an unrepresentative minority of users/residents. Also, in many cases, the professionals have already predetermined their short-list of design options and users/residents may rightly feel that all they are doing is 'rubber-stamping'. A genuinely participatory approach is time-consuming and requires the professionals to relinquish their directorial role in favour of an 'enabling' one. These are difficult changes to make for experts who are working to deadlines and who have heartfelt visions of what good buildings and their environments should look like. On the plus side, participatory exercises can be very satisfying, particularly when they employ creative methods such as 'planning-for-real' developed by the Neighbourhood Initiatives Foundation. 'Planning-for-real' enables lay people to visualise their own design preferences, and to reconcile these with the priorities of others, by constructing and manipulating simple three-dimensional scenarios. It is become increasingly possible to develop computer simulations of three-dimensional environments as a consultation tool, but one has to be careful that the consultees do not feel intimidated by the glossy technology.

The participatory approach to neighbourhood design and urban regeneration is now supported by the Department of the Environment and its success can be seen at the Eldonians' Co-operative Housing Scheme in Liverpool and the Pembroke Street redevelopment and Estate Management Board in Plymouth, among many others. Both these schemes have, through the active involvement of their residents in design, redevelopment and ongoing management, transformed high-crime 'sink' estates into attractive neighbourhoods with far fewer problems of insecurity. In Edinburgh, the Niddrie House Planning and Rehabilitation Group was a resident-led organisation which, with council support, masterminded a multimillion pound estate regeneration programme which has transformed the area physically and socially. Two tower blocks were demolished, 1970s tenement blocks were remodelled, playgrounds were built, a new housing cooperative developed homes on the sites vacated by the tower blocks, a community centre and even a community shop were opened. Crime, although not vanquished, has diminished.

4 Right-sizing   As we saw earlier when comparing urban/rural victimisation rates, crime flourishes in large anonymous environments. Small, identifiable communities seem to offer better mutual support and security to their residents, and public services seem to work better when they are decentralised to manageable neighbourhoods. There appear to be a number of reasons why right-sized neighbourhoods are safer: people can identify with 'their' community and feel they have a stake in its well being; they are more likely to observe and respond to inappropriate or offensive behaviour; they are more likely to know and support their neighbours and know who to go to for help.

The idea of dividing big cities into clusters of 'villages' is, therefore, not just a whimsical pastoral notion, but has a sound crime-preventative basis and has the potential for delivering more responsive and appropriate public services. This approach has been attempted in Islington and Tower Hamlets in London, and somewhat controversially, in Walsall. This approach to creating viable and supportive small communities is espoused by Christopher Alexander in his seminal work *A Pattern Language* (1977), in which he proposes that each identifiable neighbourhood should contain a population of no more than 7,000 people.

Figure 11.4 Niddrie House Estate, Edinburgh, after refurbishment. (Henry Shaftoe)

Figure 11.5 Niddrie House community shop. (Henry Shaftoe)

A cautionary tale of planning for short-term gain but long-term problems

One approach to planning for security is the 'ghetto of privilege' whereby certain areas are designed to be self-contained reserves which can exclude undesirables. Enclosed shopping malls with security guards and CCTV could represent 'the thin end of the wedge' of privatising public space. In California there is a downtown commercial centre which can only be reached by car – there is no pedestrian or public transport access, and in Toronto the Eaton Centre, which takes up the majority of the downtown retail area, has a list of 12,000 residents who are classified as undesirable and are banned by the 50-strong rota of security guards (Poole, 1994). The American-style fortified suburb (as seen for example in Rosemount, Chicago) has spawned its first modest British counterpart in North London where the mews entrance to an exclusive development of town houses is protected by high gates. This private response to a growing sense of insecurity, if allowed by the planners to escalate, will result in an urban patchwork of areas which are 'no-go' for rich and poor alike – surely not a desirable long-term outcome?

In summary

Planning and urban design measures alone cannot significantly and durably reduce crime and insecurity. In some cases they may merely displace the problem. Layouts and designs that work in some areas can be a criminogenic disaster in others. The Tuscan hill village concept of stuccoed clusters of housing, walled gardens and winding alleyways has not worked the way the architect intended at the Maiden Lane Estate in Camden. The design of the upper west side skyscraper apartments in Manhattan does not prove to be so appealing when it is realised on a cloud-scraping hillside above Dundee. Even the nicest 'Tudorbethan' developments such as St Mellon's in Cardiff can become ghettoes of fear and discontent if their residents live in poverty and boredom.

You cannot 'design out' crime. The results of physical planning and urban design provide the backdrop

Figure 11.6 Fortified mews, Swiss Cottage, London. (Henry Shaftoe)

against which changing social activities and dynamics evolve. There is little evidence to suggest that the design of the physical environment 'determines' people's behaviour in a such a direct cause-and-effect relationship. After all, people cause crime, not environments. Social planning (involving other disciplines and agencies) should complement physical planning, so that other human needs, not necessarily directly related to shelter and the use of space, are catered for.

Design guidance for security and crime prevention is valuable but limited if it is not augmented by user-consultation and anticipation of variations in use and side effects. People are infinitely adaptable and innovative in how they respond to built environments, but they will also overrule attempts by designers to alter their preferred use of space: many implemented landscaping and circulation plans have been undermined by local people who discovered that paths do not follow their favoured routes (desire lines) and landscape features block short cuts to where they want to go. In such cases, users will sooner or later impose their own wishes, even if it involves breaking down fences or trampling muddy paths across flower beds and shrubberies. Skate-boarders in plazas and homeless alcoholics colonising benches in enclosed shopping malls are other examples of a failure to integrate design with user need and the lack of other local facilities. Putting up signs to ban certain activities or using security officers to move people on has to be an inadequate response to bad planning and lack of integration.

Built environments need to be robust but adaptable enough to accommodate changing social dynamics and demographics. Cheap-finish, mass solutions have proved to be costly (both financially and criminogenically) in the long run. Good-quality materials and human building scales (see Alexander, 1977 for an explanation of scale) signal a respect for the intended users, and this respect is generally reciprocated.

Planners and designers should resist the creation of a divided society wherein the better-off (and allegedly law-abiding) exclude the less privileged (and so-called 'criminal classes') from large tracts of the environment by privatising what were formerly public spaces. Quite apart from the social ethics of such an approach this polarisation of space can raise levels of fear and mutual suspicion.

Planners and the planning process can provide valuable components in effective approaches to preventing crime and improving community safety, which almost inevitably require long-term, strategic and multidisciplinary interventions (cf: DoE, 1993b; Osborn and Shaftoe, 1995).

An action plan

So how can we design an optimum environment for community safety – where both actual crime and fear of crime are not major problems? Firstly, we can refer to the guidelines that have been produced and are based on research, but we should not be dogmatic in interpreting them. If possible, carry out research and consultation with people who use, intend to use, or avoid the identified environment. Appraise the context: current and intended use, variations in use according to time of day, week and season, levels and types of crime in the area, external influences from adjacent areas and transport patterns. The best that can be achieved will be a built environment, supported by the optimum number of users, which is robust and adaptable enough to accommodate and absorb activities and uses which may change over time.

For example, town centre areas which have become blighted by occurrences of vandalism, theft and predatory crime may need to be revitalised by improved supervision (say by a combination of CCTV and uniformed centre wardens, as in Coventry), new facilities or accommodation to attract citizens back into the area (including integrative activities for people who might otherwise be threateningly hanging around in the centre), as well as good urban design that avoids vulnerable locations or predatory opportunities.

There is no one blueprint for a safe community but there are many pitfalls to be avoided.

Finally, there is a view that crime adds a certain 'frisson' to the vigorous dynamics of urban living (the 'mean streets' of Raymond Chandler and film noir), but it would appear that most city-dwellers prefer to experience such excitement vicariously rather than through direct risk of victimisation. Maybe in a utopian crime-free future, people will pay to go to theme parks where, instead of being scared on ghost trains, they can wander down deserted alleys with flickering street lamps and the silhouettes of sinister looking characters outlined in the dim distance!

12 The people and the process

Robert Cowan

The city

'A city is more than a place in space,' the pioneer town planner Patrick Geddes wrote, 'it is a drama in time' (Geddes, 1905). Shaping cities, Geddes believed, was a process that should involve every citizen in a learning experience which would help to give meaning to their lives.

Geddes' influence on the development of planning was profound, but his guidance on how to establish planning as a participatory process and a learning experience was largely forgotten in the years after his death. Planning became more widely practised, but on a narrower basis. It became a profession, and the professionals enjoyed their prestige and their responsibility for helping to define the public interest in matters of development. Many of the early planners were trained as architects, and much of what we now call 'urban design' was part of their familiar practice. But as planning narrowed its focus to the processes defined in the Planning Acts, it became less concerned with conceiving and designing in three dimensions.

People and Planning (Skeffington, 1969), the influential report of a parliamentary committee chaired by Arthur Skeffington MP, suggested in 1969 that planning might reflect the public interest better if the public were consulted. Many planners welcomed this. To others, the Skeffington Report looked like a threat to their professionalism, even though its vision was of the public taking part in consultative exercises pretty much on the planners' terms.

An article by American sociologist Sherry Arnstein, published in the USA (Arnstein, 1969) and two years later in the UK, helped make the debate about partici-

pation rather more sophisticated. Arnstein presented, simply and effectively, a diagrammatic 'ladder of participation'. The ladder's eight rungs represented, from the bottom: manipulation, therapy, informing, consultation, placation, partnership, delegated power, and citizen control. Arnstein classified the bottom two of these as 'non-participation'; the next three as 'degrees of tokenism'; and the top three as 'degrees of citizen power'. This simple analysis emphasised that 'participation' could mean different things in different circumstances, and that it could be used to control the public as easily as to enfranchise it.

Strangely, the debate about participation has not become much more sophisticated since then. Public 'participation', 'involvement' and 'consultation' are used more or less interchangeably, with varying definitions, and theoretical work on the subject has had little impact on practice in the UK. The most effective attempts to make participation a reality have been in response to immediate practical needs.

In the 1970s it became clear that, whatever Skeffington might have believed, the formal planning system was an inadequate mechanism for widespread and effective public participation. People committed to making the planning and development process accessible looked for alternative ways to achieve it.

One strategy that looked promising was to make use of the education system. This, it was hoped, might provide a structure enabling children and adults to participate in planning. Pioneering educators and built-environmental professionals developed the practice of environmental education, with urban studies centres and architectural workshops among their most impressive projects. Today, some teachers, planners and designers still pursue their vision of helping people to control their own surroundings through a process of learning, but their efforts are usually significant only at the margins of the planning and development processes.

During the 1970s and 1980s a succession of initiatives explored ways of making the processes of planning, design and development more widely accessible. Planners developed planning aid as a way of giving individuals and community groups the support that they needed. Architects offered community architecture to the new community clients, or tried to make local authorities' design services more accessible and responsive. Community technical aid centres flourished for a while, then declined; as with the changing fortunes of environmental education, the cause was a combination of the vicissitudes of fashion and an altered political landscape.

The main concern of the protagonists of these various initiatives was to make professional and technical expertise available to people who did not yet enjoy its benefit. For some of them, though, the processes of planning and development, and the professions which lived off them, seemed fundamentally inequitable. The aim of these activists was, and is, to support the evolution of different and fairer relationships between landowners, developers, professionals and communities.

The experience of some of the most successful community planning initiatives shows what immense efforts can be needed to build these relationships. At Coin Street, a formerly derelict, 5.2 hectare site at Waterloo on London's South Bank, a community campaign has evolved into a not-for-profit development organisation (Brindley et al., 1996). The campaign began in the early 1970s, when Waterloo's long-established residential community realised that commercial pressures could soon overwhelm it. If the Coin Street sites were redeveloped for offices and hotels, as developers were insisting, local facilities and social networks would not survive.

Coin Street Community Builders have created a riverside walkway; a park; a designer craft market; a multi-million pound, mixed-use refurbishment scheme; and three cooperative housing schemes (the latest of which has won several awards for its architecture). Further developments will follow. The achievement has taken 20 years, including two of Britain's longest-ever planning inquiries (in the run-up to one of which the local action group was operating through 24 working groups, each concentrating on a particular aspect of the campaign). The initiative might have been doomed to failure by the lack of any one of its ingredients: a strong sense of community; various regeneration grants available for community development; effective leadership; unpaid support from sympathetic professionals; physical proximity to the centres of power and the media; the Housing Corporation's particular grant regimes; and the ownership of half the site by the Greater London Council. Even today the way the community cam-

Figure 12.1 Students discussing their proposals at Drawing on Glasgow, one of the Visions for Cities series of urban design events.

paign was transformed into a development vehicle is a matter of local controversy.

The Eldonians, descendants of Irish immigrants of the 1840s living near Eldon Street in Liverpool's Vauxhall area, have had similarly spectacular success since the 1980s in equally unusual circumstances (Cowan et al., 1988). The close-knit community had been threatened with the demolition of their homes and relocation to outlying estates, and the major local employer, a sugar refinery, had closed. They won the right to stay; refurbished some of their homes; built cooperative housing and homes for elderly people in the Eldonian Village; set up a garden market, a development trust and a local enterprise agency; and persuaded the Merseyside Development Corporation to extend its boundaries. The Eldonians flourished in the teeth of opposition from Liverpool City Council, at a time when the council was controlled by the Militant Tendency, and was ideologically opposed to housing cooperatives and community enterprise. Margaret Thatcher's government was committed to doing everything it could to frustrate Militant's plans, and supporting the Eldonians through the Department of the Environment served as a useful weapon. Other ingredients of the Eldonians' success were as varied and fortuitous as at Coin Street. They included the willingness of their architect (a community architect in the full sense of the community being, not a consultee, but the client) to work for five years before being sure that he would receive any fee.

The most impressive achievements of both the Coin Street and Eldonian communities have been their tireless perseverance against what at times have seemed like overwhelming odds. These cases serve better as inspiring examples of what can be done very occasionally in exceptional circumstances than as a guide to what can be easily replicated.

A more lasting (if unintended) legacy of community action may be seen in relation to the management and improvement of council housing. A great deal of the community action of the 1970s was a response to the sometimes inefficient, insensitive and paternalistic management and replanning by local authorities of their housing estates. The message did eventually get through to many housing authorities that the energies of their tenants could be harnessed productively. In the 1980s and the first half of the 1990s progressive thinking about housing management coincided with a government that did not like the concept of local authorities as providers of housing at all. As with the Eldonians, the willingness of tenants in several other places to take charge of their own affairs fitted conveniently with government plans to transfer the ownership and management of council

estates to new organisations in which the residents were actively involved.

To people looking for ways of opening up planning, design and development, the traditional professional boundaries between architects, planners and members of other disciplines often seem an obstacle. The use of the phrase 'urban design' has increasingly become a convenient way of stepping across these professional boundaries. The origins of its widespread use today can be traced back at least to 1979, when a forum called Architects in Planning, which had been formed the previous year, became the Urban Design Group.

In some cases 'urban design' is a new name for activities that formerly came under the headings of planning, architecture or, perhaps, civic design. As a euphemism for some aspects of planning in the 1980s, it was a convenient way of putting some of the concerns of planners on the public agenda, at a time when

Figure 12.2 Poster from a community planning project in Tyne and Wear facilitated by the Neighbourhood Initiatives Foundation in the aftermath of riots on the Meadowell Estate. (Neighbourhood Initiatives Foundation publication, funded by the Joseph Rowntree Foundation)

the government had branded anything with 'planning' in its name as the work of the devil.

'Urban design' has also been adopted as the label for a number of activities which have not previously played a significant part in the statutory planning process, and in particular some in which public participation plays an important part. Urban Design Action Teams (UDATs) are one example. UDATs are brainstorming events aimed at introducing new ideas about planning and design into the debate about the future of a particular locality. The original model was the RUDAT (Regional/Urban Design Assistance Team), devised by the American Institute of Architects in 1967 and used many times since. In the USA, a RUDAT involves bringing a team of outside experts to a town or city for a four- or five-day brainstorming exercise. The aim is to inspire interest in a new agenda for action on planning and urban design, often in communities where planning is almost unknown. Once the experts have gone, the success of the initiative depends on the effectiveness of local collaborative action (Batchelor and Lewis, 1985).

A number of UDATs have been held in the UK, with varying degrees of success. Almost always the intention has been to stimulate action in a place where, despite (or perhaps because of) the UK's sophisticated statutory planning system, a log jam of some sort is obstructing positive change.

RUDATs in the USA are governed by a strict set of rules, intended to make them effective and ethical. The rules have been developed to avoid problems of events being organised for situations for which they are not appropriate, or where there is no local commitment to the RUDAT approach; professionals joining the teams in the hope of later securing commissions; events being held with insufficient preparation; and efforts being wasted due to inadequate commitment to following up the event. The Urban Design Group, which promotes the use of UDATs in the UK, has adopted similar guidelines. But people organising brainstorming events are free to adopt any format they like, and variations on the UDAT theme have been organised under names such as 'action planning event' and 'community planning weekend'.

The initiative for a UDAT, or any other kind of urban design action event, can come from any sector (public, private, institutional, professional, voluntary or quango). Anyone can organise one, if they can attract the necessary backing and participation (Wates, 1996). Success depends on designing the event to suit local circumstances. A few examples illustrate the variety of possible applications. Burgess Park Urban Design Action Team in Southwark, London was organised by Business in the Community over three days in 1993 to generate ideas for improving a major public park. The Greater Shankill Partnership in Belfast held a weekend action planning event in 1995 on the regeneration of the Shankill Road. Hammersmith Broadway Urban Design Action Team was organised by the Hammersmith Community Trust with Vision for London, to

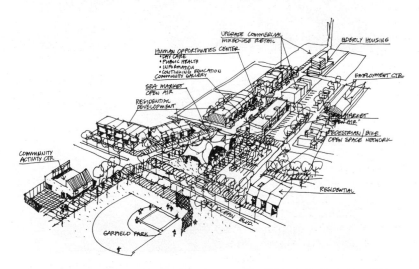

Figure 12.3 Sketch of proposals from a RUDAT (Regional/Urban Design Action Team) event held in the USA. Batchelor P. and Lewis D. (eds) (1985) *Urban Design in Action,* publication of the School of Urban Design, North Carolina State University, Raleigh, North Carolina.

generate ideas for a traffic-strangled town centre. At the first event of Birmingham's Highbury Initiative, in 1988, international specialists worked over a period of 48 hours on the opportunities and problems of Birmingham city centre with people who knew the city intimately. Eighteen months later a second event brought together many of the same 90 people to review progress. The initiative had a significant influence on city centre policy and action.

The Miles Platting and Ancoats Action Planning Event was organised with the support of Business in the Community over three days in 1995. It identified the potential of Ancoats, a run-down area of derelict land and redundant mills on the edge of Manchester city centre, to become an urban village. A building preservation trust has since been created to implement this. The three-day event followed two years of successful community development by the Miles Platting and Ancoats Development Trust. Wood Green and Alexandra Palace Urban Design Action Team in Haringey, London was organised by Haringey Council and the Urban Design Group in 1990, to generate ideas about the future of an ailing shopping street and a nearby public building and park.

A series of experimental urban design brainstorming events was organised in 1992–94 at the instigation of the then president of the Royal Institute of British Architects, Richard MacCormac (Strelitz, Henderson and Cowan, 1996). He called on schools of architecture and practising architects throughout the country to form teams with other professionals and people involved in urban renewal, and to spend an intensive three days exploring how their collaborative efforts could point to new solutions for neglected sites and wider urban areas.

The first of the events, Drawing on London, inspired a series of at least 20 more in other towns and cities, under the title Vision for Cities. In some of the events

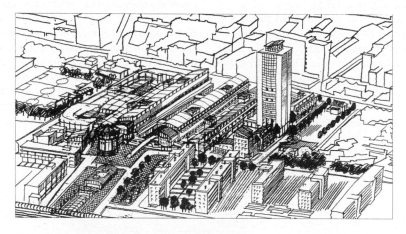

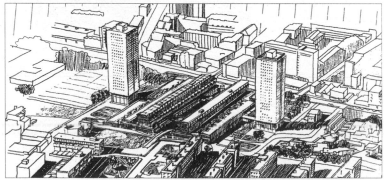

Figure 12.4 Proposals (top) by a group led by Hunt Thompson and Roger Zogolovitch to improve East London's Watney Market Estate as part of Drawing on London, with existing conditions below. (Rob Cowan)

more than 200 people took part. All the work was unpaid, and a small amount of locally raised sponsorship covered the organisers' costs. The events included, for example, Designs on Burslem (with an economic development perspective), Drawing on Glasgow (focusing on the city's midriff, where the city centre meets the suburbs), and Drawing on Poole (developing outline proposals for key sites as a prelude to a bid for funding under the Single Regeneration Budget).

At the Vision for Cities events, unlike some UDATs, consultants did not have to renounce interest in possible commissions; in some cases there was no clear brief and little preparatory work; and often little was done to ensure that the events were followed through into any sort of implementation. Some of the Vision for Cities events suffered from these omissions, remaining little more than academic exercises. In others the informality turned out to be a strength, and the results (in terms of ideas raised, experience gained, collaborations forged, expectations raised and action prompted) seemed to justify the approach.

Opportunities for organising urban design events exist in every city. An obvious responsibility to promote or support such events lies with local authorities, which can incorporate them into the planning process as a way of both facilitating public participation and opening up the discussion of issues (the three-dimensional implications of planning policies, for example) which might not otherwise be considered. Urban design action events have a potential role in, among other matters: considering the future of particular sites; investigating particular design or planning themes; preparing urban design briefs; and preparing or updating development plans.

The most striking examples of processes for producing city-wide visions of the future include several from the USA. Chattanooga Venture was launched in 1984 'to generate positive change through citizen involvement in community decision-making, encouraging citizens to participate in and take responsibility for their community by developing a vision that nourishes diversity and collaboration'. Its success led to the launch of the city's new programme, ReVision 2000, in 1993. The 1986 Philadelphia City Visions award scheme aimed 'to create designs and dreams for the City of Philadelphia' (Cowan and Gallery, 1990). It inspired the Boston Visions ideas competition, held in 1988 to encourage professions and interested citizens 'to imagine future Bostons'. Portland and Seattle have both pioneered comprehensive programmes of local and city-wide collaborative initiatives on development and urban design (Punter et al., 1996).

Attempts to emulate these in the UK include the Leeds Initiative (a civic forum promoted by the city council) and Choices for Bristol (an independent consensus-building project). Also significant are the Local Agenda 21 initiatives, in which towns and cities have responded to the call by the 1992 Earth Summit for local authorities to consult their populations about what sustainable development would mean in their particular area. The most impressive of these initiatives have been successful collaborations between people who have never before recognised that they have in common a stake in the future. The weakness of some of them has been their failure to define sustainable processes (in terms of planning, design and development) which could deliver what they have identified as the desirable, sustainable product.

In the USA the Congress for New Urbanism has set out what it sees as the correct principles for public policy, development practice, urban planning, and design. Its charter (Congress for New Urbanism, 1996) is significant in combining a considerable degree of physical prescription with a concern for the process:

> We stand for the restoration of existing urban centres and towns within coherent metropolitan regions, the reconfiguring of sprawling suburbs into communities of real neighbourhoods and diverse districts, the conservation of natural environments, and the preservation of our built legacy.... We are committed to re-establishing the relationship between the art of building and the making of community, through citizen-based participatory planning and design.

In the UK, the Urban Villages Group is similarly focused on a series of principles relating both to the physical form of development and a participatory process for achieving it.

The development process in the UK traditionally relies on developers to take the initiative. The rest of the players are often merely reactive, desperately defending the status quo for fear of the unknown. But it is becoming recognised increasingly that successful planning, urban design and regeneration depend on creative collaboration between people with common interests. In the words of *The City Set Free*:

> Who shapes cities? Politicians in central government and on local councils; civil servants; business people; accountants; engineers; institutional investors; arts organisers; creators of public art, and those who commission it; health service administrators; and the members and managers of quangos, statutory organisations, community groups and economic development agencies. Also, of course, in their own small way, planners, urban designers and architects. All these people, in doing their everyday jobs, play a part in creating the physical setting for the life of the city (Cowan,1997).

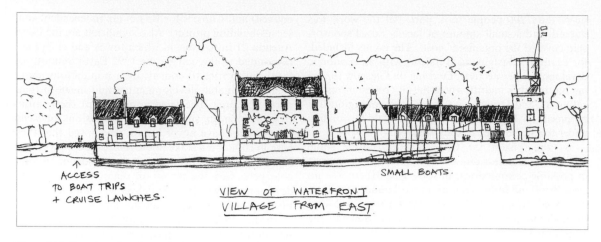

Figure 12.5 Drawing of a scheme for Inverness waterfront from Inverness Vision For Cities.

How positive their contribution is will often depend on how successfully they manage to collaborate, and on what *The Cities Design Forgot* (Cowan, 1995) has identified as the seven requirements that collaborators need: a flow of information which meets the needs of each of them; contacts with networks; knowledge of their relation to the city-wide and regional context; inspiration from experience elsewhere; access to skills and professionals; opportunity to collaborate with other people; and an acknowledged role in the process.

Collaboration should give these people a greater chance of achieving their aims: providing a better service, putting up a better building, creating more jobs, contributing more effectively to a regeneration partnership, or running a more constructive community campaign.

The City Set Free notes that:

A large number of urban regeneration projects today – including City Challenges and bids to the Single Regeneration Budget – are based on partnership, with the public, private and voluntary sectors working together. But many of those partnerships, though set up with the best of intentions, are confused as to who controls them, what the roles of the respective partners are, how they should operate, and how they can measure their success. What they lack is support and guidance in learning the arts of collaboration.

The concept of collaboration implies a new role for community organisations. No longer does it make sense to talk of 'the community', as if the residents of an area constituted the only identifiable community of interest. Nor is the conventional idea of public participation of much value, in its sense of managing policy processes in a way that allows people who are excluded from the game the dubious privilege of commenting from the sidelines. Collaboration is a game in which everyone has a right to take part, and all players have a right to a knowledge of the rules and the correct kit.

Effective urban design is not a standard product; it is a process by which people shape their environment in the way that suits them. It combines the art of design with the art of making things happen. The skills needed for the collaborative processes of shaping towns and cities do not relate only to the design of buildings, structures and spaces. They relate also to intangibles such as networks, new organisations, new working relationships, new forms of economic development, and new financial structures and arrangements. These too have to be designed. Their designers will be imaginative people skilled in such matters as management, community and economic development, law, and accountancy. Such people may well – and not unreasonably – call themselves urban designers, even though they may never draw anything. Much of their effectiveness will depend on making their own design processes open and accessible, and on recognising their roles as impresarios and facilitators of the 'drama in time' (to use Geddes' phrase) that is the life of a city.

CONCLUSION

13 Design and designers revisited

Clara Greed

The agenda revisited

The purpose of this chapter is to give a review of the issues raised in the book and to reconsider some of the questions, and problematic and unresolved dualisms raised in Chapter 1. It is also intended to add a little new material and some alternative angles on the subject, plus a bit of anecdotal reportage and 'stirring', in order to stimulate further debate as to the scope and nature of urban design and urban designers and likely future developments. In this book it has been demonstrated that a wide range of issues, topics and areas concern urban designers, beyond purely aesthetic considerations. It has been shown that urban design is an integral, indeed overarching aspect of all urban policy, and should not be seen as a 'special' add-on, after-thought, or marginalised prettification process. Issues such as sustainability, city-wide land-use zoning, urban transportation policy, and socio-economic factors have all been shown to be components of the current urban design agenda, along with the expected emphasis upon architecture, and aesthetic factors.

As to the levels of engagement in the design of the built environment, sustainability and transport issues have figured at the city-wide macro level, with many contributors arguing for a holistic approach to urban design which encompasses all aspects of (what is now) 'town planning'. The meso level has also figured strongly with an emphasis being put upon urban designers being involved in the initial policy deliberations that shape the interrelationships between land uses, districts, and zones. Thus, urban design is not to be seen as taking place in a vacuum, but should be fully integrated into the realm of location and zoning policy, which shapes the cell structure of the living fabric of the city in the first place, long before we get to the site design and development stage which has long been considered the more appropriate, yet limited, 'place' for urban designers.

Emphasis upon the micro level of urban design has been a key feature of the book, with reference to specific policy areas, housing estates, and central areas, but in this approach the contributors have always remained cognisant of the way in which (so called) small-scale, and site-specific interventions are structurally linked to overall urban strategy and policy development. The contributors have undoubtedly covered all the 'Lynch-like things' that urban designers have traditionally identified as key components of townscape. Items alluded to in the text have included (in no particular order) matters of scale, grain and density; routeways and their role as barriers or uniting interfaces; footpaths, steps, and (nowadays) ramps; public spaces, open spaces, gathering spaces, squares and malls; spaces between and flows around buildings; building materials and paving surfaces; architectural features and components; focal points, nodal points and centres; corners, edges and boundaries; mass, volume and height; and also to a lesser degree street furniture, advertisements, road signs, overhead wires, bus shelters, public toilets, parking spaces, lighting; and lots more have been mentioned in passing. Planting, landscape, ground cover, and screening, that is soft spaces, and the spaces between buildings have been referred to by several contributors and Chapter 6 has demonstrated the inseparable nature of the linkage between urban design and landscape.

In discussion of aesthetic considerations it was commented that colour was perhaps not given adequate attention (cf. Hirst, 1996, p. 9; Lancaster, 1996) however, it does figure in the discussion of building materials in relation to conservation policy (Chapter 4) and to some extent, in relation to public art. Light and lighting is another issue which sits uneasily within the discourse; this is discussed in a subsequent section later in this chapter (in the context of time and night and day in the city), and has been referred to briefly in Chapters 7, 10 and 11. Also, the issue of how to reconcile the demand for greater accessibility, especially for the disabled, with the traditional townscape features agenda has not been fully resolved. Indeed, such matters, along with detailed aspects of architectural design, building regulation, highway design, and pedestrian surfaces and textures, may all appear too detailed to be part of 'real urban design' per se. However, all these little details undoubtedly have a disproportionate influence and can be as important as the big things.

It is noticeable that many of the seminal texts on urban design, and townscape features, did not include, overtly, features needed by disabled people. We have attempted to remedy this to a degree. The lack of this emphasis in heritage texts is in contrast to more recent design guidance such as the work of Julie Fleck, Access Officer in the City of London, (*Planning Week*, 25 April 1996, letter, p. 12) where a series of groundbreaking disability design guides have been produced for one of the most historic areas of Britain. Her approach appears to be based on lateral thinking – for example, if it is impossible to drop the kerb, because of underground cabling or historic paving, then she recommends raising the road surface to increase pedestrian accessibility, and this has apparently been done in certain central area streets. The validity of inclusion of such factors is, arguably, dependent on the question of 'who' urban design is conceived as being 'for'. Sandra Manley has demonstrated in Chapter 9 that up to 5 million of the people using urban space experience some form of disability (which, incidentally, is equal to the entire population of a small country such as Norway).

Papers presented at the Streets Ahead Conference held in Bristol in 1995 explored the question of what should and should not have the right to be 'seen' on the streets. This was especially highlighted in a paper by Bromley which discussed all the unacceptable, so-called 'dirty' uses and buildings on our streets which the authorities are always trying to move, but which are vital to urban existence. The cultural anthropologist Mary Douglas long ago commented that 'dirt is merely matter out of place' (Douglas, 1966). (Compare 'weeds are merely plants whose use has not yet been discovered'.) One has to ask why there is no place in so many cities for all the so-called messy, dirty, untidy activities essential to human life, and who is making the judgment as to what is proper and what is not. The ambience and quality of an area is surely influenced by all the 'dirty' factors such as litter, dog dirt, pigeon droppings, and neglected, worn-out street furniture and signage – a theme which was discussed too, in the Streets Ahead Conference. Clearly, better maintenance and management is essential. The role of the city centre manager is key, as discussed by Kimberley Paumier in the previous volume, *Investigating Town Planning*, in relation to her role as city centre manager in the City of Bath, a UN World Heritage Site.

As to individual land uses, Alison Ravetz (Ravetz, 1974; Ravetz and Turkington, 1995) long ago commented upon the peoplelessness and impracticality of housing estates which presented an uncluttered pristine facade to the passer-by but which were hell to live in because there was nowhere to hang the washing out, nowhere for the children to play, and nowhere to mend the motorbike (Ravetz, 1974). These issues have been raised here because they have been developing in earlier volumes of the series and it will be of interest for the reader to see how they are viewed by the contributors to this one. It should be noted, however, that certain sections of the present volume have dealt with grand ceremonial spaces in which many urban designers would consider such 'visual clutter' inappropriate.

Obviously, the nature of individual buildings, and their use, all impinge upon the urban character. A particular problem in many British cities is the residue of 1960s high-rise, concrete, commercial office buildings and windswept shopping precincts, which now seem out of place as the tide of better design control, urban conservation policy and sensitive renewal sweeps across the nation's cities. There is certainly a need for close cooperation with commercial interests, property developers and owners to ameliorate the situation as the cycle of redevelopment moves swiftly on. (The concerns and agenda of the private sector property market, vis à vis the requirements of town planning policy have been thoroughly explored in the last two volumes of this series, and clearly 'the cost factor' and 'profit' rather than 'design' are key considerations.) It is important to stress both to such parties and to readers, that good design does not necessarily cost more than bad, and indeed great savings and benefits may be made in the long term in relation to maintenance and usability factors.

But what is urban design?

We have not yet resolved the question of what, exactly, urban design is, or for that matter what town planning really is. However, the book has shown more clearly the full scope and nature of urban design and has cast light on what town planning is not, where it is lacking in its present manifestation. Both 'urban design' and 'town planning' may be seen as meta-concepts, and as shorthand terms for vast, imprecisely defined fields, which are in a state of flux. It seems that everyone involved in them assumes they know instinctively what they are, but words fail them when precise definitions are requested. Also, the relationship and boundaries between town planning and urban design are still fuzzy rather than clear cut. For the purposes of professional recognition, and separation from other aligned fields, it may be important to come up with more precise definitions.

From a philosophical perspective, as discussed in earlier work (Greed, 1994), 'town planning' is a cultural construct, and an artifical reality. At the conceptual level it can be anything you want it to be, and indeed it has gone through many manifestations and incarnations. Of course at the statutory level, it is important, in terms of achieving change and having effective implementation, that both town planning and urban design are recognised as precise entities and invested with appropriate legislative powers. But, as has been discussed with reference to the imposition of prescriptive design guides, and mandatory design standards in the past, once 'urban design' becomes formalised and consequently municipalised and routinised it loses the very elements of flexibility and creativity that are so vital to making effective interventions and sensitive responses to the urban condition.

In Chapter 1, some additional 'other things which urban design might be' were included from a town planner's and community perspective (as against a pure urban designer's perspective), and these were discussed in Part III in particular. It is for the reader to decide whether these components are really part of urban design. There was, purposely, little mention, from the town planner's perspective, of 'prettying up' principles, nor of design guides, and other prescriptive interventions – partly because planners have already been condemned many times before for such approaches. Of course, by its very nature the local government planner's role in development control is bound to be fairly negative, restrictive, and bureaucratic, and yet many try to be proactive, and to do their best to promote good planning and design principles in spite of the system in which they operate.

For those planners involved in day-to-day development control, clearly, 'urban design' (or lack of it) is a matter of seeking to enforce prescriptive, regulatory control, especially over vast swathes of proposed and existing suburban and exurban housing development. Curiously, although residential development constitutes over 70 per cent of all development, and thus represents three-quarters of the building fabric of any town or city, elite architects and some urban designers have definitely given out the message, in the past at least, that a concern with mere 'housing', especially 'mass speculative housing' is quite beneath them. This may be a generalisation but certainly one picks up the message strongly that such housing is 'invisible' (presumably, along with the people who live in it) or is seen as a disgusting urban excrescence.

The 'suburbs' appear to be seen as 'boring' and uniform by the architectural elite. This is fascinating as in contrast many consider the standardised historical terraces of Georgian and Victorian town houses which constitute many an urban conservation area to fit that description exactly. Also, a desire for owner occupation of homes with gardens, was seen, not so long ago, as trivial, bourgeois, and politically inappropriate for the masses. Yet the reality is that most people nowadays, particularly in the provinces, live in such housing. Therefore it is argued that more emphasis needs to be given to urban design intervention in such areas, particularly since the vast prewar building cohort of semi-detached suburbia is now reaching a critical stage in its life span.

It is instructive in considering the future of suburban urban design, to make a digression to consider the example of North America, a more heavily suburbanised territory, and as a result to argue for greater attention to be given by urban designers in Britain to our own changing suburban situation. With continuing inner-city decline, increasing crime, racial tension and congestion, and the decline of downtown shopping streets because of retail mall development, there is a desire to recreate what has been lost – but with built-in security and social control. Within the world of bulk new housing estate development, and within popular culture there is nowadays a desire to create a total lifestyle package through an ersatz form of 'urban design', using nostalgic and homely images of a reassuring past, generated by allusions to Colonial, Prairie, Victorian, and Edwardian type features (all with garages).

Such marketing trends are epitomised by the new town of Celebration, off Highway 192 in Florida, built by the Disney Corporation and intended to embody all the best of Disneyland culture. Designed by the architect Robert Stein, and built on 5,000 acres, for 20,000 people, it satisfies a nostalgia for traditional 'small town America', with white picket fences, a Main Street USA, and everyone's favourite architectural frills. Surprisingly, it includes several 'oeuvres' by big-name international architects, plus a bewildering range of house types, creating a truly unique architectural zoo. Should such developments be seen as 'just' the next natural step from designer-towns such as Seaside, so admired by Prince Charles (built by Zyberg and Duony; see Greed, 1994, p. 168; Mohney and Easterbury, 1991)? Do such developments fulfil the ideals of the social aspects of planning, with inbuilt 'community spirit', crimeless streets, and even a selective touch of social and racial mix, provided residents are willing to sign the restrictive covenants associated with the properties and conform to the expected lifestyle? Or are such developments socially segregatory, culturally artificial and politically reactionary? Is it the beginning of the mass urban Disneyfication and the influence of television and films on the popular culture which shapes tastes in clothes, songs, food, and now apparently architecture? In the next volume, the primer on urban design, we intend to return to the design of housing estates and suburbia as a key issue of importance.

The fourth dimension and urban design

There is another 'new' dimension which some would include in urban design too, that is, four-dimensional design, namely design of *time,* and thus patterns of human activity and change and movement within cities (see the pioneering work of Belloni, 1994 on 'planning for time' in Italian cities). Its concerns include movement and traffic; employment time patterns and shop opening and closing hours; but also changing environmental processes and technologies. All of these increasingly affect employment and lifestyle trends, and thus city form and urban design.

In particular, the impact of telecommunications, the internet, and thus telecommuting (Graham and Marvin, 1996) is an area to keep an eye on for the future. Claims that telecommuting (working from home using a modem link) will render rush-hour traffic jams and central area business districts redundant are arguably overstated. Whether the internet, e-mail and related modem-based computer communication systems are really going to alter the nature of towns and cities is open to debate. At present, in Britain at least, downloading time is extremely slow and expensive, and ordinary people used to the immediacy of the television and telephone are not impressed by waiting 20 minutes for one screen of graphics to download. At present only

a minority of people use such computer-based communication systems at home – it is estimated that only around 5 per cent are regularly telecommuting by modem. But, technological advances and attempts to make systems more user-friendly are progressing by leaps and bounds. Parallels may be drawn with the growth of television ownership, as 1996 was the 60th anniversary of public transmission in Britain. At first, ownership was limited to the rich and technically minded, with less than 1 million people owning sets immediately after the Second World War, whereas nowadays most households possess more than one set. As has been commented upon above, popular culture is now a television-based culture, affecting the way we see 'reality', including ourselves and our cities.

Four-dimensional design is now an accepted area within the overarching field of 'art and design' as, for example, reflected in Time-Based Media studies at the University of the West of England. The cultural implications of time-based media and the moving image, which has such an effect on popular culture (cf. Disneyland discussion above), should not be underestimated. In Japan (the affluent 'Far West'), it is interesting that urban conservation and nostalgia are also becoming increasingly powerful forces, as manifested in 'Retro Street' near Tokyo which, like the 'Main Street, USA' concept, provides the visitor with the sights, smells and sounds of traditional small town life, albeit in this case mainly electronically generated, resulting in an experience which resembles walking through a computer game. In Britain, nowadays, people may be more familiar from television with a 'virtual' architectural world of American streets, and of Albert Square soap stage-sets than they are with the townscape around them. (Though, in fairness, if people seek to look at the architecture whilst travelling along our busy streets they may run into the car ahead.) It is curious that British town planning has considerable spatial control powers, but there are few commensurate temporal planning controls and policies, which might, for example, even out traffic flows and create a more efficient 24-hour city (Montgomery, 1994).

Light fantastic?

Lighting is a prerequisite of time management, and the 24-hour city (Montgomery, 1994; Bianchini, 1995). In Britain and other northern countries our cities are in dusk and darkness for around 50 per cent of the year, but urban design – and for that matter town planning – appear to have been, relatively speaking, primarily concerned with the daytime. Indeed, the sustainability agenda, with its emphasis upon minimal energy consumption, may be seen to be an uneasy companion for those obsessed with lighting everything to discourage crime, for those who believe using selective 'downlighting' for aesthetic purposes in historic areas, and for the full-blown '*son et lumière*' brigade, some of whom indulge in 'uplighting' on buildings creating the 'Dracula's Castle' effect! However, there are much-admired examples, too, for instance Lyon has striven to become the Second City of France, and the City of Light, and now tourists flock there just to see the very sensitively designed lighting. Taking into consideration the social aspects of planning, local communities on low incomes might resent investment in lighting for the benefit of more affluent groups within the city. Some of these conflicts are illustrated in the following example which, arguably, does not have quite the subtlety of Lyon.

Croydon, a south London borough of a third of a million population, is an area where there is considerable inner-urban poverty in certain areas and thus many demands on existing public funding. Paradoxically, it is often typified as 'boringly suburban' and culturally insignificant because it is 'south of the River'. It is one of the largest office centres in Britain, employing 125,000 office-based workers, many working within the high-rise 'mini-Manhattan' central business district, developed from the 1960s onwards. Croydon has been granted £8 million of Millenium funding (to be matched by a similar amount from international businesses, such as Nestlé, which have their headquarters there,) for the illumination of the high-rise buildings in the area, using laser skybeams and other state-of-the-art technology to create a continually changing and moving range of colour effects. (See *Estates Times* 23 February 1996, No. 1313, p. 18, article entitled 'A Light Touch' by David Crawford about 'skyline strategy'.)

In February 1997 Croydon hosted a conference entitled 'Light Fantastic', at which many of the key issues surrounding lighting vis à vis urban design were raised (summarised in *Planning Week*, 6 February 1997, Vol. 5, No. 5, p. 6). Whatever urban designers and town planners may think about this new trend, which owes much to North American influences, American designers, and undoubtedly has its roots in 'show biz' and rock concert lighting design, it is a trend which cannot be ignored as it reflects popular culture. It has gained some impetus as a result of the need to create 'grands projets' for the Millenium, with lighting projects being developed in places as diverse as Manchester, Glasgow, Portsmouth, Doncaster and, of course, Greenwich. The vast sums of money poten-

tially available have attracted the services of international designers and consultants, such as Focus Lighting and Speirs and Major from the USA, and Imagination based in London. In contrast, groups such as Planning Aid for London are keen to pursue a policy of 'community empowerment' and to press for positive involvement of local people, rather than outside contractors, in any urban design development which is ostensibly meant to be for local people.

Whatever one's views on the cultural appropriateness of such knock-out schemes, concerns are being expressed by many about the need for a coordinated lighting policy in town centres, to replace the ad hoc plethora of security lighting which has sprouted on every building. Light pollution – uncapped, badly designed street lights (including the ubiquitous globe style of lamp post found in so many 'designer schemes' nowadays) contributing to orange sky glow from conurbations, and light trespass created by unshielded overpowerful lighting – is a controversial issue of concern to groups as diverse as the British Astronomical Society, sustainability groups, and health and safety organisations (Institution of Lighting Engineers, 1996). It has been recommended that the Department of the Environment should issue policy guidance on lighting and extend development control powers (British Parliamentary Lighting Group, Bulletin, December 1996). At present, control over lighting is limited to sports facility flood-lighting, and to individual light fittings and fixtures under conservation policy. Therefore the lighting debate is an issue 'to watch' as it encompasses so many topical social, economic, cultural, functional, and environmental issues in urban design today.

Top-down and bottom-up

A particularly controversial dualism raised in earlier discussions among the team was the top-down/bottom-up (or paternalistic/participatory) dichotomy, which was inevitably linked to the visual/social dualism (and the peopleless/people-centred dualism raised in earlier volumes). Readers may feel that these dualisms are echoed in the Part II/Part III subdivision within the book, although contributors argue strongly that the division is not that clear cut and that there is an area of overlap. The contributors and editors did discuss whether, in fact, in the bad old days urban design was peopleless, to do with creating aesthetically pleasing stage sets, and very much a top-down process in which the 'designer' looked down on 'his' drawing board, taking the 'God's eye view', and thus created the Grand

Design. In contrast, one could typify the 'new urban design' as being much more to do with people's needs at street level, with functionality rather than aesthetic considerations. This was a useful organising model, but a oversimplistic image which is open to criticism. The book team agreed that there had always been urban designers concerned with people (or at least with men) and street-level accessibility, names such as Lynch (1988, originally 1960), Geddes (see Ritter, 1996), and even Le Corbusier's 'modular man' (albeit sexist, cf. EUROFEM, 1996) being cited. Perhaps one should say that there are always different groups, types, and diverse schools of thought among urban designers, and that one can, in any generation, find both top-down and bottom-up type designers, with a range of combinations in between. User-based involvement in the design process is certainly popular among the people themselves, although, as Jeff Bishop, urban design consultant, has commented (private communication on this book, 16 October 1996) because of the difficulty of developing a 'testable' theoretical model, research to explore user needs, which was pioneered in the 1960s and 1970s, has not continued as a mainstream planning research issue. However, this view might be challenged by the many minority groups, such as the Women's Design Service, in London, who are currently undertaking what they consider to be valid and fruitful research on user needs.

With reference to the dualisms set out at the end of the first chapter, it has been demonstrated that the urban design agenda is not only concerned with prestige projects in capital cities, or with urban conservation areas, but that its principles might apply equally to suburban housing estate developments and to socially deprived inner-city areas. It has been shown, particularly in Part III, that urban design is not a luxury just for rich areas/people. Good design does not necessarily cost more, and it can actually save money in terms of creating more efficient and satisfactory urban environments for everyone. Whether we can really go as far as to say that it can actually reduce crime, increase social equality, and generally improve socio-economic conditions is a complex matter which will be returned to later in this chapter. One may nevertheless argue that good design makes people feel much better about their environment, although this is hard to prove 'scientifically' to the satisfaction of the planning fraternity.

Related to this debate is the vantage point from which one sees and thus experiences the city. Envisaging oneself walking through the streets and urban spaces rather than looking at them from above soon alerts the designer to potential problems and to the true scale of the distances and heights. This street-level perspective may be gained by using two totally different methods: walking with and talking to ordinary people who use the streets such as shoppers, commuters and other pedestrians in similar sorts of area, or, more expensively, for those obsessed with the techno-fix, using CAD and virtual reality computer programmes. These enable the designer to walk through the new design to rotate it and look at it from all angles, while it is still at plan stage.

In Britain we live in an urban situation characterised both by 'European' close-knit, high-density historical development, and also by low-density, modern, suburban areas, with 'Americanisation' continuing apace, in respect of both central business district commercial development and decentralisation (out-of-town schemes). We have sought to cover many of these types of development. Both old areas (as in Chapter 4 on urban conservation) and new areas (such as in Chapter 11 on new housing estates) have been discussed. Discussions of sustainability objectives (Chapter 7) have shown that any realistic urban design strategy in this respect must be for the whole city, both urban and suburban, high-density and low-density, as the natural environment is universal and cannot be conveniently contained within spatial boundaries. As to the visual/social dualism under discussion, it is clear from the various contributions that such a division is not starkly seen as a 'problem' in the real world, within the process of policy synthesis and implementation. Chapters which specifically deal with 'art and design' (for example in Chapter 6 on Public Art) have demonstrated that for 'art' to be culturally meaningful and to work within an urban setting, it must be integrated in a manner which is relevant and inclusive of social and cultural circumstances of the vicinity. What do you think?

What qualities qualify someone to be an urban designer?

Who are the urban designers?

We have not yet resolved the question of who exactly the urban designers are. There appear to be two types. Firstly, there are those who consider themselves professionally qualified to be so, albeit without any formal professional body, or registration, as yet. Among these are established architects and planners, who have specialised in urban design, and more recently, a younger generation who have studied on new urban design courses, and therefore, innocently, consider themselves to be urban designers. Secondly, there are those who are not necessarily professionally qualified in urban design, but are likely to be professionally qualified in other fields, who have become 'reluctant urban designers' through getting involved in the sort of single-issue campaigns we have discussed in this book, such as people from 'women and planning', sustainability, disability, 'crime and design' groups, and, more recently, 'lighting designers'. By default they have all found themselves in the world of urban design, and found it to be a valuable route towards achieving their particular goals. It is for the reader to decide which of these groups are truly urban designers.

Genius?

There is a further complication. Underlying all this debate there is, undoubtedly, the ideal image of the urban designer, as 'genius', the one who can bring salvation and inspiration to the urban condition. Urban design is strongly linked to architecture and there is still a need in the architectural profession for such 'heroes', and 'great men' (Greed, 1994, p. 30). The gender dimension of this ideal type must be acknowledged as germane to any discussion of who is most likely to be doing the designing. To be a genius and distinguishable from other mortals, one must possess 'female' qualities of sensitivity and an artistic temperament but few women gain such status (Greed, 1994, p. 66; Battersby, 1989). It is fascinating that whilst it is often argued that an architect or urban designer has a 'right' to design because of at least seven years of study, in contrast the genius is apparently born with the three necessary qualities, classically defined as intuis (wisdom), cognis (knowledge) and technis (practical ability). A brief digression into the social construction of the concept of genius is called for, as the concept infuses the world of architecture and art of which urban design is part.

The concept of the 'Artist' as a 'gifted' individual, and 'genius' who is the possessor of a 'special vision' derives from the Romantic movement and was built upon in Victorian times (Abrams, 1953; Babbit, 1947; Peckham, 1970). Whilst some men were being given 'star' status, established women artists were increasingly marginalised, their work demoted to the secondary realms of 'craft' rather than 'art' (Anscombe, 1984). Several authors have catalogued the marginalisation of women in art (Greer, 1979, Spender, 1982; Chadwick, 1990; Broude and Garrard, 1982). The idea of individual male creativity was further bolstered in the twentieth century in the popular mind in books and films, such as Irvine Stone's accounts of the lives of Van Gogh and Michelangelo who were clearly mad,

male, macho figures (Stone, 1961). The image of the fiery, bearded, eccentric, male genius affected twentieth-century concepts of the real architect, the town planner, and possibly the socialist too. Nowadays, it is not enough just to be 'good', to be recognised as 'great' as an artist or architect one must have a suitably packaged 'biography' (Wayte, 1986 and 1989) so that a couple of squiggles on a piece of paper can be interpreted correctly. One can see a 'star system' at work in the built environment professions, especially in architecture, surveying and town planning, which generally only creates famous men. Paradoxically, though the 'genius of the city' as shown on the RTPI coat of arms is a woman (Greed, 1994, p. 1).

There is a tendency for each new generation to come up with what it believes to be the definitive, perfect solution, and in the process there is always a need to disparage the ideals of the previous generation and to prove that they got it hopelessly wrong. As discussed in previous work (Greed, 1994, p. 138) each new generation of architects and planners produces its own 'stars', 'brat packs' and 'new kids on the block'. As can be seen from the approaches to urban design expressed in this book, nowadays, some would question the 'star system' of 'the great designer' and instead would see the essence of good urban design practice to be that of involving, listening to, and working with the 'users', that is, the public, the residents – as well as being creative, inspired, and professionally competent. This approach is exemplified in the discussions of the process of urban design in relation to 'the people' as found in Part III.

Designing people

Having discussed – albeit inconclusively – the tangled issue of who has the right to be an urban designer, we will now discuss the likely impact, or power, of urban design on ordinary people. Urban designers are likely to be working, as earlier discussed by Marion Roberts, in a range of local and central government departments, some of which will be town planning offices, and also in the private sector. In addition, there has been an increase in opportunities within the voluntary sector, campaign groups, and in relation to a range of ad hoc 'special' government programmes, related to urban renewal.

The current SRB (Single Regeneration Budget) and related Urban Programme and City Challenge inner-city renewal initiatives can potentially make considerable amounts of money available to community groups. But areas have to bid and compete with each other for funding, and then spend the money in a relatively short period of time (Oatley, 1996). In this situation 'quick-fix' solutions are likely to be seen as more likely to win funding, than gradual, long-term community empowerment programmes. In the current political and economic climate there is an expectation of quantifiable results and measurable outputs, and therefore ostensibly 'provable' theories such as environmental determinism have been dusted off and put back on the agenda. The validity of environmental determinism as a theory, and the wider issue of the extent to which urban design policy can actually shape or even change people's lives and behaviour is discussed below, with particular reference to 'crime and design'. This is particularly important in evaluating the validity of the ideas and policies put forward by contributors in Part III.

'Crime and design' is definitely one of the more controversial of the new manifestations and applications of urban design, as discussed by Henry Shaftoe in Chapter 11. Some are suspicious of single-issue and problem-solving, quick-fix applications of urban design. Some see urban design being 'coopted' by the police, who are desperately looking for instant solutions with guaranteed results. In particular, there has been some concern that an oversimplistic version of urban design has developed which, apparently, can be applied directly to high-crime areas. In fact, as the author explains, one cannot take 'crime and design' in isolation but must relate the policy to wider concerns and strategies in relation to housing, community development, education and employment. Nevertheless, there has undoubtedly been political pressure to introduce, and the provision of considerable government finance, to carry out anti-crime schemes. Some are fearful that when such schemes do work, the problem is not solved but simply moved elsewhere, or that, in creating a fortress mentality, other more legitimate urban functions (such as young people simply 'hanging out' and innocently socialising) are severely curtailed (Kenvyn, 1995). Women's groups have been particularly concerned that many of the measures seem more concerned with protecting property rather than people, as reflected in the DoE Circular 5/94 *Designing out Crime.* For example, shuttering shop windows reduces ambient light in streets and creates a threatening, inhospitable street environment for women who wish to go out in the evenings (Bedminster High Street in Bristol being a classic local example).

Returning to 'crime and design', one other issue must be raised which may influence one's judgement of how to view it and indeed how to receive other topics in the book too. One of the reasons that urban design lost out in the battle for domination of the planning profession in the postwar period is that it was falsely accused of offering more than it could deliver. As explained within the context of the social aspects of planning in Chapter 11 of *Introducing Town Planning,* some planners and architects set great store by environmental determinism, that is, the idea that one could shape and improve human behaviour through the way the built environment was designed. For example, on the positive side, it was imagined that if residents arriving in the postwar new towns were put into houses at relatively high-density, if the footpaths on the 'Radburnised' estates ran straight past everyone's front doors, and if the houses were grouped into neighbourhood units, then, hey presto, they would rapidly develop a sense of community spirit.

On the other hand, environmental determinism can also be used to explain why people are as they are in existing, non-planned areas. A priori, it was apparently assumed by some sociologists that the poor, run-down quality of the existing inner-city environment 'made' the residents commit crime, and engage in vandalism and violence. Of course, from a feminist perspective, many have asked why, if this was so, it was only young males – and not the whole population – who were so affected to undertake acts of violence, crime and vandalism. Furthermore, why was it that they usually chose young females, families and the elderly, who were *also* residents of the area, as their victims? And why did the sociologists and urban researchers seem relatively unconcerned with the victims as against the aggressors in their studies? (These issues are discussed in Greed, 1994, in relation to the gender-biased nature of the professional subcultures of town planning and urban sociology, and the way urban problems and policies are identified and prioritised.)

Some planners appeared to imagine that planting lots of trees, providing community centres, or designing housing estates in a certain way, would actually change people's characters and make society better. (Not, note providing better childcare facilities, after school facilities or improved public transport.) Planners were accused of playing God, and were seen as an easy target for the New Left which emerged within the profession in the 1960s and 1970s. It was assumed that the environmental deterministic type planners ignored deeper economic and political constraints, and imagined simplistically that one could achieve 'salvation by bricks' – i.e. design and build one's way out of urban social problems. The accusation of environmental determinism is still heard whenever anyone broaches the subject of 'crime and design' and campaigners such as Alice Coleman, who undertook the experiment of redesigning the Mozart council estate in inner London, in particular have been much maligned (Coleman, 1985; Markus, Teymur and Woolley, 1988). Enthusiasm for American gurus such as Oscar Newman has endured, albeit much criticised (Newman, 1973). Coleman herself is viewed as an environmental determinist by many commentators, and is seen as creating grandiose, top-down schemes on behalf of the people, in the 'grand manner' tradition, although, interestingly, her approach to urban design is social rather than aesthetic.

However, if one looks at the phenomenon of environmental determinism more closely it may be argued that the town planners and architects involved (unlike some urban sociologists) never did pretend that urban design would solve all society's problems. It may be concluded, for example, that the neighbourhood unit was a good functional concept for organising large numbers of people in a short space of time, but that, with the growth of the motorcar and greater mobility and choice in society, few would want to limit their social contacts only to others in the neighbourhood. (It must be said, though, that many mothers and young children found the arrangement very helpful in providing instant friends.) With regard to solving inner-city problems it is generally acknowledged nowadays that there are many other economic, social, cultural and political factors to take into account. Perhaps the answer is that every professional group can do its bit, and that, relatively speaking, there is some value in seeking to design out crime, provided the initiative is supported and backed up by other policies to tackle poverty and unemployment. As quoted in *Introducing Town Planning* Maurice Broady, a sociologist disquieted by the belief in the apparently magical powers of environmental determinism, stated, 'architectural design, like music to a film, is complementary to human activity, it does not shape it' (Broady, 1968).

This chapter, so far, has sought to make visible some of the latent subplots and debates running through the book, particularly in relation to the question of the power and limitations of urban design and the issue of who the urban designers are and by what right they are so called. We have not put forward any proposals for change, nor any prescriptive policies. As stated, this is not the purpose of this volume, and, in fact, many of the threads will be taken up again in the next volume in which there will be a more prescriptive, and advisory approach. However, in the final section certain guidelines and principles contained within the various chapter contributions are drawn out. Readers are also recommended to refer to the Manifesto in Chapter 1,

page 8 in order to understand the basic objectives and principles which motivate urban designers. Indeed, several contributors have already included their own lists of objectives and 'wish lists', as in Chapters 2 and 3, and the reader is advised to reconsider these. Readers are encouraged to compare these objectives and statements with their own goals, and relate them to their own experience and understanding of urban design and its manifestations in the built environment.

Conclusion: reflection and direction

Taking stock

This book has explored many aspects of the field of urban design. The chapters broadly cover aspects and issues which would be expected in such a text, for example conservation, design control, public participation, regeneration and recent history. Other topics have emerged from the editors' own specific concerns and interests. For example, the chapters on public art and women arise form the editors' previous research interests, the first being an emergent area within the practice of urban design and the second a much-neglected topic, both in theory and practice.

As explained in Chapter 1, the aspect of the book which differentiates it from other collections is its emphasis on user responses to urban environments. The editors make no apologies for this shift: too many accounts of design initiatives and schemes stop with the triumphant photographs of openings and do not consider how well such schemes have fared in the long run. This book has sought to make a small step in redressing the balance of academic discussion away from the first part of the design process to an examination of the whole, which includes design in use. Although the chapters have covered quite different aspects of urban design, there are a number of common themes which emerge between chapters. These are set out below and are linked to guidelines for the future.

Common themes

The first draws in the relationship of urban design to planning. These themes are listed below:

1 The relevance of design to all scales of development
The clear message arising in a number of chapters, from Tony Lloyd-Jones' historical account onwards, is that urban design is about all scales of development. Strategic design decisions can be crucial to an entire

city, as in the case of Barcelona, or to its city centre, as in Glasgow or Birmingham, or to a local neighbourhood, as in Dublin's Temple Bar. Urban design is not just about providing pedestrianisation and bollards: it is also about the structuring of towns, cities and urban areas. This means that the study of urban design is intrinsic to the planning profession, rather than simply being a detailed add-on. Planning and design are not necessarily sequential; in many cases they will be simultaneous.

2　Design controls need reforming using urban design ideas　Design controls are embedded in different aspects of planning legislation, as Matthew Carmona's chapter shows. As Richard Guise and Sandra Manley point out in relation to conservation, design controls are also vested in different bodies. Again this suggests that urban design issues are closely related to planning.

Both Guise and Carmona argue that design controls need to be reformed using ideas that have evolved in urban design theory. Carmona suggests that there is a trend in this direction at the moment, with a move away from elevational control towards a plan-led system which allows for the possibility of enforcing design guidance and design briefs. However, much more could be done on this front to unify legislation into a coherent framework.

In a similar vein, Sandra Manley also points out that some legislation for the disabled does have an impact on the public realm. Yet again, this is only a beginning and much more could be done. The use of her suggestion for an external audit could provide a straightforward tool for analysis and action.

3　Effectiveness of design interventions: principles versus prescription　Many chapters refer to the need to think about design principles rather than to jump into prescription. Both Guise and Roberts demonstrate that a desire to conserve the past does not mean that a strict rule book has to be adhered to. It is possible for conservationists to preserve important buildings and to reinterpret the character of an area through the reuse of building types, as with the Berlin block and the Glasgow tenement.

Whilst Hugh Barton suggests certain design standards for providing for a more sustainable form of development, these standards are based on principles rather than arbitrarily defined rules. In a similar vein Henry Shaftoe casts doubt on the efficacy of any one strategy to combat crime and suggests that a combined approach may offer the most success. Likewise, Rob Cowan has stressed the importance of planning *with* people rather than *for* people.

4　Importance of aesthetic experience　As might be expected in a book which introduces urban design, each chapter articulates the importance of different aspects of the aesthetic, sensory experience of the environment and demonstrates that such experience cannot be divorced from other planning decisions. At its crudest this means that design is not an add-on or optional extra. Public art, for example, which is used like a 'badge' on a building appears to be simply that, an afterthought. Access for the disabled, similarly, appears clumsy if it is only thought about as an addition to a scheme. Likewise, landscape should not be seen as just dealing with the 'bits left over', but should be an integral aspect of urban design, as discussed in Chapter 6 by Ian Thompson.

Both Hugh Barton and Sue Cavanagh's chapters demonstrate the importance of early strategic decision-making to urban design concepts. In this way a layout cannot be made sustainable or woman-friendly if certain basic decisions are inappropriate – for example if housing is located a long distance from employment opportunities, or from public transport. In this sense the social and the aesthetic are intertwined.

This also suggests that most planning decisions have a design implication. The location of land uses in space, whether they are separated in a low-density sprawl, or compacted in a mixed-density city core, automatically has implications for a potential range of design solutions. Town planners are therefore in a position of facilitating design decisions, even if they are ostensibly only interested in forward planning or economic issues.

5　Importance of process　The extent to which the design process is one that is exclusive to professionals has been explored in the last chapter of this book. Rob Cowan has suggested that successful collaboration means making things happen and that involving people in design implies a partnership rather than comments from the sidelines.

Whilst we have examined a range of topics and issues which are each of importance to the study and practice of urban design, it may help readers to point out some omissions. We have not, for purely practical reasons, unrelated to our original intentions, considered the vital role of landscape and the relationship of urban design to landscape architecture in detail. Neither have we considered the meanings associated with urban space and the relationship of urban design to identity and subjective experience in the imaginative sense.

These shortcomings are indicative of the need for a broadening of the urban design agenda beyond the notion of making people-friendly places. Tony Lloyd-

Jones has suggested some items which might be placed on such an agenda – to these we have added our own.

Urban design: A future agenda

Perhaps the most pressing problem arising from current demographic projections is the pressure for new housing developments. Decisions as to whether new settlements will have to be built outside of the major conurbations to accommodate the projected rise in the number of households, or whether they can be accommodated within the boundaries of existing urban areas are of major importance in terms of determining the future design agenda.

On the one hand, the design of new settlements offers the opportunity to think anew of how we might want to live and to rephrase questions which were only asked at times of great physical renewal, as after both world wars. On the other hand, the accommodation of an increased number of households within existing towns and cities suggests a different type of vision – one that might, perhaps, be concerned with mixed-use, high-density living and a greater reliance on public transport, coupled with a more urban existence. In the light of mass car ownership, and greater frustration with increasing traffic jams, delays and inconvenience due to road works, parking problems and road rage, there is certainly continuing pressure from ordinary people, as well as the sustainability and environmental lobbies for greater restraint in the use of cars and for entirely new approaches to transport to be investigated.

This book has given some examples of successful regeneration of town centres – Birmingham being the most obvious. If, as many commentators agree, the revitalisation of town centres continues and the need to use cars is reduced, then a great deal more of urban areas will have to become mixed-use. The design implications of tightly-knit mixed-use development need more exploration in terms both of building types and of urban form.

It has already been suggested that, whether planning new settlements or using existing derelict or vacant land, the problems of transport pollution and congestion and the relationship of transport/land-use planning to environmental sustainability need to be tackled in a thoroughgoing way. As Hugh Barton has argued, movement is an essential component of urban design and the design of movement systems which are integrated into the urban fabric provides a challenge for transport planners and engineers as well as urban designers.

The chapter on urban regeneration raised the issue of the competition which now exists between cities in transnational markets. Whilst the chapter pointed to some ways in which individual cities were striving to retain and reinterpret their identity in the face of such competition, perhaps the biggest formal challenge on the design agenda is that of homogenisation.

This is not only a problem of having the same shops and chain stores in every High Street, but a more profound issue connected with the globalisation of culture. As building materials become easier to obtain from different parts of the world and as images, fashions and other points of reference become more widely transmitted, the distinctive aspects of locality become displaced. Furthermore, local communities are no longer defined by the dominance of a local industry (if, indeed, that could ever have been an adequate way of categorising all the members of a neighbourhood, or town). The challenge facing urban designers is to engage with the 'placelessness' of many places and to try to design something which is at least distinctive, or memorable. As has been discussed, television has led to a standardised, bland, global culture, but the development of the internet may yet lead to more interactive, participatory, creative and varied forms of electronic cultural expression, and new forms of virtual reality which provide an escape from the urban pressures of actual reality.

The other side of modern cultural experience is that of the commercialisation or commodification of each aspect of the urban landscape. Guise and Manley have discussed how certain conservation practices contribute to a feeling of unreality in conservation areas, as standardised, historically inaccurate exteriors are unwittingly reproduced. The unfortunate aspect of such inept methods of conservation is that they tend to provide a visual association with other more artificial environments such as the Victorian street reproduced in the heritage park or the fantasy world of Disney.

The creation of such fantasy environments (as discussed above, in relation to Disney's Celebration township) has been characterised as a feature of post-modern existence – a feature which distinguishes our contemporary culture from the heroic age of modernism, which Tony Lloyd-Jones discussed in his historical survey. Another feature of post-modernism which we have barely touched on in this book is that of the information age. As already mentioned, there has been much speculation – in journalistic circles at least – that, with the greater use of digitised media, basic structures of social existence such as the home/work relationship would change. Were such changes to take place, with a greater use of home working and home shopping, for example, then the structures of urban life would change. This could have quite profound implications for the overall arrangement of our towns and cities. Since these changes have not yet occurred, perhaps it is sufficient to draw attention to them as possible areas of note.

The pattern of regeneration projects in Western Europe has also been touched on in this book. Much regeneration effort, in Britain at least, has been expended on derelict industrial sites and on housing estates. Whilst these two are manifestations of some distinctly poor areas of the environment, there are other areas which are also of poor quality and may become the focus of attention in the future. The interwar suburbs which ring most of the towns and cities in England and Wales provide an example of environment which could rapidly become obsolete as patterns of movement and household sizes change.

Another social trend is the emergence of greater social inequality, and thus differentiation in terms of lifestyle and more extreme urban spatial contrasts between domicile areas of different social groups. Although in Britain such divisions are generally related to matters of social class and regional disparity (Oatley, 1996) in North America, in spite of 30 years of equal rights legislation, there are growing, and marked contrasts within cities on racial lines, generally correlated to poverty factors, particularly in large cities such as Chicago and Los Angeles. In Britain it is interesting from an urban design perspective that in many ethnic minority areas, especially those such as Bradford and East London, which are the home of people of Indian-subcontinent origin, there is a demand for a new sensitivity in design guidance and development control to take into account different traditions in terms of architectural style, places of worship and house type. Such demands may be equally motivated by socially deprived or wealthy ethnic minority groups. Significantly, Prince Charles pops up again in this context, in supporting the recent construction of one of the largest and most ornate Hindoo temples outside India in Neasden, West London, which will surely have an influence on our conceptualisation of urban architecture and valid townscape.

The extent to which finance will be funnelled into areas of poor environmental quality is uncertain. The recent change of government may bring a change in thinking about development and a move away from the dominance of the free market. Because of this uncertainty, it is difficult to forecast who will be involved in urban design in the future and precisely what work they will be doing.

This book has made the argument that definitions of urban design are fluid and that the range of people involved in urban design may be wide. Some – ordinary members of the public taking part in an UDAT, or an investment banker taking a major decision – may not be designers in the conventional sense at all. This does not mean to say that the involvement of a trained designer is irrelevant. As has been argued in the introduction, the editors do not eschew the idea of a design training. Instead, we recognise that urban design is a complicated activity which requires the establishment of generative ideas and concepts which the design process can then elaborate and change. This book has not tackled the issue of how to design – rather it has looked at much of the context of urban design, its history, its place in the planning system and some current contexts for practice as well as issues and debates.

How to design is a large topic and one with which many students, when faced with a blank sheet of paper and their checklist of ideas and requirements, need urgent help. In our next volume we shall set out to provide that help, for which this volume was a preparation.

Creating future realities

In the final section it is appropriate, indeed expected, in the tradition of this series, to provide some Visions of the Future, for readers to think upon. The previous section has already identified some guidance, based upon tackling practical issues which have come up in the course of the book. As to the wider, visionary, brainstorming question of what cities ought to be like, it is not the place of this book to provide a blueprint, or model, for the ideal city of the future, and it would be presumptuous to do so. Indeed, all cities are different, and all individuals have different views on this matter. Readers who wish to investigate this further might consult the last chapters of earlier volumes in this series, all of which conclude with some suggestions and ideas on this topic. Also, the next volume on urban design, which, as stated, will take the form more of a primer and therefore will be more prescriptive, should, in due course, be consulted. However, here are some thoughts as an envoi to the book.

Generally, the recommendations on this matter discussed in previous volumes in the series, may be summed up as advocating as the 'ideal city form' a city of 'everyday life', a functional, human-scale, multi-centred city, a 'city of short distances' with an emphasis upon fuller provision of public transport. These still hold true. Such aspirations would involve a movement towards greater mixture of land uses, an element of dezoning, combined with a return to a multi-nucleated (many-centred) urban cell structure at district, local and neighbourhood level. This would provide a more even and available distribution of retail, employment, education and leisure facilities throughout the city, which would, in turn, generate fewer car journeys. Who knows what form transport, public or private, might take in the future – solar power? teleportation? bicycles? – over and above this we need to think of ways of designing cities that reduce the need to travel in the first place, by whatever means. Such an arrangement would create an environmentally more sustainable city, where there was less need to travel to work either by car or by transmat beam. The greater subdivision of cities into smaller, viable, local areas within this multi-nucleated city structure, would, perhaps, engender greater local democracy and accountability and therefore, perhaps, greater social equality, less local unemployment. Such a city form would make life easier for women and other carers who at present have to juggle and organise their daily round within spatially decentralised and disparate city forms, as they seek to combine work and home, and have to travel themselves (and/or ferry children on necessary journeys) between school, home, shops, work, leisure, recreation and other social facilities. Environmentally, this would be a far more sustainable city form. A greater sense of identity, belonging, and ownership within local areas might generate a stronger sense of civic pride and awareness of one's surroundings, leading to greater public demand for 'good urban design', public art, usable public open space, integrated landscape – and for accountable, well-organised management and maintenance which is so vital to maintaining the quality and ambience of an area.

Questions, and details as to what urban design would be like in the future, whether the building form would remain low- to medium-rise or whether we would see a return to high-rise and high densities within these new urban centres, is a complex issue which is left for the reader to speculate upon. However, it is a significant trend for the future that there appears to be a return of enthusiasm for high-rise in some circles at least. In February 1996 the Pretronas Building in Kuala Lumpar became the tallest building in the world at 445 metres, with 1.6 million square metres of floorspace, incorporating offices, shops and apartments and a mosque. Such a project in South East Asia is seen by many as being entirely appropriate as a reflection of the power and land-space pressures of a fast growing Tiger Economy (*Planning Week*, 31 October 1996, p. 14, and originally reported in *Planning Week* on 12 and 19 September). There is debate in Britain over the possible construction of a 400-metre high 'Millenium Tower', 94 storeys high, proposed at the Baltic Exchange in London, designed by Norman Foster. Foster also designed the 984 ft high, Commerce Bank HQ in Frankfurt, currently under construction, and also vying to be the tallest building in Europe. An emphasis upon a renaissance of high-rise in Britain seems to many to be a misplaced and inappropriate project – in the more restrained, conservative, and conservation-obsessed context of late-twentieth-century England, against the background of a much weaker economy and our declining, disillusioned post-industrial western culture. The messages put out by this and other mega-scale Millenium scheme proposals should be reflected upon by the readers as they say a great deal about the nature of our culture and civilisation. However, the future is not fixed, it is up to us as urban designers, planners, architects and citizens to design urban reality for the 21st century.

Bibliography

Abrams, M (1953) *The Mirror and the Lamp: Romantic Theory and Critical Tradition*, Oxford University Press, Oxford.

Access Committee for England (1992a) *Access Policies for Local Plans* Access Committee for England, London.

Access Committee for England (1992b) *Building Homes for Successive Generations Criteria for Accessible General Housing*, Access Committee for England, London.

Addenbrooke, P (1981) *Urban Planning and Design for Road Public Transport*, Conference of British Road Passenger Transport, London.

Alcock, A, Bentley, I, Murrain, P, McGlynn, S and Smith, S (1985 and 1992 new edition) *Responsive Environments*, Architectural Press, London, in association with Oxford Brookes University, Oxford.

Aldous, T (1988) *Inner City Regeneration and Good Design*, HMSO, London.

Aldous T (1992) *Urban Villages: A Concept for Creating Mixed-use Urban Developments on a Sustainable Scale*, Urban Villages Group, London.

Alexander, C (1977) *A Pattern Language – Towns, Buildings, Construction*, UCLA, California.

Almack, K and Grainger, P (1995) *Safety Check: A Practical Handbook on Woman's Safety*, STRIDE, Nottingham.

Anderson, S (ed.) (1978) *On Streets*, MIT Press, Cambridge, Mass.

Anscombe, I (1984) *A Woman's Touch: Woman in Design From 1860 to the Present Day*, Virago, London.

Appleyard, D, Lynch, K and Myer, J (1964) *The View from the Road*, MIT Press, Cambridge, Mass.

Arnstein, S (1969) 'A ladder of citizen participation in the USA', *Journal of the American Institute of Planners* (July 1969), also published in the *Journal of the Town Planning Institute* (April 1971).

Arriola, A (1994) 'Contemporary Public Art and Public Space – Spain', in Holman, V (ed.), *Transcript of Conference Proceedings Public Art – the New Agenda*, 18 November 1993, University of Westminster, pp. 13 – 17.

Arts Council (1989) *An Urban Renaissance: 16 Case Studies*, Arts Council, London.

Arts Council (1996) *Commissioning Art Works in London*, Arts Council for England in collaboration with the Public Art Forum, London.

Ashworth, W (1968) *The Genesis of Modern British Town Planning*, Routledge, London.

Askew, J (1996) 'Case Study: King's Cross', in C. Greed (1996) (ed.), *Implementing Town Planning: The Role of the Town Planning in the Development Process*, Longman, Harlow.

Babbit, I (1947) *Rousseau and Romanticism*, World Publicity Company, Cleveland, Ohio.

Bailey, N, Barker, A and MacDonald, K (1995) *Partnership Agencies in British Urban Policy*, UCL Press, London.

Baines, C and Smart, J (1991) *A Guide to Habitat Creation*, The London Ecology Unit.

Ball, S and Bell, S (1995) *Environmental Law*, Blackstone, London.

Banham, R (1960) *Theory and Design in the First Machine Age*, Architectural Press, London.

Banham, R (1976) *Megastructures: Urban Features of the Recent Past*, Thames and Hudson, London.

Barton, H, Guise, R and Davis, G (1995) *Sustainable Settlements: a Guide for Planners, Designers and Developers*, University of the West of England, Bristol, / Local Government Management Board, Bedford.

Bassett, K (1993) 'Urban Cultural Strategies and Urban Regeneration: A Case Study and Critique', *Environment and Planning A* Vol. 25, pp. 1773–88.

Batchelor, P and Lewis, D (1985) (eds), *Urban Design in Action*, North Carolina State University, Raleigh, North Carolina.

Bath City Council (1993) *Cherishing Outdoor Places, A Landscape Strategy for Bath*, Bath C.C., Bath.

Battersby, C (1989) *Gender and Genius: Towards a Feminist Aesthetics*, The Woman's Press, London.

Bee, S and Rowland, J (1994) 'Participation and Reality', *Urban Design Quarterly* No. 49, January, pp. 26–7.

Bell, C and Bell, R (1972) *City Fathers: The Early History of Town Planning in Britain*, Pelican, Harmondsworth, p. 284.

Belloni, C (1994) 'A woman-friendly city: politics concerning the organisation of time in Italian cities', proceedings of *Woman in the City: Housing Services and Urban Environment,* OECD (Organisation for Economic Cooperation and Development), Paris.

Bentham, G (1986) 'Public Satisfaction and Social, Economic and Environmental Conditions in the Counties of England', *Institute of British Geographers – Transactions*, 11 (1) pp. 27–36.

Berman, M (1984) *All that's Solid Melts into Air: the Experience of Modernity*, Verso, London.

Bianchini, F (1995) 'The twenty four hour city', *Demos Quarterly*, Issue 5.

Bianchini, F, Fisher, M, Montgomery, J and Warpole, K (1991) *City Centres, City Cultures: the Role of the Arts in the Revitalisation of Towns and Cities,* 2nd edn., Centre for Local Economic Strategies, Birmingham.

Bianchini, F, Dawson, J and Evans, R (1992) 'Flagship projects in urban regeneration,' in Healey, P et al.

(1992) (eds), *Rebuilding The City: Property-led Urban Regeneration*, E and F N Spon, London.

Bianchini, F and Parkinson, M (1993) (eds) *Cultural Policy and Urban Regeneration in Western Europe*, Manchester University Press, Manchester.

Biddulph, M (1996) 'An evaluation of a public sector residential layout guide', *Urban Design International*, Vol.1, No.2, pp. 145–62.

Billingham, J (1996) 'Review – World Cities: Berlin', in Alan Balfour (ed.) *Urban Design* 58 April, p. 36.

Blowers, A (1993) (ed.), *Planning for a Sustainable Environment*, A Report from the Town and Country Planning Association, Earthscan Publications Ltd, London.

Bohigas, O (1987) *Strategic Metastasis* in Hortet, L and Adria, M (eds), *Barcelona: Spaces and Sculptures 1982–86*, Ajuntament de Barcelona, Barcelona. pp. 11–12

Booth, C, Darke, J and Yeandle, S (1996) *Changing Places: Women's Lives in the City*, Paul Chapman Publishing, London.

Bowlby, S (1989) 'Gender issues and retail geography', in Whatmore, S and Little, J (eds), *Geography and Gender*, Association for Curriculum Development, London.

Boys, J (1991) 'Dealing with Difference,' *Built Environment: Women and the Designed Environment*, 16 (4), pp. 249/256.

Branch, M (1975) *Urban Planning Theory*, Dowden, Hutchinson and Ross, Stroudsburg, Pa.

Breitbart, M M and Ellen-Pader, J (1995) 'Establishing Ground: Representing Gender and Race in a Mixed Housing Development', *Gender, Place and Culture*, 2 (1), pp. 5/20.

Bright, J, Maloney, H, Pettersson, G and Farr, J (1985) *After Entryphones*, Safe Neighbourhoods Unit, London.

Brindley, T, Rydin, Y and Stoker, G (1996) *Remaking Planning*, 2nd edn., Routledge, London.

Bristol (1995) 'Streets Ahead: International conference on the environmental, human, and economic aspects of street management and design', University of the West of England, Bristol.

British Parliamentary Lighting Group (December 1996) *Bulletin*, Swan House, 207, Balham Road, London SW1 7BQ. 0181 675 5432.

Broadbent, G (1990) *Emerging Concepts in Urban Space Design*, Van Nostrand Reinhold, London.

Broadbent, G (1991) *Deconstruction: A Student Guide*, Academy Editions, London.

Broadby, M (1968) *Planning for People,* NCSS/Bedford Square Press, London.

Bromley, R (1995)) 'Street vendors, public policies, and private initiatives', Paper presented at *'Streets Ahead'* International conference on the environmental, human, and economic aspects of street management and design', University of the West of England, Bristol.

Broude, N and Garrard, M (1982) *Feminism and Art History: Questioning the Litany*, Harper and Rowe, New York.

Brunt, R and Rowan, C (1982) (eds), *Feminism, Culture and Politics,* Lawrence and Wishart, London.

Buard, Lebhar and Le Guay (1989) *Architectures Capitales – Paris 1979–1989*, Electa Moniteur, Paris.

Buchanan, P (1988) 'What city? A plea for place in the public realm', *Architectural Review,* No. 1101, October 1988.

Buchanan, P (1992) 'Barcelona, a city regenerated', *Architectural Review* Vol. 191, No. 1146, August 1992, pp. 11–14.

Building Research Establishment, P J Littlefair (1991) *Site Layout Planning for Daylight and Sunlight: A Good Practice Guide*, BRE, Watford.

Burdett, R (1991) 'Architecture of the Public Realm: Frankfurt Museums 1980–1991, Catalogue Notes', The Architecture Foundation, London.

Burgess, J and Harrison, C M (1988) 'People, Parks and the Urban Green: a study of popular meanings and values for open spaces in the city', *Urban Studies* (25) pp. 455–473.

Burgess, J (1994) *The Politics of Trust: Reducing Fear of Crime in Urban Parks*, Working Paper No. 8, Comedia Demos Study: The Future of Urban Parks and Open Spaces, Comedia, Stroud.

Businaro, U (1994) *Technology and the Future of Cities*, Commission of the European Communities, Brussels.

Bynoe, I, Oliver, M and Barnes, C (1991) *Equal Rights for Disabled People*, Institute for Public Policy Research, London.

Calthorpe, P (1993) *The Next American Metropolis*, Princeton Architecture Press, New York.

Campbell, B (1995) 'Little Beirut', *The Guardian Weekend*, 1 July 1995, pp. 14/21.

Carmona, M (1991) *The London Docklands, An Experiment in Incremental Urban Planning,* Institute of Planning, Nottingham University, Nottingham, Unpublished M.A. Dissertation, pp. 133–6.

Carmona, M (1996a) 'Controlling Urban Design – Part 1: A Possible Renaissance? *Journal of Urban Design*, Ed Oc, T, Vol. 1, No. 1, pp 47–74.

Carmona, M (1996b) 'Controlling Urban Design – Part 2: Glasgow's Renaissance', *Journal of Urban Design*, Vol. 1, No. 2.

Carr, S and Lane, A (1993) *Practical Conservation: Urban Habitats*, Hodder and Stoughton, London, Sydney, Auckland.

Caulton, J (1995) 'Urban design's soft city', *Urban Design Quarterly* No. 55, October 1995.

Cavanagh, S, Debono, J and Jaspert, J (1988) *Thinking of Small Children: Access, Provision and Play*, We Welcome Small Children Campaign, LB Camden, Women's Design Service, London.

Cavanagh, S (1992) *Designing Housing for Older Women*, Women's Design Service, London.

Cavanagh, S and Ware, V (1990) *At Women's Convenience: A Handbook on the Design of Women's Public Toilets*, Women's Design Service, London, pp. 9–17: 'From Cesspools to Restrooms'.

Cervero, R (1989) *America's Suburban Centres: The Land Use Transportation Link*, Unwin Hyman, London.

Chadwick, G (1978) *A Systems View of Planning: Towards A Theory of the Urban and Regional Planning Process*, Pergamon, Oxford.

Chadwick, W (1990) *Women, Art and Society,* Thames and Hudson, London.

Chapman, D W and Larkham, P J (1993) *Discovering the Art of Relationship: Urban Design, Aesthetic Control and Design Guidance*, University of Central England, Birmingham.

Cherry, G (1974) *The Evolution of British Town Planning*, Leonard Hill, London.

Cherry, G (1988) *Cities and Plans: the Shaping of Urban Britain in the Nineteenth and Twentieth Centuries*, Edward Arnold, London.

Cherry, G (1995) 'Town planning and planning ideals in 20th century Britain', *International Report*, May 1995.

Cheshire County Council (1974) *Planning Standards: Roads*, Cheshire County Council.

Church, C and McHarry, J (1994) 'Indications of Sustainability', *Town and Country Planning*, July/August 1994, Town and Country Planning Association, London, pp 208–9.

Clarke, F (1995) 'Pulling Back from the Brink', *Town and Country Planning*, July 1995, Vol. 64, No. 7, p. 186.

Clifford, S (1993) *Places: The City and the Invisible London*, Public Art Development Trust and Common Ground, London.

Coleman, A (1985, 1990) *Utopia on Trial: Vision and Reality in Planned Housing*, Hilary Shipman, London.

Colomina, B (1992) (ed.) *Sexuality and Space,* Princeton Papers on Architecture, Princeton University School of Architecture, Princeton, New Jersey.

Colquhoun, I (1994) *Urban Regeneration*, Batsford, London.

Comedia (1991) *Out of Hours, A Study of Economic, Social and Cultural Life in Twelve Town Centres in the UK,* Comedia, Stroud.

Comedia (1995) *The Future of Public Libraries Project: Libraries in a World of Cultural Change,* UCL Press, London.

Congress for New Urbanism (1996) *CNU Charter,* CNU, Charleston, South Carolina.

Congressional Digest (1989) *Americans with Disabilities Act.* 68 (12): 289–314, Federal Publications, Washington.

Conway, H (1996) *Public Parks*, Shire Garden History, Princes Risborough.

Coombes, T J, Farthing, S M and Winter, J (1994) *Environmental Quality and Facilities on New Housing Estates*, Town and Country Planning Working Paper No. 18, Bristol Polytechnic, Bristol.

Cork, R (1991) 'Art in the City' in Fisher, M and Owen, U (eds) *Whose Cities?,* Penguin, Harmondsworth.

Costello, A (1994) 'Community Based Charettes' *Urban Design Quarterly,* No. 49, January 1994, pp. 18–19.

Coulson, M (1980) 'Space Around the Home', *Architects Journal*, 24 and 31 December 1980, pp. 1245–60.

Coupland, A (1996) (ed.) *Reclaiming the City,* E & FN Spon, London.

Cowan, R, Hannay, P and Owens, R (1988) 'The Light on Top of the Tunnel', *Architects' Journal,* 23 March 1988.

Cowan, R (1995) *The Cities Design Forgot: a Manifesto,* Urban Initiatives, London.

Cowan, R (1997) *The City Set Free*, Civic Design Exchange, London.

Cowan, R and Gallery, L (1990) (eds), 'A Vision for London', *Architect's Journal*, 14 March 1990.

Cowan, R and Billingham, J (1996) 'The Urban Design Agenda', *Urban Design Quarterly*, No. 58, April 1996, pp. 10–11.

CPRE (Council for the Protection of Rural England) (1995) *Local Attraction: The Design of New Housing in the Countryside,* CPRE, London.

Crane, D (1960) 'The Dynamic City', *Architectural Design*, Vol. 30.

Crawford, M (1992) 'All the World a Mall? in Sorkin, M (1992) (ed.) The New American City and the End of Public Space. *Variations on a Theme Park*, Noonday, New York.

Creese, W (1967) *The Legacy of Raymond Unwin*, MIT Press, Cambridge, Mass.

Crouch, D (1994) *The Popular Culture of City Parks*, Working Paper No. 9, Comedia Demos Study: The Future of Urban Parks and Open Spaces, Comedia, Stroud.

Cullen, G (1961) *Townscape,* Architectural Press, London.

Cullen, G and McKinsey & Company (1984) *The Potential for Glasgow City Centre,* Scottish Development Agency, Glasgow.

Cullen, G and Hunter, P (1994) *The Investment Performance of Listed Buildings*, English Heritage, London.

Cullingworth, J B (1975) *Environmental Planning 1939–69, Vol. 1, Reconstruction and Land Use Planning*, HMSO, London.

Cuthbert, A (1996) 'An Interview with Manual Castells', *Cities*, February 1996, pp. 3–10.

Dacorum Borough Council (1995) *Residential Area Character Study (draft)*, Dacorum B.C., Hemel Hempstead.

Davis, A (1982) *Women, Race and Class*, Women's Press, London.

Davies, L (1996) 'Equality and Planning: Gender and Disability', in Greed, C (ed.), *Implementing Town Planning*, Longman, Harlow.

Dawson, J (1994) 'Dublin', in Harding, A, Dawson, J, Evans, R and Parkinson, M (1994) *European Cities Towards 2000: Profiles, Policies and Prospects*, Manchester University Press, Manchester.

Department of the Environment (1932) Department of Building originally) *Residential Roads and Footpaths*, DB32.

Department of the Environment (1973) *Circular 82/73: Bus Operation in Residential and Industrial Areas*, HMSO, London.

Department of the Environment (1977) *Residential Roads and Footpaths: Layout Considerations*, (Design Bulletin 32, updated 2nd edn. 1992), HMSO, London.

Department of the Environment (1980) *Development Control: Policy and Practice*, Circular 22/80.

Department of the Environment (1985) *Access for the Disabled*, Development Control Policy Note (DCPN) No. 16, HMSO, London.

Department of the Environment (1990) *This Common Inheritance*, HMSO, London.

Department of the Environment (1991) *Development Control Study: Time for Design, Monitoring the Initiative*, HMSO, London.

Department of the Environment (1992a) *Planning Policy Guidance (PPG1): General Policy and Principles*, HMSO, London.

Department of the Environment (1992b) *Planning Policy Guidance, PPG12: Development Plans and Regional Planning Guidance*, HMSO, London.

Department of the Environment (1992c) *Development Plans: A Good Practice Guide*, HMSO, London.

Department of the Environment (1992d) *Access and Facilities for Disabled People: Approved Document M*, HMSO, London.

Department of the Environment (1993a) *Circular 8/93: Awards of Costs Incurred in Planning and Other (Including Compulsory Purchase Order) Proceedings*, HMSO, London.

Department of the Environment (1993b) *Crime Prevention on Council Estates*, HMSO, London.

Department of the Environment (1994a) *Quality in Town and Country, a Discussion Document*, DoE, London.

Department of the Environment (1994a) *Planning Policy Guidance (PPG13): Transport*, HMSO, London.

Department of the Environment (1995a) *Quality in Town and Country, Urban Design Campaign*, DoE, London.

Department of the Environment (1995b) *Consultation Paper: Planning Policy Guidance Note 6 (Revised): Town Centres and Retail Development*, DoE, London.

Department of the Environment (1995c) *Regional Planning Guidance (draft RPG3): Strategic Guidance for London Planning Authorities*, HMSO, London.

Department of the Environment (1995d) *The Use of Conditions in Planning Permissions*, Circular 11/95.

Department of the Environment (1997a) *Planning Policy Guidance: General Principles and Practice*, PPG1.

Department of the Environment (1997b) *Planning and Policy Guidance 7: The Countryside – Environmental Quality and Social and Economic Development*.

Department of the Environment (1997c) *The Design Improvement Controlled Experiment (DICE): An Evaluation of the Costs and Benefits of Estate re-modelling*, London: Price Waterhouse Consultants, for the Department of the Environment.

Department of the Environment and Department of National Heritage, *Planning Policy Guidance: Planning and the Historic Environment* (1994) PPG 15, HMSO, London.

Department of the Environment and Department of Transport (1992 originally 1977) *Design Bulletin 32 Second Edition: Residential Roads and Footpaths: Layout Considerations*, HMSO, London.

Department of the Environment and Department of Transport (1994) *Planning Policy Guidance Note 13: Transport*, HMSO, London.

Department of the Environment and Housing Research Foundation (1976) *Design Guidance Survey*, HMSO, London.

Department of the Environment and Ministry of Agriculture, Fisheries and Food (1995) *Rural England, A Nation Committed to a Living Countryside*, HMSO, London.

Department of Environment and the Welsh Office (1994) *Planning out Crime*, Ciricular 5/94.

Department of Transport (1995a) *Transport Statistics for Great Britain*, HMSO, London.

Department of Transport (1995b) *National Travel Survey for 1995*, HMSO, London.

Devas, N and Rakodi, C (1993) (eds), *Managing Fast Growing Cities*, Longman, Harlow.

Dormer, P (1992) 'Lipstick on the face of a gorilla', *The Independent* Wednesday 9 September 1992, p. 10.

Dorment, R (1995) Review of HG, *Observer*, 17 September 1995, reproduced in cuttings from *The Edge Supplement to Theatre Record*, 24 September–7 October 1995, pp. 10–11.

Douglas, M (1966) *Purity and Danger: An Analysis of the Concepts of Pollution and Taboo*, (reprinted 1966), Routledge, London.

Dresser, M and Ollerenshaw, P (1966) (eds), *The Making of Modern Bristol*, Redcliffe Press, Bristol.

Driedger, D (1989) *The Last Civil Rights Movement: Disabled People's International*, Hurst, London.

Dunlop, R (1995) 'Public Art in the Urban Environment, with particular reference to transport systems', unpublished PhD thesis, University of Westminster, London.

Dunster, D (1989) 'History City', *Architects' Journal* 8 November 1989, pp. 34–54.

Dyos, H J (1976) *The Study of Urban Form*, Arnold, London, p. 34, footnote 100 for research on water supply at that time.

Economakis, R (1992) (ed), *Leon Krier: Architecture and Urban Design 1967–1992*, Academy Editions, London.

Ecotec (1993) *Reducing Transport Emissions Through Planning*, HMSO, London.

Edwards, B (1992) *London Docklands: Urban Design in an Age of Deregulation*, Butterworth, London.

Edwards, T (1906, 1922) *Good and Bad Manners in Architecture,* Cassell, London.

Eisenman, P (1993) *Re-working Eisenman,* Academy Editions, London.

Eisenstaedt, P (1985) *Eisenstaedt on Eisenstaedt,* Abbeyville Press, New York.

Ellis, see Williams Ellis

Ellin, N (1996) *Postmodern Urbanism,* Blackwell, Oxford.

English Heritage (1993) *Conservation Area Practice,* English Heritage, London.

English Heritage (1994) 'What is a conservation area partnership?', *Conservation Area Partnership Schemes,* Leaflet No. 1, From English Heritage, 23 Savile Row, London W1X 1AR.

Essex County Council (1973) *A Design Guide for Residential Areas*, Essex County Council, Chelmsford.

EUROFEM (1996) 'Moving Towards a Gender Conscious City', paper presented at 'European Coalition on Gender Issues for Habitat II, Istanbul: The City Summit', Habitat II in association with Eurofem Network, Ministry of the Environment, Helsinki, Finland.

Evans, R 'Birmingham' in Harding, A et al. (1994) (eds), *European Cities towards 2000: Profiles, Policies and Prospects,* Manchester University Press, Manchester.

Farthing, S and Winter J (1988) 'Residential Density and Levels of Satisfaction with the External Residential Environment: A Research Report on New Private Sector Housing Schemes in West Totton', *Faculty of the Built Environment Working Paper No. 11*, University of the West of England, Bristol.

Farthing, S, Winter, J, and Coombes, T (1994) 'Coordinating Facility Provision and New Housing Development: Impact on Car and Local Facility Use' in Farthing (ed.) , *Towards Sustainability Conference Papers*, Faculty of the Built Environment WP38, University of the West of England, Bristol.

Feaver, W (1995) Review of the HG, *Observer,* 17 September 1995, reproduced in cuttings from *The*

Edge Supplement to Theatre Record, 24 September–7 October 1995, pp. 10–11.

Fearns, D (1993) *Access Audits: a Guide and Checklists for Appraising the Accessibility of Buildings for Disabled Users,* Centre for Accessible Environments, London.

Finkelstein, V (1993) 'Disability: a social challenge or an administrative responsibility?', in Swain, J, Finkelstein, V, French, S and Oliver, M (eds), *Disabling Barriers – Enabling Environments,* Sage Publications, London, in association with the Open University.

Fisher, M and Rogers, R (1992) *A New London,* Penguin, London.

Fordham, G (1995) *Made to Last: Creating Sustainable Neighbourhood and Estate Regeneration,* Joseph Rowntree Foundation, York.

Frampton, K (1985) *Modern Architecture: a critical history,* Thames and Hudson, London.

Franc, K A (1994) 'Questioning the American Dream: recent housing innovations in the United States', in Gilroy, R and Woods, R (1996) (eds), *Housing Women,* Routledge, London.

Frankum, P (1992) 'Marsham Street Brake on Plan Access Policy' *Planning* 11 September, Ambit Publications, Cheltenham.

French, S (1993) 'Can you see the rainbow?' The roots of denial, in Swain, J, Finkelstein, V, French, S and Oliver, M (eds), *Disabling Barriers – Enabling Environments,* Sage Publications, London, in association with the Open University.

Frey, H (1994) 'Transforming a City', *Interface,* March 1994, University of Strathclyde, Glasgow.

Frick, D (1995) 'Berlin: Town Planning under Particular Conditions', *European Planning Studies* 3(4), pp. 427–39.

Galloway, M and Evans, B (1991) 'Glasgow City Centre', *Urban Design Quarterly,* Issue 37, January 1991, pp. 10–15.

Galloway, M (1993) 'The Crown Street Regeneration Project', *Town and Country Planning* June 1993, pp. 140–41.

Geddes, P (1905) 'Civics: as applied sociology', *Sociological Papers* 1904, Macmillan, London.

Gerz, J and Shalev-Gerz, E (1994) *The Hamburg Monument against Fascist Germany,* Gerd Hatje, Berlin.

Gibberd, P (1967 first published 1953) *Town Design,* Architectural Press, London.

Gillespies (Consultants) (1990) *Glasgow City Centre and The Clyde, Continuing the Renaissance,* Scottish Development Agency and Glasgow District Council, Glasgow.

Glasgow City Council (1990) *Glasgow Central Area Local Plan (Draft),* Glasgow City Council, Glasgow.

Glasgow City Council (1991) *Merchant City: Policy and Development Framework,* Glasgow City Council, Glasgow.

Glasgow City Council (1996) working drafts of the *Revised Glasgow City Centre Local Plan,* Glasgow City Council, Glasgow.

GLC (Greater London Council) (1986a) *Changing Places: Positive Action on Women and Planning,* GLC, London.

GLC (Greater London Council) (1986b) *Town Centres and Shopping Attitudes Survey: Preliminary Results,* GLC, London.

Goldsmith, S (1963, 1967, 1976) *Designing for the Disabled,* RIBA Publications, London.

Goodey, B (1974) *Where You're At,* Penguin, London.

Gosling, D (1996) *Gordon Cullen: Visions of Urban Design,* Academy Editions, London.

Gosling, D and Maitland, B (1984) *Concepts of Urban Design,* Academy Editions, London.

Graham, S and Marvin, S (1996) *Telecommunications and the City: Electronic spaces, Urban Places,* Routledge, London.

Grant, M (1995) *Urban Planning Law,* Sweet and Maxwell, London.

Greed, C (1991) *Surveying Sisters: Women in a Traditional Male Profession,* Routledge, London.

Greed, C (1994) *Women and Planning: Creating Gendered Differences,* Routledge, London.

Greed, C (1996a) (ed.) *Implementing Town Planning: The Role of Town Planning in the Development Process,* Longman, Harlow.

Greed, C (1996b) (ed.) *Investigating Town Planning,* Longman, Harlow.

Greed, C (1996c) *Introducing Town Planning,* 2nd edn., Longman, Harlow.

Greed, C (1996d) 'Toilets and townscape: townscape and taboos' *Planning History,* Vol. 18, No. 1 pp. 14–18.

Greed, C (1996) MA/Postgraduate Diploma in Town and Country Planning – Unit 3, *Equal Opportunities,* RTP1, Joint Distance Learning Unit, London.

Greenberg, S (1995) 'Time's arrows', *Blueprint,* October 1995, p. 24.

Greer, G (1979) *The Obstacle Race: The Fortunes of Women Painters and Their Work,* Farrar Straus Giroux, New York.

Griffiths, J (1995) 'Griffiths Flies Kite for Role in Improving Urban Design', 30 June 1995, *Planning,* No. 1125, pp. 6–7.

Griggs, R (1995) 'Public Art: A Review of Local Authority Implementation', unpublished MA thesis, School of Urban Development & Planning, University of Westminster, London.

Gummer, J (1994) 'More Quality in Town and Country', *Department of the Environment News Release 713,* 12 December 1994, DoE, London.

Gummer, J (1995) 'The Way to Achieve "Quality" in Urban Design', *Department of the Environment News Release 162,* 30 March 1995, DoE, London.

HM Government (1990) *This Common Inheritance: Britain's Environmental Strategy*, HMSO, London.

HM Government (1994) *Sustainable Development: the UK Strategy,* HMSO, London.

Hall, P (1988) *Cities of Tomorrow,* Basil Blackwell, Oxford.

Hall, A C (1990) *Generation of Design Objectives,* Anglia College Enterprises Ltd, Chelmsford.

Hall, P (1992) *Urban and Regional Planning,* 2nd edn., Routledge, London.

Hall, P (1995) 'Planning and urban design in the 1990s', *Urban Design,* No. 56, October 1995.

Hallyburton, G and Dally, D (1992) *A Comparative Study of Urban Design in Selected Cities*, ISO-CARP, The Hague.

Hanna, J (1996) 'Whose streets are they anyway?', *The Geographical Magazine,* June 1996, pp. 18–20, with reference to the 1993 Traffic Calming Act.

Harding, A, Dawson, J, Evans, R and Parkinson, M (1994) (eds), *European Cities Towards 2000: Profiles, Policies and Prospects,* Manchester University Press, Manchester.

Harrison, C M and Burgess, J (1995) *Accessible Natural Greenspace in Towns and Cities,* English Nature Research Reports, London, No. 153.

Harvey, D (1975) *Social Justice and the City,* Arnold, London.

Harvey, D (1989) *The Condition of Postmodernity,* Blackwell, Oxford.

Hass-Klau, C, Nold, I, Böcjer, G and Crampton, G (1992) *Civilised Streets: A Guide to Traffic Calming,* Environmental and Transport Planning, Brighton.

Hayden, D (1980) *What would a Non-Sexist City be like? Speculations on Housing, Urban Design and Human Work*. Women and the American City, University of Chicago Press, Chicago.

Hayden, D (1995) *Redesigning the American Dream*, Norton, London.

Hayden, D (1995) *The Power of Place: Urban Landscapes as Public History*, The Massachusetts Institute of Technology Press, Massachusetts.

HBF and RIBA (House Builders Federation and Royal Institute of British Architects) (1990) *Good Design in Housing*, London, HBF.

Healey, P (1994) Integrating the Concept of Social Diversity into Public Policy, Issue paper. High Level Conference. 'Women in the City: Housing, Services and the Urban Environment', Paris, November 1994. OECD, Paris.

Heap, D (1996) *An Outline of Planning Law*, Sweet and Maxwell, London.

Heath, J (1992) (ed.), *The Furnished Landscape: Applied Art in Public Places*, Bellew in collaboration with the Crafts Council and the Arts Council, London.

Hedicar, P and Curtis, C (1995) *Residential Development and Car-based Travel: Does Location Make a Difference?*, Oxford Brookes University, Oxford.

Hellman, L (1995) [Cartoon] *Building Design*, No. 1225, 16 June 1995, p. 9.

Hewison, R (1987) *The Heritage Industry*, Methuen, London.

Hillier, B and Hanson, J (1984) *The Social Logic of Space*, Cambridge University Press, Cambridge.

Hillman, M and Whalley, A (1983) *Energy and Personal Travel*, Policy Studies Institute, London.

Hillman, M, Adams, J and Whitelegg, J (1991) *One False Move*, Policy Studies Institute, London.

Hirst, C (1996) 'Unity, purity, and a splash of local colour', *Planning Week*, Vol. 4, No. 18, 2 May 1996, p. 9.

Holman, V (1994) (ed.), 'Public Art – The New Agenda', transcript of Conference at Institute of Education, 17 November 1993, University of Westminster, London.

Holmes-Siedle, J (1996) *Barrier Free Design*, Butterworth Architecture, Oxford.

HOLSA (1992) *Barcelona, '92 Barcelona*, Barcelona Olympic Holding SA.

Holt, G (1988, with updates) (ed.), *Development Control Practice*, Ambit Publications, Gloucester.

Home Office Crime Prevention Centre (1994) *Police Architectural Liaison Manual of Guidance*, HMSO, London.

Hooks, b (1982) *Ain't I a Woman: Black Women and Feminism*, Pluto Press, London.

House of Commons, Command 9498 (1985) *Royal Fine Art Commission; Twenty Second Report, October 1971 – December 1984*, London, HMSO.

Howard, E (1960, originally 1898) *Garden Cities of Tomorrow*, Faber, London.

Hulme Regeneration Ltd (1994) *A Guide to Development: Hulme, Manchester*, HRL, Manchester.

Imrie, R (1996) *Disability and the City: International Perspectives*, Paul Chapman, London.

Imrie, R and Wells, P (1993), 'Disablism, planning, and the built environment', *Environment and Planning C: Government and Policy*, Vol. 11, pp. 213–31.

Institution of Lighting Engineers (1996) *Guidance Notes for the Reduction of Light Pollution*, Lennox House, 9 Lawford Road, Rugby, Warwickshire, CV21 2DZ, tel. 01788 576492.

IPPR (1996) *Citizens' Juries: Towards Best Practice*, Working paper from IPPR, tel. 0171 470 6100.

Jacobs, J (1992, originally 1961 and 1984) *The Death and Life of Great American Cities: the Failure of Town Planning*, Peregrine Books, London.

Jenks, M (1983) 'Residential Roads Researched' *Architects Journal*, 29 June 1983, pp. 35–67.

JRF (Joseph Rowntree Foundation) (1993) *Lifetime Housing*, Available with accompanying video from JRF, The Homestead, 40 Water End, York, YO3 6LP.

Karn, V and Sheridan, L (1994) *New Homes in the 1990s*, Joseph Rowntree Foundation, York.

Karn, V and Sheridan, L (1995) *Housing Quality, a Practical Guide for Tenants and their Representatives*, Joseph Rowntree Foundation, York.

Katz, P (1994) *The New Urbanism: Towards an Architecture of Community*, McGraw Hill, New York.

Kelbaugh, D (1989) (ed.) *The Pedestrian Pocket Book*, Princeton University Press, New York.

Kenvyn, I (1995) 'The street as arena for adolescent rite of passage', paper presented at 'Streets Ahead: International conference on the environmental, human, and economic aspects of street management and design', University of the West of England, Bristol.

Kira, A (1975) *The Bathroom*, Penguin, London.

Koolhaas, R (1990) *Projets Urbains (1985–1990)*, Collegi d'Arquitectes de Catalunya, Barcelona.

Koolhaas, R and Mau, B (1995) *Small, Medium, Large, Extra Large*, Office for Metropolitan Architecture, Rotterdam (ed. J. Sigler).

Kostof, S (1991) *The City Shaped: Urban Patterns and Meanings through History*, Thames and Hudson, London.

KPMG, Peat Marwick and The Safe Neighbourhoods Unit (1990) *Counting out Crime: the Nottingham Crime Audit*, KPMG, London.

Krier, R (1984) *Urban Space*, Academy Editions, London.

Kunzmann, K and Lan, R (1994) 'Frankfurt', in Harding, A (et al.) (eds), *European Cities Towards 2000: Profiles, Policies and Prospects*, Manchester University Press, Manchester.

Lacey, S (1995) (ed.), *Mapping the Terrain: New Genre Public Art*, New Bay Press, Seattle, Washington.

Lancaster, M (1996) *Colourscape*, Academy editions, VCH Publishing, London, and see *Architectural Design* journal on 'colour in architecture' in Vol. 121).

Lane, P and Peto, M (1996) *Environment Act 1995*, Blackstone, London.

Latham, I (1995) 'The surreal city: Rem Koolhaas at Euralille', *Architecture Today*, No. 55, February 1995, pp. 19–25.

LB Greenwich (1994) *Designing for Personal Safety*, LB Greenwich, London.

LBDRT (London Boroughs Disability Team) (1991), 'Access for all: Special Feature', *Community Network*, 8 (3), Autumn 1991, Town and Country Planning Association, London.

LCC (London Country Council) (1928) *Public Conveniences in London*, Report of Medical Officer of Health, London County Council, London.

LDR/HLN Consultancy (1988) *Pedestrian Movement and Open Space Framework*, City of Birmingham.

Lacey, S (1995) (ed.), *Mapping the Terrain: New Genre Public Art*, New Bay Press, Seattle, Washington.

Leach, B (1989) 'Disabled people and the implementation of local authorities' equal opportunities policies', *Public Administration*, Vol. 67, pp. 65–77.

Lee, T (1968) 'Urban Neighbourhood as a Socio-Spatial Scheme', *Human Relations*, 21, pp. 241–67.

Little, J, Peake and Richardson, P (1988) *Women and Cities: Gender and the Urban Environment*, Macmillan, London.

Lloyd-Jones, T (1966) 'Curitiba – sustainability by design', *Urban Design*, No. 57. January 1996, pp. 26–32.

Local Transport Today, 12 October 1995.

Loew, S (1995) 'Lille bidding high for urban quality', *Planning*, No. 1149, 15 December 1995, pp. 20–21.

Loftman, P and Nevin, B (1993) 'Inter-city competition – intra city inequality', *Town and Country Planning* 62(12) December 1993, pp. 324–5.

Loftman, P and Nevin, B (1995) 'Prestige Projects and Urban Regeneration in the 1980s and 1990s: a review of benefits and limitations', *Planning Practice and Research,* Vol. 10, Nos. 3/4, pp. 299–315.

Lucan, J (1991) *OMA – Rem Koolhaas: Architecture 1970–1990,* Princeton Architectural Press, New York.

LWPF (1993) *UDP Policies,* Broadsheet 7, Women's Design Service, London, in association with London Women and Planning Forum.

Lynch K (1960, new ed. 1988) *The Image of the City,* MIT Press, Cambridge, Mass.

Lynch, K (1980) *Managing a Sense of Region*, MIT Press, Cambridge, Mass.

Lynch, K (1987) *Good City Form*, MIT Press, Cambridge, Mass.

Lynch, K and Hack, G (1984) *Site Planning* (3rd edn.), MIT Press, Cambridge, Mass.

Manley, S (1996) 'Walls of exclusion: the role of local authorities in creating barrier-free streets', *Landscape and Urban Planning*, Vol. 35, Nos. 2–3, August 1996 pp. 132–52.

Markus, T. Teymur, N and Woolley, T (1988) (eds), *Rehumanising Housing,* Butterworth, Oxford.

Martin, L and March, L (1972) (eds), *Urban Space and Structures*, Cambridge University Press, Cambridge.

Massey, D (1992) 'A Place Called Home?', in Massey, D (1994) (ed.), *Space, Place and Gender,* Polity, Cambridge, pp. 157–73.

Matrix (1984) *Making Space: Women and the Man Made Environment,* Pluto, London.

Mayhew, P and Maung, N (1992) *Surveying Crime: Findings from the 1992 British Crime Survey,* Home Office Research and Statistics Department – Research Findings No. 2.

Mayhew, P, Mirrles, B and Maung, N (1994) *Theories in Crime: Findings from the 1994 Births Crime Survey,* Home Office Research and Statistics Department – Research Findings No. 14.

McDowell, L (1992) 'Multiple voices speaking from outside and inside "The project"', *Antipode: A Radical Journal of Geography,* 24 (1) January 1992.

McGonagle, D (1996) 'On reading Temple Bar' in *Temple Bar: The Power of an Idea*, Temple Bar Properties Ltd, Dublin.

McKie, L and Edwards, J (1995) 'The "roll" of the public toilet in the engendered city', paper presented at the British Sociological Association Conference at Leicester University, April 1995.

Meadows, D (1968) *Limits to Growth*, Club of Rome.

METRAC (1994) (Metro Action Committee on Public Violence Against Women) *Women's Safety Audit Pack*, Metro Toronto Council, Toronto.

Middleton, D (1982) (ed.), 'Urban design', *The Cornell Journal of Architecture*, Rizzoli, New York.

Milner, J and Urquhart (1991) 'Architectural education: What about access?', *Access by Design*, Vol. 56, pp. 17–18, Centre of Accessible Environments, London.

Miles, M (1991) *Art for Public Places: Critical Essays*, Winchester School of Art Press, Winchester.

Miles, M (1996) 'Imaginative interventions: art and craft in urban design', *Urban Design International* Vol. 1, No. 1, pp. 81–8.

Miller, M (1992) *Raymond Unwin: Garden Cities and Town Planning*, Leicester University Press, Leicester.

Mills, G (1994) 'Fuel savings from park and ride schemes', in Farthing, 5 (ed.) Towards Sustainability Conference Papers, Faculty of the Built Environment WP38, University of the West of England, Bristol.

Milroy, B M and Wismer, S (1994) 'Communities Work and Public/Private Sphere Models, *Gender, Place and Culture* 1 (1) pp. 71–90.

Ministry of Health (1933) *Circular 1305/33: The Town and Country Planning Act*, HMSO, London.

Mohney, D and Easterbury, K (1991) *Seaside: Making of a Town in America*, Phaidon, London.

Montgomery, J (1994) 'The evening economy of cities', *Town and Country Planning*, Vol. 63, No. 11, pp. 302–7.

Montgomery, J (1995) 'The story of Temple Bar: creating Dublin's cultural quarter', *Planning Practice and Research* 10(2), pp. 135–172.

Moore, V (1995) *A Practical Approach to Planning Law,* Blackstone, London.

Morgan, and Nott, S (1995) *Development Control: Law, Policy and Practice*, Butterworth, London.

Moro, P (1958) 'Elevational Control', *Architects' Journal*, Vol. 127, p. 203.

Morton, D (1991) 'Conservation areas, has saturation point been reached?', *The Planner,* Vol. 77, No. 175.

Moughtin, C (1992) *Urban Planning: Street and Square,* Butterworth Architecture, Oxford.

Murrain, P (1996) 'Congress for the New Urbanism', *Urban Design International* Vol. 1, No. 2, June 1996.

Murray, K and Willie, D (1991) 'Choosing the Right Approach', *Landscape Design,* May 1991, pp. 21–3.

MVA Consultancy (1991) *BRITES: Bristol Integrated Transport and Environmental Study,* Avon CC, Bristol CC, etc, Bristol.

Myerscough, J (1988) *The Economic Importance of the Arts,* Policy Studies Institute, London .

Nairn, I (1955) *Outrage,* Architectural Press, London.

Newman, O (1973) *Defensible Space: People and Design in the Violent City,* Architectural Press, London.

Newman, O (1974) *Community of Interest – Design for Community Control,* NACRO conference paper, London.

Newman, O (1995) 'Defensible Space – a new physical planning tool for urban revitalisation', *Journal of the American Planning Association,* Vol. 61, No. 2, Chicago.

Newman, P and Thornley, A (1995) 'Euralille: "Boosterism" at the centre of Europe', *European Urban and Regional Studies,* Vol. 2, No. 3.

Newman, P and Thornley, A (1996) *Urban Planning Europe: International Competition, National Systems and Planning Projects,* Routledge, London.

Nicholson-Lord, D (1987) *The Greening of the Cities,* Routledge, London and New York.

Nisancioglu, S Takmaz and Greed, C (1996) 'Bringing down the Barriers', *Living in the Future: 24 Sustainable Development Ideas for the UK*, UK National Council for Habitat II, London, pp. 16–17 (summary of presentations in Birmingham and Instanbul).

Oatley, N (1996) 'Regenerating cities and modes of regulation', in Greed, C (ed.) *Investigating Town Planning,* Longman, Harlow, Chapter 4.

O'Conner, J and Wynne, D (1996) *From the Margins to the Centre: Cultural Production and Consumption in the Post-Industrial City,* Arena, Hampshire.

Olin, L (1990) Untitled keynote speech at Avenues for Investment: Landscape Design as a Catalyst for Development, Landscape Institute National Conference, Durham.

Oliver, M (1990) *The Politics of Disablement,* Macmillan, London.

Oliver, MN (1993) 'Redefining disability: a challenge to research', in Swain, J, Finkelstein, V, French, S and Oliver, M (1993) (eds), *Disabling Barriers – Enabling Environments,* Sage Publications, London, in association with the Open University.

Oliver, P, Davis, I and Bentley, I (1981) *Dunroamin' – the Suburban Semi and its Enemies,* Barrie and Jenkins, London.

OPCS (Office of Population Census and Surveys) (1988a) *Surveys of Disability in Great Britain,* Report 1, 'The Prevalence of Disability among Adults', HMSO, London.

OPCS (1988b) *General Household Survey*, HMSO, London.

Osborn, S and Shaftoe, H (1995) *Safer Neighbourhoods? Successes and Failures in Crime Prevention,* Safe Neighbourhoods Unit, London.

Ostler, T (1994) 'Making Designs on a Safer City', *Geographical,* July 1994, pp. 29/31.

Painter, K (1988) *Lighting and Crime: The Edmonton Project,* Middlesex Polytechnic, London.

Painter, K (1989) *Lighting and Crime Prevention for Community Safety: The Tower Hamlets Projects,* Middlesex Polytechnic, London

Painter, K (1989) *Crime Prevention and Public Lighting with Special Focus on Women and Elderly People,* LB Hammersmith and Fulham and Urbis Lighting.

Palfreyman, T and Thorpe, S (1993) *Designing for Accessibility – an Introductory Guide,* Centre for Accessible Environments, London.

Parkes, M (1996) *Good Practice Guide to Community Planning and Development* LPAC (London Planning Advisory Committee), London.

Peckham, M (1970) *The Triumph of Romanticism: Collected Essays,* University of South Carolina Press, Charlotte.

Phillips, P (1988) Out of Order: The Public Art Machine, *Art Forum* 27, pp. 92–7.

Pirie, A (1993) *Planning the Built Environment: Women's Safety,* Briefing Paper 1, Crime Concern, Swindon.

Plowden, S and Hillman, M (1996) *Speed Control and Transport Policy,* Policy Studies Institute, London.

Poole, R (1994) *Operation Columbus – Travels in North America,* West Midlands Police.

Power, A and Turnstall, R (1995) *Swimming Against the Tide,* Joseph Rowntree Foundation, York.

Prince of Wales (1989) *A Vision of Britain,* Doubleday, London.

Public Art Commissions Agency (1991) *Context and Collaboration: The International Public Art Symposium,* Public Art Commissions Agency, Birmingham.

Punter, J V (1990a) *Design Control in Bristol,* Redcliffe Press, Bristol.

Punter, J (1990b) 'The Privatisation of the Public Realm', *Planning Practice and Research* 3, pp. 9–13.

Punter, J (1996) 'Developments in urban design review: The lessons of the West Coast of the United States for British Practice', *Journal of Urban Design,* February 1996.

Punter, J, Carmona, M and Platts, A (1994) 'Design Policies in Development Plans', *Urban Design Quarterly*, Issue 51, July 1994, pp. 11–15.

Punter, J, Carmona, M and Platts, A (1996) *Design Policies in Local Plans: A Research Report*, DoE, HMSO, London.

Punter, J and Carmona, M (1997) *The Design Dimension of Local Plans: Theory, Content, and Best Practice for Design Policies,* E & F N Spon, London.

Quillinan, J and Wentges, R (1996) 'The Community Origins of the Temple Bar Project', in Quinn, P (1996) *Temple Bar: The Power of an Idea*, Temple Bar Properties Ltd, Dublin.

Rabinovitz, J and Leitman, J (1996) 'Urban planning in Curitiba', *Scientific American*, Vol. 1274, No. 3, 10 March 1996.

Ramsay, M (1991) *The effect of Better Street Lighting on Crime and Fear: a Review*, Home Office Crime Prevention Unit Paper 29.

Rapoport, A (1982) *The Meaning of the Built Environment,* University of Arizona Press, Tucson.

Ravetz, A (1974) *Model Estate: Planned Housing at Quarry Hill,* Leeds, Croom Helm, London, in association with Joseph Rowntree Foundation.

Ravetz, A (1980) *Remaking Cities*, Croom Helm, London.

Ravetz, A and Turkington, R (1995) *The Place of Home: English Domestic Environments 1914–2000,* E & FN Spon, London.

Relph, E (1976) *Place and Placelessness*, Pion, London.

Reyburn, W (1989) *Flushed with Pride: The Story of Thomas Crapper,* London, Pavilion Books.

RFAC (Royal Fine Art Commission) (1990) *Planning for Beauty: The Case for Design Guidelines,* HMSO, London.

RIBA (Royal Institute of British Architects) (1995) *Quality in Town and Country, a Response to the Secretary of State for the Environment,* RIBA, London.

Rights Now (March 1996) *Campaign Update,* produced by a consortium of independent organisations campaigning to end discrimination on the grounds of disability, Rights Now, 12 City Forum, 250 City Road, London, EC1V 8AF.

Ritter, P (1996) '"Patrick Geddes", The Sensitive Future,' *Newsletter of 'Education' Generation Group,* January 1996, pp. 45–57, Perth, Australia, produced by P Ritter architect and planner.

Roberts, M (1991) *Living in a Man-Made World: Gender Assumption in Modern Housing Design,* Routledge, London.

Roberts, M and Marsh, C (1995) 'For art's sake: public art, planning policies and the benefits for commercial property', *Planning Practice and Research,* Vol. 10, No. 2, pp. 189–98.

Roberts, M, Marsh, C and Salter, M (1993) 'Public art in private places: commercial benefits and public policy', University of Westminster Press and AN Publications, London.

Roberts, M, Nice, S, Lloyd-Jones, T and Erickson, B (1996) 'The city as a multi-layered complex of simple units', Urban Utopias: New Tools for the Renaissance of the City in Europe, European Conference Proceedings, November 15–17 1995 Berlin, European Commission DGXII and TVFF, Berlin.

Robson, B (1975) *Urban Social Areas,* Oxford University Press, Oxford.

Rosenberg, F (1992) *Architect's Choice,* Thames and Hudson, London.

Rossi, A (1989) *The Architecture of the City,* MIT Press, Cambridge, Mass.

Rowe, C (1982) 'Programs vs. paradigm', in MIddleton, D (1982) (ed.), 'Urban design' in *The Cornell Journal of Architecture,* Rizzoli, New York.

Rowe, C and Koetter, F (1984) *Collage City,* MIT Press, Cambridge, Mass.

Rowland, J (1995) 'The urban design process', *Urban Design,* No. 56, October 1995.

Royal Commission on Environmental Pollution (1994): Transport and the Environment. Oxford University Press, Oxford.

RTPI, (1988) *Access for disabled people,* Practice Note No. 3, Royal Town Planning Institute, 26, Portland Place, London, W1N 4BE.

RTPI (1989) *Planning for Choice and Opportunity,* RTPI, London.

RTPI (1993) *The Character of Conservation Areas,* RTPI, London.

RTPI (1995) *Planning for Woman,* Practice Advice Note No. 12, RTPI, London.

Ruskin, J (1849) *Seven Lamps of Architecture,* Dent, London.

Saunders, P (1989) 'The Meaning of Home in Contemporary English Culture', *Housing Studies,* 4 (3), pp. 177–92.

Scott Brown, D (1990) *Urban Concepts,* Academy Editions, London.

Scottish Office (1994a) *National Planning Policy Guideline NPPG1: The Planning System,* SO, Edinburgh.

Scottish Office (1994b) *Planning Advice Note PAN 44: Fitting New Housing Development Into The Countryside,* SO, Edinburgh.

Scottish Office (1994c) Planning Advice Note PAN 46: *Planning for crime prevention,* SO, Edinburgh.

Selwood, S (1992) 'Art in Public', in Jones, S (1992) (ed.), *Art in Public, Why, What and How,* AN Publications, Sunderland.

Selwood, S (1995) *The Benefits of Public Art: The Polemics of Permanent Art in Public Places,* Policy Studies Institute, London.

Sharp, T (1940) *Town Planning,* Penguin, Harmondsworth.

Shaw, P (1991) *Percent for Art – A Review,* The Arts Council, London.

Skeffington, A (1969) *People and Planning, Report of the Committee on Public Participation in Planning,* HMSO, London.

Slessor, C (1993) 'Irish Reels', *Architectural Review* (192) 1151, pp. 46–49.

Smithson, A (1978) (ed.), *Team X Primer*, Studio Vista, London.

Social Trends (1995) *Social Trends* 25, HMSO, Office of Population, Census and Surveys, London, (annual, also on CD).

Sola-Morales, I (1987) 'Matters of Style', in Hortet, L and Adria, M (1987) (eds), *Barcelona Spaces and Sculptures (1982–1986)*, Ajuntament de Barcelona and Joan Miro Foundation, Barcelona.

Southampton Directorate of Strategy and Development (1991) *Women and the Planned Environment: Design Guide*, Southampton City Council.

Spaull, S and Rowe, S (1992) *Silt-Up or Move On. A Report by Single Homelessness in London* (SHIL), SHIL, London.

Spender, D (1982) *Women of Ideas: and What Men Have Done to Them*, Routledge and Kegan Paul, London.

Sprieregen, P (1965) *Urban Design and the Architecture of Town and Cities*, McGraw Hill, New York.

Starkman, N (1993) 'Espaces Publics', *Paris Projet,* No. 30–31, APUR, Paris.

Stedman-Jones, G (1971) *Outcast London: A Study in the Relationship between Classes in Victorian Society*, Oxford University Press, London.

Steinman, S L (1995) Compendium in Lacey, S (ed.), *Mapping the Terrain: New Genre Public Art*, New Bay Press, Seattle.

Stimmann, H (1995) 'New Berlin Office and Commercial Buildings', in Burg, A *Downtown Berlin – Building the Metropolitan Mix*, Birkhauser, Berlin.

Stone, I (1961) *The Agony and the Ecstasy: A Biographical Novel of Michelangelo*, Collins, London.

Stones, A (1992) 'Revising the Essex Design Guide', *Urban Design Quarterly*, No. 44, September 1992.

Strathclyde Regional Council (1995) *Glasgow City Centre Millennium Plan, Transport Strategy*, Strathclyde Regional Council, Glasgow.

Strelitz, Z, Henderson, G and Cowan, R, (1996) *Making Cities Better: Visions and Implementation*, Vision for Cities, Leicester.

STRIDE (Safe Travel for Women, Nottingham); Hammersmith and Fulham Crime and Safety Unit; Metrac, Toronto.

Stringer, B (1994) 'Public conveniences – search for a suitable role', *The Urban Street Environment*, Sept/Oct 1994, pp. 27–29.

Swain, J, Finkelstein, V, French, S and Oliver, M (1993) (eds), *Disabling Barriers – Enabling Environments,* Sage Publications, London, in association with the Open University.

Swansea City Council (1993) *Sites: Enhancement and Sculpture and Monuments,* Swansea City Council, Swansea.

Taylor, H (1994) *Age and order: the public park as a metaphor for a civilised society*, Working Paper 10, Comedia Demos Study: The Future of Urban Parks and Spaces, Comedia, London.

Taylor, M (1995) *Unleashing the Potential: Bringing Residents to the Centre of Regeneration,* Joseph Rowntree Foundation, York.

Teagle, W G (1978) *The Endless Village*, Nature Conservancy Council.

Telling, A E and Duxbury, R (1991) *Planning Law and Procedure*, Butterworth, London.

TEST (1987) *Quality Streets*, TEST, 177 Arlington Road, London NW1 7EY.

Thomas, L and Cousins, W (1996) 'A new compact city form', in Jenks, S, Burton, R and Williams, K (1996) *The Compact City*, Spon, London.

Tibbalds, F (1992) *Making People-Friendly Towns: Improving the Public Environment in Towns and Cities,* Longman, Harlow.

Tibbalds, F Colbourne, Karski and Williams, (1990) *City Centre Design Strategy (BUDS)*, City of Birmingham.

Townshend, T (1984) 'Glasgow's Model Future', *Architects' Journal*, 21 November 1984, pp. 43–47.

Townshend, T (1995) 'Representing the Past', unpublished paper given to the conference on teaching and research in urban design, University of Manchester, Manchester.

Townshend, T (1995) 'Gummer Sets Out his Mission for Planners', *Planning Week*, Vol. 3, No. 25, 22 June 1995, p. 1.

Trench, S and Ball, R (1995) 'Buses and traffic calming', in Trench, S, and Taner, O, *Current Issues in Planning,* Volume II, Gower, Aldershot.

Tschumi, B (1994) *Event-cities (Praxis)*, MIT Press, Cambridge, Mass.

Tugnutt, A, and Robertson, M (1987) *Making Townscape: a Contextual Approach to Building in an Urban Setting*, Mitchell, London.

Tutt, P and Alder, D C (1993) N*ew Metric Handbook: Planning and Design Data*, Butterworth, London.

Ulrich, R S (1983) 'View through surgery window may influence recovery from surgery', *Science*, Vol. 224, pp. 420–21.

Unwin, R (1920) *Town Planning in Practice,* T Fisher Unwin, London.

URBED (1994) *Vital and Viable Town Centres: Meeting the Challenge,* Urban and Economic Development Group in association with Department of Environment, 1994, HMSO, London.

Valentine, G (1991) 'Women's Fear of Public Space Built Environment', *Women and the Designed Environment,* 16 (4), pp. 288/303.

Venturi, R (1988) first published 1968) *Complexity and Contradiction in Architecture*, Butterworth Architecture, London.

Venturi, R (1996) *Incongraphy and Electronics upon a Gerneric Architecture: a View from the Draft Room,* MIT Press, Cambridge, Mass.

Venturi, R, Izenour, S and Scott Brown, D (1977, first published 1972) *Learning from Las Vegas*, MIT Press, Cambridge, Mass.

Vidler, A (1978) 'Scenes of the streets', in Anderson, S (ed.), *On Streets*, MIT Press, Cambridge, Mass.

Walmsley, D J (1988) *Urban Living: the Individual in the City,* Longman, Harlow.

Ware, V (1988) *Women's Safety on Housing Estates,* Women's Design Service, London.

Wates, N and Knevitt, C (1986) *Community Architecture,* Penguin, Harmondsworth.

Wates, N (1996) *Action Planning,* The Prince of Wales's Institute of Architecture, London.

Watson, S with Austerberry, H (1986) *Housing and Homelessness: a Feminist Perspective,* Routledge and Kegan Paul, London.

Wayte, G (1986) 'Stories of genius: some notes on the socialisation of fine art students', in Farran, D, Scott, S and Stanley, L, *Writing Feminist Biography, Studies in Sexual Politics,* Manchester University Press, Manchester.

Wayte, G (1989) 'Becoming an artist: the professional socialisation of art students', unpublished PhD thesis, University of Bristol.

WCD, (1987) *The Implementation of Access Legislation in Local Authorities in Wales,* Access Committee for Wales, Welsh Council for the Disabled, Llys Ilfor, Crscent Road, Caerphilly, Mid Glamorgan CF8 1XL.

WDS, *Women's Design Service Broadsheet Design Series,* current publications available from:

Westminster, *MA Urban Design Course*, Degree Document, London: University of Westminister.

Westwood, S and Williams, J (1996) *Imagining Cities: Scripts, Signs and Memories,* Routledge, London.

WGSG, Women and Geography Study Group, Institute of British Geographers (1984) *Geography and Gender – An Introduction to Feminist Geography,* Hutchinson, London.

Wilkoff, W L and Abed, L W (1994) *Practising Universal Design,* Van Nostrand Reinhold, New York.

Williams Ellis, Clough (1928) *England and the Octopus,* Dent, London.

Williams Ellis, Clough (1938) *Britain and the Beast*, Dent, London.

Williamson, C (1995) 'Urban Design in Central Milton Keynes', unpublished MA thesis, University of Westminster, London.

Willmott, P and Young, M (1976) *Family and Class in a London Suburb*, 3rd edn., Mel Mentor, London.

Wilson, E (1991) *The Sphinx in the City: the Control of Disorder and Women*, Virago, London.

Winter, J, Coombes, T, and Farthing, S (1993) 'Satisfaction with space around the home on large private sector estates: Lessons from surveys in Southern England and South Wales, 1985–89' *Town Planning Review* 64 (1), pp. 65–88.

Wohl, A (1983) *Endangered Lives: Public Health in Victorian Britain*, Dent, London.

Women's Design Service, Second Floor, Johnson's Yard, 4, Pinchin Street, London, E1 1SA.

1   Race and Gender in Architectural Education

2   Planning London: Unitary Development Plans

3   Challenging Women: City Challenge

4   Antenatal Waiting Areas

5   Participation in Development

6   Training and Building Design and the Construction Industry: Routes for Women

7   UDP Policies: Their Impact on Women's Lives (LWPF report January 1994)

8   Designing Out Crime (LWPF report April 1994)

9   Public Places, Future Spaces: Older Women and the Built Environment

10   Women as Planners: Is More Better? (LWPF report July 1994)

11   Street Lighting and Women's Safety

12   Are Town Centres Managing? (LWPF report October 1994)

13   Sisterhood, Cities and Sustainability (LWPF report January 1995)

14   Residential Neighbourhoods: A Place for Children (LWPF report April 1995)

15   Government Urban Funding: Winners and Losers (LWPF report July 1995)

16   Public Surveillance Systems

17   Local Pride: The Role of Public and Community Art

Wood, L (1994) *The Lady Lever Art Gallery: Catalogue of Commodes,* National Museums and Galleries on Merseyside, Liverpool.

Wooley, T. (1985) *Community Architecture: An Evaluation of the Case for User Participation in Design,* unpublished PhD Thesis, Oxford Polytehnic (Oxford-Brookes University), Oxford.

Woolley, T (1994) 'Innovative housing in the UK and Europe', in Gilroy, R and Woods, R (eds), *Housing Women,* Routledge, London.

Worpole, K, Greenhalgh, L and Landry, C (1995) *Libraries in a World of Cultural Change,* The Future of Public Libraries Project, Comedia, UCL Press, London.

Worksett, R (1969) *The Character of Towns: an Approach to Conservation,* Architectural Press, London.

Young, J (1992) 'The Counter-Monument: Memory against Itself in Germany Today' in Mitchell, W J T (ed.), *Art and the Public Sphere,* University of Chicago Press, Chicago. pp. 49–78.

Zucchi, B (1992) *Giancarlo de Carlo,* Butterworth Architecture, Oxford.

Zukin, S (1993) *Landscapes of Power: from Detroit to Disneyworld,* University of California Press, Berkeley.

Appendix I: Government and official publications

Policy Guidance Notes and Circulars

PPGs (Planning Policy Guidance notes)

The ones most mentioned by contributors were PPGs 1, 3, 6, 12, 15, and 17; the following is a selection, not a complete list.

N.B. PPG 1 'General Policy and Principles' as revised in 1996 contains a significantly larger element on urban design. See paras. 11–15.

1   General Policy and Principles (1988, revised 1992, and updated in 1997)
2   Green Belts, 1998 (revision 1994)
3   Land for Housing (revised 1992 as 'Housing')
4   Industrial and Commercial Development and Small Firms
5   Simplified Planning Zones (redrafted 1992)
6   Town Centres and Retail Developments (updated 1993, and revised 1996)
7   Rural Enterprise and Development (revised 1992 as 'The Countryside and Rural Economy')
8   Telecommunications
9   (Previously, 'Regional Guidance for the South East' (moved to RPGs – Regional Planning Guidance notes) Now PPG 9 'Nature Conservation'
10 Strategic Guidance for the West Midlands (moved to RPGs) to be replaced
11 Strategic Guidance for Merseyside (and see RPGs)
12 Local Plans (revised 1992 as 'Development Plans and Regional Planning Guidance')
13 Highways Considerations in Development Control (update 1994 'Transport')
14 Development on Unstable Land
15 Planning and the Historic Environment (1990 and subsequent updates)
16 Archaeology and Planning
17 Sport and Recreation
18 Enforcing Planning Control
19 Outdoor Advertisement Control
20 Coastal Planning
21 Tourism
22 Renewable Energy
23 Planning Pollution Control
24 Planning and Noise

These are constantly being updated and revised, especially PPGs 1, 6, and 13. There are several other new ones which have not been included as they are not directly relevant to urban design.

N.B. Check current Department of the Environment lists for updates, current Circulars, and additional PPGs not referred to in this book (see the annual *Building, Housing and Planning* catalogue, HMSO). The Department of the Environment was renamed the Department of the Environment, Transport and the Regions in 1997 by the new Labour Government. Frequently, consultative drafts are produced by the Department of the Environment in an ongoing process of updating existing PPGs and creating new ones reflecting current policy issues.

Regional Planning Guidance

There are series of RPGs but RPG 3, produced in draft in 1995, *Strategic Guidance for London Planning Authorities* is the main one mentioned in the text.

Scottish Office

The Environment Department of the Scottish Office issues NPPGs (National Planning Policy Guidance) like the PPGs in England, and also PANs (Planning Advice Notes – not to be confused with the RTPI's own series of PANs). Note Carmona, in particular, refers to Scottish Office publications. Full list of Scottish Office planning policy documents is to be found in Cullingworth and Nadin, *Town and Country Planning in Britain* (Routledge, 1994 and forthcoming update).

NPPG 1, 1994, *The Planning System* (like PPG 1)

PAN 44 *Fitting New Housing into Development in the Countryside* (1994)

PAN 46 *Planning for Crime Prevention* (1994)

Circulars

This is a selective list, based on Circulars mentioned in individual chapters, plus other key Circulars. Nowadays key policies statements are more likely to appear in PPGs than Circulars or Command papers (White Papers). Please note this is only a small selection.

42/55 Green Belts
50/57 Green Belts
56/71 Historic Towns and Roads
82/73 Bus Operation in Residential and Industrial Areas
24/75 Housing Needs and Action
4/76 Report of the National Parks Policies Review Committee
36/78 Trees and Forestry
22/80 Development Control: Policy and Practice
38/81 Planning and Enforcement Appeals
10/82 Disabled Persons Act
22/83 Planning Gain (replaced by 16/91)
1/84 Crime Prevention
14/84 Green Belts
15/84 Land for Housing (cancelled by PPG 3)
22/84 Memorandum on Structure Plans and Local Plans (See PPG 12)
1/85 The Use of Conditions in Planning Permission
2/86 Development by Small Businesses
8/87 Historic Buildings and Conservation Areas: Policies and Procedures
3/88 Unitary Development Plans (cancelled by PPG 3)
15/88 Town and Country Planning (Assessment of Environmental Effects) Regulations
12/89 Green Belts
7/91 Planning and Affordable Housing (cancelled by PPG 3)
16/91 Planning and Compensation Act 1991: Planning Obligations
17/92 Planning and Compensation Act 1991: Immunity Rules
8/93 Awards of Costs incurred in Planning other Proceedings (including Compulasory Purchase Orders)
5/94 Planning Out Crime

7/94 Environment Assessment: Amendment of Regulations
1/97 Planning and Compensation Act 1991: Planning Obligations.

Command Papers

This only includes those mentioned in this particular volume. There are also many more specifically on town planning, although over the last ten years the trend has been to put key policy statements in PPGs rather than Department of the Environment Command Papers, but other departments and ministries also produce relevant White Papers. A full list is to be found in Cullingworth (1994); and in the HMSO *Building, Housing and Planning* annual catalogue.

1971 A Fair Deal for Housing
1977 Policy for Inner Cities Cmnd 6845
1990 This Common Inheritance Britain's Environmental Strategy Cmnd 1200
1992 (and annually) This Common Inheritance: The First Year Report
1994a Sustainable Development: The UK Strategy Cmnd 2426
1994b Climate Change: The UK Programme, Cmd 2427
1994c Biodiversity: The UK Action Plan, Cmd 2428

Practice Guides

'Development Plan: A Good Practice Guide', DoE, 1992
'Environmental Appraisal of Development Plans: A Good Practice Guide', DoE, 1994
'PPG 1: A Guide to Better Practice', DoE, 1995.

Acts referred to in this volume or of relevance

1909 Housing and Town Planning Act
1919 Housing and Town Planning Act
1925 Bath Corporation Act
1935 Restriction of Ribbon Development Act
1932 Architects Registration Act
1946 New Towns Act
1947 Town and Country Planning Act
1949 National Parks and Access to the Countryside Act
1952 Town Development Act
1953 Historic Buildings and Ancient Monuments Act
1954 Town and Country Planning Act
1957 Housing Act
1967 Civic Amenities Act
1968 Countryside Act
1969 Housing Act (General Improvement Areas)

1970 Chronically Sick and Disabled Act
1968 Town and Country Planning Act
1971 Town and Country Planning Act
1972 Local Government Act
1974 Town and country Amenities Act
1974 Housing Act (Housing Action Areas)
1976 Local Government (Miscellaneous Provisions) Act
1978 Inner Urban Areas Act
1980 Highways Act
1980 Local Government, Planning and Land Act
1981 Disabled Persons Act
1982 Local Government (Miscellaneous Provisions) Act
1982 Derelict Land Act
1985 Housing Act
1986 Local Government (Access to Information) Act
1986 Housing and Town Planning Act
1988 Housing Act
1988 Local Government Act
1989 Local Government, and Housing Act
1990 Town and Country Planning Act
1990 Planning (Listed Buildings and Conservation Areas) Act
1990 Environmental Protection Act
1991 New Roads and Street Works Act
1991 Planning and Compensation Act
1992 Local Government Act
1993 Housing and Urban Development Act
1993 Traffic Calming Act
1994 Local Government (Wales) Act
1995 Environment Act
1995 Disability Discrimination Act

Regulations and Orders

DOE (Department of the Environment) (1981, 1986, 1989) *Town and Country Planning (Determination of Appeals by Appointed Persons) (Prescribed Classes) Regulations 1981, 1986 and 1989,* HMSO, London.
DOE (1985) *The Building Regulations* 1985, HMSO, London, SI 1065/1985, updated as DOE (1992) *The Building Regulations* 1991, SI 2768/1991 (see Appendix III).
DOE (1987) *Town and Country planning (Listed Buildings and Buildings in Conservation Areas) Regulations,* HMSO, London.
DOE (1987) *Town and Country Planning: Use Classes Order* (UCO), HMSO, London, SI 764/1987.
DOE (1987) *Town and Country Planning (Appeal) (Written representations Procedure) Regulations,* HMSO, London.

DOE (1988) *Town and Country Planning General Development Order* now superseded by two documents, namely:
DOE (1995) *Town and Country Planning (General Development Procedure) Order,* HMSO, London
DOE (1995) *Town and Country Planning (Permitted Development) Order,* HMSO, London.

Other Sources

Worldwide

The recent Habitat II conference in Istanbul in 1996 has produced a range of documents, some of which are relevant to design. Also note that the Rio conference brought to world attention environmental issues and sustainability.

European Planning Controls

EC Directive 85/337 on Environmental Assessment 'The Assessment of the Effect of Certain Public and Private Projects on the Environment' is applied in Britain under 'Assessment of Environmental Effects Regulation' No.119 of the 1988 Town and Country Planning Regulations. (All EU legislation must be embodied in relevant domestic state legislation, and in case of dispute the EU takes precedence.)

Article 119 of the Treaty of Rome established the principle of equal opportunities, and the Equal Treatment Directive 76/207 details the scope of application.

1987 Single European Act.

Also note reference is made to various building codes and planning regulations in other European countries by the contributors, such as in relation to the reconstruction of Berlin.

North American Legislation

This is of particular relevance in respect of access issues.

1973 Rehabilitation Act, Section 504 (in relation to disability and access).

1990 Americans with Disabilities Act.

Note also that different US state have different local codes, and zoning regulations in relation to disability and access rights.

Also note importance of Bill of Rights, Constitution and Civil Rights in disability access and therefore in effect upon urban form.

Appendix II: Disability

Explanation

This appendix provides additional and more comprehensive information on governmental and official guidance and regulations in respect of disability access, than was possible within the context of Chapter 9, which dealt more with matters of policy and practice. The first section covers the background legislation and requirements for planners, with particular reference to the salient sections in each PPG. Information is then given from a recent survey as to the extent of actual implementation of policy drawing on work by Linda Davies.

The next section deals with the problem of the Building Regulations. This is essential background and of great concern to many in the built environment professions, but possibly not appropriate for inclusion in the main core of the chapters on urban design per se. The situation undoubtedly has implications for urban designers, however, and will be of interest to other readers from areas such as construction, building, and architecture. The last section takes the issues forward by providing a checklist of more specifically site-related considerations to be taken into account when designing for access. This material may be seen to be more suitable for the detailed approach to be adopted in the next volume but because it links specifically to the topic of disability discussed in this volume it is included here.

Requirements and expectations

According to the Royal Planning Institute's Practice Advice Note No. 3 *Access for Disabled People*:

> Disability includes a wide range of conditions: it covers more than the obvious such as blindness or confinement to a wheelchair. Breathlessness, pain, the need to walk with a stick, difficulty in gripping because of paralysis or arthritis, lack of physical co-ordination, partial sight, deafness and pregnancy can all affect a person's mobility in the environment.

Access for the disabled will also benefit parents with buggies and the elderly.

Provision of access for people with disabilities is a fact which must be taken into account in determining a planning application as required under Section 76 of the 1990 Town and Country Planning Act. Section 4 of the Chronically Sick and Disabled Persons Act, 1970 first required builders to provide disabled access to, and within, buildings, with particular reference to parking, and sanitary conveniences (toilets). This was only required 'as far as is practical and reasonable', which may be seen as an escape clause, and there was not enforcement of the act. This was followed by the Disabled Persons Act of 1981, which led to the insertion of additional requirements into the planning legislation of the time, as represented nowadays by Section 76. As a result, local planning authorities are required to draw the attention of developers to the provisions of the 1970 Act, and also to relevant design guidance, with particular reference to the relevant Building Regulations (Davies, 1996). British Standard BS5810 *Access for Disabled People*, last updated in 1992, sets out the principles, and Linked Document M of the Building Regulations translates these standards into design requirements.

The government has also produced several design guidance reports such as Development Control Planning Note 16, *Access for the Disabled* (DoE, 1985, DCPN, 16), and if you look very closely, it is also possible to find several encouraging statements hidden within the PPGs. However, the RTPI itself has produced PAN No. 3, *Access for the Disabled*, and many voluntary groups have produced a range of design guides and policy documents related to the built environment, such as the Centre for Access Environments, the Access Committee for England (who produced *Access for Disabled People*) and Women's Design Service. Arguably, planning well for people with disabilities and other minority groups should be all part of the professional code of conduct of the professional town planner. Planning for all minority groups should also be strongly supported from central government, via the DoE and backed up by appropriate PPG statements of policy and intent.

Planning Policy Guidance

Since the question of DoE guidance and support through the PPGs is so crucial in getting validation for UDP policies which deal with social issues, a selection of the main references in the PPGs to minorities and social issues is now given. (The PPGs themselves are listed in Appendix I.) This list may be seen to be parallel to Tables 3.2–3.4 on the extent to which PPGs provide guidance on urban design issues. It is for the reader to compare each list and consider whether there is any correlation between the two, and thus any evidence of integration of social and visual issues at central government level. At present, the editor considers the links are merely incidental, perhaps accidental, and somewhat tenuous, suggesting that there is a need for a major rethink on all this at DoE level.

PPG1 *General Policy and Principles* says in paragraph 55 'the development of land and buildings provides the opportunity to secure a more accessible environment for everyone, including wheelchair users, and other people with disabilities, elderly people, and people with toddlers or infants in pushchairs'. However, it does not make it clear what exactly these 'opportunities' are, and how they relate to concrete measures. This PPG is seen as somewhat negative because it also implies that it is the role of the Building Regulations, not the planners, to deal with these issues.

Recent government advice (PPG1, 1997a) takes a more positive view of the scope of planning authorities in securing an accessible environment than previous guidance. For the first time it is mentioned that improved access will be beneficial to everyone, not just those with disabilities. This must be taken into account within the development control and development plan processes. The impression is still given that what happens about the insides of buildings, is, strangely, not part of the concern of planners. Yet, as argued convincingly by Imrie (1996), disability and accessibility issues have become part of what many ordinary people expect to be a high priority for urban designers, even before aesthetic considerations. Changes may be coming, as a new Directive is currently being produced for the

European Union which may radically alter the situation by requiring the insides and outsides of buildings to be looked at together under new combined planning and building regulations, but this may be a long way off.

PPG3 *Housing* talks about 'developers considering whether the internal design of housing, and access to it, can meet the needs of the disabled, whether as resident or visitor'. Significantly, at the time of writing there are proposals to extend Document M regulations to new private housing development, as until now residential development, which constitutes 75 per cent of all building stock, has been excluded. Paradoxically, the PPG goes on to state 'the Government looks to the Building Regulations and not the planning system to impose requirements'.

PPG12 *Development Plans and Regional Planning Guidance* is the most useful one of all for giving 'space' for social issues to be taken into account. Policy guidance prior to Circular 22/84 'Memorandum on Structure Plans and Local Plans' (replaced by PPG12) was concerned only with land use and development issues. Any other factors such as social considerations in the form of equal opportunity issues were considered to be outside the remit of the Planning Acts and were therefore *ultra vires*. Central government guidance at that time was such that although policy plans could take social considerations into account, planning control should concern itself only with the use applied for, and not with the user of the land.

PPG12 paragraph 5.48 states that

the Regulations [on the preparation of development plan documents] also require planning authorities to have regard to social considerations in preparing their general policies and proposals in structure plans and UDP Part I documents [the policy aspect]. But, in preparing detailed plans too, authorities will wish to consider the relationship of planning policies and proposals to social needs and problems, including their likely impact on different groups in the population such as ethnic minorities.

PPG15 *Planning and the Historic Environment* paragraph 3.28 has a short section on increasing access for people with disabilities to historic buildings, stating, 'it is important in principle that disabled people should have dignified easy access to and within historical buildings', but again is quite apologetic and ambivalent about but what this might entail in practical terms. Significantly, English Heritage have produced a useful document *Easy Access to Historic Properties* which makes practical suggestions on location of entrances, use of handrails, and use of paviers and large paving slabs to create accessible, yet historical, ground surfaces. Likewise, the City of London Corporation has produced *Designing the City*, a guide for disabled access along the narrow streets of the city of London. In streets where layers of history – not to mention cabling – lie a few inches below the surface, it is suggested that it is sometimes more practical to raise the roadway (carriageway) rather than to lower the pavement. However, PPG15 is seen as one of the most promising as it deals with 'old' buildings, (admittedly only 'historical ones') whereas the Building Regulations only apply to new buildings.

The report *Development Plans: A Good Practice Guide* issued in relation to development plan preparation is also of significance (DoE, 1992). Paragraph 3.79, states, within a discussion of social issues and the 'particular sections of the population' to be considered in relation to the implications for plan making, that 'perhaps children, women and homeless people should be added to the list'.

One factor which may affect the acceptance of policies by the DoE is the question of where to put them in the development plan written statement. Separate chapters on women, race or disability may allow more space and detail to be given to these issues, but at the same time this approach might marginalise them. Incorporation of topics within mainstream chapters, for example on housing, employment and transport, leads to integration, but may also lead to less detail, or, at worst, a mandatory sentence added at the end of each page to the effect that 'the needs of minorities must be taken into account', which is too vague to have any effect. Lambeth Borough Council initially adopted the separate chapter approach in the mid-1980s but thereafter preferred to integrate special needs policies for women, and other groups, throughout their development plan, in accordance with the preferences indicated in the above '*Development Plans – A Good Practice Guide*', paragraph 3.79. There is, of course, the benefit of the additional safeguard that the policies are less likely to be eliminated in a local authority cost-cutting exercise but this needs to be balanced against policies being 'lost' within the development plan, if not separately prioritised. (Indeed, some would argue that it is better to try to put them in twice, once on their own, and once under the relevant topic heading in the hope that at least one version will ge through he Local Inquiry stage.)

Extent of implementation

The following section gives a brief summary of Davies' findings (Davies, 1996) which are fully set out in the previous volume in this series, *Implementing Town Planning*. This appendix also draws on material assem-

bled for the RTPI Joint Distance Learning Unit produced by Clara Greed in 1996 (Greed and JDL, 1996).

After 1986 when the London boroughs commenced their Unitary Development Plan, the London Group Access Officers felt it was very important that access policies should be considered across borough boundaries and produced a number of policies which it hoped would be adopted by London boroughs. The overall strategy is twofold:

1 To encourage access throughout the authority for everyone, including wheelchair users and people with disabilities
2 The authority is determined to ensure that people with access difficulties are not prevented from playing a full role in the life of the community.

It was against that background that Linda Davies carried out her research in 1992 to investigate the extent to which Unitary Development Plans were incorporating policies for access for the disabled, in parallel with studying the situation with regard to women.

As to *Transport*, parking spaces for the disabled in off-street car parks with more than 20 parking spaces were pursued in Newham, Bromley and Wandsworth Borough Councils. Sensitive local policies such as the need to design riverside walkways (and public areas) for the needs of the disabled were sought in Wandsworth Borough Council.

In the area of *Housing*, in the Draft Unitary Development Plans all of the six London boroughs, which were the focus of the author's London research, had drafted polices requiring that all new single-storey houses would be built to mobility standard, in accordance with the Department of the Environment's Housing Directorate Occasional paper 2/74. Most boroughs – four out of six – drafted policies to provide access for people with disabilities into new buildings, conversions or premises to which the public have access. By comparison, in some of the metropolitan boroughs, authorities were keen to draft quoted policies for encouraging disabled persons' housing within large-scale residential developments (Wolverhampton, Coventry, Kensington and Chelsea, and Bromley were notable here).

In the area of *Recreation, Leisure and Movement,* all of the six London boroughs had access policies. Most popularly they were policies concerned with the need to provide access for people with disabilities in converted and newly constructed buildings for leisure and recreational use.

In the area of *Retail* Kensington and Chelsea Borough Council pointed out that shopping centres are public places and it is important that high standards prevail. Policies in this area often overlapped or complemented those found under *Conservation and Development.* Occasionally, reference was made to Part M of the Building Regulations, particularly if shopfront design policies were being promoted by the council. In four of the six London boroughs, policies required that all shopfronts should be accessible to wheelchair users. Two of the metropolitan boroughs (Oldham Borough Council and Manchester City Council) requested in their draft plans that toilet facilities for shoppers with disabilities should be provided in new retail developments of more than 1,000 square metres floor space. Wandsworth Borough Council stated that it had become the norm to request, in new shopping developments, amongst other things, a range of facilities for people with disabilities, including toilet facilities, ramped accesses, reserved parking spaces, etc.

Building or planning or designing?

As can be seen, implementation of policy has not been spectacular in extent. It is often said that one of the main reasons for lack of achievement is that many of the standards and 'rules' which affect disabled access, are administered through the Building Regulations, and not through town planning. Indeed, PPG3 warns, 'the government looks to the building regulations and not the planning system to impose requirements'. Should the planners seek to impose detailed Building Regulation-like controls on planning decisions they are likely to find that their requirements are ruled to be *ultra vires* (outside the scope of planning law). One is most likely to find 'planning for the disabled' in evidence in the case of housing schemes where the local housing authority, a housing association, or the local health authority, has a role as 'developer' itself, in respect of providing accommodation for disabled or elderly people. The effects might be extended to the estate as a whole in cases where the development in question is mixed, with a nominated percentage of 'special housing' within the so-called 'normal' housing, and where the planning gain is in operation.

However, many concerned parties have argued that it is too late to leave detailed design matters to the second stage after planning, when the plans go to the building control officer for scrutiny. Also, the 'culture' of building control is hardly famed for its social awareness, and the regulations were primarily developed to deal with structural matters, fire and safety, not to facilitate people's ease of use of buildings. Indeed, quite apart from the social side of the debate, fulfiling the requirements of Section 76 might lead to substantial changes in the external appearance and layout of a building, thus putting the matter back in the court of the planners. For example, a requirement for adequate internal access might require the building of a lift, and its 'wheel house' might prove to be a bulky visual element on the roof line, and so the design might need to go back to the planners again, particularly if the building is located in a conservation area. Likewise, compliance with external disabled parking and access requirements might substantially affect the overall plot ratio of the development and have landscaping and highways implications. A ramp should have not more than a 1 in 12 slope, though level access is to be preferred, but with the option of steps too for those who find it easier to hold on to a rail and work their way up steps than to tackle a ramp. In practice, however, ramps are often steeper and the route to them is strewn with obstacles and changes of level. Relevant regulations include BS5588 part 8, code of practice on means of escape from buildings, BS 5776 on powered stairlifts and BS6460 on lifting platforms for when a lift cannot be used, as in an emergency or fire. See the table at the end of this Appendix which compares the Building Regulations with town planning controls.

Also a range of regulations from the EC Workplace Directive, and related 1992 Health and Safety at Work Regulations affect those with disabilities as well as the able-bodied and will shape the design of new buildings. There are also various guidelines, such as the Traffic Directive, with implications for access around buildings. In 1991 the Institute of Transport produced *Towards a Barrier Free Environment,* which also provides useful guidelines for external access in relation to road and car park design. Design Note 18, *Access for Disabled People to Educational Buildings,* published in 1979 by the Department of the Environment, gives guidelines, although many colleagues cite problems of compliance in older accommodation. Clearly, it is necessary to use whatever legislation is available from whatever source, for, as yet, there is no comprehensive legislation.

The Building Regulations

The British Standards are linked to the Building Regulations. For example, BS5810 on disability access is the basis of 'linked' Document M of the Building Regulations, BS6465 'Sanitary Installations' (which includes design standards, and level of provision guidelines) for all toilets, both public conveniences and private toilets, is likewise linked to Approved Document G 'Hygiene', under Schedule 1 of the 1984 Building Act, which is the basis of the 1985 Building Regulations (updated in 1992). The Approved Documents run from A–M. In other words, the Building Regulations provide no standards of their own, rather they refer to British Standards and other

Codes of Practice as the basis of their standards, that is they are 'linked documents'. As discussed in the text, it is argued that some Building Regulations and British Standards are relevant to urban design and town planning, although, strictly speaking, they come within the realms of building control as they relate to the insides of buildings (reflecting the insides/outsides dualism identified in Chapter 1).

Part M of the Building Regulations (1992) specifies the arrangement of access to individual buildings. The regulations have been incrementally updated in the last few years and since 1991 have recognised the existence of sensory impairments. The current requirements represent a considerable improvement, although many people would argue that they do not go far enough. The regulations specify minimum standards for access to non-residential buildings, including the provision of a level approach, access within the building and the provision of facilities such as sanitary conveniences.

Although the Building Regulations do provide at least a minimum standard of provision of access and facilities, there are a number of problems in practice. First, at the stage of Building Regulations approval much of the initial design work for a particular building has already taken place. This encourages the designer who has not considered access as an integral part of the design to find technical solutions to meet the regulations, so that the development project can go ahead with the minimum of delay. Many people would argue that considerations regarding access should be considered at the planning stage, rather than at the time of submission of an application under the Building Regulations.

A second problem is that the regulations do not at present require new houses to be accessible. This omission may be rectified if new regulations currently under discussion are introduced. However, the new requirements may only relate to the larger home and may offer only a partial solution. The principle of the 'lifetime home' has been explained clearly by the Joseph Rowntree Foundation (1992) and by the Criteria for Accessible Housing proposed by the Access Committee for England (1992 a and b). The intention, suggested by both bodies, is that every home should be built to a standard of 'visibility' so that in time people with disabilities would have the freedom to visit their friends and relatives without the fear of being unable to get through the front door or visit the WC. The intention would not be to ensure that every house was built to be completely accessible to a wheelchair user, but the adoption of the criteria would ensure that homes would be more adaptable and it would be possible to alter the house if a future resident needed much provision. A 'lifetime home', as its name suggests, would apply the principle of universal design by taking into account the needs of people of all ages and abilities throughout their lifespan.

The detailed specifications set down in the regulations are also regarded by many people with disabilities as very much a minimum standard. Regrettably, any set of rules specifying certain standards of provision is almost always influential in design terms. The designer, even if motivated to provide access to a higher specification, may be pressurised by the client for financial reasons to keep to the minimum provisions. The result is often rather mean standards of access and poor designs that are obvious 'special needs' provisions.

A final problem with the regulations is that, even when all requirements have been met by the designer, many disabled people do not find the finished building particularly accessible. The much acclaimed Tate Gallery at St Ives in Cornwall is an example of a building found to be difficult in access terms, and audits of even recent buildings have found imperfections and failures to meet the minimum requirements. In addition the regulations do not address matters such as the difficulty of opening doors with closure devices, which have been designed to act as checks to the spread of fire. These doors are needed for fire safety reasons, but they can render a building almost inaccessible to a wheelchair user or someone with lower than average strength or stature.

The regulations need to be revised to include considerations of such omissions and to resolve the conflicts between the requirements of different sets of regulations.

Regrettably, there is also some evidence to suggest that many architects, designers of buildings, and planners who may be deciding whether a particular building should obtain planning permission have little familiarity with the concepts of accessible design. The fault may lie with the way in which built environment professionals are educated (Milner and Urquhart, 1991) and the lack of emphasis given to such issues in courses. Bearing this in mind a checklist of matters that should be taken into account by the designer of a new building is put forward in Appendix III as a starting point and a list of recommended reading is given. All built environment professionals should have some knowledge of the principles of barrier-free design. The need for the designer to be aware is obvious, but planners may feel that this matter can be left safely in the hands of building control staff. However, planners and urban designers will often be called upon to make judgements about the quality of a building and be in a position to influence the designer of a building at a very early stage in its conception. The checklist gives some basis of making judgements about the accessibility of particular buildings and suggests ways of promoting the idea of a universal approach to design which goes beyond the basic requirements of the

Building Regulations. Bearing in mind the fact that many buildings which are the subject of applications to planning authorities are not designed by qualified architects or designers this advice may be particularly useful.

See: DOE (1985) *The Building Regulations* 1985, London: HMSO, SI No. 1065/1985, updated as DOE (1992) *The Building Regulations* 1991, SI 2768/1991.

Other guidance on disability and design

Development Control Policy Note 16 (1985) *Access for Disabled People*
Access for Disabled People (ACE, Access Committee for England)
Access for Disabled People: Design Guidance Notes (ACE, Access Committee for England)
See also other current ACE publications
Check all Centre for Accessible Environments publications, 35, Great Smith Street, London SW1P 3BJ.
Check all Women's Design Service design guides (in bibliography).
The RTPI has produced a PAN (Practice Advice Note) *Access for Disabled People* (RTPI 1985, updated as PAN No. 3. 1988) and also *Planning for Women* (RTPI 1995, PAN No. 12).
Read the various topic sections of the *New Metric Handbook: Planning and Design Data* which include

detailed dimensions on requirements (Tutt and Adler, 1993, and forthcoming update). For example see diagrams 5.3 and 5.4 of dimensions and 'reach' of wheelchair users. These are design matters affecting both the insides and outsides of buildings.

Relevant Legislation

1970   Chronically Sick and Disabled Persons Act
1970   Equal Pay Act
1975   Sex Discrimination Act
1976   Race Relations Act
1981   Disabled Persons Act
1986   Local Government (Access to Information) Act
1995   Disability Discrimination Act

British Standards

BS 5810   Access for Disabled People
BS 6465   Sanitary Installations
BS 5776   Powered Stairlifts
BS 5588   Means of Escape from Buildings
BS 6460   Lifting Platforms
BS 6465   Sanitary Installations Part I: Revision 1995
BS 6465   Sanitary Installations Part II: Draft Revision.

Table 1 Difference between planning and building control process

Planning control process	Building control process
Local policies and planning variations (this may result in varying provision and uncertainty for users)	National objectives and standards (people know what to expect)
Standards measured against approved plan appl ies to most types and ages of land use and development	Measured against national criteria applies to new built, rebuild and major structural repairs and extensions. Various exemptions
Developers/builders need to find out planning requirements	Developers know what is expected nationwide
Long approval process before work starts	Once plans are deposited work can start or can start with simple provision of notice
Work in progress seldom inspected	Work in progress inspected
Public can inspect plans and plan register	Plans are not open to public
Clients and public involved think they know about plannning	Decisions seen as technical and unlikely to be understood
Consultation and public participation	No such outside liaison
Councillors must approve decisions	Officers make final decision
Planners must consult with many groups	Only consult with fire service
Concerned with physical and various social, economic and environmental factors and other on- and off-site issues	Structural factors, fire and safety
Mainly land-use control and external design control	Mainly internal and structural design control
Must advertise major changes	Can make changes, relaxations
Can approve phases of plan	Must approve whole scheme
Some control over future provision/fate of conditions	Cannot control management or maintence of access features

Appendix III: Advice to the designer of buildings

Guidelines on how to achieve access

1 **Design holistically** Consider access requirements as an integral aspect of the design of the building and not as a 'special needs' or technical requirement. Embrace the idea of universal design and use the Building Regulations as a guide and not as a rule book. Recognise that accessible solutions should also be aesthetically pleasing and avoid design of external or internal features that have an institutional appearance. Demand better design from the suppliers of equipment such as stairlifts, automatic door openers, handrails, textured flooring, lifts etc. Note that since the passing of the Americans with Disabilities Act (1990) in the USA, considerable improvement has already taken place in the design and availability of products. The cost of these products is also gradually decreasing as demand increases. If designers in the UK followed this approach it is likely that manufacturers would respond in a similar way.

2 **Conduct audits** Undertake a detailed building audit of an existing building to raise your own awareness of the matters of importance before designing a building or judging the performance of a building designed by someone else.

Audit checklists can be obtained from the Centre of Accessible Environments or the Access Committee for England. These can act as a useful starting point, but may need to be adapted for local circumstances and different building types. Visit buildings and spaces which users and designers agree represent good practice.

3 **Consult with building users** Talk to the users of buildings, including people with disabilities. Many areas have local access groups representing people with disabilities who will be pleased to discuss a particular scheme at a formative stage. Undertake post-occupancy evaluations on completion of all design schemes and use the results to refine designs in the future or make adaptations.

4 **Obtain design guidance documents and advice** Seek advice from the various organisations who have specialist knowledge of accessible design, such as the Centre of Accessible Environments, and obtain current copies of design guidance documents. Some local authorities produce useful design guides such as *Accessible Ealing* and the *City of Westminster's Mobility Guide* which are specifically geared to the needs of architects and developers.

5 **Provide choice** Provide as much choice of means of access as possible and choice of routes through the building to cater for a variety of users. Remember that people with different types of disability may have different needs, e.g. ramps may be difficult for some ambulant disabled people to negotiate and many people with visual impairments prefer well-designed stairs to ramps. Consider ways of resolving conflicts of interest between the needs of different groups of people with different disabilities and between the demands of various regulations.

6 **Design for legibility** Design a legible building so that everyone can find their way about easily. Aim to make life easier for people with all types of impairment by careful design. Large buildings with complex floor plans such as education buildings, hospitals and buildings to which the general

public have access should be provided with land-mark features to assist legibility. Entrances should be clear to avoid confusion. Colour and contrast in the use of materials for interior design can assist legibility, but should not be relied upon to make a complex building legible.

7 **Inform the user**   Provide clear, accessible signage when necessary, recognising that people with visual impairments may need alternative forms of signage. Remember that the building may be used by people with learning difficulties as well as sensory or physical impairments.

8 **Design for adaptability**   Allow as much space as possible for future adaptations; a flexible design which can be adapted in the future is likely to be a long-term, more sustainable solution.

This point is particularly applicable to the design of new dwellings., A typical narrow-fronted dwelling designed by a developer is difficult to extend or adapt to the needs of the user. A wider-frontage dwelling does not necessarily occupy more space, but allows more scope for adaptation (Barton, Davis and Guise, 1995).

9 **Avoid on-site errors**   Provide good on-site supervision, preferably including training for builders and all involved in the construction process. Mistakes on site, such as the precise detailing of a threshold or the gradient of a ramp can render a building almost inaccessible. Building control staff do inspect work for compliance but mistakes often occur on site.

10 **Provide a maintenance plan**   Access problems can occur in even the best-designed buildings if the people responsible for subsequent maintenance and management of the building do not have an understanding of the reasons for provision. The designer can help to avoid these problems through the provision of a maintenance plan.

Adaptation and reuse – resolving conflicts of interest

Designing new buildings in a manner which takes into account the need for access is relatively straightforward if the designer adopts the principle of the universal need for access. More complex problems often result from adaptations and changes of use of existing buildings, particularly where the building concerned is a listed building or is situated within a conservation area. Aesthetic demands may then conflict with the needs of users and prove particularly challenging. Planners and conservation officers will often be in the position of making judgments on planning applications or listed building consents in which access is an issue. The following questions might act as a guide in making such decisions.

Is the use appropriate?   Consider whether the building or site is suitable for the use proposed, bearing in mind the requirement to achieve access at an early stage in the process. For example adapting a Grade 1 listed building for a use which requires very high levels of public access in some circumstances may not be compatible with the maintenance of the integrity of the building. However, few buildings or historic areas can survive without some alteration over the years. Managed change can be expected in the life of a building or conservation area. Most of the finest listed buildings have survived changes such as the installation of modern drainage and toilet facilities, lighting, central heating and computer installation and yet they continue to enrich our streets because they have been successfully adapted to meet modern needs. Similarly, conservation areas have had to adapt to modern demands associated with vehicular access or new users. Access adaptations may fall into the same category as other modern adaptations. However, they do represent a challenge to the designer and alterations must be handled sympathetically to avoid conflicts revolving around aesthetic issues.

How much would the alterations cost?   Taking into account realistic estimates of the cost of securing reasonable access from the initial conception of the project is particularly important in relation to listed buildings and conservation areas. Add-on afterthoughts such as poorly designed ramps are more likely to damage listed buildings and the use of poor-quality materials in relation to the adaptation of buildings or streets is more likely to create aesthetic conflicts if full costs are not considered at the outset. Possible sources of grant aid can also be explored if the costs are realistically assessed from the conception of the project.

Can the change be temporary?   Permanent adaptations are not always necessary and in some cases reversible provisions can be acceptable. Bearing in mind the improvement in the design of modern equipment such as stairlifts in the last five years, partly stimulated by increased demand, it may be more desirable in some cases to consider reversible, temporary solutions that do not irretrievably alter the fabric of a building. More permanent changes can then be considered at a later date.

Is the design proposed in sympathy with the design of the building or conservation area?   The design challenge to incorporate access provisions means that the designer must have a full understanding of the character of the building or area. Some buildings, by virtue of their design, will require more robust solutions. Alterations to symmetrical buildings, for example, must respect the form of the building and avoid breaking the symmetry. Innovative solutions should be considered and purpose-designed solutions applied when necessary. This does not always mean the rejection of a simple modern design or use of a modern material. Such a solution may in some cases be preferable to an inept attempt to create a new feature that mimics the character of a building slavishly. Generally, the scheme is more likely to be acceptable in aesthetic terms if a high-quality material is used and the scheme becomes indistinguishable from the original building or area.

What to do if access is impossible   In some circumstances it may be impossible for all users to gain access. Historic sites such as castles, forts and ancient city walls by their very nature will be impregnable. In these circumstances it may be possible to allow a degree of access, such as has been achieved on the historic city walls at Chester, where visitors with disabilities can gain access to part of the city walls. Alternatively, visitors will disabilities might be provided with interpretive material so that an appreciation of the building or site can be gained.

Index of themes

There are four indexes of significance to the urban design movement. They are themes, places, people and groups.

Index of places, sites and spatial associations

Index of people (authors, designers, planners and architects)

Index of groups, initiatives, campaigns and institutions